uncommon cures
for everyday ailments

From the Editors of
Bottom Line / Health

Bottom Line
Books

A ROUNDTABLE PRESS, INC. BOOK

For Roundtable Press
Directors: Julie Merberg, Marsha Melnick, Susan E. Meyer
Production Editors: John Glenn, Meredith Wolf Schizer
Design Concept: Martin Lubin
Production: Laura Smyth
Researchers: Elizabeth Barrett, Bob Condor, Deborah Crooks, Carol Kauder, Jim Moscou, Jacqueline Stenson, Elizabeth Yow

Written by Curt Pesmen

ISBN 0-88723-348-1

Bottom Line® Books publishes the advice of expert authorities in many fields.
The use of a book is not intended as a substitute for personal medical advice. Before making
any decision regarding your health, please consult a physician or another qualified healthcare practitioner. Every effort is made to ensure the accuracy of telephone numbers,
addresses and Web sites listed in this book, but they change frequently.

Bottom Line® Books is a registered trademark of Boardroom® Inc.
281 Tresser Blvd., Stamford, CT 06901

Printed in the United States of America
10 9 8 7 6 5 4 3 2

I went to a bookstore and asked the saleswoman, "Where's the self-help section?" She said if she told me, it would defeat the purpose.

—George Carlin

Contents

CHAPTER 1:

CHAPTER 2:

CHAPTER 3:

CHAPTER 4:

CHAPTER 5:

Preface

In today's world of wellness, medical history is not rewritten so much as it is constantly updated. Currently, some 34 of the 125 medical schools in America—including schools at Yale and Harvard—offer courses in alternative medicine. Over time, this broader-based approach to healing will lead millions of Americans to think anew about what they do with—and to—their bodies.

Most of the treatments and suggestions that you will find in this book can be classified in a variety of ways: Natural, new age, alternative, folk, traditional, homeopathic, holistic or complementary—or as some combination of one or more of these categories. In several cases, you will find out about uncommon uses for quite commonplace treatments. But, most specifically, you will find an abundance of advice from doctors, healers and other health practitioners on how to look at medical problems in different ways than you might have in the past.

The focus is on what works, and why. For in the hundreds of uncommon treatments and cures for everyday ailments accumulated here, there is much wisdom and a lot of science. But there is also tradition and faith and, we think, an uncommonly large lot of healing advice.

■ Where to Find What You're Looking For

First, the introduction gives you brief descriptions of 15 of the healing practices most often referred to in the chapters that follow. Resources are listed for each modality, should you wish to contact experts in a specific field or explore any of the treatments in more depth.

Chapter 1, on "Staying Young, Staying Fit," explores the world of longevity and provides you with anti-aging tips, while Chapter 2, the heart of this book, contains practically 1,000 uncommon treatments, cures and methods for easing everyday ailments. Chapters 3 and 4, "Especially for Women" and "Especially for Men," cover gender-based conditions with a focus on new ways to treat "old" conditions. Chapter 5, "Money-wise Ways to Wellness," gives health-conscious readers dozens of ideas not only for saving lots of money on health care costs, but also about rethinking where to turn for help in our increasingly fragmented health care system. However you choose to use this book, we do expect, and hope, that you will use it often.

Introduction

If you are new to the world of alternative medicine, the 15 healing methods that follow may at first seem less scientific than those you are accustomed to using. That is to be expected. But over the next decade, be assured that doctors of all kinds will be incorporating a number of these modalities into their practices. Note that we don't say "replacing." Because the best doctors and hospitals will be broadening their scopes to practice complementary medicine. It is not exclusionary medicine, nor is it magic. Over time it simply may be a better blend of what's good for what ails you.

ACUPRESSURE

A hands-on medicine that is at least a few thousand years old, acupressure evolved as a blend of massage and acupuncture (see following page). It is designed to unleash or lift the restrictions that injury has placed on the body's flow of energy. It is also used for preventive health.

While it is based on the same principles of energy flow as acupuncture, acupressure uses fingers, knuckles or blunt-edged instruments instead of needles. Pressure is applied to specific locations on the body, called meridian (or acupressure) points, which correspond with the patient's diagnosis. Both specific, easily located symptoms, such as neck and shoulder pain, or nonspecific symptoms, such as menstrual problems, may be treated with acupressure.

The pressure can be extremely light—just the weight of the finger—or deeper, like a massage. The touch will encourage the free flow of the body's energy, or chi, in places where it is blocked. Sometimes called shiatsu, this type of massage includes pressure applied to specific areas of the body also targeted in acupuncture.

One advantage of acupressure is that it can be a form of self-care—that is, it can be administered at home, which is important to many people who suffer from chronic pain. Perhaps most important to acupressure practitioners and Americans unfamiliar with alternative remedies is the fact that acupressure is immediately understandable. It makes sense: When we bash a toe or burn a thumb in the kitchen, we instinctively grab the painful parts and *hold on*, tightly, in order to blunt the hurt. And you don't have to know anything about meridians or endorphins to know that this works, at least temporarily.

Acupressure Resource

The Acupressure Institute
1533 Shattuck Ave.
Berkeley, CA 94709
800-442-2232; 510-845-1059 (in California)
www.acupressure.com

ACUPUNCTURE

Acupuncture is a lot more than needles, and it offers a lot more than pain relief. A complete medical system that stretches back at least 3,000 years, acupuncture is a technique of medical treatment based on traditional Chinese medicine. Disciples of the method and the use of related treatments moved to other Asian countries around A.D. 1000. In China today, many hospitals have two wings: One devoted to acupuncture, the other devoted to Western, or allopathic, medicine.

Although it is used to treat illness, reduce pain and manage chronic conditions, a cornerstone belief of acupuncture is the promotion of good health through preventive measures. In brief, acupuncture uses very fine needles, pressure, heat and exercise to restore or redirect energy in the body that is believed to directly and indirectly affect health.

Three kinds of energy—yin, yang and qi— are central to the core doctrine, as is the belief that 12 main meridians run through the body and carry an energy force that affects the workings of internal organs and tissues. Altogether, acupuncturists use nearly 1,000 designated points in their treatment in an effort to bring the energy force back into balance. Depending on the severity of the condition in question, a treatment can include anywhere from 1 to 10 or 20 or more procedures. You can think of meridians as feedback loops of energy—a communication through the whole body, telling it what to do and what's going on. Sometimes things get stuck, and needles in the right spots can clear up the problem, whether it's too much energy or not enough. One theory is that acupuncture works by stimulating endorphins, those natural, morphine-like painkillers found in the brain.

Regardless of the patients' individual illnesses, acupuncturists never treat a symptom without relating it to weaknesses in other parts of the body. Acupuncture is truly a holistic form of medical treatment.

Acupuncture Alert

Although it is extremely rare for an acupuncture patient to suffer any kind of adverse reaction to the slender needles used in most procedures, one recent case in medical literature has reminded acupuncturists to be a bit more vigilant.

In the British medical journal *The Lancet*, a doctor described a disturbing incident that resulted in a patient's death. One of the needles passed through the patient's sternum (breastbone) by mistake and pierced the heart. There was no reason for the acupuncturist to have known that the patient had a congenital defect—a hole in the sternum—as these kinds of defects are difficult to detect. But the incident reminded acupuncturists everywhere of the potential for problems in what is normally a worry-free treatment.

To locate qualified acupuncturists in your area, contact:

American Association of Oriental Medicine
909 22nd St.
Sacramento, CA 95816
866-455-7999 (toll free)
916-451-6950 (tel)
916-451-6952 (fax)
www.aaom.org

For information about specific schools of acupuncture, at which your practitioner may have trained, contact:
The Council of Colleges of Acupuncture and Oriental Medicine
7501 Greenway Center Dr., Suite 820
Greenbelt, MD 20770
301-313-0868 (tel)
301-313-0869 (fax)
www.ccaom.org

■ "Acupuncture Lite"

Not everyone will take to needle therapy right away, especially Westerners who are new to the idea of energy medicine and healing "flows" throughout the body. For this reason, acupuncturists in North America (and elsewhere) have learned how to use heat, magnetic waves, ultrasound, lasers and suction rather than needles to stimulate acupuncture points. Plus, even some acupuncturists say that needles are not always the best way to treat an ailment.

Even though these alternate methods have been dubbed by some as "acupuncture lite," they should not be taken lightly. They may turn out to be a particularly powerful way of helping acupuncture spread its message—and its powers—to millions of former skeptics in years to come.

BIOFEEDBACK

In this new age of interactive technology, biofeedback should be more popular than it is. Consider this: Biofeedback is a minimally high-tech way for people to peer inside their bodies noninvasively—and then take simple actions to control their vital functions, including heart rate, pulse, blood pressure, muscle action and brain waves. In addition to treating heart disease, biofeedback can help treat sleeping disorders, headaches, back pain, urinary incontinence, digestive disorders and temporomandibular joint syndrome (TMJ).

Biofeedback practitioners hook up sophisticated instruments to the client's head or chest (or other body area) to gauge the level of brain or heart activity. The equipment used varies depending on the ailment. In any case, the procedure is painless. Biofeedback practitioners can take such measurements as muscle tension, brain waves, body temperature and heart activity and display the data on a monitor for the patient. By following the monitor's readings—for example, a blinking red light or a beeper—the patient can see how deep breathing and other relaxation techniques impact his or her physiology in ways too subtle for ordinary detection. With this information in hand, the patient can amplify the appropriate technique to noticeably impact his or her condition.

Over time—generally 10 to 12 sessions—patients and clients, once aware of their own physiological reactions, learn to alter and control their responses through relaxation, deep breathing, imagery or meditation. The more they practice, the more adept they will become, since using the biofeedback method is as much a skill as a medical therapy. In effect, biofeedback enables people to consciously change physiological and biological responses that Western scientists once considered unchangeable. In so doing, people can greatly improve their health as they gain control over their bodies and minds.

How to Find a Biofeedback Practitioner

To locate qualified biofeedback practitioners in your area, contact:
The Association for Applied Psychophysiology & Biofeedback
10200 W. 44th Ave., Suite 304
Wheat Ridge, CO 80033
800-477-8892 (tel)
303-422-8894 (fax)
www.aapb.org

■ Biofeedback's Future

Biofeedback has come a long way since its discovery in the 1930s and its more heady development in the 1960s. Now, thanks to technological progress, biofeedback is poised to offer patients even more control over bodily responses and reactions. It appears that thousands of clients may soon be able to receive instant readouts of the gases in their blood while they practice the technique.

Biofeedback professionals in Boulder, Colorado, and in New York City are now using machines called oxycapnometers to teach patients how to control their breathing patterns (and relaxation responses) more efficiently and

more precisely. Why is this very important? Because when a person's carbon dioxide level is unbalanced, it can cause all kinds of other problems. So, rather than measuring mere chest movements or sweat responses of the skin, as is done now by biofeedback, practitioners who have access to oxycapnometers can show patients the changes in their bloodstream and nervous system before heavy breathing or nervous sweating sets in. This means that patients can cut off the effects of stress even earlier in the process.

Now all that remains is to figure out a way to bring the price of the machines down to levels that clinics under managed care can afford. Right now, the typical cost of an oxycapnometer can easily surpass $10,000.

CHIROPRACTIC CARE

When you cut off a piece of a hanging mobile, it will shift to rest at a new point of balance. When your body suffers a physical trauma, small or large, it too finds a different balance to compensate for the change. This new alignment can result in pain and dysfunction over time, if not immediately. The point of pain isn't necessarily the location of the problem. A part of the body may experience pain because it is compensating for the trauma to another part, which may feel fine.

A skilled chiropractor will locate the area of imbalance and correct it with musculoskeletal manipulation. Contrary to common assumption, chiropractic care is not all about the back. It *uses* the spine, however, as the primary means for its practitioners to effect changes in health. Chiropractors use the spine to correct imbalances

How to Find a Chiropractor in Your Area

For a reliable referral, contact:
American Chiropractic Association
1701 Clarendon Blvd.
Arlington, VA 22209
800-986-4636
703-276-8800 (tel)
703-243-2593 (fax)
www.acatoday.com

International Chiropractors Association
1110 N. Glebe Rd., Suite 1000
Arlington, VA 22201
800-423-4690
703-528-5000 (tel)
703-528-5023 (fax)
www.chiropractic.org
E-mail: chiro@chiropractic.org

affecting the rest of the body—knees, ankles, hips, shoulders, elbows, even migraine headaches resulting from improper alignment of the neck. These changes are made possible by "unblocking" the pathway of nerves from the brain to all other parts of the body.

Chiropractors may treat specific conditions and make people feel better, but their goals are more general. The basic premise of the chiropractic system is that through gentle adjustments, or "treatments," practitioners are able to realign spinal vertebrae that have become displaced through injury, poor posture, lack of muscle tone or stress and are causing a disruption of nerve function. Through massage and manual manipulation of the vertebrae to relieve pressure on nerves, chiropractors enable the body to tap its immense curative powers.

Chiropractors believe that their treatments enable the immune system to perform optimally, helping patients better arm themselves against insults to their good health.

In addition to anecdotal evidence of the benefits of chiropractic care, a major US government agency, the Agency for Health Care Policy Research, announced in the mid-1990s that chiropractic therapy *works* for many patients, at least for musculoskeletal problems. This type of endorsement has led insurance companies and interested others to take a new look at a not-so-new profession.

CRANIOSACRAL THERAPY

As powerful directors of the body's actions, the head and spine contain our most important communications pathways. That is the founding belief of craniosacral therapy, a modern kind of bodywork that was derived from what used to be called cranial osteopathy.

Craniosacral therapy consists of gentle, noninvasive, hands-on massage that corrects imbalances in the fluid system that connects the brain and spinal cord. Unlike Swedish massage, which focuses on the muscles, or Rolf therapy, which focuses on the alignment, craniosacral therapy focuses on a membrane, or sac, that contains cerebrospinal and other important fluids of the nervous system.

The therapy, developed in the early 1970s by osteopath John Upledger, D.O., is based on belief in the disputed existence of the craniosacral system, which, like the respiratory system, cardiovascular system or nervous system, is believed to influence the development and performance of the body. Therapists say imbalance or restriction in the craniosacral system, sometimes dating back as far as birth, can potentially cause any number of sensory, motor or neurological disabilities.

The therapist uses a very gentle touch to detect restrictions and then subtle movements, often on the plates of the skull, to assist the hydraulic forces of the craniosacral system and encourage the body's natural healing powers.

Applied by itself or in concert with other kinds of bodywork, craniosacral therapy can be used to help relieve whiplash, head and neck injuries, temporomandibular joint syndrome (TMJ), balance problems, effects of trauma and a host of other disorders. Today, a variety of health professionals perform craniosacral work, including osteopaths, chiropractors, acupuncturists and physical therapists.

HERBAL MEDICINE

Once you find out, or are reminded, that aspirin was developed from extracts of the willow bark tree, you may begin to view herbal medicine a little differently. Around most of the world outside North America, in fact, herbal, or botanical, medicine *is* traditional medicine. To the contrary, in our culture, we have come to think of our pharmaceutical-based, increasingly high-tech healing system as "traditional" and the other systems around the globe as "alternative."

In herbal medicine, "herb" means any plant —or any part of a plant—that is used to make medicine, food flavorings or aromas (for aromatherapy). You can find herbs in whole form, extracts, tinctures, oils, ointments, teas and tablets. Because everyone's physiology is different, some experimentation is necessary to find the right herbal remedies for you.

The chemicals that occur naturally in herbs have been observed and studied for centuries, but have only recently achieved "scientific" recognition by American doctors and researchers. Despite great strides in the acceptance and understanding of using herbs as medicine, there is no licensing body to regulate herbal medicine in the US. Thus, herbs—some

Check Your Craniosacral Therapist's Credentials

The premier practitioners of craniosacral therapy have usually attended classes at:
The Upledger Institute
11211 Prosperity Farms Rd., Suite D-325
Palm Beach Gardens, FL 33410
800-233-5880, ext. 90012
561-622-4334 (tel)
561-622-4771 (fax)
www.upledger.com
E-mail: upledger@upledger.com

quite powerful—can now be bought in health food stores, supermarkets, herb shops and specialty drugstores. Herbs are regulated as dietary supplements, like vitamins, not as drugs, even though some of them can have the same effect as drugs. (In brief, manufacturers can't make curative claims on the label.)

Care must be taken when seeking advice from an herbalist, for training can be quite varied, or even lacking. Consumers should be prepared to research herbal medicines on their own before starting any kind of serious regimen. Consider including a naturopath in your decision, as naturopathic education includes training in both herbal medicine and physiology in a medical school–like setting. And always consult with any doctor who may be treating you for a particular ailment before going on an herbal regimen.

In the near future, we can foresee that many more people will experiment with herbal medicines for everyday ailments like coughs, colds, sore throats, menstrual problems, minor cuts, scrapes and burns. In such cases, natural herbal remedies may be as effective, no more expensive, and have fewer side effects than conventional over-the-counter drugs.

For information on sources, contact:

American Botanical Council
P.O. Box 144345
Austin, TX 78714
800-373-7105
512-926-4900 (tel)
512-926-2345 (fax)
www.herbalgram.org

Herb Research Foundation
4140 15th St.
Boulder, CO 80304
800-748-2617
303-449-2265 (tel)
303-449-7849 (fax)
www.herbs.org

■ How to Buy Fresh Herbs

Since herbs lose their essential oils, and thus their efficacy, over time, fresh is best. Whenever possible, shop for herbs in herb shops or in the busiest natural food shops. According to herbalists, you want to use herbs as close as possible to the time they were harvested.

The standard rule is that you should never buy more of an herb at one time than you will likely use in a year. Better yet, if you have easy access to an herb store, buy medicinal herbs in amounts that will be consumed within three months.

Of course, buying fresh herbs and mixing concoctions at home is trickier and more time-consuming than buying prepackaged varieties of aloe, echinacea, ginkgo biloba and peppermint leaf, for example. But if you have the time and energy, you may find that growing your own fresh herbs will dramatically enhance your health.

6 Using a baster, transfer the liquid into small, dark-glass dropper bottles. (Many pharmacies sell, or will special order, these dark bottles.) Store the tincture in a cool, airy place out of direct sunlight. Now you are ready to treat family members from your own kitchen dispensary.

■ How to Prepare Herbal Tinctures

Tinctures are herbal preparations made for medicinal purposes using fresh or dried herbs and, usually, alcohol. Throughout this book, you will come across a number of remedies that recommend using herbal tinctures. You can make tinctures yourself at home, but it is strongly advised to enlist an herbalist's help for safety reasons, as well as to answer questions of potency.

The basic process is as follows:

1 Start with finely cut or powdered herbs in a wide-mouthed jar (general rule is 8 oz. dried herb per 1 quart alcohol/water).

2 Fill the jar with a 50–50 mixture of food-grade grain alcohol and water (this is the general rule for dried herbs only), and close tightly.

3 Shake the jar each day, a few minutes at a time, a few times each day, for at least 14 days.

4 After two weeks, strain this mixture into a bowl. Also squeeze the excess moistened herb through a cheesecloth into the bowl.

5 Take the liquid in the bowl and strain again into a jar, this time through a coffee filter to capture the small particles that remain.

■ How Strong Are Herbal Remedies?

Truth be told, few people know the actual strength of herbal remedies. One big problem in herbal medicine today is the lack of comparative standards. Three bottles of echinacea herbal extract, for instance, could have widely varying potency, yet exactly the same price, leaving the consumer not knowing which is strongest or weakest.

Standardization of herbal products is a thorny issue because the natural foods and herb industries do not want to invite too much government influence or intervention. Nevertheless, consumers have a right to know what they are buying. You must rely on consumer research and a trustworthy vendor for advice on which brands have the best reputation for product quality. Or, of course, you can grow your own.

HOMEOPATHY

"Like cures like." If an entire healing system's principles could be shrunk into a three-word proverb, this is what the homeopath's creed would be. The theory is that if a substance produces symptoms of disease in a healthy person, it will cure a sick person suffering from those same symptoms. Homeopathic medicines are derived from some 1,500 plant, animal or other natural substances (e.g., minerals), with the intent of triggering the body to fight disease.

In the late 1700s a German doctor, Samuel Hahnemann, formulated the principles of homeopathy as a counter to prevailing medical practices at the time. Today, after numerous ups and downs in popularity, homeopathy enjoys a broad following in Europe and other parts of the globe, but not quite so broad a following in North America. In fact, the American Medical Association (AMA) was formed in 1846 in part to thwart the growth of homeopathy.

Some people refer to any natural remedy as homeopathic, but this is a misnomer. Classical homeopathy treats a patient with one substance at a time (many commercial remedies combine more than one substance) in an extremely diluted and extremely safe solution. Remedies commonly come in the form of small pills you dissolve under your tongue or as a tincture.

Homeopathic remedies are made by crushing the curative substances, mixing them with alcohol or water, then repeatedly diluting and vigorously shaking them. Homeopaths differ in determining appropriate formulas for dilution but agree on the counterintuitive principle that the more it's diluted, the more potent it becomes.

Manufacturers list the dilution formula on the packaging, where "C" means 100 and "X" means 10. An arnica remedy labeled 6C, for example, was made by mixing one drop of arnica to 100 drops of water. Then one drop of that solution was mixed with 100 drops of water and so on, for a total of six times. In most circumstances, the final solution no longer contains molecules of the original substance, but homeopaths say it does contain the "imprint" or energy of the substance. People who have a hard time believing homeopathic theories insist its remarkable actions are the result of the placebo effect.

In general, because the remedies are so diluted, it is difficult to imagine an overdose, although there are a few things to watch out for. In some instances, certain homeopathic treatments should not be taken for more than a week at a time. If a remedy is working, it may first produce a "healing crisis," where the symptoms magnify for a few hours or days before going away completely. It's important to stick with the remedy through the "aggravations" and not use another form of treatment, which may counter the homeopathic one. Also, if you have the wrong remedy and take it for an extended period of time, it may "prove" itself, that is, manifest the symptoms that it would otherwise cure in you.

Medicines can be ailment-specific (those you find in drugstores or health food stores) or matched to a person's overall internal health, or "constitution." The precise formulas can be derived only after having a formal interview with a homeopath or naturopathic physician. (For the record, the FDA has expressed concern over use of homeopathic remedies for serious illnesses and diseases, and encourages consumers to be sure they are working with a licensed practitioner.)

Note: Coffee is an antidote to homeopathic remedies. If you want to try homeopathy, say bye-bye to your café latte.

NATUROPATHY

Yes, naturopaths favor natural healing techniques. But that does not mean they are not well-versed in science. Naturopathic healing combines elements of herbal medicine, acupuncture, nutrition, bodywork, homeopathy and exercise. Like many alternative modalities, naturopathy treats by supporting and enhancing the patient's inherent ability to heal and maintain good health.

All illness has a cause which can be physical, emotional, mental or spiritual, or a combination of some or all of these. Symptoms indicate the body's attempt to fight the disease—they are not the disease itself and should not be suppressed. The naturopath seeks to treat root causes, not symptoms. Naturopathy is one of the few complementary medicines (like chiropractic) that require its practitioners to complete four-year, postgraduate training with admission requirements similar to those of US medical schools.

Having been available in the US for about 100 years, naturopathy has had a resurgence in the past two decades. There are now 12 states (plus the commonwealth of Puerto Rico) that will license naturopaths, including Arizona, Oregon, Washington and Hawaii, with more to follow in the near future.

Using a prevention-oriented and cause-versus-symptom approach to care, naturopaths take detailed medical histories of patients, unlike any you are likely to undergo in an HMO. Naturopaths believe in the body's ability to cure itself and regard disease as a violation of natural law. Any number of conditions respond well to naturopathic healing, including colds, flu, allergies and digestive ills, as well as particular

How to Find a Qualified Naturopath

There are only three colleges of naturopathic medicine in the US that are recognized by the US Department of Education and accredited by the Council on Naturopathic Medical Education (CNME):

Bastyr University, 14500 Juanita Dr. NE Kenmore, WA 98028, 425-823-1300 (tel) 425-823-6222 (fax), www.bastyr.edu

National College of Naturopathic Medicine 049 SW Porter St., Portland, OR 97201 503-552-1555 (tel), www.ncnm.edu

Southwest College of Naturopathic Medicine and Health Sciences, 2140 East Broadway, Tempe, AZ 85282, 480-858-9100 (tel), www.scnm.edu

To locate a naturopath in your area, contact:

The American Association of Naturopathic Physicians
3201 New Mexico Ave. NW, Suite 350
Washington, DC 20016
866-538-2267,
202-895-1392 (tel)
http://naturopathic.org

autoimmune diseases such as rheumatoid arthritis. The future looks bright for naturopathic medicine—and for its increasing pool of patients.

ORIENTAL MEDICINE (also called Asian Medicine)

When you think of Oriental medicine, you may be inclined to think of acupuncture. That is partially correct, but doesn't tell the whole story. First, Oriental or Asian medicine is more about energy, or what the Chinese call *qi,* pronounced "chee," which is the life force that Asian medical healers work to change and strengthen. Oriental medicine looks at health as the integration of body, mind and spirit.

It follows a structured hierarchy of categories that represent the body and its functions. In theory, these categories keep each other in a cyclic series of checks and balances, like an unending game of rock-paper-scissors. When one element dominates, as is often the case, there is imbalance, which leads to disease. The goal of the doctor of Oriental medicine is to determine, through intensive questioning and examination, which properties are out of balance—and then prescribe herbs and dietary changes to support the weaker ones and subdue excessive ones.

In the area of herbal medicine, practitioners of Asian medicine choose herbs for nutritional value as well as medicinal qualities. The herbs may contain vitamins and nutrients, but they also serve to prod the body's immune system, circulation and metabolism.

Over the years, you may also have heard (and used) the terms *yin* and *yang* without truly knowing what they mean. In Asian medicine, yin refers to things, including foods, that are nourishing and moistening and that have the capacity to slow metabolism. Yang, by contrast, refers to nutrients and foods that are stimulating and that tend to speed up metabolism.

Note: Oriental or Asian medicine (a broader category than traditional Chinese medicine) includes the healing principles of countries other than China, including Tibet and Japan.

Oriental / Asian Medicine Resources

For information on Asian medicine principles and products, contact:

Institute for Traditional Medicine
2017 SE Hawthorne Blvd.
Portland, OR 97214
503-233-4907 (tel)
503-233-1017 (fax)
www.itmonline.org

American Association of Oriental Medicine
909 22nd St.
Sacramento, CA 95816
866-455-7999 (toll free)
916-451-6950 (tel)
916-451-6952 (fax)
www.aaom.org

THE PILATES® METHOD

A combination of rehabilitation, strength-building and postural exercise, the Pilates (pronounced pih-LAH-teez) method was popularized by professional dancers. Yet, in recent years, Pilates—founded in 1923 by Joseph Pilates—has caught on in a big way with countless other fitness-oriented people. These yoga-inspired exercises focus on enabling a person's body to feel "longer and stronger," no matter what the person's height, by building a strong, lean abdomen and by working joints individually. The use of a fitness machine known as the Reformer, which uses body weight as resistance, accentuates the "lengthening" part of the workout.

How to Find a Pilates Instructor

The Pilates Center
4800 Baseline Rd., Suite D206
Boulder, CO 80303
303-494-3400 (tel)
303-499-2746 (fax)
www.thepilatescenter.com

The Pilates Studio
2121 Broadway, Suite 201
New York, NY 10023
212-875-0189
www.pilates-studio.com

"Mat" classes incorporate the theories and motions of Pilates, without using Reformers. These classes cost significantly less and still offer many of the benefits of a Reformer class. The goal of Pilates is to teach you a healthier way to move in everyday life. By strengthening parts of the body that are overlooked and overwhelmed, you will gain balance and alignment. Pilates increases circulation, strength, range of motion, flexibility, coordination and stamina.

The orthopedists and athletic trainers are among the health professionals who regularly refer clients to Pilates instructors for joint and spine work. When working on an injured joint, an instructor will break down the structural imbalance of the joint, before trying to build it

back to its full strength. The Pilates exercises will be set up to work specifically on the joint's weakest link. Toughened abdominals may be considered a bonus by some, but Pilates veterans view them as an anchor of sorts—at the core of the program.

REFLEXOLOGY

For most people who have heard about the healing technique of reflexology, their first thought is of the soles of their feet as a remote control of sorts for pain located in other parts of the body. That is true enough for a quick snapshot of the practice, but not nearly broad enough, for reflexology can also be applied through the hands. The difference? Some believe that the hands, being in almost constant touch with things both soft and hard, benign and abrasive, have lost their responsiveness over the years. The feet are regarded as more sensitive to touch, and thus a better site for the treatment.

Reflexology Referrals

For more information, write or call:
American Reflexology Certification Board
P.O. Box 740879
Arvada, CO 80006
303-933-6921
www.arcb.net

International Institute of Reflexology
5650 First Avenue North
P.O. Box 12642
St. Petersburg, FL 33733-2642
727-343-4811
www.reflexology-usa.net

In brief, the practice of reflexology applies gentle pressure to specific areas of the feet (usually) to treat a range of conditions, from joint pain to immune problems to infertility. The treatment's goal is to reorient and balance the energy flow within the body. The soles of the feet are believed to hold miniature maps for entire bodily systems that work best when they work together.

ROLFING THERAPY

In one word, Rolfing therapy is about realignment, or, in another word, balance. Rolfing is not massage or deep tissue work, although that's how people have incorrectly described it in the past. Named for its founder, Ida Rolf, this therapy works to realign segments of the body that injury, emotional trauma and poor postural habits have forced out of balance. Ideally, each of the body's sections are "stacked" so that the centers of gravity match up precisely—no head jutting forward, no hunched shoulders. Think of an imaginary pole running through your body, providing support and serving as an anchor.

Rolf practitioners manipulate the major muscle groups and fascia (tissue under the skin, wrapping the muscles) by using hands, fists and elbows. But sessions are not, by their nature, painful. That is a misconception that has plagued the profession, unfairly, for many of its more than 50 years of existence. In the 1980s and 1990s, Rolf therapists worked to soften their techniques some, without straying from the original goals of the therapy: To bring a part (or parts) of the body to where it precisely belongs and set up a new pattern of movement.

Rolfing bodywork is reinforced by Rolfing movement integration, in which the practitioner teaches the client new ways of moving—walking, sitting at a computer, playing a sport—to avoid reestablishing the former problematic muscular tension. Most Rolf therapists will incorporate some movement in treatment, and about one-third of therapists are certified in Rolf movement integration. Some will focus on movement alone, leaving out the bodywork.

Usually, a patient's head and neck feel lighter after treatment and the torso feels lengthened. Formerly, Rolfing was practiced in 10, and exactly 10, sessions. Today, however, Rolfers will vary a bit from that rule, although they state that one or two sessions are simply not enough to effect any kind of lasting change.

How to Find a Rolfer

The Rolf Institute of Structural Integration
5055 Chaparral Ct., Suite 103
Boulder, CO 80301
800-530-8875
303-449-5903
www.rolf.org

THERAPEUTIC TOUCH

Therapeutic touch is a modernization of ancient religious/healing rites known as "laying on of hands." Only with today's practitioners, religious belief is not required.

Approximately 50 years old, the theory behind therapeutic touch is based on the idea of a complex energetic life force that surrounds and flows through all of us. In the therapy a healer can "feel energy imbalances" by passing his or her hands lightly on or over the afflicted part of the patient's body. These imbalances may present themselves in a number of ways, practitioners say: Tingling, tightness, heat, cold or electric shock.

The therapist doesn't so much "heal" the patient as facilitate the patient's own healing by gently manipulating and restoring the integrity of his or her energy field. This technique entered the mainstream when its chief proponent, Dolores Krieger, PhD, taught a graduate class in therapeutic touch at New York University in the mid-1970s.

Research has shown this type of touch to be effective at relaxing the patient, reducing anxiety and changing the patient's perception of pain. It was introduced to doctors and patients at the prestigious Columbia–Presbyterian Medical School in New York City in the mid-1990s (in conjunction with standard surgeries), and yet to this day has faced serious scientific challenges from medical skeptics.

Prior to a procedure, the healer goes into a meditative state. Then, before any touching, the healer focuses intently on healing the person being treated. Finally, the practitioner "reads" the patient's energy field and transfers healing energy back into the person, as needed. This transfer of energy from healer to patient is supposed to result in better health. Of course, a healer's hands must be sensitive, and his or her mind must be open to working with other forms of medicine—sometimes those that are considered conventional.

Therapeutic Touch Information and Referrals

Barbara Brennan School of Healing
500 NE Spanish River Blvd., Suite 108
Boca Raton, FL 33431
800-924-2564
561-620-8767
www.barbarabrennan.com

VISUALIZATION AND GUIDED IMAGERY

Visualization is quintessential mind/body healing. When it works, it demonstrates how one can use the mind's eye to form images that help effect physiological changes. The unconscious plays an undeniable role in wellness and healing, as evidenced by results attributed to the placebo effect and the power of suggestion. Rather than writing these off, guided imagery attempts to lock in and focus the mind's ability to help heal the body.

Albert Einstein once said, "Imagination is more important than knowledge," and this is the credo of the Academy for Guided Imagery. Difficult to measure, of course, the success of visualization (also called guided imagery) in the West has been bolstered by related research in fields such as biofeedback and meditation. In those practices, patients also use images to effect (measurable) bodily changes.

In visualization therapy, patients who suffer from headaches, chronic pain and even cancer are told that they can contribute a lot to the healing they are hoping to achieve. Images used—such as tiny video-game characters "gobbling up" diseased cells in the body, or a pair of "inner hands" holding or supporting an injured or diseased organ—can be a lot more than palliative. Visualization has become both a self-help mechanism and a tool of Eastern and Western medicine. In the years ahead, research may be able to move this method forward to the status now enjoyed by its more mechanized cousin, biofeedback.

Visualization Resources

Imagery International
1574 Coburg Rd., Suite 555
Eugene, OR 97401
www.imageryinternational.org

Academy for Guided Imagery
30765 Pacific Coast Highway, Suite 369
Malibu, CA 90265
800-726-2070
www.healthy.net/agi

The Mind/Body Medical Institute
824 Boylston St.
Chestnut Hill, MA 02467
866-509-0732
617-991-0102
www.mbmi.org

YOGA

Currently booming in health clubs and fitness classes in the US, yoga has ancient roots. While it has long been known for its unusual poses and deep breathing exercises, yoga's goals remain akin to those of Indian yogis some 5,000 years ago: An integration of body and mind that results in spiritual growth and health. The aim may not always be to soothe sore joints or muscles, but such tangible results are often experienced.

Breath in yoga is so much more than oxygen. Called "prana," the breath is considered

to be the interface between the spirit and the physical body. It is a life force. The controlled breathing in yoga eases tension, nervousness and anger, and provides relaxation, better concentration and, yes, more oxygen to the bloodstream.

The various postures of yoga are designed to work every muscle in the body. The poses are carefully sculpted positions—some simple, some contorted—held for several seconds or several minutes. The body stretches and relaxes, allowing energy to flow through in ways not normally reached in everyday life. As a whole, the discipline is often credited with improving the function of entire bodily systems, such as circulation, digestion or metabolism.

Hatha yoga, the physical aspect of yoga philosophy that most people refer to with the word "yoga," incorporates a number of principles designed to bring better health. There are numerous schools of hatha yoga—Astanga, Iyengar and Bikram are a few of the more popular ones—that follow the teachings of different gurus and stress varying elements of the yoga poses. Many of the yoga references in this book will pertain specifically to ideas based on Hatha principles.

Yoga Resources

Yoga Research and Education Center
PO Box 2513
Prescott, AZ 86302
928-541-0004
www.yrec.org

Iyengar Yoga National Association of the US
800-889-9642
www.iynaus.org

A NOTE ABOUT ALTERNATIVE TREATMENTS...

■ *Telling Your Doctor All for Better Health*

Surprisingly, nearly 50% of those who use acupuncture, herbs or chiropractic healers fail to tell their primary care doctors that they are using alternative treatments—largely out of embarrassment or fear of being reprimanded by a traditional authority figure.

However, according to recent research at Oregon Health Sciences University, telling the whole truth is more important than these consumers know. One reason is that many herbs and supplements may adversely interact with prescription medicines, and doctors have no way of knowing what is in the body unless their patients tell them. In rare cases, there may be problems combining herbal and allopathic (Western) medicines. You may be better off with no treatment at all or taking a single kind of medication by itself.

CHAPTER 1

Staying Young, Staying Fit

In this section, you will find treatments for conditions that are most often age-related, as well as suggestions for preventing disease, extending your youth—and your life.

ALZHEIMER'S DISEASE

■ An Everyday Herb Enters the Scene

When Alzheimer's disease strikes, it targets the memory first, then other parts of the brain, in a methodical attack on behavioral and other neurological functions. Difficult to diagnose and to treat, Alzheimer's is the most common of the degenerative diseases of the brain. Some doctors are hopeful that rosemary, an herb that commonly enhances dishes from chicken or fish to pasta and potatoes, can help slow the progression of the disease.

It appears that rosemary contains compounds that prevent the breakdown of a neurotransmitter that is deficient in Alzheimer's patients. James Duke, PhD, one of the leading botanists in the US, even believes that eating rosemary over many years can reduce a person's risk of developing Alzheimer's.

■ Ginkgo for Stronger Cognitive Skills

Several studies have shown that ginkgo biloba extract, taken from the leaves of the ginkgo tree, can help some people with Alzheimer's disease by slowing their rate of mental decline. In one study, nearly 30% of the people who took 120 mg of the extract for at least six months improved on cognitive tests, whereas only 13% of those taking a placebo showed improvement.

Music Makes a Difference

Music therapy can temporarily bring dementia and Alzheimer's patients back to reality and help them relate to their families. It may even reduce their need for medication.

Often, patients who have lost verbal ability still can sing or make music. Music therapists are trained musicians who create live music with patients. Drum circles are one way music therapists restart the communication process for Alzheimer's patients, who may beat to their own rhythm at first but eventually get in sync with each other.

There are many colleges teaching music therapy, and these therapists are board certified. For more information about music therapy, contact: American Music Therapy Association at 301-589-3300, www.musictherapy.org.

■ Decelerate the Trend with Vitamin E

High doses of vitamin E supplements may also delay Alzheimer's disease. A recent study found that 2,000 IU of vitamin E, taken daily, slowed the rate of disability among patients with moderately severe Alzheimer's by seven months, on average. Patients on the vitamin E regimen were able to maintain daily functions, such as dressing themselves and handling

money, for longer than Alzheimer's sufferers who were not taking the E supplements. Due to the possible interactions between vitamin E and various drugs and supplements, as well as safety considerations, check with your doctor before starting this vitamin therapy.

ANTI-AGING

■ "Nuts" to Growing Older

In recent years, a handful of new nutrients, vitamins or antioxidants have been shown to help delay the age-related breakdown of skin, muscle and many other of our cells. *Among them:* Selenium, a trace mineral prevalent in Brazil nuts, is said to promote immune responses. An average Brazil nut has 70 micrograms of selenium, more than the recommended daily amount of the mineral. Eating just one or two of these nuts a day is an easy first step in an anti-aging plan.

■ Chew More, Eat Less, Live Longer

It's known that obesity cuts millions of lives short, but only in lab animals have scientists been able to confirm that extreme caloric restriction extends life span. Perhaps that is plenty of proof for some people, however, to think about how to eat less, over a lifetime, without going on a diet.

One good solution: Chew more. Much more. Most of us chew food an average of only seven times before swallowing (go ahead, count at your next meal). If we chewed each mouthful 20 or 30 times, as some dietitians recommend, our average caloric intake (in the US) could be cut from more than 3,000 calories per day to closer to 2,000 or 2,500. (And we would feel full on less food.) Less food taken in means a lot less resultant weight. And perhaps brighter prospects for longevity, as well.

Living Longer, Stronger

By exercising regularly, postmenopausal women can reduce their risk of premature death by as much as 30%, according to a recent study of more than 40,000 women in Iowa. Even

women who were physically active only once a week were more likely to live longer. But those women who exercised the most, and the most intensely, had the greatest reductions in premature death, especially from respiratory or cardiovascular disease.

Pycnogenol Power

Not so long ago, many nutritionists scoffed at the idea of anti-aging antioxidants—those nutrients found in foods and supplements that could delay aging by slowing the normal rate at which skin, the cardiovascular tissues and organs break down. But then, scientists discovered that Pycnogenol, a product that contains vitamin-like flavonoids, is a powerful pill. It is said to combat aging, heart disease, hair loss and skin damage.

Too new to have any real long-term research behind it, Pycnogenol is gaining favor due to recent studies at the University of South Florida medical school and the University of Arizona. Researchers suggest taking 1.5 mg of Pycnogenol daily per pound of body weight. (You should also check with your doctor before you begin taking it.)

Undernutrition for Longer Life?

In the world of anti-aging medicine, the remarkable does not always turn out to be practical. At least not yet. For already there is one method of dramatically extending lives in lab animals: Undernutrition, or feeding the animals half as much as they would like to eat, at every meal. This is not starvation, though, because the researchers use supernutritious food and are careful to supply all necessary nutrients.

As a result, over the years, scientists have found that mice that were supposed to live 14 months, for example, went on to live for four years after being put on an undernutrition-without-malnutrition diet. The federal government has given the okay to test the nutrient-dense, low-cal regimen on apes, but not yet on humans.

But would such a diet be practical for mammals like us—over 20 or 30 years, say? Or would it adversely affect the enjoyment of life too much, for the sake of an extra decade or two of life? Perhaps we'll know by the year 2010, when a major phase of the National Institute on Aging's ape research on life span is completed.

■ *Powerful Three-Pill Shortcut*

Now that antioxidant vitamins and supplements have been studied in clinical settings for more than 15 years, there is more evidence on how to use supplements wisely to slow the aging process. In brief, antioxidant nutrients help delay the normal oxidation (breakdown) of cells that occurs inside the body, which often accelerates the aging process. Experts in nutrition and aging suggest a three-pill strategy that touches most of the important bases:

■ A multivitamin that contains at least 100% (and up to 200% is okay) of the RDA amounts of the B vitamins (including B-6), beta-carotene, folic acid, vitamin C and vitamin D.

■ Vitamin E that contains 100 to 400 IU, a safe dosage.

■ Calcium, which—in addition to keeping bones strong—may have anticancer properties, according to recent research. One 600- to 700-mg supplement a day is usually sufficient, in addition to eating yogurt and plenty of leafy greens.

■ *New Antioxidant Discovery*

Alpha lipoic acid is a chemical that the body naturally produces, and it is a powerful antioxidant. Not only does this acid forestall the degeneration of cells, it also boosts the antioxidant power of vitamins C and E. You can find alpha lipoic acid at health food stores. Follow package instructions for appropriate dosages and be sure to consult with your doctor.

Sweat as Anti-Aging Medicine

A long-awaited verdict is in: Exercise doesn't just help you feel better; it measurably slows down the aging process. After studying 20 exercising men for more than 20 years, Dr. Lawrence Golding of the American College of Sports Medicine found that their key measures of VO2 max (the body's oxygen-processing limit), flexibility and strength all held up surprisingly well over...decades! We now have solid evidence that some of the changes associated with aging are not inevitable.

Flexibility, researchers say, is the bodily characteristic that changes most dramatically with age (besides looks, that is); and it is the one thing, they add, that does not have to decline with age. Most heartening is the fact that the subjects in the above study showed great flexibility regardless of whether they started the program at age 25 or 60!

ARTHRITIS

■ *Walk This Way*

It may not make sense at first, but when arthritis makes your joints ache all over, a workout of sorts may be in order. Researchers at the Hospital for Special Surgery in New York City recently studied more than 100 people who had arthritis of the knees. Half were put on a walking program; the other half did not partake in regular exercise. After eight weeks, the walkers reported decidedly less pain and less reliance on pain medication. Also, they were able to walk farther without pain than they had been able to do in the experiment's pretest.

Celery Tonic

For such a seemingly mild-mannered vegetable, celery packs a surprisingly strong medicinal punch. Celery seed contains at least 12 compounds that have anti-inflammatory effects, which makes celery desirable as a natural treatment for arthritis. You can take celery seed in extract form, available in herb shops and health food stores, or you can eat the stalks themselves. Four stalks of celery a day should deliver healing benefits.

European Cure Catches On

With three out of four people over the age of 65 classified as arthritis sufferers to some degree, any supplements that offer relief for stiff, painful joints would be welcomed by millions in the US. No wonder, then, that in recent years interest has grown markedly in the naturally occurring glucosamine and chondroitin.

These supplements—a sugar (glucosamine) and a substance found in connective tissues (chondroitin)—are extensively taken in Italy, Germany and France, where they are said to both relieve pain and go one big step further: They purportedly help cartilage to regenerate. It is difficult to document these claims scientifically (drug companies are hesitant to fund research on natural substances that cannot be patented and marketed "exclusively" for profit); but The Arthritis Foundation in the US has gone so far as to say that results on glucosamine are quite promising.

Dosage: To ensure quality (and purity), ask a pharmacist for the pharmaceutical grade of glucosamine and chondroitin sulfate. They come in tablet or capsule form. A common dosage is 500 mg of glucosamine three times a day, and 250 mg of chondroitin two or three times a day.

Cayenne: A Pepper Pain Blocker

Among its many uses, cayenne is touted by numerous herbalists for its impressive efficacy against many kinds of pain, especially chronic pain, which is why it is well suited as a remedy for arthritis. Cayenne contains a compound called capsaicin, which, among other things, blocks pain impulses from traveling to the brain. As a bonus, the pepper is said to boost the production of endorphins, the natural painkillers produced by the body after exercise.

Green Tea Prevention

Recent research performed at Case Western Reserve University's School of Medicine indicates that green tea may both prevent the onset of arthritis and reduce the severity of its symptoms. The reason is that polyphenols—antioxidants found in green tea—possess anti-inflammatory properties. So starting the day with a cup of green tea can do a world of good.

Don't Overlook Vitamin D

Recent research has shown that some individuals who have arthritis may also be deficient in vitamin D. In a large-scale study, people who consumed little vitamin D were three times more likely to see their arthritic knees take a turn for the worse than those who ingested high levels of the vitamin. (This may be exacerbated in winter, when typically people don't spend as much time outdoors, since the sun helps the body to produce vitamin D.) Salmon and sardines are rich in the vitamin, as is milk. If you're not getting enough vitamin D in your diet, taking a supplement of 400 IU per day is also a good idea.

■ Putting an "Old" Hormone to New Use

Pregnenolone, like estrogen and testosterone, is a steroid hormone naturally produced in our bodies from the cholesterol we have stored up inside. Despite the name, it has nothing to do with pregnancy, and is produced equally among men and women. Like other hormones, its production wanes with age. Some 50 years ago, in a number of experiments, pregnenolone was used as an effective, gradual treatment for rheumatoid arthritis patients.

Now, with spurred interest in other hormone supplements, pregnenolone is getting a second look as a treatment for rheumatoid arthritis, especially from doctors and patients who are concerned about the side effects of cortisone (which indeed works more quickly to relieve pain). If your internist or orthopedist is not familiar with pregnenolone's effects, you might ask for a referral to an endocrinologist.

■ A Root for Pain Control

It may not be high tech, but a poultice made of ginger root (or heated ginger root and olive oil), steamed and laid into a cloth, can help ease the pain of rheumatoid arthritis, especially among patients who must restrict the use of allopathic pain medications, such as aspirin and steroids. Multifaceted ginger has long been considered an aid for both circulation and relaxation. The fact that it may calm inflamed joints is not so surprising.

■ An Herbal, Fatty-Acid Solution

To ease tenderness and pain in swollen joints, consider a little-known extract of borage seed oil: Gamma linolenic acid (GLA). Herbalists and naturopaths have known about it for years, and now some internists and rheumatologists are also becoming fans of the oil. Judging from recent studies, GLA, taken in large doses, has a marked effect on pain and swelling of afflicted joints. As with acupuncture, however, the "cure" won't come right away. It may take from 6 to 12 weeks to feel real results. The dosage used in the study was 2.8 g per day (that's grams, not milligrams). Check this dose with your doctor or other health practitioner, and ask about possible side effects and drug–herb interactions.

Estrogen—An Unlikely Ally

Women over the age of 65 who took estrogen over the long-term post-menopausally were found to have had a nearly 40% reduced risk of osteoarthritis of the hip in a study of more than 4,000 subjects. This is a critical finding because weak hip joints and fractured hips are responsible for millions of late-life health problems and hospitalizations. Osteoarthritis of the hip joint, usually a result of wear and tear over a lifetime, may be postponed by taking estrogen supplements: The theory is that estrogen helps the cartilage in joints remain elastic. Due to certain risks, estrogen therapy may not be appropriate for you. Consult your doctor.

A Berry Fine Arthritis Remedy

Lip-smackingly sweet cherries, blueberries and blackberries are a flavorful alternative remedy for reducing swollen joints caused by arthritis. The secret ingredient? Flavonoids. These brightly colored compounds found in berries increase fatty acids in your system, which can affect muscle tissue and lessen swelling.

Spice Up Your Life

Spicing up your sandwiches, burgers and other entrees with plenty of onions and garlic can both fire up the taste and cool down an arthritic condition. Both these foods are high in sulfur, which absorbs toxins that may be irritating joint tissues.

A Two-Step Supplement Painkiller

If painkillers and other drugs have got you down, it may be time to try a supplemental approach to managing arthritis pain. CoQ-10 (coenzyme Q-10) has been gaining fans in recent years because of its reported ability to stabilize cell membranes and thus prevent cells from breaking down in the joints. (Anti-aging experts also note this effect.)

In addition, a supplement called quercetin can help block the release of histamines into the blood, which means less inflammation, experts say. Both substances are available in health food stores.

Suggested dosage: 30 mg of CoQ-10 daily; 100–500 mg of quercetin daily. Check with your doctor to see if these supplements are appropriate for your condition.

Reflexology to the Rescue

No, reflexology does not have solid scientific evidence to back up its use for treating painful conditions. But if you understand a bit about how acupuncture works—by interrupting and redirecting paths of healing energy through the body—you may find yourself a fan of this foot-based massage modality. Reflexology can be especially effective if you suffer from the recurrent joint pain caused by arthritis.

In brief, the practice of reflexology is based on channels, or zones of the body, that can be accessed through directed massage of certain points on the feet. It is said that a "map of the body" exists on both feet, one side mirroring the other. After a reflexologist takes a complete medical history and directs you to a comfortable chair, he or she preps your feet and gets you accustomed to the sensation of applied pressure. A one-hour massage session, repeated over three successive weeks, is a typical time frame in which to treat osteoarthritis. Happy feet can make for happier joints!

No Potatoes, No Tomatoes

If your joints are feeling a little achy, clean out your refrigerator. According to nutritionists, plants from the nightshade family, such as potatoes, eggplant, peppers and tomatoes, contain solanine, a little-known inflammatory agent that can sometimes exacerbate arthritis.

Oiling the Joints

Just like the Tin Man, people with arthritis may need to oil their joints. But not just any oil will do. Avoid consuming corn and peanut oils, which contain large quantities of arachidonic acid, a substance produced by the body during an inflammatory attack. Because of this, corn and peanut oils may actually exacerbate arthritis symptoms.

Instead, opt for evening primrose and flaxseed oils; both are rich in the omega-3 fatty acids also found in fish. If you don't want to add fish to your diet three times a week, supplementary capsules, available in many drugstores and in health food stores, can be taken daily.

Feldenkrais for Better Mobility

If chronic pain from severe arthritis is cutting down on your ability to move about, consider going to a Feldenkrais practitioner. A type of physical therapy, Feldenkrais operates on the assumption that you can learn different movement patterns and break bad habits—such as relying too heavily on one side of your body or certain muscles—that may be contributing to pain and recurring injuries.

Feldenkrais therapists work with patients to extend their range of motion and loosen stiff joints by using unique tissue massage techniques and guided stretching exercises.

A Devil of a Cure

For temporary relief of minor arthritic pain, devil's claw, also known as cat's claw, acts as an anti-inflammatory agent and has an analgesic effect. The extract, which can be purchased at health food stores, should be taken orally three times a day. Alternatively, you can make a tea by mixing 1 to 2 grams of the dried, powdered root with a cup of boiled water. Drink one cup of tea three to four times a day.

A Hot Cup of Relief

Drink away stiffness with a hot cup of willow bark tea. Willow bark contains salicylates,  the potent ingredient in aspirin. To brew the tea, add 1 teaspoon of dried willow bark to a cup of boiled water. Steep for 5 minutes, then strain before drinking. You can safely sip up to three cups a day.

Caution: If you're already taking aspirin or another anti-inflammatory drug, consult your doctor before taking willow bark.

A Healing Wrap

A spa-like treatment can soothe stiffness and soreness in arthritic joints. To give yourself a healing wrap:

1 Wrap the area—your wrist, for example—in a bath towel.

2 Place your wrapped wrist under a stream of hot, but not scalding, water until the towel becomes saturated.

3 Relax and let the damp heat ease the pain until the towel begins to cool.

During a serious arthritis attack, you can repeat the process once every hour.

Skip the Wheat

Are you sidelined because of pain in your hip? Go gluten-free. Gluten, a protein in wheat, has been found to trigger allergies that can exacerbate arthritic conditions. Try avoiding wheat-based breads, pastas and doughs, and your hip may begin to loosen up.

Too-Strong Solution?

A controversial arthritis remedy is dimethyl sulfoxide (DMSO), a chemical solvent derived from wood pulp. The solvent helps to reduce inflammation when massaged into arthritic joints. However, some physicians believe that the chemical can cause cataracts if used too frequently. Ask your doctor for advice before applying DMSO to swollen joints. (Some would also advise a second opinion.)

Improve Balance as You Age

Tai chi (or *tai chi chuan*) is an ancient, graceful martial art widely practiced in China, especially by elderly Chinese. Tai chi is also gaining favor in the US as a way for people of all ages, but especially those over 60, to improve balance and posture.

Tai chi combines a series of slow, measured movements of the arms, torso and legs. Many of these movements involve standing for a time on one leg. Merely standing on one leg for 20 to 30 seconds is normally difficult for many older people to do, but tai chi practitioners get better at it as they age. Classes are available in most medium-to-large US cities.

Homeopathic Help from Poison Ivy

Admittedly, it is difficult to imagine how ingesting extract of the poison ivy plant could help relieve the pain and stiffness of early-morning arthritis episodes—the kind that fade as you get up and move around. But for years homeopaths have prescribed rhus tox, a heavily diluted formulation of the poison ivy plant that has brought favorable results.

Suggested dosage: 6X or 30C.

An ACE Cure

Antioxidants are more than vitamins, arthritis doctors say. Much more. Antioxidant nutrients in foods and in supplements may help reduce age-related and "free radical" cellular damage to the cartilage surrounding painful joints—resulting in less pain and freer movement over time.

The approach favored by some doctors is known as ACES, for vitamins A, C, E and the mineral selenium. Recommended (and generally safe) dosages are:

- Vitamin A: 5,000 IU per day
- Vitamin C: 500 mg per day
- Vitamin E: 400 IU per day
- Selenium: 200 mcg per day

Note: Higher doses of selenium can be harmful to some people.

BALANCE PROBLEMS AND AGING *See also* **Vertigo**, *page 219*

■ *The Simple Stork Test*

Perhaps the best exercise to perform in later life is to simply stand on one foot for as long as possible, and then switch to the other foot and repeat. Easy as it sounds, this drill helps improve balance, muscle strength and flexibility—traits that are known to decline in late life when not used (and possibly cause falls). The so-called Stork Test has also been used by researchers at the National Institute on Aging to gauge subjects' rate of aging. Absent practice (starting at 15 seconds per foot, graduating to 15 minutes or more), the younger you are, the longer you will be able to stand there looking like a stork.

■ *A Helpful Yoga Pose*

It is never too late to improve your balance and coordination. The tree pose, practiced in hatha yoga, is a simple way to build confidence in your gait and posture as you age:

1 First, while standing with your bare feet parallel to each other, shift your weight to your left leg, and place the heel of your right foot against your left ankle.

2 Slowly slide your right foot up the left leg, gently helping it along with your right hand until it feels snug against your left knee or thigh. (You can hold on to a chair or table with the other hand for balance, if necessary.)

3 Let your arms hang straight down and fix your eyes straight ahead at an object in the room—the focus will help your balance. Breathe slowly and deeply.

4 Raise your arms over your head, slowly, trying to keep them as straight as possible. Bring the palms together.

5 Breathe deeply while holding this variation-on-a-tree pose as long as possible. It may be only a few seconds at first. But after you repeat with the opposite leg, and practice, you will notice improvements fairly quickly.

Remember: Age-related declines in balance are often noted by researchers in the absence of exercise. This serves as a counterattack!

BLOOD CLOTS

■ *Exercise a Solution*

We've long known that workouts are good for the heart, but only now are researchers focusing on what *exactly* makes heart vessels narrow, leading to dangerous blood clots and heart attacks. One of the answers is inactivity. When 44 men and women over age 65 were placed on a thrice-weekly walking or jogging program for six months in a recent study, they were markedly less likely to suffer blood clots than those who only did flexibility exercises. Moreover, the blood of the walkers and joggers was found to be less likely to clot in the morning—the time of day when heart attacks are most likely to occur.

Note: These substantial benefits disappeared once the exercise routines were stopped.

BONES, MUSCLES AND AGING

BUILDING STRONG BONES

■ *Preventing Osteoporosis—Precisely*

A recent change in federal guidelines calls for more calcium in our diets than was previously thought sufficient. Formerly, 800 mg was the standard recommendation for healthy bones for adults, even though most adults consume only 500 mg to 700 mg a day, researchers say.

The new numbers:

- Adults under 50 should get 1,000 mg daily.
- Adults over 50 should get 1,200 mg.
- Teenagers should get 1,300 mg!

Translation: Adults should now have four servings a day of low-fat milk, yogurt, low-fat cheese or other calcium-rich food, including fortified orange juice. To ease the load, try splitting a cup of yogurt for breakfast and lunch (or dinner) as a sweet side dish.

CARING FOR MUSCLES

■ *Arnica: A Gentle Way to Treat Pain*

After a workout or activity that is too strenuous, homeopathic remedies made from the arnica plant can help reduce or stave off feelings of soreness that become more common as one ages. In addition to reducing the throbbing or stinging associated with sharp bruises (such as a black eye), arnica also works to reduce swelling around the locus of the pain. Suggested dilution is 30C taken orally once or twice a day, as needed. You can find arnica tablets at most health or natural food markets, and even in a few grocery stores. The arnica gels and ointments, which can be applied topically to reduce muscle pain, are also widely available.

ENDURANCE PROBLEMS

■ *Chinese Root Enhances Performance*

It is no secret that as we age, our bodies slowly lose muscle and tend to build pockets or layers of unwelcome fat. One way to combat this—in conjunction with a regular exercise program—is to start taking a supplement made from a Chinese root, ciwujia, that can help boost fat metabolism and training performance. It has been utilized by mountain climbers to good effect; in animal studies, it has been

Building Muscle After Age 40

Weight lifting is not just for the young. Gerontologists and others who study aging now know that muscles built when you are 40, 50 and 60 can help more than just your self-esteem. Developed leg, trunk and arm muscles help protect older bodies from injuries related to frailty. These muscles help keep bones, which peak in density between ages 21 and 30, stronger longer.

Indirectly, new muscles also improve balance, reducing the chances of a dangerous fall in late life. Even lifting 5- or 10-pound dumbbells or using ankle weights four or five times each week can make a noticeable difference.

For safety reasons, those over 60 should lift weights only under a doctor's supervision.

shown to boost endurance. Results of human trials in both China and the US will soon tell us how effective the supplement may be. In the meantime, it can be found in health food stores under the trade name Endurox.

As a fat fighter, the root is said to shift metabolism during exercise from burning carbohydrates to burning fat. Not a bad trade-off for most middle-agers.

EYES AND AGING
See also Eye Conditions, page 112

■ Relaxing the Huxley Way

Take it from Aldous Huxley, the author of *Brave New World* and *The Art of Seeing:* Eye exercises can be not only relaxing, but also necessary for healthy vision as you age. One simple workout is called "palming," which was first popularized by Huxley back in the 1940s. Although it never caught on as mainstream visual therapy, eye doctors today continue to give the practice high marks.

First, close your eyes, then cover them with your palms—with the lower palms resting on the cheekbones. (This keeps the eyeballs from being rubbed inadvertently.) To further the relaxation, try placing your elbows on a desk or table. Maintain this position for 30 to 60 seconds, and repeat whenever you feel tired.

In addition to relieving eye strain and fatigue, your vision may improve for a time following the workout.

A Hint to Stave Off Presbyopia

The eyes, for better or worse, are true biomarkers. As such, the lens of the eye steadily hardens and thickens with age and usually begins to cause vision problems in a person's early 40s.

Close-up vision is the first to become fuzzy, as the lens has stiffened and is unable to respond fully to the muscles "tugging" at it to focus. This condition is known as presbyopia, sometimes called middle-age farsightedness.

In the field of behavioral optometry, however, some patients have been able to improve their eyesight in middle age through vision therapy and low-light visual exercises.

Not every optometrist is familiar with these exercises, and results are not yet guaranteed. But if you have the time, inclination and a disdain for corrective lenses, you may want to try working with a behavioral optometrist. Therapy sessions (some in darkened clinic rooms, where you practice tracking objects in flickering light) may last from a few weeks to a few months.

■ Blinking for Better Vision

Why think about a blink? Because it may boost your vision, eye doctors say, especially if you do a lot of close-up, near-focus, eye-straining computer work or reading. Blinking lubricates the eyes naturally, with tears, and it also rests them by shutting out light, if only for a tenth of a second at a time.

Try this easy exercise: First, blink six or so quick, flickering blinks; then close your eyes for a few seconds. During a tough day at work, after long spells on the computer or after hundreds of pages of reading, repeat the blinking drill every 20 minutes or so. Sure, you blink automatically. But adding a few here and there, experts believe, may also slow the effects of aging upon the eyes.

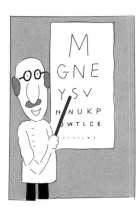

■ *Playing Safe*

The newest—and safest—way to protect your eyes from sports (and other) injuries, especially from such things as tennis balls and racquet balls that we don't react to as quickly in middle age, is to toughen up your glasses or goggles. *Here's why:* In recent tests, glasses made of high-index plastic shattered when hit by tennis balls flying at 40 mph; those made of glass shattered when hit by balls traveling at 89 mph. Meanwhile, polycarbonate lenses withstood tennis ball missiles fired at 130 mph!

CATARACT PREVENTION

■ *Sunglasses—Made in the Shade(s)*

While cataracts can strike in middle age, they are much more commonly diagnosed after age 65. Explaining the condition to patients, eye doctors sometimes compare the gradual clouding of the eye lens with adding drops of milk to a glass of clear water, one drop at a time, with each drop signifying a year's worth of aging.

Eventually the clouding of the lens can lead to blindness, though it is easily treatable with surgery. To postpone the condition, however, it helps to develop sound sunglass habits starting in one's 20s and 30s.

In bright sunlight, try to always wear good sunglasses with dark lenses. Clinical research has shown that eyes suffering from years of overexposure to ultraviolet rays are more likely to develop cataracts.

A New Lens for Murky Ones

A surgical technique for cataract sufferers that ophthalmologists are using is to replace the murky, cloudy lens of the eye with a thin, pliable, *foldable* intraocular lens.

In a way, it's the next step in the evolution of contact lenses, from the formerly rigid to the softer, and now the soft, disposable lenses. Only with cataract surgery, the foldable lenses remain in place for life.

They are inserted while folded through a tiny incision—the smaller the incision, the less trauma and faster recovery—then unfolded and placed behind the cornea. Eyesight is improved immediately.

Caution: As with any surgery, make sure your doctor has performed many of these procedures before you opt to try it.

■ *C Is for Cataract Control*

Research has found that vitamin C may help combat a myriad of diseases, including cancer and heart disease. And limited evidence suggests it may even ward off blindness. A study of 247 women, ages 56 to 71, showed that those who took vitamin C supplements for 10 years or more had 80% fewer cases of early to moderate cataracts than women who did not take supplements. More studies are needed to corroborate the link. Until then, experts say the findings offer more reason to include plenty of vitamin C–rich foods and drinks in your daily diet.

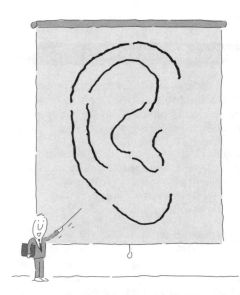

HEARING LOSS, AGING-RELATED

See also **Ear Conditions,** page 107

■ *Long-Term Hearing Protection*

Because hearing loss is often so gradual as to go unnoticed for decades, preventing age-related declines isn't commonly taught in medical schools. Nor is it practiced by most family doctors or internists. But audiologists—specialists in measuring hearing and fitting hearing aids—point out that lifestyles have made modern

middle-aged men and women pay more attention to their ears.

Consider: Noise above 85 decibels can have negative effects, while personal stereos, construction jackhammers and rock concerts have all been measured at 110 decibels. *Bottom line:* Think seriously about using earplugs when mowing the lawn, attending concerts, or if, by chance, you work in a kennel filled with yelping dogs. Drugstore-bought earplugs will help; custom-fitted ones (from an audiologist) will be more comfortable, more expensive and more effective.

HEART DISEASE PREVENTION

■ *Oatmeal Is Here to Stay*

Long before oatmeal was promoted in television ad campaigns, doctors knew that the fiber in oatmeal was good for the cardiovascular and digestive systems. Now science has caught up with folklore. Research from Rush–Presbyterian–St. Luke's Medical Center in Chicago has shown that eating one large bowl of oatmeal daily can lower overall blood cholesterol readings by 6%.

Every bit as important, oatmeal as heart helper can raise one's HDL (high-density lipoprotein, or "good")  cholesterol level by as much as 15%. What's more, these readings don't track any additional health benefits you might accrue by adding such extras as strawberries, bananas or other sweet, fibrous fruits to your bowl of oatmeal.

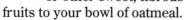

■ *The Prudent Post-Workout Cooldown*

First, congratulate yourself for having started and stuck with an exercise program. Now keep in mind one often-ignored caveat, courtesy of exercise physiologists: A proper cooldown period after exertion is not only important, it could be lifesaving. Heart irregularities and heart attacks sometimes occur after exercise, for want of a smooth deceleration of the heart rate.

Critical hints: Avoid standing still or sitting down immediately after you've exercised heavily—that includes post-workout sessions in the sauna or whirlpool. Instead, walk slowly for at least five minutes after a rigorous workout, especially if you are middle-aged or older or have known heart problems.

■ *Exercising the Heart—Gradually*

Most people realize that the better shape they're in, the less likely it is they'll get winded doing everyday things like walking up a flight of stairs. Therefore, exercising is probably the best way to keep yourself breathing freely. But if you find that you are still short of breath every time you run up a flight of stairs or go for a brisk walk, you might not be working out effectively.

The best way to increase your cardiovascular health is gradually. If you are running a mile very quickly one day, and taking a leisurely stroll the next, you are not going to build endurance. Exercise physiologists (and cardiologists) recommend the following:

1 Estimate your target training intensity (target heart rate).

2 Subtract your age from 220, then multiply the result by 65% (your lower limit) and 85% (your upper limit).

3 Start exercising at the lower limit and gradually work up to your upper limit over a period of several weeks—or longer if you still feel exhausted at the lower levels.

You should breathe easier after just a few weeks. If you are still gasping for breath, you might have exercise-induced asthma or a more serious condition. *Note:* Before you begin any exercise program, it's important to be evaluated by a physician.

TRIGLYCERIDE CONTROL

■ *"Tri"ing Harder*

In recent years, more and more doctors have begun recording and reporting patients' blood levels of triglycerides as well as their cholesterol levels. A wise move, since this fatty substance in the blood can, in high amounts, lead to coronary artery disease and heart attack. So be sure to ask about your level at your next checkup: 100 to 200 is thought to be the prime target level, and lower is better.

Three ways to keep your "tri" level down:

- Regular aerobic exercise

- Cut down on saturated fats and sugars

- Increase intake of the omega-3 fatty acids (found in tuna, sardines and flaxseed oil)

HIGH BLOOD PRESSURE PREVENTION

■ *Simply Suck Air*

One of the simplest, most-often overlooked strategies to prevent high blood pressure is, literally, right under your nose—deep breathing exercises. Try the following technique, adapted from Chinese medicine:

1 Take a slow, deep breath through the nose, allowing the lower sections of the lungs, then the rest of the lungs, to fill with air.

2 Exhale slowly, for 10 seconds, either silently, or with an audible sigh, to remind yourself that the lengthy breath has been completed.

3 Repeat these inhale/exhale workouts four to five times a day, even if only for a few minutes at a time (at red lights in traffic or perhaps each time the E-mail beeps).

The potential health benefits include lower blood pressure, increased relaxation and heightened immune defenses, according to practitioners of Chinese medicine.

HORMONAL DEFICIENCIES

■ DHEA: Too Good to Be True?

It's true that we all have lower levels of certain hormones as we age. Women and doctors have known that for decades—as they've experimented with estrogen replacement. In recent years, there's been a big buzz about DHEA (*dehydroepiandrosterone*), a hormone-like substance produced by the adrenal glands. Like estrogen, DHEA levels fall in middle age and later. And some studies have shown that people who took DHEA capsules "for replacement purposes" reported enhanced memory, improved energy, increased sex drive and reduced body fat. DHEA is now available in health food stores, being marketed as a "nutrient." That's the good news.

The not-so-good news is that, like estrogen, DHEA can be powerful stuff, with little-known, long-term effects. Scientists are not even certain what DHEA does throughout the body—and at what ages. So appropriate replacement doses are, at best, anybody's educated guess. Too good to be true? In small doses (10 mg to 25 mg a day), under a doctor's care, maybe not. In larger doses (50-mg supplements daily), it is probably not safe. In all cases, consult your doctor before taking any amount of DHEA.

IMMUNITY

■ Vitamin E for Senior Supplementation

Although immune strength typically declines with age, there are many ways to prolong youthful responses of the immune system. One proven method is to take 60 to 200 IU of vitamin E daily, as a separate supplement, beginning in your 60s.

That suggestion is based on exciting recent data from the federal government's nutrition research center at Tufts University, where two different measures of immunity were boosted after subjects took vitamin E over an eight-month period. Responses to skin tests and to a hepatitis virus were decidedly more vigorous among the E supplement group—which is one of the first times researchers have linked *cellular* responses with a vitamin supplement. Still, check with your doctor before taking the highest experimental amount, just to be safe.

INCONTINENCE

■ An Idea with Bounce

Strengthening the pelvic muscles is a key strategy in controlling urination and involuntary leakage. One valuable—and fun—exercise is

---

bouncing on a mini-trampoline or rebounder for 5 to 10 minutes daily. You will likely notice a difference within the week.

■ Biofeedback Beats Incontinence

Many patients have had great success using biofeedback to control urinary and fecal incontinence. A trained practitioner can teach a patient to become more aware of breathing rates and bodily tension in order to control emotional responses to stress, which may contribute to incontinence. Learning the biofeedback techniques may take up to 15 sessions.

Surgical Solution

A new surgical procedure can solve an emotionally traumatic problem: Incontinence. Surgeons implant a pacemaker-like device in the abdomen. The device sends electrical impulses to the nerves at the base of the spine that control the bladder, regulating its function.

If your doctor feels you would benefit from this expensive surgery, your insurance company may cover it because the procedure is FDA-approved.

■ Pelvic Pointers

Kegel exercises are praised by health practitioners as a means to prevent incontinence difficulties in both women and men. Male patients can use Kegels to strengthen pelvic muscles before prostate cancer surgery. (Gen. Norman Schwarzkopf swears that his daily Kegel routine allowed him to normalize within weeks of his radical prostatectomy.) Women can perform Kegels when experiencing any sign of symptoms.

The exercise is easy. Slowly contract the pelvic floor muscles as if you were halting urine flow (or actually practice during urination). Hold for 10 seconds, repeat several times. You can do Kegels while standing, sitting or lying down. Doing a five-minute set three times each day can produce satisfying results.

MEMORY LOSS

■ A Three-Step Brain Boost

First, remember that minor memory lapses that occur with age are normal and are not usually an indication of a serious condition like dementia or Alzheimer's disease. Some gerontologists liken the lapses to information overload—when our mental computers temporarily run out of storage space. It happens.

Here's a three-step plan that might help counter midlife memory slippage:

1 Exercise regularly, to boost blood flow throughout the body. Better blood flow to your brain has been shown to give a boost to mental function.

2 Try ginkgo biloba supplements (following package directions), which enhance blood flow to the brain and may improve memory.

3 Ask your doctor about taking phosphatidylserine—a fatty substance that has been shown to halt memory loss (and at times improve memory) in those who have suffered such deterioration. Suggested dosage is 200 to 300 mg per day, but it may take a few months to notice improvement.

Note: If your doctor is not familiar with phosphatidylserine, he or she may want to substitute L-acetyl carnitine, an amino acid, as a three-times-a-day supplement (500 to 1,000 mg in each dose).

■ Zinc Can Bring Mindful Zing

When many people age, they may suffer nutritional deficiencies for the first time. Either their eating habits decline somewhat, or their bodies are less efficient at processing and absorbing nutrients. That is one reason why federal researchers advise everyone—but especially older men and women—to think more about zinc. Recent research has shown that zinc supplements can improve memory and clarity of thinking in cases of deficiency. Check with your doctor about side effects.

Dosage: 15 mg a day has been tested as safe and effective.

■ Use Your Home to Remember Better

Experts in aging like to remind us from time to time that often when we think we've forgotten something, we haven't. It's merely been "misplaced," or blocked by the interference from all the knowledge we've gained over a lifetime. That is one reason why gerontologists suggest a literal home remedy for boosting memory.

If you need to remember a list of 10 objects, say, pretend you are walking through your home. Visualize your walk and mentally stop and pick up each object from a familiar place in your house—for example, a can of paint in the hallway, a box of tissues from the top of the wine rack, and so on. The journey with occasional stops (in familiar surroundings) becomes easier to remember than an abstract list.

Researchers say that this linking of familiar and unfamiliar works especially well among the memory-impaired elderly, so you can just imagine the memory boost it can provide to those of us in need of only a little fine-tuning now and then.

■ Using Ginkgo to Boost Memory

Currently approved in Germany to treat memory loss and anxiety, among other conditions, the use of ginkgo biloba as medicine dates back at least 500 years, to the Ming dynasty. The leafy extract is said to enhance memory by boosting blood flow to, and through, the brain. Store-bought formulations of the extract are the most popular, herbalists report, since it takes bundles of leaves to make each small dose. Suggested dosage is 40 to 120 mg daily as a tonic.

Ginkgo Safety Alert

Although ginkgo biloba has been shown to boost mental alertness and memory in many cases, it can sometimes be harmful. Usually, a 40 mg dose twice a day would be considered safe. But when taken by people who are also taking aspirin regularly, the combined blood-thinning effects can cause blurred vision or other problems.

So if you suffer from any recurring bleeding problems, such as an ulcer, or if you're taking aspirin, vitamin E or prescription blood thinners, consult your doctor before trying ginkgo.

■ *Helpful Fatty Supplement*

It may be easier to take than to spell—phosphatidylserine—and in the long run, it may be well worth taking. That's the belief of doctors who have studied age-related declines in memory. Phosphatidylserine is a nutritional supplement, not a drug; as such, it is more widely known in alternative than in conventional medicinal circles.

In short, it is a fatty substance that may halt memory declines and even bring memory improvements (at least among those who have already suffered some decline). You may see results over the course of two or three months.

It is too soon to tell whether this supplement, available at health food stores, can help prevent memory decline from occurring in the first place.

METABOLISM CONCERNS

*See also **Obesity,** page 184*

■ *Try a Trick of the Mind*

With age, the stomach doesn't shrink, or stretch, as much as it becomes sluggish. It's part of an overall slowdown that takes place in the digestive tract, and with metabolism. At age 50 or 60, you just don't burn calories as

easily as you used to, which is why sly nutritionists and personal trainers offer this trick of the mind (and body) to help you lose weight or maintain a healthy weight in middle or old age: Start thinking about food consumption and physical exercise as *one metabolic activity*. Of course, they're intimately connected, but most people don't think of them that way.

If you do start to link up food and fitness thoughts throughout the day, week and year, you will notice a change in your behavior. You won't count calories or fat grams as much as overall energy, or energy you ought to expend on exercise. If you are sedentary all day and only work out once a week, rethink the heavy power lunches. Over time you'll be more comfortable with your body—and your weight as well.

SENSORY CONCERNS

KEEP A YOUTHFUL SENSE OF SMELL

It's a fact of aging: Eyesight deteriorates. And taste buds fade a bit, too, making food taste more bland. What most people don't know, however, is that our sense of smell, too, fades in our 50s, 60s and beyond.

The good news is, you can do something to preserve your sense of smell: Take zinc. Research has shown that zinc plays a significant role in preserving the sense of smell, and that people become deficient in zinc as they age. The suggested amount, for those thought to be slightly deficient, is 20 mg daily.

SEXUAL MATTERS
*See also **Sexual Concerns**, page 188*

INHIBITED SEXUAL DESIRE

■ *Sex and Self-Esteem*

ISD, or inhibited sexual desire in the parlance of sex experts, is one of the sexual problems most frequently cited by aging men and women. Drugs or purported aphrodisiacs alone cannot "cure" the trouble. Testosterone levels in men and estrogen levels in women drop in middle age, but that isn't the whole story. Often, sexual desire has as much to do with self-esteem as it does with hormones.

The first thing individuals and couples should try when analyzing a loss of desire is to gauge how they are feeling about themselves, physically and mentally. Is there a life event—job or family occurrence—that is interfering with the ability to relax and enjoy good sex? If so, that issue needs to be addressed.

Next, sex therapists say, try to work on your body to help boost your musculature as well as your self-esteem. The stronger your body, the better you'll feel about it.

Finally, commit to keeping a sexual desire diary. For at least a week, write down everything during the day that stimulates interest or desire for sex—and rate it from 1 to 10 in terms of its power. Even fleeting images from a newspaper or TV ad should be logged. If you feel adventurous, share your diary with your partner. It's a great way for couples to communicate deeply personal desires without saying them aloud.

PERFORMANCE ANXIETY

■ *A Relaxing Approach*

Performances usually occur on stage, on screen or in an arena. Ideally, sex should not be viewed as a performance, where one partner performs, while the other acts interested but passive. And even though erections *do* take longer to rise in one's 40s and 50s (and longer to reappear between acts of intercourse) than in one's 20s and 30s, it is not something to fear. Just knowing the physiological facts helps assuage feelings of inadequacy.

Another way to ease anxiety about sex in midlife is to shift to what Oakland sexologist Bernie Zilbergeld, PhD, calls "pleasuring the soft penis." It's a pre-Viagra sex therapy trick that's quite successful, even if it isn't exactly common. The goal for a man (and his partner) is to not focus on erection, but on receiving pleasure in a flaccid state. He doesn't have to "perform" at all as he or his partner massages his genitals in a relaxed, warm state. When thought of as an exercise, it's often less threatening to anxious partners—and in just a few sessions, surprisingly effective.

■ *Smoother Moves*

Because some sexual changes are inevitable with aging, it helps to prepare for them before they have a chance to rob you of spontaneity—

and pleasure. Start with sexual response: It slows down for both men and women in their 40s, almost imperceptibly, but enough for people to worry about performance in ways they didn't think about in their 20s. Men fear their erections may not be firm enough, fast enough. Women may begin to lose vaginal moisture in middle age, causing them concern about painful intercourse and whether arousal is happening.

One underused but wildly successful tool recommended by sex therapists in recent years is Astroglide, a water-based sexual lubricant that is a lot more than petroleum jelly. It is often described as "realistic" by first-time users; the bonus is that it can be used by both sexes.

Eros is another highly realistic lubricant—one that is silicone-based but "fully condom compatible," in the words of sexual health experts.

Further, many couples find that applying these lubricants offers partners creative sensual possibilities.

SKIN PROBLEMS

*See also **Skin Conditions**, page 193*

AGE SPOTS

■ *Peeling Your Skin*

Not surprisingly, the mere thought of using any kind of acid on the skin is frightening to many people. But since the early 1990s, dermatologists and researchers have used alphahydroxy acids (AHAs)—naturally found in many fruits—quite safely and effectively to help slow the process of skin aging and to restore a more youthful appearance. In other procedures, known as peels, a solution of mild topical acid

is applied to the skin, which in turn reddens and abrades the skin's top layers.

The use of these peels has branched out from the face to the neck, chest, arms and legs—anywhere that discoloration and wrinkles have taken hold. Dermatologists also say that the peels can remove precancerous spots on the skin, a helpful preventive measure.

Nonprescription forms of AHAs are found in many cosmetic creams, though their effectiveness in these formulations is not documented.

Essential News About Essential Oils

Throughout the cosmetics industry, you'll hear praise for the power of citrus fruit compounds to help keep skin healthy and young looking. One warning demands attention: When some women and men use citrus peel essential oils—such as grapefruit, mandarin and tangerine—on their face in the sun, the pigment of their skin may be altered or "stained" by the combined oil and sun exposure. In some instances, the discoloration can be irreversible, according to dermatologists. They suggest, in short, avoiding the citrus peel oils altogether in summer, when heading out-of-doors.

■ *Temporary Remover*

If you do not care to experiment with permanent fixes for age spots, stretch marks and other skin imperfections, but want a quick fix for a day at the beach, there are solutions. And, say some dermatologists, there is no need to buy the heavy-duty cover-ups that require a prescription.

A much more elegant, inexpensive way to cover up imperfections is to buy a concealer from a cosmetics company such as Clinique. Try Advanced Concealer or City Block.

Note: Both are waterproof, a big must for sun-savvy frolicking in the water.

New, Safer "Laser Lift"

Through most of the 1980s and 1990s, laser face-lifts were regarded by traditional plastic surgeons as unproven, temporary, hype-laden solutions to problems of sagging skin. Finally, in the late 1990s, advances in laser technology led certain surgeons and dermatologists to speak more highly of the potential of new, CO_2 laser surgery to smooth the skin and minimize wrinkles. The doctors stopped short, however, of deeming it equal to a surgical face-lift.

Surgeons have been praising the effects of a newer treatment, using the element erbium in place of CO_2 for "laser resurfacing" to minimize the effects of aging. Because the erbium laser is absorbed by the skin more rapidly than are other lasers, there may be less pain and reddening after the procedure—and less anesthesia used during the procedure. Plus, instead of two-to-four weeks of recovery typical after other laser resurfacings, erbium laser patients may recover in as little as one-to-two weeks.

Costs for full-face treatments may drop, once scores of doctors order the equipment—and after thousands of case histories are collected.

For more information, contact the American Society of Plastic Surgeons at 888-475-2784 or www.plasticsurgery.org.

WRINKLING

■ *New Approach to a Younger-Looking Neck*

Even after a face-lift, many women and men continue to "look their age" because of the tell-tale wrinkles and lines below the face, on and about the neck. (Face-lifts don't always lift enough skin.) Recently, though, plastic surgeons and dermatologists have had success in improving the appearance of wrinkling skin on the neck by giving their clients injections of Botox, a toxin made by the bacteria that causes botulism, of all things.

It works by temporarily paralyzing certain muscles that cause wrinkles, in this case, platysma muscles of the neck. Dermatologists and plastic surgeons say that safety is not a problem when a well-versed and experienced physician does the treatment. (The doctor should be board-certified and have performed at least 50 of these procedures prior to yours.) For information or referrals, check with:

■ The American Society of Plastic Surgeons at 888-475-2784 or www.plasticsurgery.org

■ The American Society for Dermatologic Surgery at 800-441-2737 or www.asds-net.org

■ The American Academy of Facial Plastic and Reconstructive Surgery at 703-299-9291 or www.facial-plastic-surgery.org

■ An Aromatherapy Approach

Many people get their first whiff of frankincense inside a dimly lit massage room at a spa. The scent is as mysterious as it is relaxing. And now aromatherapists and other skin care professionals say that essential oils from the frankincense tree have an added benefit: They help to reduce the fine lines of aging on the skin. Mixed with a carrier oil, such as sweet almond oil or cold-pressed olive oil (in a standard ratio of 2% essential oil to 98% carrier), and applied twice a day, frankincense is a fragrant alternative to other anti-aging potions for the skin.

■ Can Estrogen Help Smooth Fine Lines?

While not a widely publicized benefit of hormone replacement therapy (HRT), much younger looking, less wrinkled skin appears to be one of the side effects. In fact, one recent study of 4,000 women showed that those who took estrogen were 30% less likely to have wrinkles and dry skin than women who did not take estrogen after menopause. (Some doctors believe estrogen supplements may build collagen, the connective tissue in skin that diminishes with age.)

Caution: Check with your doctor about the possibility of other, potentially harmful side effects of HRT.

■ Promising Japanese Vitamin Treatment

Just when American women thought they were up to speed on alphahydroxy acid (AHA) cosmetics that help keep skin looking younger longer, a new skin formulation has jumped into the fray. Over the years, AHAs, or fruit acids, have been shown to slough the surface skin layers lightly while cleansing, providing a more youthful appearance. Now it appears that a form of concentrated vitamin C, mixed with a form of magnesium, helps maintain youthful skin as well as, or perhaps better than, AHAs.

The new formula is called Mag C, and it is patented by Japanese researchers. It doesn't irritate the skin, and actually penetrates the dermal layer to help undo sun damage. Mag C is applied twice each day to firm and smooth facial skin. Ask your dermatologist about this and other "cosmeceuticals," the hottest category of aging-related skin products.

■ Mix Your Own Wrinkle Cream

Glycolic acid is a member of the alphahydroxy acid family and is a naturally occurring substance that most often comes from sugar cane. Glycolic acid helps reduce the appearance of tiny facial lines by sloughing away dead skin cells. One product known to reduce wrinkles, age spots and scars is a mixture of glycolic acid and hydroquinone, a depigmenting agent and antioxidant. You can mix your own formula easily. Although lotions containing alphahydroxy acids can be quite costly, both glycolic acid and hydroquinone are available inexpensively, over the counter.

To mix your own wrinkle-reducing cream, mix 98% glycolic acid with 2% hydroquinone.

■ *A Natural Anti-Wrinkle Mask*

Applied once a week, this mask will help smooth out fine lines and prevent the occurrence of new ones. Mix one tablespoon of honey and one half teaspoon of nutmeg and apply to the face. Leave on for 20 minutes, then lightly tap the face all over with your fingers to stimulate and improve circulation. Remove the mask with warm water and a washcloth. The grainy texture of the nutmeg sloughs off dead cells, while the honey, a natural humectant, draws moisture from the air and into the skin.

■ *Aloe Anti-Wrinkle Mask*

The property that allows the aloe plant to survive the dry desert is its ability to draw moisture from the air—so imagine what it can do for your skin. Mix equal parts of cosmetic-quality aloe (not burn gel) from the health food store with vegetable glycerin. Apply the mixture to your face and leave on for 20 minutes.

The aloe will help reduce fine lines, pitting and scarring. After three months of daily use, your skin will look firmer, smoother and younger.

■ *Milk for Sun-Damaged Skin*

The sun, a major cause of aging, tends to leave skin dried out and wrinkled. Naturally fatty dairy products can help plump up cells and moisturize depleted skin. Spread buttermilk or plain yogurt straight onto the skin. Leave it on for 20 minutes, then rinse well with warm water.

■ *Guacamole Facial*

Next time you eat an avocado, don't throw away the peel. A naturally fatty fruit, avocado is also rich in vitamins, and the green pulp left attached to the peel has the highest concentration. Scrape off the pulp, and apply it directly to the skin. The abundant oils lubricate and soften the skin—the most basic step in preventing wrinkles.

An Electric Face-Lift?

Whether it's called electric stimulation or electrotherapy, the medical practice of dispensing low (and safe) levels of pulsed electricity to the skin can help reduce wrinkles and aging lines. Of course, doctors and plastic surgeons say electrotherapy is no substitute for a face-lift. Even so, others point out that by stimulating certain acupuncture points on the face, the muscle contractions that follow indeed strengthen those muscles and temporarily "tighten" the facial skin. The more youthful look that follows, however, does not last much longer than a few weeks. Repeat procedures can be costly, as much as $200 per session.

■ Homemade Essential Oil Combo

Herbalists, aromatherapists and more than a few dermatologists agree: Sometimes the natural essential oils do as good a job of arresting skin damage as the steeply priced designer cosmetics. This combination facial oil is a favorite around Europe, and is gaining in popularity in the US.

> 8 drops geranium oil
> 5 drops lavender oil
> 5 drops carrot seed oil
> 4 drops chamomile
> 2 drops sandalwood
> 1 drop patchouli
> ¼ cup hazelnut oil (or apricot kernel)
>   as the carrier oil

Remember: Essential oils are *strong* stuff. The standard dilution guideline is 2% essential oil to 98% carrier oil, which may be hazelnut oil, cold-pressed sesame oil or another oil of your choice.

■ Refine Wrinkles in Sensitive Skin

If your skin is irritated by alphahydroxy acids or standard moisturizers with preservatives or fragrance, try this natural skin softener. Mix one ounce of a light but moisturizing carrier oil (apricot kernel works well) and four drops of neroli, chamomile or geranium oil. This should help increase skin turnover without redness or irritation.

■ Put the Spring Back in Your Skin

The natural aging process, sun exposure and smoking often cause skin to lose elasticity. Two essential oils are especially useful for restoring a youthful glow. Add a few drops of neroli, from the flower of the orange plant, or geranium essential oils to your base oil or moisturizer to help slough away dead skin and generate new cells.

■ Medication for Aging Skin?

Tretinoin, more commonly known by its trade name, Retin-A, has long been a staple for teenagers suffering from acne. But many dermatologists prescribe the topical version of the drug Renova to older patients to diminish the appearance of such nuisances as stretch marks, wrinkles, age spots and even freckling. The FDA approved Renova in 1995 for use in improving the look of skin damaged by sun exposure.

Renova works by regenerating collagen in the skin and sloughing off dead skin, essentially ridding the skin of sun-damaged cells and allowing the healthy cells underneath to mature normally. To determine whether Renova will work for you, it's best to consult your dermatologist.

Side effects include temporary peeling, redness, blistering and increased sensitivity to the sun.

For general questions, check out the Web site, www.tryrenova.com.

■ *Vitamin C Fights Wrinkles*

Few wrinkles are caused by aging alone. Usually, exposure to sun and pollution (such as cigarette smoke) speeds the otherwise natural aging process, adding wrinkles. Research now shows that topical vitamin C can help protect skin against wrinkles, and reduce the appearance of existing lines.

Topical vitamin C usually comes in the form of serums, gels or creams, which may contain anywhere from 5% to 10% of the vitamin. These solutions can help skin retain elasticity and firmness, making the skin appear smoother.

SKIN CANCER PREVENTION

■ *Mole Census Reduces Your Risks*

Call it a dermatologist's hunch that's been proven true: People with 50 or more normal-looking moles are three times as likely to develop melanoma skin cancer as are those with 25 or fewer moles. A recent study in the *Journal of the American Medical Association* also pointed out that having just one abnormal-looking mole doubles a person's risk of developing melanoma, while having 10 or more such moles increases the odds by more than 10.

Bottom line: Have a dermatologist examine, photograph and track any moles or age spots anywhere on your body at least once a year.

■ *Sun Block—Not Just for Summer*

Back in the dark ages of skin care, the 1960s and 1970s, before sun protection factors (SPFs) became ubiquitous, tanning was the name of the game. But even though SPFs now reach sky high, to 40 and above, they are still not used often enough. Typically, most people apply them only in summer, or in winter if they visit tropical locales. Meanwhile, across the US, skin cancer rates are rising. The point is that sun damage and related wrinkling accrue over years, not months—and spring, winter and fall account for three-quarters of every year. So get in the habit of moisturizing, with SPF 15 and above, beginning in young adulthood. And, as dermatologists remind us, it's never too late to start.

CHAPTER 2

Treatments for Everyday Ailments

ABSCESSES AND SORES

MOUTH, CHEEK AND GUMS

■ *Mouth Sore Brush-off*

Research shows that sodium lauryl sulfate (SLS), the detergent commonly found in commercial toothpastes, may dry out the lining of the mouth and gums. Without this protective layer, foods and drinks that are highly acidic can attack sensitive gums and cheeks. To protect your teeth—and your mouth—switch to a toothpaste that doesn't contain SLS.

You can also use homemade toothpaste: Mix equal amounts of hydrogen peroxide and baking soda, and dip your brush into the paste.

■ *Natural Winter-Ready Therapies*

The coldest season brings on the highest number of cold and canker sores. Aromatherapists suggest applying tea tree oil at first outbreak, then three or four times each day. Some cold sufferers also claim that zinc lozenges (commonly used to alleviate cold symptoms) have worked to calm down canker outbreaks.

■ *Raspberry Relief*

Herbalists all over swear by highly astringent raspberry leaf gargle for soothing mouth sores. To prepare this beneficial rinse:

1 Add a heaping teaspoon of dried raspberry leaves (available at health food stores and tea shops) to a cup of boiled water.

2 Let the tea steep for 30 minutes, then strain.

Gargle a mouthful for one minute, three times a day. By the next day, you will see—and feel—results. This soothing gargle will also relieve angry abscessed areas and the irritation caused by new braces.

Note: Keep the tea refrigerated between treatments, and make up a new cup for each day's use.

■ Lysine Cure for Viral Sores

For speedy healing of mouth sores associated with a viral infection, supplement your diet with lysine tablets. Lysine is an amino acid that blocks arginine, another amino acid that fuels the herpes virus. Lysine tablets are available in most health food stores and nutrition centers. Take a 500 mg dose three times a day until the sore disappears.

■ Tea for Two Treatments

The herbal balm for healing a herpes outbreak? Lemon balm. It's rich in antiviral properties that battle the herpes virus. Look for tea bags in your health food store. You may drink up to three cups a day. For an effective spot treatment, place a lemon balm tea bag that's been soaked in warm water directly onto the blisters for 15 minutes.

■ A Goldenseal Heal

Rinse your mouth out with goldenseal tea. Goldenseal is a popular herb used to treat colds and boost the immune system. Why? It contains a natural antibiotic known as berberine, making it a great solution for sores and spots associated with infection and illness. Brew tea from a teaspoon of dried goldenseal and hot water, then strain and refrigerate the liquid. Use the chilled tea as a mouth rinse, three to four times a day until the area is healed.

SKIN SORES

■ Go Bananas!

If a skin irritation is driving you crazy, go to the produce store and buy some extremely ripe bananas. The bananas' enzymes and high sugar content will kill bacteria, help draw out toxins and dry up any "weeping" or oozing associated with a sickly sore.

Mash up the fruit or scrape the inside of the peel, then apply it directly onto the sore. Cover the area with gauze and surgical tape. Leave the treatment on overnight—uncovering and cleaning the area in the morning—and you'll see much improvement.

■ Tea Tree Treatment

Tea tree oil, found in health food stores and in pharmacies, is an antidote to skin irritations: Its antimicrobial properties make it a powerful antidote to all sorts of abscessed areas. (It is also widely used in aromatherapy to lift moods.) For abscesses, apply a drop directly to the area with a cotton swab in the morning, and again in the evening.

■ Casting Call for Plaster of Paris

The material that makes up plaster casts for broken bones contains some valuable, often overlooked healing properties, according to homeopathic doctors. Plaster of paris, or calcium sulfate, is a tissue salt (in the medical sense) that acts as a blood cleanser and wound healer to treat abscesses and "weepy" sores.

Note: This remedy may promote discharge at first, but that's normal in the healing process. Suggested dilution is 6C, or as labeled on the homeopathic product packaging.

ALCOHOLISM

■ Benefits of Combined Natural Therapies

Along with medical help from a physician or psychotherapist, acupuncture has been beneficial during alcohol withdrawal and the detoxification period. In particular, it can minimize stress-related cravings that will recur from time to time during detoxification.

While the appetite is suppressed (a common occurrence during withdrawal), vegetable and fruit juices, warm broths, soups and herbal teas, including chamomile, valerian root and skullcap, are suggested. (One of the goals of detox is to replenish fluids and increase intake of alkaline foods.)

In addition, taking an amino acid supplement, L-glutamine, is often advised, as it can be helpful in reducing cravings for both alcohol and sugar.

■ Herbal Remedy for Constant Cravings

Research shows that pueraria, otherwise known as kudzu vine, diminishes alcohol cravings. The vine is also thought to relieve hangovers. An herbalist or an expert in Chinese medicine can help you locate pueraria capsules or a tincture, and can outline an individual course of treatment—in combination with other therapies if necessary—to control alcohol addiction.

ALLERGIES
*See also **Hay Fever**, page 142*

GENERAL ENVIRONMENTAL ALLERGIES

■ Cleaning Products to Blame?

If you or a family member notice outbreaks of allergy-like symptoms while housecleaning (or the day after), you may be suffering from a tough-to-diagnose environmental illness. Excess exposure to detergents and cleaning solutions may be contributing to the condition. A new, and highly controversial, medical specialty—clinical ecology—has developed over the past 20 years to provide additional expertise to patients, allergists and other doctors. Patients are advised to substitute organic foods for commercially prepared ones, and natural-based cleaning products and homemade scrubs for commercial cleaners.

For a list of alternative cleaning products, write or contact:

■ The Ecology Center, 117 N. Division St., Ann Arbor, MI 48104 (734-761-3186, www.ecocenter.org).

■ Washington Toxics Coalition, 4649 Sunnyside Ave. N., Suite 540, Seattle, WA 98103 (206-632-1545, www.watoxics.org).

Negative Energy, Positive Results

Do you feel you have more than your share of allergies? You could be surrounded by too much "positive" energy. *One solution:* Try using a negative-ion generator, which emits tiny, invisible, odorless and electrically charged particles into your home or office.

Negative ions, environmental air experts say, actually stick to irritants and allergens, forcing them to adhere to surfaces instead of remaining free-floating. Once they stick, you can sweep or dust the allergens away. The ion generators can be obtained through mail-order catalogs, Internet suppliers and allergy clinics.

■ A Lymph Massage Boost

If your allergy symptoms such as sinuses and congestion are lingering, and you suspect that your condition is bogged down by poor diet and/or an especially high pollen count, take a cue from Europeans who are similarly afflicted. Drs. Emil and Estrid Vodder developed lymph (or lymphatic) massage in the 1930s as a way to help detoxify the body. The light-touch, "feathery" massage technique is said to work on and in the body, *between* the surface of the skin and muscles, to help remove metabolic waste, toxins and allergens from tissues—quickly. You can request this type of massage from a growing number of massage therapists.

■ Acupressure Allergy Relief

An especially powerful acupressure point that is used to help clear the sense organs sits just beyond the fleshy part of your hand between the forefinger and thumb. Simply press one thumb against this point on the opposite hand (for 15 to 30 seconds) to help open up your sinuses.

A more direct approach favored by acupressure therapists is to press clean fingertips to the sides of the nose, slightly above the nostrils, for about a minute at a time. Do the same to your sinuses, slightly above each eyebrow.

■ Bee Pollen Power

Besides its ability to boost energy, bee pollen is said to help prevent allergies. Naturopaths and others often recommend it. Try adding a teaspoon of the sweet granules (now widely available in health food stores) to your daily diet during allergy seasons. If you are especially sensitive to pollen, start with only a few granules. *Caution:* You should avoid bee products altogether if you are allergic to bees.

■ Detoxify for Allergy Prevention

Many naturopaths and Ayurvedic doctors recommend fasting between seasons to cleanse the system and prepare for the changing weather and vegetation. Complete abstention from food is not practical for many people, so consider doing a cleanse instead. Some painless ways to help detoxify include:

- Eating a large salad or plate of steamed vegetables for dinner each night.

- Drinking organic apple juice mixed with a scoop of psyllium seed husks in the morning and night. Psyllium seed husks are nondigestible and are exceptionally effective in cleansing the walls of the intestinal tract.

Another herb effective in cleansing the colon is cascara sagrada.

Fresh, Spicy Solution

Paying special attention to your diet during allergy season could alleviate your symptoms. Try cutting back on mucus-producing foods like dairy products and orange juice. On the other hand, pour on the salsa: Spicy foods help thin mucus and aid breathing. Finally, take your eating cues from what's growing—right now. Ayurvedics believe it is best, and most healthful, to eat with the seasons.

Potent Herbal Decongestant

If you suffer from stopped-up sinuses and bronchial passages caused by the first signs of spring and late summer, consider a natural decongestant: Ma Huang. This traditional Chinese medicinal herb contains a similar stimulant to many over-the-counter allergy medications found in the West and acts much like adrenaline to stimulate circulation. *Caution:* Because Ma Huang is a powerful herb that can raise your blood pressure and heart rate, check with your physician before taking the treatment. (See *Ma Huang's Woes*, page 58.) For hay fever relief, take *no more* than 0.6 g three times a day.

For a milder effect, many naturopaths and herbalists suggest using formulations that contain the whole plant—not just the root.

An A-peeling Remedy

"I can't believe I ate the whole thing." That's what some are saying about an unusual allergy remedy that calls for consuming an entire orange—peel and all. The rind and pulp are loaded with vitamin C, essential oils and bioflavonoids, making a combination antihistamine and decongestant. Select organically grown oranges to ensure that the peels will be pesticide-free.

Drowning Congestion

Feeling so stuffed up you can't even think straight? Take a break and drink to your health. Consuming extra fluids helps to thin mucus and drain sinuses. Water or herbal tea are your best bets. Experts suggest drinking at least eight cups a day during an allergy attack. *Please note:* Coffee and caffeine-laden soft drinks can have a dehydrating effect on the body.

Need Relief? Try Acupuncture

It's the drug-free alternative for allergy relief: Acupuncture. Inserting and stimulating needles in the sinus areas of the face will balance and correct energy flow, diminishing inflammation of passages and improving the immune system's response to allergens. However, it's not a quick fix: Up to 15 sessions, say experts, may be necessary before you notice any improvement.

■ *Breathe Again—Thanks to Homeopathic Pulsatilla*

Whether from seasonal allergies or congestion from the common cold, a homeopathic remedy may relieve sinus stuffiness. The powerful prescription? Pulsatilla, a circulatory aid, gets the body's fluids moving to break up congestion in the sinuses. Take a 30C dilution three times a day. You should feel your sinuses becoming clearer after just a few doses.

■ *Go Ahead, Inhale*

It's the minty-fresh allergy remedy: The menthol in peppermint or spearmint helps to relax and open air passages. To maximize the healing power of mint:

1 Put a few drops of essential oil in a pot of hot, steaming water.

2 Place your head covered with a towel about 10 inches above the bowl, and deeply inhale the scented steam.

A few minutes of this mint-based kitchen inhaler should provide marked relief.

■ *A Preseason Plan*

Long before allergy shots became common, practitioners of Asian medicine prescribed natural ways to prevent, or minimize, allergy symptoms. This two-step plan includes a tea and a digestive remedy, following the belief that many allergy symptoms go beyond the sinuses.

For the tea, combine one-eighth teaspoon each of cumin powder, coriander powder and fennel seed powder in one cup of water. Steep the herbs for five minutes into a tea and sip it after breakfast. (If you don't like the taste, you don't need to drink it hot; lukewarm is fine.)

The second part of the five-day plan is Xiao Yao Wan, a Chinese medicine herbal remedy that works to minimize symptoms of both sinus and hay fever, among others. Xiao Yao Wan is available at Chinese herb shops and pharmacies, and is becoming increasingly available at specialty health product stores.

■ *Improve Your Air Conditioning*

When suffering from allergies, you need all the allergen-free air you can get. That includes improving the air you breathe, courtesy of air conditioners. When using an air conditioner in the car, run

---

Ma Huang's Woes: When Bad Things Happen to Good Herbs

In the mid-1990s, as many Americans began to discover the effects of Ma Huang to treat asthma and other ills, numerous marketers decided to combine this energizing Chinese herb with caffeine (and other stimulants) and to sell the herb combos as diet aids and energy pills. And that's where trouble began: When Ma Huang (also known as ephedra) is combined with caffeine, it can result in such side effects as increased heart rate and blood pressure and jittery, overactive nerves. In fact, nearly two dozen deaths were associated with a suspected overdose of the combined stimulants, forcing the FDA to ban these products. And rightly so.

Herbalists point out that taken by itself—as directed by naturopaths, allergists and other health practitioners—herbal Ma Huang can ease bronchial congestion caused by allergies and asthma. And quite often it can do so without side effects. Chinese healers have known this for centuries. Problems crop up in natural medicine circles when marketing gets in the way of medicine.

it for at least a few minutes with the windows *open*. This is a quick-and-easy way to clean and improve the air quality you will be breathing in the enclosed space. At home, make certain you keep air conditioning filters clean, changing (or cleaning) them even more often than manufacturers suggest.

ITCHY, WATERY EYES

■ *A Watery Eye for a Watery Eye*

Based on the homeopathic principle that a minute dose of what causes symptoms can help to cure them, once the immune system is activated and targeted, homeopaths suggest swallowing allium cepa tablets derived from the all-time greatest eye irritant, onions. Take a 30C preparation once or twice a day, and you'll see the difference—clearly.

■ *Eyebright Solution*

An herb from the figwort family, eyebright is also known as euphrasia. Homeopaths recommend this herb for the treatment of watery, red eyes associated with colds and allergies—even viral infections like conjunctivitis.

Note: Bacterial conjunctivitis should be treated with antibiotic eyedrops.

Eyebright is full of niacin, manganese, potassium and ascorbic acid, and is known to have astringent, antihistamine and antiviral properties. Take 35 drops of a tincture orally three times a day for relief, or a 30C tablet once or twice a day.

■ *Take the Sting out of Allergies*

Although taking freeze-dried stinging nettle may sound like it will cause sniffles and sneezes, herbalists swear by it. Stinging nettle provides relief not only for itchy, irritated eyes, but also for scratchy throats caused by seasonal allergies. (It is also rich in iron and trace minerals.) Take one 435 mg capsule

A British Cure

For many allergy sufferers, a treatment known as Enzyme Potentiated Desensitization (EPD) has provided long-term relief when more traditional forms of allergy treatments have failed. EPD was first introduced in England in the 1960s; since then, it has been used in that country and others as a treatment for many types of allergies, including those caused by food, chemicals and inhalants, such as pollen.

EPD treatment is a series of injections of tiny amounts of allergens combined with an enzyme that helps kick in the immunizing effects of the allergens. The number and frequency of the injections depend on the type and severity of the allergies. Studies now being conducted in the US, according to FDA guidelines, show that EPD's overall success rate is 75% to 80%.

Patients preparing for EPD treatment must undergo a series of medical tests to ensure that there are no preexisting conditions, such as hormonal dysfunctions, which may interfere with the treatment. In addition, patients must follow strict dietary and/or environmental guidelines before and after each injection—to help avoid any potential allergens.

At the time of this writing, there are only about 70 doctors in the US who are trained to administer EPD. That number should grow quickly once the FDA approves the method. To get a list of physicians who perform the procedure, you can fax The American EPD Society at 505-820-7315. This organization will not give advice or answer questions by phone.

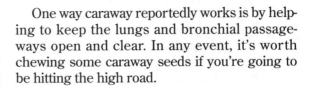
every two to four hours as needed. Or, try drinking a few cups of stinging nettle tea, available from health food stores.

Cranialosteopathy Treatment

It's all in your head. That's the theory behind cranialosteopathy, a hands-on touch therapy that works to adjust slightly the bones of the skull and face, which helps relieve sinus pressure and promote drainage for some. Depending on the severity of your allergies, you may need frequent treatments—once a week—during high allergy season. And you may also need to supplement the therapy with other remedies that work to suppress reactions to environmental allergens.

ALTITUDE SICKNESS

■ Carry Caraway

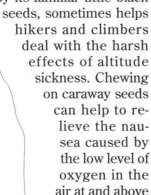

Caraway, an unlikely member of the parsley family distinguished by its familiar little black seeds, sometimes helps hikers and climbers deal with the harsh effects of altitude sickness. Chewing on caraway seeds can help to relieve the nausea caused by the low level of oxygen in the air at and above 10,000 feet.

One way caraway reportedly works is by helping to keep the lungs and bronchial passageways open and clear. In any event, it's worth chewing some caraway seeds if you're going to be hitting the high road.

ANEMIA

■ Liquid Iron—An Uncommon Option

Besides increasing one's intake of dark green leafy vegetables and small portions of (preferably organic) meat, those with iron-deficient anemia can look for what's called "food source" liquid iron. This often overlooked supplement is available at better natural food stores. Follow package directions.

ANXIETY See also *Stress, page 206*

■ Needlework Induces the Relaxation Response

Needlepoint may relieve stress as well as meditation can. Researchers have found that needlepoint, knitting and other gently repetitive activities break the flow of rapidly changing conscious thought that normally fills our

A Prescription for Calm Confidence

Severe or chronic performance anxiety can be paralyzing. Fortunately, beta-blockers—often prescribed by physicians to lower blood pressure in patients with hypertension—can help control performance anxiety and keep you calm, cool and collected when used in low doses. For more information on this drug therapy, ask your physician.

minds. This produces the same effect as meditation, involving lower blood pressure and heart rate, slower breathing and the feeling of calmness, a combination known as the relaxation response. *Best:* Choose an activity you enjoy, and spend at least 20 minutes a day on it.

■ Scents and Sensibility

Scientific research shows that different scents work directly on the brain to stir memories, moods and emotions. In fact, some odors actually slow brain wave activity to the alpha range—the same frequency induced during meditation. A few scents to soothe and quiet: Vanilla, geranium and bergamot. Just place two or three drops of essential oil on a cotton ball, and take a whiff when you're feeling out of sorts.

■ Purple Reigns

Sweet-smelling lavender is a favorite of aromatherapists to ease nervous tension and soothe stressed-out senses. How can you get the benefits? For a relaxing do-it-yourself rubdown, mix two to three drops of essential oil of lavender into a cup of almond oil and massage the solution into your temples and feet. Add a few drops of essential oil to a hot, steamy bath after a day of being hassled at the office. Or

On Pins and Needles?

A visit to an acupuncturist may lift your spirits. Twirling and manipulating needles inserted into various points throughout the body can work to correct energy imbalances that might be the cause of physical and mental disorders. What are the hot spots? The ear and elbow—two crucial centers of psychological function.

Pushing the Right Buttons

Jin shin acupressure may provide a release from deeply rooted emotional problems. According to practitioners, the body can physically store an emotional trauma or trouble. In performing this type of therapy—using the hands to apply deep pressure to different parts of the body—a professional can provide an emotional release.

Where does a practitioner focus attention? Emotional armor tends to be found around the head, hip, abdominal and chest areas.

take a few deep breaths from a bowl filled with lavender potpourri. Place it on your desk to infuse your office with the relaxing aroma of lavender throughout the day.

■ Magnesium Therapy

According to nutritionists, anxiety disorders and susceptibility to emotional upset may be the result of a magnesium deficiency. A simple blood test, administered by your doctor, can diagnose this condition. The prescription? A 400-mg magnesium supplement daily—available at drugstores and health food stores. Also, add some extra servings of foods rich in magnesium to your diet, such as fish, nuts, dried apricots and whole grains.

An Herb to Relax With

Through the centuries from the mountain villages of Asia to the bustling cities of Germany, valerian has been used as a sedative for all sorts of anxiety-producing conditions. Commonly taken in liquid form (as an extract obtained by boiling or as tea), valerian has a strong taste and odor, which has led modern fans of the herb to try taking it in prepackaged doses available in health food stores.

Be patient: You may need to increase your dosage after starting with the lowest recommended dose. And as with any medicine related to anxiety, don't rely on it for extended periods of time without talking with a doctor or health professional. There may be more to the anxiety than simply nerves.

Blow It Off

Is excess anxiety draining your energy? Just blow it away using this simple technique. When you inhale, let the breath travel to a point of tension. Imagine that the breath absorbs the pressure and stress you're feeling. When you exhale, picture the tension getting carried away along with the breath. Continue breathing deeply for a few minutes, letting the air travel to tension trouble spots and whisking them away.

Aromatherapy In a Hurry

Relaxation...ahh, the smell of it. Studies show that scent works directly on the brain and can significantly alter mood—at times almost instantly. The following essential oils are known particularly for their calming and relaxing properties.

- clary sage
- vanilla
- neroli
- basil
- lavender

Banish Stress from Head to Toe

Anxiety is a product of confusion in both the mind and body. So in order to eliminate stress, you need to restore order to both. Progressive muscle relaxation forces you to use your muscles and your brain to systematically reduce anxiety and restore calm.

It sounds a lot more complicated than it is. Simply lie down in a quiet room if possible, or find a peaceful place where you can sit comfortably without interruption.

Start at the top of your head, and move down to your toes, tightening and then relaxing your muscles. Here's how: Tighten your facial muscles and hold for five seconds, then release. Repeat with your shoulders, arms and hands, followed by your butt, hips and thighs; and then your calves and ankles; your feet and toes should be last.

Next, reverse the process, starting from your toes and tightening each muscle one by one moving up the body (to your feet, then calves, etc.) without releasing them. Once you've tightened up all your muscles, hold your body taut for five seconds, and then release the muscles, one by one from head to toe.

Finish by taking deep, slow breaths until you don't even remember why you ever felt stressed at all.

Put a few drops of any of the oils on a cotton ball and store in an old pill bottle. Whenever you need to de-stress in a hurry, open the bottle and breathe in the scent.

PANIC ATTACKS

■ Visualization to Relieve Anxiety

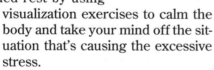

Your heart is hammering, your mouth is very dry and all you can think of is a way to escape—right now. While you may not be able to make a clean getaway, you could take a needed rest by using visualization exercises to calm the body and take your mind off the situation that's causing the excessive stress.

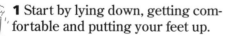

1 Start by lying down, getting comfortable and putting your feet up.

2 Breathe in gently but deeply through your nostrils and exhale slowly out of your mouth.

3 Continue breathing as you imagine the sights, smells and sensations related to something that brings you pleasure—your last vacation, a favorite spot on the beach or hiking a secluded trail in the Adirondacks.

Let your mind truly wander for 10 minutes while you calm down and regain composure. The secret, say experts, is visualizing something that *you* find relaxing and soothing. An afternoon at the beach, after all, is not everyone's idea of paradise.

Biofeedback to Counter Panic Attacks

Biofeedback has been proven to help people with anxiety disorders and those prone to panic attacks by teaching them how to relax. First, electrodes attached to the body measure breathing rates and electrical impulses in the skin that change with perspiration levels. These sensors feed into a computer monitor that allows you to watch your stress levels increase and decrease. After 5 to 10 treatments, you can learn to recognize what relaxation feels like—and how to bring yourself into that state when anxiety strikes.

During office therapy, and later at home, patients learn how to slow down their breathing and respiratory system, which in turn helps to slow the racing heart, the fluttering stomach and the churning intestines. By practicing these breathing and relaxation techniques, patients can slow down the release of adrenaline and other hormones that intensify a panic attack.

Over time, by learning how to slow down the cardiovascular and endocrine systems, patients may be able to prevent panic attacks altogether or greatly alleviate them.

■ Seeing the Light

Golden white light, according to the holistic healing experts, is the universal image of relaxation and healing. When your world starts spinning out of control, try visualization:

1 Imagine a white light shining down on your head. It may take a minute or two to see a true "picture." Give yourself the time.

2 Feel the warmth bathing your forehead and face.

3 Then, picture the light moving down your whole body—from your head to the tips of your toes—washing away anxiety and worries as the light travels through you.

A Drug-and-Therapy Approach

Now that panic attacks are becoming more familiar among psychotherapists and patients alike, a second stage of therapies is emerging to treat them. In the early to mid-1990s, many psychiatrists reported success in treating panic disorders with new kinds of antidepressants, such as Prozac and a few similar drugs that affect how the brain processes the neurotransmitter serotonin.

It now appears that combining medication and talk therapy brings more success to those suffering panic attacks. The problem is that many health insurance plans are not as willing to reimburse patients for long-term psychotherapy as they used to be, even in the face of the new research. With panic disorders, it is known that cognitive therapy helps prolong feelings of control, which is especially helpful after medication has lessened panic-related symptoms.

For more information, contact The National Institute of Mental Health at 800-64-PANIC or 866-615-NIMH, www.nimh.nih.gov

■ Better Breathing Eases Anxiety

Here is one often overlooked way to help switch off the panic button: Yoga-type breathwork. It turns out that shallow, short breathing is one of the main signs of a panic attack. However, by consciously breathing deeply, you can calm your body and mind. Try this helpful technique:

1 Imagine a point below your belly button.

2 Inhale deeply through your nostrils into your abdomen to reach that point.

3 Then, exhale even more slowly through your mouth.

Concentrate on your breathing and block out everything else for a peaceful and meditative moment.

Responses Make a Dent

For patients who have panic attacks and have been slow to respond to standard psychotherapy and/or medications, yoga and breathwork therapies can provide long-term relief from what seems like paralyzing fear. The first goal of such relaxation-oriented therapy is to reduce the number of panic attacks. Often, the added effect is a reduction in the severity of attacks. Those who teach yoga, relaxation and breathing exercises to those with panic attacks believe that major breakthroughs occur when sufferers begin to regain a sense of control over their bodies and lives. Like the disorder itself, the newfound control starts from within.

ASTHMA

■ A Stimulating Prescription

Ephedra has caused a lot of controversy in modern-day America. As a stimulant, it has been used as a weight-loss aid in products that claim to boost metabolic rates. But it also raises blood pressure and heart rates, which poses a danger to those with health problems. In 2003 the FDA banned dietary supplements containing ephedra.

Still, for centuries, the Chinese have used the herb in its natural state (Ma Huang) to heal respiratory ailments like asthma, as it opens airways for easier breathing. Before you try Ma Huang, however, talk with your doctor.

Also, check with your doctor to make sure that any preexisting health conditions will not be exacerbated by this powerful herb.

■ Tea to Loosen Up

Try black tea. That's what many asthma sufferers turn to for relief from tightening in the chest. Black tea contains chemicals related to the stimulant theophylline, which is also the basis of many modern medical asthma remedies. Three or four cups of black tea can open airways and ease breathing.

■ Ginkgo Goes a Long Way

Although herbalists and doctors won't go so far as to claim that ginkgo tea (from ginkgo biloba leaves) can cure asthma outright, when used regularly it has been shown to help patients cut down on prescribed medication. Aside from its purported effects in boosting blood flow, ginkgo taken three times a day for weeks or months at a time (ask your doctor how long would be best for you), relaxes the lungs and helps keep the breathing passageways clear.

A SIX-POINT PREVENTION PLAN

When it comes to asthma, your own home may play a major role in triggering attacks. Here are six ways you can clean up, clear out and create a healthier home.

1 Clean your pet

If you have a pet—particularly a cat—it is so important to bathe him once a week. Research shows that it's not their fur but their saliva that contains allergens, including pollen picked up outside on their paws. When cats groom themselves, they spread allergens from their saliva onto their fur. So, the cleaner your cat keeps himself, the more you'll need to wash him.

Coping with Biofeedback

After practicing biofeedback techniques for a few weeks, many asthma patients can reduce their fears and increase control of their breathing during attacks, recent research shows. Asthma attacks can induce great anxiety among sufferers and can lead to repeated emergency room visits—especially when medication is lagging and breath is short. Patients who have practiced biofeedback, however, have shown that they can increase their inhalation and, at the same time, decrease the severity of their wheezing attacks. In some cases, experimental subjects have been able to decrease their dependence on medication.

2 Tear up the carpet

Dust mites, microscopic critters that live on dust particles, cause a lot of allergies and asthma attacks, say physicians. Ripping up carpets and removing drapes that trap dust can reduce the number of mites tickling your nose and throat. Opt instead for throw rugs and blinds that can be washed easily—and wash them regularly!

3 Sleep "alone"

There's something else in the bed with you: Millions of dust mites. Covering mattresses, pillows and box springs with plastic covers provides a barrier between you and the offending creatures. Also, washing linens frequently on the hot cycle will rinse away mites from sheets and pillow cases.

4 Repel the roaches

Catch that cockroach. In addition to other insidious traits, it appears that the cockroach—in particular its feces and shell—contains allergens that trigger asthmatic attacks. Set traps, changing them even more frequently than the package instructions say. And in areas where you see cockroaches, clean thoroughly to guard against allergic reactions.

5 Keep the great outdoors, outdoors

During pollen season, don't bring the outdoors in. After extended periods in the park or backyard, leave your shoes outside, shower off the pollen from your body and hair and change your clothes as soon as you come inside. This reduces the chances of the pollen working its way into your sinus passages, eyes and bronchial tract.

6 Close the windows

Do everything you can to insulate your environment against the elements. Close your windows and use an air conditioner so you're not breathing pollen-laden air. Regularly replace the filters to keep the air conditioner from pumping allergens into your home. Do the same with the humidifier, which otherwise might be circulating allergy-causing molds into the air.

ATTENTION DEFICIT DISORDER (ADD)

■ Martial Arts Moves May Make a Difference

In this era when Ritalin is so often prescribed to control erratic behavior of children and adults who suffer from attention deficit disorder (ADD), research done at the University of Akron in Ohio has shown that karate may be another treatment to combat ADD. In a small study of clinically hyperactive children over a 10-week period, researchers found that those who took karate lessons, for unexplained reasons, learned to control their impulsive behavior better than children of the same age who did not receive the training.

Although the study was limited to children and needs to be repeated among other groups in other locales, the results point to a potential treatment that has gone virtually unnoticed—martial arts as behavioral medicine!

BACK PAIN

GENERAL MUSCLE PAIN

■ The Quick Prescription

Feel a twinge or crick from overdoing it in the gym or in the garden? Follow these osteopathic rules for overcoming minor back pain:

■ If it hurts when you wake up in the morning, get moving with easy (nonbouncing) stretches, a swim or a leisurely walk. This situation suggests that your muscles need more use to work out the tension.

■ If the pain develops over the course of the day, rest is the prescription. Within a few days, the pain should begin to subside.

Pinpoint the Source of Back Pain

Is your back thrown out of whack? According to acupuncturists, the spasms and pain could be caused by energy imbalances in the body. The remedy? Needles placed in the back of the leg will relieve tension and pain in the back. You should feel immediate relief. In order to stabilize the body's systems, however, you will need to go for more treatments—maybe more than 10.

■ Better Abs for a Better Back

According to experts on back pain, many lower-back injuries result from weak abdominal muscles. The lack of strength in the abs makes the back do more work than it's supposed to—leading to mild pain and posture problems that can develop into an injury. Abdominal crunches (sit-ups performed slowly—hands crossed on chest, knees bent—25 per day minimum) will work the set of muscles that should be bearing the brunt of the work, instead of your lumbar spine.

Also try pelvic tilts to loosen and strengthen lower abs:

1 Lie on your back with knees bent and together, feet flat on the floor.

2 Suck in your stomach while pressing your lower back into the floor.

Try to complete 15 repetitions, building up to three sets as you become stronger.

■ P. T. for the Time-Pressed

Here is a do-it-yourself physical therapy regimen: Stand up straight, put your hands on the small of your back for support and lean back. This easy movement neutralizes stress on lower back muscles and gives quick relief for minor aches and pains. It can (and should) be performed at least three times a day, according to physical therapists.

■ Hot and Cold Healing

To ice or not to ice, that is the question. According to some experts, you can successfully ease muscle pain by doing both at the same time. Wet a T-shirt with hot water. Wring it out and place it on your back. Now put an ice pack on top of the warm T-shirt. This technique keeps the skin and muscles from being frozen. Keep the hot/cold pack on the area for 20 minutes, then remove it for 40 minutes before beginning the treatment again if necessary.

A Buzz Against Backache

If you've been frustrated by so-called standard treatments for general backache, you might want to try TENS. Otherwise known as Transcutaneous Electrical Nerve Stimulation, the treatment is delivered via small machines that emit electrical impulses, which in turn can lessen pain sensations from muscles. Just strap on the wallet-sized device to the aching area often for quick relief (some sufferers, however, keep the machines on affected areas all day). See a physical therapist for a "prescription" and information on how to rent a TENS machine.

■ *Have a Ball—Or Two*

Pulled your back muscles straining to hit that overhead net shot on the tennis court? Well, put away that racquet for a while, but hang on to the tennis balls for a therapeutic self-massage:

1 Put two tennis balls in a sock, and knot the open end.

2 Lean with your back against the wall—placing the sock between your back and the wall.

3 Move your back up and down, rubbing your muscles against the tennis balls, applying pressure that's comfortable.

You can also lie on your back on the floor, placing the balls beneath a pressure point, such as the lower back or the upper shoulders. Then, use your weight to work the point.

■ *The Door Stretch*

After a long day sitting at a desk, your back can feel cramped, tired and pinched. A good upper-body stretch can alleviate some of the muscle tension and provide relief.

1 Open up a sturdy door that will bear your weight.

2 Place your feet together six inches from the edge of the door, facing it.

3 Put a hand on each knob and lean back, letting the upper body muscles stretch and relax.

Hold the pose for 10 seconds, and repeat three to four times.

■ *Two Back-Saving Stretches*

You don't have to take yoga classes at the health club to benefit from back stretches. The first, the Cobra, is done while lying face down, palms at shoulder level:

1 Lift your head *slowly*, then your shoulders, and chest, as if in a half push-up.

2 Arch your back, again very *slowly*. Hold this position for five seconds.

The second stretch is done while lying on your back, with arms at your sides:

1 Slowly and steadily lift your legs up and back over your head until your knees are bent near your ears.

Biofeedback for Your Back

It's a vicious cycle: Being in pain makes you tense, which makes soreness and muscle stress even worse. Biofeedback can help people suffering from chronic back problems learn to stop guarding against the pain, thereby reducing muscle tension. Small, painless electrodes applied to the sensitive area track levels of tension in the muscle. A computer monitors the stress so you can see how tense your muscles are, and what you can do to alter the patterns on the screen (and in your musculature). A professional biofeedback practitioner can help you learn how to relax muscles, using breathing techniques to improve your condition.

2 Hold for a few counts, and slowly release.

Doing these stretches just a few minutes a day can relieve stiffness. *Note:* These yoga stretches are good preventive moves, but may be too much if you are already suffering from acute back pain.

All the Right Moves

A Feldenkrais practitioner will teach you how to move correctly while helping relieve muscle pain. This specialized type of physical therapy evaluates your movement patterns to see what stress you place on your back during day-to-day activities. Next, Feldenkrais instructors teach you how to move differently, alleviating stress on overused or injured muscles and extending your range of motion.

■ How a Juice Fast May Help

When back pain is caused by stress or tightened muscles, and not from bulging disks or bone disease, some naturopaths and other alternative health practitioners recommend to patients a (temporarily) lighter diet or a juice fast. Both back pain and tightness can be a result of congestion in the lower torso—from the intestines or other organs pressing toward the back.

A three-day fast, medically supervised and supplemented with glasses of fresh fruit juice, vegetable juices or spring water four or five times a day, has been shown to bring marked pain relief. According to naturopaths, fasting prods the release of toxins from the kidneys, colon, bladder, skin, sinuses and lungs.

■ If You Can't Stand the Seat...

One solution to moderate bouts of back pain, often overlooked because it is so simple, is a 15-minute walk. Physical therapists at Kaiser Permanente Health Care point out that after sitting in one spot for hours, all the upper body weight has been pressing down on the vulnerable lower back muscles. It's not enough to walk to the water cooler, microwave or espresso cart. A 15-minute walk (25 minutes is even better) promotes healing by encouraging blood to circulate all through the vertebrae and lower torso, nourishing tired, fatigued muscles and tissues. You need blood pumped through the area to outsmart "office backache." If you're worried about the boss missing you, take a memo recorder with you and do some work as you stroll.

Shock Therapy Lite

You might call it friendly shock therapy. It's also known as electric galvanic stimulation (EGS). Portable EGS machines, used by various physical therapists on spastic muscles of the spine, send a safe dosage of electric current into the afflicted muscle, forcing it to contract. The therapist then keeps the muscle in contraction until it becomes fatigued, alleviating both pain and spasm. Treatments, though not universally effective, can range from 15 to 60 minutes.

■ A Handy Solution to Heavy Loads

Now that commuting often means lugging around a briefcase *and* a 10-pound computer case (with accessories), many people put undue stress on their backs. One way to counteract the lower-back strain and pressure of carrying too much weight is to hold the handles of the cases with just your thumb and last three fingers. This physical therapists' trick leaves the index finger "floating," but, more important, it usually results in better, more erect posture while lugging a load. Why? Because there's less compression on the lower vertebrae.

Caution: This is not advised if the load is truly weighty, as with heavy luggage, because you'll be sacrificing too much strength by not using the index finger.

■ Don't Sit Tight, Sit Right

As we age, maintaining the back becomes ever more important, and words such as "ergonomic chairs" begin to take on greater meaning. The fact is, sitting is not good for the spine. So if you have a choice, at certain times during the workday or at home, stand rather than sit. If you must sit, do it correctly:

■ Use a chair that supports your lower back and enables your feet to rest flat on the floor.

■ Keep your knees at or above hip level.

■ Use footrests, such as phone books or firm foam pads, for 15 to 20 minutes every hour.

■ Use armrests when you can.

Finally, get up and move around at least once an hour, stretching a bit here and there.

Oh, My Aching Back...or Is It?

When we experience muscle aches the day after an intense workout, the cause of the pain is clear. But with what doctors call "referred pain," the source of your suffering may surprise you. Referred pain is pain that originates in one area of the body, but is felt in another. This can occur in parts of the body that share the same nerve pathways. A well-known example is the ache in the left arm that can accompany a heart attack.

Here is a list of pain sources that may be felt in parts of the back (among other places in the body):

SOURCE OF PAIN	WHERE IT CAN HURT
liver, gallbladder	right shoulder
heart	neck, shoulder, upper back
wrist	shoulder
kidney	back (below the ribs)
abdomen	upper back, right shoulder
lungs	back

■ Back Belts—Not Just for Weight Lifters

In recent years you probably have seen more and more workers wearing flexible, lightweight back-support belts. Do they really work to prevent injury? The answer appears to be good news for those interested in sound midlife back care.

A six-year study of 36,000 Home Depot employees (men and women) showed that those who wore fabric back belts for support had one-third fewer injuries to their backs than those who did not wear the belts. The study also found that the belts helped both men and women who perform any kind of lifting on the job. The belts cost from $20 to $40 and can be purchased at most sporting goods stores.

A Softened Hard Massage

Sometimes images are tough to shake. Take Rolf therapy, for instance. While it rose to minor national prominence in the early 1970s, anybody who remembers it probably recalls that it involved painful applications of deep tissue massage, using knuckles and elbows as instruments. True enough, but times have changed.

Many of the top Rolf practitioners today are known for having a rather light touch, without giving up any of the guiding principles of their profession. When that touch is combined with an overall focus on body alignment, and listening to clients' problems over multiple sessions, persistent lower back pain can disappear. It's more than massage, but a lot less painful and perhaps more effective than you thought.

■ Get Your Hips and Hamstrings into Play

Both serious and weekend athletes have known for years that strong abdominal muscles can help prevent backache. The reasoning is simple: The more stress and weight your stomach muscles can handle, the less pressure is exerted on the lumbar spine. But less common is the knowledge, gleaned from athletic trainers and physical therapists, that flexible hamstrings and hip flexor muscles can also prevent back pain and injury.

To work the hamstring muscles (back of the thighs), perform a skier's stretch:

1 While leaning your back against a wall, slowly bend your knees, as if you are about to sit down on an invisible chair.

2 When your knees reach a 90-degree angle, hold the position for 20 to 30 seconds, being careful not to bend the knees further.

3 Slowly rise and repeat 10 to 12 times.

To work the hip flexors:

1 Begin by sitting on the floor, your legs should be straight and splayed out, forming a 60-degree angle.

2 Bend forward, attempting to lower your torso down to the ground (slowly!), reaching out to touch the ground between your feet. If you are tight, try putting a pillow or two under your buttocks to free up your lower back.

3 Sit up slowly and repeat 10 to 12 times.

After performing these helpful exercises three to four times a week for a few weeks, you'll be at a lower risk for serious back injury.

LOWER-BACK PROBLEMS

■ Acupressure for General Relief

Acupressure, like its ancient Chinese relative, acupuncture, promotes healing throughout the body by stimulating channels of energy known as meridian points. But where acupuncture uses thin, sterile needles, acupressure relies on the fingertips to do the probing.

Sometimes you can even provide your own massage relief. For lower back pain:

1 Stand and place your hands on your waist, with thumbs in back and fingers to the front.

2 Next, find the cordlike bands of muscles about two inches off from the center of the spine. Press the *outer* edges of these muscles with the thumbs, directing the pressure toward the spine.

A few minutes of acupressure should be sufficient to trigger better blood flow and the body's release of painkilling endorphins.

Note: Such acupressure is not suited for certain back injuries, including herniated disks. Discuss this treatment with your doctor.

■ *Safer Sitting*

Is your desk job exacerbating existing lower-back pain? Physical therapists suggest sitting with a support, like a small pillow, in the curvature of your lower back. This simple lumbar support trick helps to maintain the correct curvature of the spine and to take pressure off the lower back, alleviating tension and pain. Specialty stores such as The Better Back Stores, 303-442-3998; Relax the Back, 800-222-5728; and medical supply stores (see Chapter 5) sell lumbar supports in a wide variety of sizes and prices.

■ *A Quick, Easy, Effective Stretch*

Get a leg up on lower back problems. Tight hamstring muscles can pull on your pelvic bone, resulting in abnormal movement patterns that put stress and strain on the lower back. To prevent lower back strain, try the following stretch:

1 Lying on your back, bend your right leg at a 90-degree angle, with your left foot flat on the floor.

2 Clasp your hands behind your right knee and bring it to your chest.

3 Attempt to straighten your right leg as much as you can, and hold the stretch for five counts. Return your right leg to the floor.

4 Repeat three times on the same leg, then switch legs and repeat the entire process.

Pilates Heals Sciatica

When you mention the word sciatica, many people think that it is a condition that is one step away from surgery. Symptoms include a stabbing, radiating, electric-type pain that typically shoots out from the lower back into the buttocks and down the thigh—sometimes as far as the foot. When the condition is severe and doesn't respond to less invasive treatments, surgery may sometimes be necessary.

Other times, however, instructors in the Pilates method of exercise can, over the course of several weeks, help realign the tissues of the lower back to relieve pressure on the sciatic nerve. At the same time, the Pilates approach works to strengthen and lengthen rows of muscles along the spine and in the abdomen, building tissue to help take pressure off the original source of sciatic pain.

Ultrasounding Muscle Spasms

If a muscle spasm has you flat on your back, catch the wave—an ultrasound wave. A small but increasing number of physical therapists around the US can work out muscle kinks using an ultrasound machine.

This unit—basically the same as the one used to track fetal development in pregnancy—creates vibrations that increase circulation deep in muscle tissue. The added circulation, according to therapists, creates heat in the area to relax too-tight muscles.

■ The Yogi Berra Squat Solution

While baseball catchers might squat so frequently during a season that it puts a strain on the lumbar section of the back, some Chinese medicine practitioners and chiropractors recommend five minutes of squatting per day for people with nagging lower back pain. Place your feet about hip-width apart and slowly drop to a full squat, resting your weight on your heels. Rest your arms on your knees, though you might have to use them to keep your balance until you become accustomed to the position. Gradually work your way up to five minutes per day.

MUSCLE SPASMS

■ Pheasant Tail Relief

Take it from rain forest healers of Central America: Much in nature can help relax the back and, in particular, back spasms. One of the better botanical medicines is a plant known as pheasant tail, plentiful in Belize and found in ethnic or other herb shops in the US.

Mix boiled pheasant tail leaves and water into a leafy compress. Apply directly to the skin to help relieve sore back muscles.

Make a mash from the center vein of the leaf, and apply it directly over tight muscles.

SHOULDER AND BACK PAIN

■ Stretch It Out at Your Desk

When your back or shoulders hurt from too much computer work, try this stretch to loosen up, once every couple of hours:

1 Raise your forearms from the keyboard, hands toward the ceiling.

2 Push your arms back, join and lock hands behind your head, and try to squeeze your shoulder blades together. Hold the position for five seconds, relax and repeat a few times.

■ Bend Them, Shake Them

This move is embarrassingly easy to perform, but tough to do in front of an audience, such as a dozen office mates. Start by standing, then dropping your hands to your sides. Relax and take a few deep breaths. Then shake your arms and shoulders for five (what seem like extremely long) seconds. Relax and repeat a few more times, until your shoulders and arms get a little bit rubbery. If you simply can't do this exercise at your work space, do "the shake" during a bathroom break.

BAD BREATH

INTERMITTENT OR AFTER MEALS

■ A Nice Spice

Anise, or aniseed, belongs to the parsley family but tastes like licorice. Like parsley, anise is a little-known but effective breath freshener. But unlike parsley, the breath-cleansing power of anise is contained in the flowering seeds, not in the leaf. Often, Indian restaurants offer anise seeds to diners after a meal instead of mints.

Chew a pinch or two after particularly pungent meals. It will aid your digestion a bit, too, at no extra charge. Aniseed is available at the spice counter of many supermarkets.

■ Freshen Up with Clove

A potent, pleasing, aromatic herb often used by cooks, clove has many valuable properties, from stimulant to antiseptic to breath freshener. Herbalists suggest that one leaf put into your mouth after a garlic-laden lunch or dinner freshens breath for hours. Pick up some cloves at your local herbal shop.

RECURRENT BAD BREATH

■ Spooning for Better Breath

You already know about brushing and flossing the teeth to reduce bad breath. If you're brushing to no avail, try brushing your tongue. Or if you're a purist, try "tongue scraping." What apparently began as a West Coast fad has caught on among many dental hygienists, dentists and, of course, cosmetic companies. Tongue scrapers have made their way into chain drugstores and health food stores nationwide. The scrapers may help get rid of bad breath—and help prevent it as well. Scrapers cleanse tongues of millions of tiny bacteria that most people miss when they freshen up their mouth, morning and evening.

What the cosmetics companies don't tell you is that a spoon will work nearly as well.

■ Baking Soda Breathwork

For fresh breath, mix together baking soda and ground cinnamon. Scoop the mixture onto your toothbrush and brush away lunchtime bad breath, or your morning coffee breath.

■ Beating Bad Breath

Do your dates flinch when you whisper sweet nothings in their ears? It may be your breath, not your choice of words, that's turning them off. Try this concoction for a fresher approach:

In a one-sixth-ounce bottle, mix equal parts of pure essential oils of peppermint, spearmint, star anise and lemon. Shake well. Then add two to three drops of the mixture to a glass of water. Take a healthy swig, gargle and rinse well.

Indian Toothpick

Take a hint from India: Twigs from the native neem tree and the oils within can help fight infections associated with gingivitis or other periodontal problems. It's a low-tech, highly effective dental "tool." People from India often chew on the tree's twigs for on-the-spot relief. In the West, you can sample the extract in an imported toothpaste known as Auromere. Health food stores and Indian-American markets carry the paste.

BODY ODOR

Deodorizing Naturally

A homemade or natural deodorant may be the key to sweet-smelling success. The following all-natural solutions can keep you smelling swell as they kill the bacteria that cause body odor. Dab any of the following under your arms at least once a day for the best results:

- Witch hazel or rubbing alcohol, both of which are antiseptic.

- Tea tree oil, which is antimicrobial.

- Green tea extract (or tea bags, in a pinch).

- Bergamot essential oil, an antiseptic.

- Apple cider vinegar, which changes the pH-level (measure of alkalinity and acidity) of skin to a higher level of acidity so that bacteria grow less readily.

Note: These are deodorants only, not antiperspirants, so they won't prevent you from sweating.

Time to "Change Your Oil"

Of course you can try to snuff out excessive body odor with deodorants from the drugstore, but did you ever consider that both the problem and solution may lie inside the body? Some nutritionists suggest a food-based remedy that has mostly to do with fats and oil.

Eating excess fats in food, especially saturated fats in dairy foods and meats, can cause body odor. Make a conscious effort to replace those fats with olive oil or sunflower seed oil. As for margarine, make sure that it is polyunsaturated.

Mineral Aid for Aromatic Relief

Time to tone down the wetness of excess perspiration? One exceedingly simple remedy worth trying is to take 20 to 30 mg of zinc supplements daily. It is believed that zinc deficiency can cause people to sweat excessively. Chelated zinc tablets are better absorbed by the body.

An Odor-Fighting Formula

One wise use of the essential oils is to fight body odor produced by underarm bacteria. Using a clean glass bowl or beaker-shaped glass, mix together 2 tablespoons witch hazel,

2 tablespoons apple cider vinegar (the vinegar scent fades quickly!), 12 drops grapefruit seed extract, 3 drops tea tree oil, 2 drops essential oil of lemon, and 2 drops essential juniper oil. Use a cotton ball to apply this deo-dorant mixture, or pour it into an atomizer bottle.

Note: It's best to test this mix-ture first on your wrist to check for skin sensitivity. If you are sensitive, or if you prefer a different scent, consider using lavender or rosemary essential oils.

BONE FRACTURES

■ *De-stressing Stress Fractures*

Distance runners, gymnasts and other ath-letes involved in intense weight-bearing activ-ity and prolonged pressure on the bones risk sustaining a stress fracture. These injuries can sideline an athlete for many months. But now, a device that relies on sonic healing can help them get back into action much more quickly.

The Exogen Bone Healing System (which is available at www.smith-nephew.com) utilizes low-intensity ultrasound waves to boost the body's natural bone-repair process. The ultra-sound works as a mechanical force that helps fuse bone. The patient places the head of the small battery-powered device on the skin over the fractured area, and then turns it on for about 20 minutes a day until the fracture is healed—usually in about two to three months.

One study found that stress fractures in patients using this therapy healed up to 38% faster than those in patients using dummy devices. By speeding up healing, experts say, this sonic therapy may help prevent the need for extensive rehabilitation, bone grafts and other costly procedures.

BRUISING

■ *Herbal Healing Helpers*

Arnica and calendula both help to speed the healing of bruises and act as anti-inflam-matories, though arnica is a more popular alternative. The chemicals in the herbs will in-crease your circulation, wash-ing away blood and damaged skin cells that collect under the surface of the skin.

Massage a dab of arnica or calendula cream or ointment (sold at health food stores and

An Electrifying Way to Speed Healing of Fractured Bones

After you break an arm or leg, have your X rays read and your cast applied, the typical 10 to 12 weeks of healing time seems interminable. Fortunately, some orthopedists and other doctors have found a way to speed the meshing and mending of broken bone—using electricity as medicine.

In electrotherapy, small (and safe) doses of electric current are dispensed via a compact office machine (a transcutaneous electric nerve stimulator, TENS) through electrodes placed on the body near the fracture. The stimulation apparently speeds the healing process, by helping new bone fragments grow faster and attach to each other more quickly. It is common practice in Russia, but not yet in the US. That may change in due time.

many pharmacies) onto the bruised area three times a day. Don't use arnica on open wounds or broken skin; it interferes with healing.

■ A Valuable Vegetable

An unusual and effective treatment for a bruise can be found in your pantry: Onions. It seems that the same chemicals that cause eyes to water can be absorbed through the skin. A slice of yellow onion placed on a fresh bruise for 15 minutes can help stimulate the lymphatic flow, flushing away excess blood. Apply the onion immediately after the bump or impact to increase the efficacy of this treatment.

■ Bruise Juice

Did you run into the sharp edge of your desk or coffee table again? Take a seat, relax and have a tall, cool glass of pineapple juice.

Containing bromelain, an enzyme that has anti-inflammatory properties, the juice will help to reduce swelling and the redness of a fresh bruise.

■ Sprig Cleaning

Sprigs of parsley don't often get the chance to star at the dinner table. More likely, they are an afterthought, a punctuation mark of the meal. But the next time you have an unsightly, painful bruise, crush and chop a handful of chilled parsley sprigs and apply them straight to the bruise. In the same unspectacular but efficient fashion in which it attacks bad breath, parsley goes to work taking the color out of the bruise, often within 24 hours.

■ Put Comfrey to Work

For those who have bruises that they would like to fade quickly, comfrey can provide two-pronged assistance. An ancient remedy for a variety of skin ailments (it contains allantoin, which encourages skin repair), more recently comfrey has been shown to have anti-inflammatory properties. In fact, Commission E, Germany's version of the FDA, now says comfrey is useful for treating bruises as well as sprains. While applying ice to the bruise, brew some comfrey tea and soak sterile gauze in it. After icing for a while (a few 20-minute sessions should help), apply your comfrey compress.

BURNS *See also First Aid, page 123*

■ *An Herbal Ointment*

Chinese herbalists recommend covering scalds and burns with Ching Wan Hung ointment. Apply the ointment, available at many natural foods stores (and at Chinese pharmacies), directly to a clean burn. The ingredients are a secret, but according to herbalists, the ointment heals burns quickly.

■ *French Fries for Fire-Damaged Skin?*

Not quite, but raw potatoes that are washed, cut and pressed on a burn can bring soothing relief almost instantly. Thin slices work best to cover the burn in a compress, but this remedy should be reserved for small burns. Any burn larger than a couple of inches across should be treated by a doctor or other health professional.

■ *Beyond Aloe*

In addition to gel from the leaf of an aloe vera plant, lavender oil will also help to keep a burn from blistering. For small burns—on a finger, for example—apply two or three drops of lavender oil directly to the area.

For larger burns, including sunburn, dilute the oil before applying, or it may dry out your skin. Dilute lavender oil by mixing one ounce of essential lavender oil with one ounce of aloe vera juice. Then, apply the diluted oil to the affected area.

■ *Milk Is Better than Ice*

With a minor burn, such as the ones you get in the kitchen or from hot engines in the garage, hold the ice water and turn to the milk jug instead. While both will soothe the irritated skin, the fat in the milk provides a much-needed liquid coating at the site of the burn. Cloths dipped in cold milk will provide quick relief for minor burns.

For more serious burns, keep the wound loosely covered with sheets or clothing en route to the doctor or hospital.

CANCER

■ *A Chinese Electrochemical Treatment*

For a few decades now, doctors in China have treated some types of cancer with a process called electrochemical treatment (ECT). Now, the treatment is being tested in the US, thanks to the National Center for Complementary and Alternative Medicine (NCCAM) at the National Institutes of Health.

The City of Hope National Medical Center in Duarte, California, received a small grant to conduct a pilot study of the technique using rats and mice as subjects. Dr. Chung-Kwang Chou and his

Hyperbaric Chambers—The New Healing Ward

There's a painless treatment for speedy healing of serious third-degree burns: Oxygen. A hyperbaric chamber contains pressurized, 100% oxygen that stimulates new blood vessel and tissue growth. A patient may need a series of treatments, sitting in a chamber for an hour or so. This therapy not only helps the healing process but can also cut down on the number of reconstructive surgeries a burn victim may require.

researchers inserted electrodes into the animals' tumors and sent a tiny electrical charge (around 10 volts) through the electrodes for 30 minutes to several hours. The study showed that, depending on the placement of the electrodes and the dosage of electrical current, ECT was effective in reducing the size of the tumors.

Recently, City of Hope began human testing, although the trials have not been advertised and the test group is extremely small, given the legal constraints. So far, results from the human trials have been consistent with the animal trials and with other studies conducted in countries such as China. Widespread acceptance of ECT could provide cancer patients with a less invasive alternative to surgery, radiation and chemotherapy treatments, potentially at a lower cost and with fewer side effects. For information on ECT clinical trials, call:

■ City of Hope National Medical Center, 626-301-8497 or 626-359-8111.

Receive results of the pilot study and other studies involving cancer from:

■ The National Center for Complementary and Alternative Medicine at the National Institutes of Health at 888-644-6226 or http://nccam.nih.gov.

A Free Cancer-Free Shopping Guide

Eating healthfully is becoming easier all the time. Now you can order a free set of grocery shopping lists—developed by nutritionists—that offer various combinations of foods and food groups with potential anticancer advantages.

Brochures on fiber, veggies, phytochemicals and other topics are also available.

Contact the American Institute for Cancer Research at 800-843-8114, 1759 R Street NW, Washington, DC 20009, Att: Publications.

You can also access information through its Web site at www.aicr.org.

■ Minimize Nausea from Chemotherapy Treatments

It is not yet standard protocol at the country's major cancer treatment centers, and it may never be, but many patients who undergo chemotherapy may be helped in overcoming subsequent nausea by drinking caraway tea. Herbalists, pointing to anecdotal evidence, say that caraway has long been considered a digestive tonic. It may also help soothe the stomachs of cancer patients by relieving intestinal spasms.

Caraway leaves can easily be found at herbal stores, or look for caraway tea at well-stocked tea shops.

Acupuncture Restores Immune System Health

An antidote for the side effects of chemotherapy is pain-free—even though it involves a few needles—acupuncture. Chemotherapy irradicates cancer cells as well as white blood cells—the body's infection fighters. But acupuncture can stimulate immune system function. According to practitioners, in some cases, normal white blood cell counts may be restored to a healthy level within one to two sessions. However, some patients may need longer to stimulate their immune system.

CANCER PREVENTION

■ *Cooking with Care*

There are many foods that may help prevent cancer. Also following certain rules when cooking may guard against the disease. Studies show that grilling meats, fowl or fish over hot charcoal will release chemicals that may increase your risk for cancer. Plus, fat dripping onto charcoal produces carcinogen-laden smoke.

It is not necessary to avoid grilling altogether. Instead, use hard woods, which burn at lower temperatures, in your grill; opt for low-fat meats; and put a sheet of aluminum foil underneath your food to catch drippings before they drop onto the coals.

■ *Tea for Cancer-Free Cells*

Next to lots of fresh fruits and vegetables, put tarragon tea, rich in caffeic acid, on the list of possible cancer fighters. In addition to spicing up dishes with the fresh or dried herb, drink a few cups of tarragon tea every day. Steep the herb in a cup of hot water and strain before sipping.

■ *Broccoli Sprouts Come of Age*

Given the impressive research that surfaced in the late 1990s showing that broccoli sprouts contain vast amounts of anticancer chemicals, it might be time to rethink at least some of your menus. The sprout-growing industry will have to catch up with demand, but this much is clear: Studies done at the Johns Hopkins Medical Center show that broccoli sprouts have at least 30 times the concentration of the anticancer substances found in mature broccoli. A handful of the sprouts on a sandwich each day, or in a salad, will be beneficial to the detoxifying systems in your body.

Some resourceful people are growing their own broccoli sprouts. The seeds are available from mail order companies like The Sprout House at 800-SPROUTS, or www.sprout house.com.

■ *Combating Colon Cancer*

We know now that eating low-fat, healthful meals lowers overall cancer risk, but can we go further to specify which foods will protect which vulnerable body parts? Yes, to a degree, nutritionists say. *One example:* For people who have a family history of colon cancer, or those who are trying to prevent a recurrence, try combining soy foods with turmeric, a spice that is gaining in popularity in the US. While soy foods have been linked to lower rates of colon, breast and prostate cancers, turmeric contains a powerful antioxidant called curcumin. That nutrient, which prevents cellular damage, has been linked to lower rates of colon cancer. A casserole or stir-fry containing both soy and turmeric could provide a one-two punch.

■ *Calcium for More than Strong Bones*

The anticancer properties of calcium have been building excitement in research circles since the late 1980s. Now, gastroenterologists and others recommend that patients who have colon polyps or other increased risk factors for colon cancer should consider taking more calcium. Whether taken in the form of milk products, dark green leafy vegetables, sardines, salmon or supplements, calcium appears to reduce the development of substances in the colon that can lead to the formation of polyps or cancerous growths. Dietitians recommend 1,000 to 1,200 mg a day of calcium.

CARPAL TUNNEL SYNDROME

■ *Don't Squeeze, Do Stretch*

If a wrist is sore from too many hours at the computer, using a hand grip or squeeze ball is just the thing *not* to do. Most practitioners discourage such "stress-busters" because the motion only aggravates already pained ligaments and muscles in the overused wrist and hand. Instead, take frequent breaks from continuous typing or mouse maneuvering (stopping for a few minutes every half hour or a full 15 minutes every two hours), and perform one of two stretches: ·

When B6 Is Bad

While doctors have often prescribed vitamin B6 (up to 300 mg) to patients with carpal tunnel syndrome, recent research shows that it may be time to back off the B6. In a study of 125 factory workers, no link was observed between blood levels of B6 in the blood (and thus throughout the body) and pain from carpal tunnel syndrome. Moreover, high dosages of B6 can cause nerve damage—and 300 mg is far above the recommended dietary allowance of up to 2 mg a day. The syndrome often responds to splinting, aspirin or ibuprofen, ergonomic aids, rest and relaxation or muscular therapy.

1 Gently push the right palm and fingers backward with the left palm until you feel a slight tugging in the right wrist. Then gently push forward on the back of the right hand. Repeat on left hand and wrist as needed.

2 Hold your hand in front of you with the palm facing out. Slowly perform a clawing motion several times. Repeat with other hand if needed.

Weight Loss Eases Carpal Tunnel Pain

Extra pounds may aggravate the symptoms of carpal tunnel syndrome. More fat between your tissues can reduce the space in the tunnel in your wrist, putting more pressure on the median nerve and exacerbating pain and numbness. If you're suffering from carpal tunnel syndrome and you're overweight, talk to your doctor about safe and healthy weight-loss methods.

■ *Hawaiian Isles Solution?*

Pineapple contains bromelain, a protein-dissolving enzyme that has been credited with joint-pain relief because of its anti-inflammatory properties. It is also a potential remedy for carpal tunnel syndrome sufferers. A daily therapeutic dose is 250 to 1,000 mg in supplement form between meals.

■ *Supplementary Advice*

Vitamin B6 is important for fat and protein metabolism, plus the formation of new blood cells. Some patients with carpal tunnel pain have a B6 deficiency. If this deficiency is contributing to your pain, studies have shown that daily supplementation of 100 mg of B6 for three months, plus 50 mg of vitamin B2, can reduce symptoms. (If the carpal tunnel patient has normal B6 readings, the supplementation won't make a difference.)

■ Quick Reach for Relief

Technically, it's known as spanning. But informally, this simple exercise is known as instant PT—physical therapy. Pianists, other musicians and keyboard jockeys all have benefited from it—so what are you waiting for?

Spanning is simply reaching your arms straight out in front of you, keeping them at shoulder level, and spreading your fingers as far apart as possible. Relax the digits, and do it again, five times in all. The goal is to counteract the cramping your hands and fingers have silently endured all day, week or year.

The Rolf Approach

Even though most cases of carpal tunnel syndrome seem centered in the wrists, palms and fingers, a reduction of that pain might be accomplished by treating other areas. An alternative to surgery that is gaining favor with health care practitioners nationwide is the Rolf system of bodywork. This program of structural integration treats the problem in a more holistic manner. Rather than trying to work on one tendon, or a single locus of tightened, inflamed tissue in the "tunnel" of the wrist through which the median nerve and several muscle tendons pass, the Rolf method attends to the fingers, wrist, arm, shoulder and thorax.

Through a series of massage sessions, rolfing reworks the relationship among all those body parts. The goal is to bring the inflamed and injured tissues to a point where they can reside comfortably again, and heal.

■ Self-Massage—Acupressure Style

When you spend too many hours at the keyboard or on the assembly line and your wrists feel locked up with aching pain, you may be able to rub it away. Here's an acupressure treatment worth trying, adjusted for self-treatment. In addition to pain, it may reduce associated swelling and inflammation as well, if practiced daily.

Using the uninjured (or less painful) hand, press and rub two spots in the middle of the other wrist, above and below, that are located two-and-a-half finger widths from the wrist joint. One spot is just about where your watch face rests (feel for the "valley" of tendons); the other spot is on the inner forearm (on the arteries). Press both spots simultaneously, using thumb and fingers; then release. Repeat as needed. Most important, keep it up every day until the pain lessens or vanishes.

CHAPPED LIPS

■ Vitamin E Oil Smoothes Them Out

Instead of automatically settling for a lipstick-type protector for chapped lips, try vitamin E oil when you get home from a day in the great outdoors. Or apply it to your lips *before* you brave the elements. *Note from the skin pros:* Vitamin E-enriched lotions don't contain nearly as much vitamin E as the oil.

You can find the oil in health food stores, herb shops and some well-stocked pharmacies. For treatment, rub the oil in softly and slowly, and remember to fully cover the lower lip line.

■ *Three-Step Lip Moisture Tip*

When chapped lips pass the point of dry, when they start to flake, peel and hurt, regular lip balm will no longer do, especially during the winter months. Here's a three-step method from skin experts.

1 Slough off the flaky skin by using a damp washcloth and massaging gently in a circle.

2 To restore skin tone and eventually moisture, apply a 0.5% hydrocortisone ointment (available in pharmacies) twice a day. *Note:* Products that contain alphahydroxy acids can help keep lips smooth.

3 Finally, to help the healing and to seal and retain moisture, frequently and generously apply lip balm that contains protective waxes (such as beeswax) and sunscreen.

Most people don't realize that, unlike the rest of the face, the thin skin of the lips produces no oil of its own, so it can use your help.

CHRONIC FATIGUE SYNDROME

■ *Behavioral Therapy Surprises Many Sufferers*

Though the causes of chronic fatigue syndrome (CFS) are still elusive, researchers recently made a surprising finding about cognitive behavioral (talk) therapy: It works as well or better than some standard treatments for CFS. A recent British study showed that, over a yearlong period, the CFS patients who engaged in talk therapy in order to reverse negative thinking showed higher activity levels and better sleep patterns than patients who received standard relaxation therapy or other standard medical treatment. It is not a cure, experts remind patients, but cognitive therapy can ease the burden of CFS.

CIRCULATION PROBLEMS

■ *Treating Cold Hands and Feet Gingerly*

For a winter warmer, try drinking ginger tea before going outside in those coldest winter months, or take a 500-mg ginger capsule in the morning. Benefits to circulation accrue  over time, not right away, so ginger is a good habit to get into.

In addition to taking supplements, try using it as a seasoning in vegetables and soups—or stir a slice into your tea.

Biofeedback for Raynaud's Syndrome Sufferers

Raynaud's Syndrome is a painful circulatory disease that causes color and temperature changes in the fingertips and toes (they turn blue). It is also known as arterial spasm, and it can be difficult to treat. Biofeedback, however, can help alleviate the symptoms by teaching you how to control the blood flow to your hands and feet. On average, 5 to 10 biofeedback sessions with a trained practitioner are necessary to learn the powerful behavioral-medicine technique.

■ Treat with Good Hands—Your Own

Borrowing a tip from Ayurvedic healers of India, you can give your circulation (and possibly your immune system) a boost with self-massage, using sesame oil. This self-massage is said to promote energy flow by stimulating certain points on the body that are similar to acupuncture points. Using sesame oil adds an antioxidant boost.

Here's how to perform the self-massage:

1 Fill a squeeze bottle with sesame oil and plunge it into a sinkful of hot tap water to warm it.

2 Strip down, place a towel over a chair and sit down.

3 Massage the oil into your skin, from the head down.

Use the balls, not heels, of the hands as your applicators (that is the place where the fingers meet your palms). Make smooth, long strokes down the arms and legs, circular rubs over your head, joints, abdomen and chest. Avoid the genitals, and use long strokes over as much of the back as you can reach. Spend extra time on toes and feet! Vigorously rub the soles while rolling the toes between your slippery fingers.

Let oil sink into skin for at least 10 minutes before showering off. Many practitioners apply some graham flour (found in health food stores) to aid in the rinsing. If time allows, top off the treatment with a 15-minute soak in an Epsom-salted bath.

■ A Hot, Hot Soak

Chase away the winter chills with a well-seasoned bath. Stir a teaspoon or two of cayenne pepper or spicy ginger powder into your bathwater and soak.

One warning: The oils in cayenne and ginger will generate heat in the water which could make the bath too hot to handle if mixed with very warm water.

A New Age Winter Warm-up

In midwinter, the power of suggestion combined with relaxation can translate into real warmth. At least that's what recent research from the University of Alaska at Anchorage shows. When a person is in a state of deep calm or meditation, the temperature of his or her toes and fingers tends to rise, as much as seven degrees in five minutes. (That's because the nervous system pumps less adrenaline during *true* relaxation, allowing blood vessels to dilate and warm blood to "pool" in the extremities.) But alas, this biofeedback trick of the mind takes time to learn.

Interested? You can start by meditating twice a day for 20 minutes. Then, take your hand temperature one day by taping a thermometer to the outside of your middle finger. First, tense your muscles from head to toe; then, relax those muscles in the same order and take your hand temperature again. After a month or so, there's a good chance you'll see—and feel—biofeedback results that you can take to the ski slopes and back.

COMMON COLD *See also* **Cough,** *page 92, and* **Sore Throat,** *page 204*

GENERAL COLD SYMPTOMS

■ *Go for Goldenseal*

To help fight the viral infection that causes the common cold, goldenseal is a natural choice because it's loaded with berberine, a botanical antibiotic. Make an infusion from a teaspoonful of dried goldenseal and hot water. Let the mixture steep for 10 minutes before straining. Drink three cups a day until you bounce back.

As an alternative, take one-half to one teaspoonful of goldenseal tincture twice a day. Simpler still, goldenseal capsules are available at health food stores—and increasingly at drugstores as well.

■ *Echinacea Update*

At the first sign of the sniffles or a stuffy feeling in your head, crack open the echinacea. This popular herbal cold remedy stimulates the immune system to fight an infection before it causes congestion, chills and the need to pull the covers over your head. Take one to three capsules every two hours for best results as soon as symptoms start. Waiting too long can render the treatment ineffective, as can taking echinacea for long periods of time—it is most effective with short-term use.

■ *Two Herbs Can Be Better than One*

According to herbalists, goldenseal and echinacea are the dynamic cold-fighting duo. But beware of the formulations on the market that combine the two herbs: Sometimes taking two "anti-cold" herbs offers no more cold-fighting ammunition than a single one. Echinacea must be taken much more frequently than goldenseal to really "do in" a cold. And in high quantities, goldenseal can be toxic and leach vitamin B from the body. To get the most from both herbal remedies, take them in separate doses according to a physician's advice or package instructions.

Like Cures Like—In the Shower, Too

In Germany, not long ago, researchers discovered an odd connection. Cold showers help prevent colds. Basically, they had subjects take a hot shower, then turn on cold water for the last two minutes. After a yearlong study, researchers found that these folks had significantly fewer colds than their hot-shower counterparts. Theory has it that not only was circulation improved, but so was the flow of white blood cells, which fight infection.

■ *Good Ol' Garlic*

The jury is still out on whether garlic can ward off evil spirits and vampires, but some alternative practitioners believe that garlic can help fight the common cold. Chew or swallow a whole clove every couple of hours. The goal when you have a bad cold? You want to have garlic breath.

Join a Group, Prevent a Cold

You would think that the more people you come into contact with during the cold season, the greater your chances of catching a cold. Not so, according to a recent study. People who had six or more social roles were four times less likely to get colds when exposed to the cold virus than people who had only one to three social roles. *Note:* It was not the number of friends that mattered, but the number of different social roles people played, such as wife, mother, coworker, soccer coach and so on. The more diverse social networks people were part of, the greater their resistance to upper respiratory infections, and the stronger their immune systems.

■ Open Senses on the Go

Can't smell? Can't taste? Sprinkle a few drops of eucalyptus essential oil onto a cotton ball and store in an old pill bottle. When you begin to feel congested, uncap the bottle and take a few deep breaths of the mentholated oil. You'll feel your passages open, and your senses will quickly return.

■ Make a Runny Nose Run More—Then Less

Stuffy nose? It might be the right time to try nasal irrigation (sometimes called nasal douching). Don't be frightened; it's simple, say holistic physicians who recommend it. It will cleanse sinus passages, soothe inflammation and reduce congestion. In your kitchen or bathroom:

1 Make a solution mixing one-half teaspoon of salt and one-half cup of warm water in a small paper cup.

2 Bend the lip of the cup to make a small spout.

3 Tilt your head back and to the right, then slowly pour the salt water into your left nostril. The water will flow out of your right nostril. If it flows down the back of your throat instead, tip the top of your head farther to the right.

4 Refill the cup and tilt your head back and to the left to cleanse your right nasal passage in the same manner. Blow your nose when done to help clear the water.

Repeat once daily until congestion subsides.

■ Liquid Aid

What is the often-invoked but too-often-ignored rule for overcoming the common cold? Drink lots of fluids. In fact, doing so actually does a lot of good to stimulate the body's ability to drain the lungs and sinuses. *The prescription:* At least eight glasses a day of such liquids as herbal tea, water or fresh fruit and vegetable juices.

■ Herbal Energy Booster

Sick and tired. Tired and sick. To stave off the sluggish feelings that surface with even the mildest cold or viral illness, it may help to take three 500-mg doses of ginseng daily. And although there are four main types of ginseng, it is American ginseng that stimulates the immune system and is purported to give the body the energy boost it needs while battling infection.

A Homeopathic Boost to Avoid Getting Sick

When stress and fatigue begin to take their toll, and you're starting to feel run-down, it's aconite to the rescue. This homeopathic remedy strengthens the immune system and gives you energy so you won't fall prey to the cold that's making its way through the office. Take a 30C preparation three times a day when you think you're coming down with something—or to guard against infection if your family is sick.

■ Working with the Elements

Heat and wind. Can you feel them when you're fighting a cold? According to Chinese medical principles, when the body is overcome by these elements, the imbalance causes a cold. To achieve a more healthful harmony, you might try Yin Chiao Chieh Tu Pien, a cold formula made from forsythia and honeysuckle that is believed to push heat and wind from the lungs and respiratory tract. When you first feel a cold coming on, take six tablets every three hours. This treatment should keep the cold virus from taking hold in your system. It's easy enough to find in the Chinatowns of major cities and in well-stocked herb shops.

■ Spicy Cold Therapy

Do you have a cold? Then feel the burn of cayenne pepper. This scorching seasoning—in its rawest forms—gets the body's fluids flowing, which in turn works to drain stuffy sinuses. Even tiny airways leading in and out of the lungs will open up a bit in answer to cayenne's call. Sprinkle powdered cayenne or a drop or two of liquid extract into your favorite soup for super spicy therapy.

■ Elderberry Cold Fighter

As a natural replacement for over-the-counter cold concoctions, swallow a tablespoon of sambucol extract every few hours. Sambucol, from brightly colored elderberries, is loaded with bioflavonoids and vitamin C—a powerful pair that herbalists believe work in concert to knock out the viral infections that cause colds. Find sambucol at your local health food store.

■ Better Way to Use Vitamin C

With all the talk over the years about vitamin C and the common cold, those who have studied the vitamin's effect mostly suggest taking the vitamin *once a cold sets in*.

There are two things to remember about vitamin C therapy for colds.

■ Vitamin C has not consistently been shown to *prevent* colds. Its value lies in helping to reduce symptoms and their duration once you are afflicted.

■ Most people don't take enough vitamin C to do them any good. For a "treatment" dose, take 1,000 to 2,000 mg a day—in two or four 500-mg doses—in order to shorten the duration of the cold and minimize severity of symptoms.

Note: At high levels of vitamin C intake, up to 3,000 mg a day or more, diarrhea becomes a frequently cited side effect.

Decongestant Vapor—Better than Steam

When it comes to colds and deep-down congestion, some steam is better than others—in this case, with eucalyptus, made from the gum tree (and a popular essential oil). Boil one quart of water, preferably distilled, and remove from heat. Add 5 to 10 drops of eucalyptus oil, stir and pour into a large pot. Test the heat with your hand before placing your face over the pot. Once the water has cooled to a comfortable temperature, drape a towel over your head to trap the steam as you breathe in the decongesting vapors. *Bonus:* Your face will get a mini-detoxification treatment in the process.

Hot Tip on Cold Cures

Antihistamines aren't forever. If and when a cold moves out of the sinuses and down to the chest, that's your cue to drink fluids and consider using a steam vaporizer—and to stop taking antihistamines. The millions of Americans who continue to take antihistamines after a cold has migrated southward may actually aggravate infections lower in the respiratory system.

Acupressure for Nasal Relief

If you've ever prevented a sneeze by pressing inward on the mustache area of your upper lip with your index finger, you're aware that pressure applied to the skin can affect the sinuses and nasal passages. The same theory underlies the idea of self-administered acupressure for the common cold, in which both hands are used. Here's how to perform it:

1 Start with your middle fingers at the base of the cheekbones, directly below the iris of each eye.

2 Next, press all four fingers upward and hold for up to 30 seconds.

3 Then release and repeat.

The goal is to reduce both congestion and pain related to the sinuses. You should feel immediate relief, but this depends on how congested you are. (The technique is more effective at the onset of a cold than three days into one.) Likewise, the number of repetitions needed depends on the severity of congestion.

Treat Your Cold Gingerly

Trade in your bottle of ginger ale for a steaming hot cup of ginger tea. Ginger is known to boost immune system activity and may well help your body beat a cold. Stir two teaspoons of grated ginger root into a cup of boiling water and allow the mixture to steep. Strain and sip. For extra soothing and sweetness, add a teaspoon of honey.

Catch That Cold Before It Catches You

At the first sign of a scratchy throat or spike of a fever, a dose of gelsemium may put you on the road to a quick recovery. This homeopathic remedy treats many cold and flu symptoms that strike when defenses are down. Take a 30C preparation three times a day until you're back on your feet.

RUNNY EYES

A Runny Eye for a Runny Eye

For the watery eyes that sometimes accompany colds, homeopaths recommend allium cepa tablets. Derived from onions, this treatment works on the homeopathic principle that "like cures like"—that a trace amount of what causes a condition can cure it. The theory in brief involves stimulating one's immune system, then directing it toward a specific organ, condition or system. *The prescription:* A 30C preparation once or twice a day.

SNEEZING

■ *A Hands-on Way to Beat Sneezes*

When you feel a sneeze coming on, don't hold your breath. Instead, work the acupressure point in the fold between your forefinger and thumb to alleviate sniffles and other cold symptoms. Use your right hand to apply pressure to the fold on your left hand for at least a minute. Then repeat the technique, switching hands.

Also, try pressing on your face beside each nostril for relief of similar symptoms.

CONCUSSION (Mild)

■ *Flower Remedy to the Rescue*

If you or a family member suffers a minor concussion, or a wicked tennis ball to the head or similar sports injury, you might try a flower-based medicine known as Rescue Remedy. Developed by Edward Bach about 100 years ago, flower remedies are not quite herbal and not quite homeopathic. Yet they combine the flower essences and pure water into medicine.

Rescue Remedy is a combination of five such flower remedies, and it is one of the most commonly cited treatments in the first-aid kits of herbalists and naturopaths. It has even been known to help people who have suffered shock. Follow directions on the eye-dropper bottle. The remedy is available at most health food and natural food stores, as well as herb shops.

Note: Neurologists believe there's no such thing as a "slight" concussion. Head injuries are serious and should be diagnosed appropriately.

Bodywork for Recovery

After a fall or a car accident, victims who have hit their heads sometimes present their doctors with vague symptoms from seemingly minor memory loss to a "heaviness" that permeates their mood almost daily. They can't seem to connect with the world—even weeks after the supposedly minor event. Pilates Method exercise is one way to help the brain (and body) recuperate over time, by focusing on proper posture, breathing, muscular strength and alignment—while working around the specific injury site.

Concussions are not exactly minor events. The brain has been shaken and typically recoils against the inner portion of the skull. In working with clients who have had concussions, Pilates instructors take care to keep the neck and head aligned and structurally sound. Following treatment, clients often feel as if they've broken through the temporary mind/body dissociation that occurred with the initial injury.

■ *Magnetic Infrared Therapy for Pain Relief*

Much more advanced in Japan than in the US, magnetic therapy—using small magnets to effect changes in energy in the body—has been shown to offer relief to patients who have suffered concussions and other forms of serious head trauma. The common treatment requires the patient to sleep on a mattress that has waferlike magnets stitched into the fabric.

Often used in combination with "far infrared" light, the two modalities purportedly complement one another to change the flow of lymph and other bodily fluids to speed healing.

Healing magnets are available in many health food stores and back care specialty stores (such as The Better Back stores, 303-442-3998 or Relax the Back, 800-222-5728, www.relaxtheback.com), or through catalogs (such as The Sharper Image, 800-344-4444, www.sharperimage.com).

Craniosacral Therapy for Mild to Severe Head Trauma

After an auto accident, fall or sharp bump to the head, your body will take a longer time to heal than you might expect. A concussion is, in fact, a serious injury, even if it is described by a doctor or nurse as "mild."

The emerging field of craniosacral therapy has helped a number of patients recover after a concussion by treating the brain (cranium) and spinal cord (the sacrum lies at the base of the spine) as one unit—a unit that was injured in its entirety—as opposed to focusing on the head alone.

Gentle, sensitive, knowing massage along the nerve centers of the body can search for blockages and help erase the aftereffects of concussion.

CONSTIPATION

■ Aloe Relief

Among its myriad uses, the humble aloe plant can help end bouts of constipation fairly quickly. Instead of the gel, you want dried aloe latex, which can be found at health food stores, herb shops and some grocery stores. Taken orally, it works by stimulating the muscles of the colon to contract, and should be used only on occasion. (For repeated use, it is safer to take fiber products like psyllium.)

Typical dosage of aloe powder is 250 mg to 500 mg, starting with the lowest dose and working upward.

■ Ginger Compress

A warming ginger compress can help stimulate sluggish bowels. To make one, set two gallons of water on the stove to boil. While the water boils, grate four tablespoons of fresh ginger root into a cheesecloth pouch. Dip the ginger pouch in the hot water, then wring the juice out of the pouch back into your pot. Remove from heat and return the pouch to the pot to steep. Dunk a thick towel into the water, wring out and place over abdomen until it cools. Reheat water and repeat the process four times.

■ An Acupressure Exercise

Here's a hands-on way to relieve the pressure and gas of constipation, and to keep the bowels moving. It's an acupressure exercise, performed on the floor.

1 Lying on your back with knees comfortably bent, find the spot three finger widths below the navel.

2 Press this spot slowly, firmly, downward—into your body—using all your fingertips at once.

3 Breathe deeply, release and repeat.

Performed over days or weeks, the exercise will help prevent constipation from recurring.

A Caution About Natural Laxatives

Not long ago, Rob McCaleb, president of the Herb Research Foundation, made a startling pronouncement. He wrote, in the pages of a leading natural health magazine, that some herbs, including senna, cascara sagrada and rhubarb, may be hazardous to your health when used as laxatives. McCaleb was simply reminding herb users that "natural" does not necessarily mean safe. In this instance, these natural laxative extracts should not be taken for longer than 8 to 10 days, McCaleb said. The herb senna, in fact, has been cited in a number of deaths in recent years, even though fatalities are extremely rare.

■ Saltwater Solution

Beyond the prune juice and commercial preparations, one simple method of relieving constipation starts at the kitchen sink. As soon as you get up in the morning, add two teaspoons of table salt to a quart of water, then drink up. Follow this up with a minifast, until the intestines empty out—usually within a few hours.

Note: This remedy is not for regular bouts of constipation. *Caution:* People with congestive heart failure, kidney disease or high blood pressure may not tolerate the additional salt.

■ Turning It Around

Strengthening of the abdominal, pelvic and lower back muscles can help relieve irregularity. Asian doctors recommend this simple waist-turning exercise to clear up constipation problems.

1 Stand with feet slightly turned out at hip width, and bend the knees a bit (kneecaps no farther forward than the toes).

2 Keeping the upper body upright, place your hands on your hips.

3 Rotate the torso clockwise, then repeat the same move counterclockwise.

4 Next, lean the torso to the side, first moving to the right then to the left.

Beginners should try 10 turns in each of the four moves, twice per day. Some devotees work up to 200 daily turns.

■ Root Relief

For recurrent bouts of constipation, before you reach for the over-the-counter drugstore treatments, and after you've eaten more fiber for a day or two, why not try to stimulate and normalize bowel function with a natural product? Herbalists and naturopaths often recommend tinctures (extracts) of any of the following herbs:

- angelica root

- dandelion root

- chicory root

Each of these should be taken as a 20- to 30-drop dose in a small cup of water, three times a day. If one doesn't work for you, try another—but don't combine them.

Reflexology Relieves Constipation

Try this three-step reflexology method to relieve occasional constipation.

1 While sitting in a comfortable position, pour some moisturizing lotion on your hands and work into the feet over a period of 5 to 10 minutes, kneading, stroking and squeezing along the way. Dust with foot powder, massaging until the lotion is absorbed.

2 Press both thumbs deeply into the center of the sole, into each foot's arch, one at a time, and hold for three minutes. This region of the foot is said to correspond with the intestines, according to principles of reflexology, the ancient medical art that uses reflex areas in the foot to affect organs throughout the body.

3 As you work on your feet, take time to close your eyes, breathe deeply and imagine your intestines relaxing. "See" yourself flowing freely down a river, along a path, wherever you wish to visualize. Think of this as the mindful laxative.

COUGH
See also **Common Cold**, *page 85,* and **Sore Throat**, *page 204*

GENERAL COUGH SYMPTOMS

Yup...Chicken Soup

Instead of a few spoonfuls of cough medicine, how about a cup of hot chicken soup? Yes, your mother was right: Chicken soup will cure what ails you. The protein in chicken contains cystine, an amino acid similar to acetylcysteine, a drug that thins mucus and clears lungs. A bowl of steaming hot chicken soup helps release fluids within the body that will drain your chest of fluid and make mucus less likely to settle in lungs and become infected.

A Sweet but Smelly Cough Syrup

Finely chop one onion, place it in a pot and cover it with honey. Put the lid on the pot and warm the mixture on low heat for 40 minutes. Take as needed, one spoonful at a time, until the cough feels better. Onions are high in resins that have expectorant and antimicrobial properties. When taken warm, they increase blood flow to the chest and throat.

Get to the Root of Your Illness

Osha root stimulates the circulatory system, causing perspiration, chasing away chills and breaking up mucus in sinuses and lungs. Plus, this herb soothes sore tissues. Take a teaspoon of osha root tincture two to three times a day to remedy coughs, sore throats, congestion and other cold symptoms.

When you're run-down and feeling under the weather, indulge in a massage. Not only does this touch therapy relax and revive tired, sore muscles, it has a medicinal effect as well. Massage stimulates the lymphatic system to flush away toxins and infections and stimulates the immune system to carry cells to fight bacteria. At least that's what massage therapists and some naturopathic healers claim.

■ Tea Thyme Treatment

More than a mere spice or entree seasoning, thyme has antiseptic properties that often are overlooked. (Next time you're in a pharmacy, check the ingredients label on a Listerine bottle for thyme.) Thyme may help prevent infection and worsening of nagging coughs. Although you probably have dried thyme in your spice rack, herbalists suggest brewing fresh or dried leaves into a tea, and sipping it throughout the day until the cough is tamed.

■ Homemade Expectorant

If you're looking for a cough remedy that is powerful enough to work quickly and yet is gentle enough for children, herbalists recommend anise, or aniseed. Taken in tea form, it adds a little anesthetic quality to the remedy. Simply heat the seeds or leaves in water, let steep for several minutes, then strain the leaves and sip.

Although the herb is safe when taken in tea medicinally for up to a week, chronic use of anise can be toxic. (In stronger, essential oil form, two or three drops taken orally are safe,

but 30 or 40 drops are not.) Check with your doctor if you have a persistent cough, as it may be a sign of a more serious problem.

■ Family-Sized Portion of a Potion

Fancy yourself a chef? Cook up your own herbal cough-and-cold syrup. Follow this recipe:

1 Combine equal parts of honey and wild cherry bark syrup to form the base.

2 Next, mix in two grams of ground apricot seed, an ounce of garlic tincture and an ounce of osha root tincture.

3 Store in a tightly closed container.

Take two teaspoons every few hours during a coughing spell.

■ Sage Advice

Used by Native Americans during purification rituals, white sage is also one of the best natural antibiotics to rub out infection. Make an all-purpose white sage solution using 30 to 60 drops of tincture mixed in a cup of warm water. Either drink the brew as a tea or gargle with it.

Massage for Organs

Sometimes even the most potent antibiotics can't help a stubborn case of bronchitis. Visceral massage—or organ massage—could help stimulate the congested area of the lungs and break up the infection. A massage therapist (trained in therapeutic massage) will be able to do this for you. Just don't be surprised if you spend much of the next day coughing—that's part of the recovery process.

■ The Daily Rind

Tangerine rinds—and other citrus fruits like oranges and lemons—contain essential oils, bioflavonoids and vitamin C that naturally clear out stuffy sinuses and respiratory tracts. Grind or grate each of the peels (they can be combined if you wish), then add a teaspoonful of the zest to a cup of herbal tea. Or combine with wild cherry bark syrup for a fruity cough formula.

■ Oregano Quiets a Cough

The herb oregano can be a powerful cough soother. Make a tea with a teaspoon of dried oregano steeped in a cup of hot water. Strain before sipping. You may drink up to three cups a day during a cold or coughing spell.

■ Powerful Kitchen Poultice

To help break up congestion in the lungs, thinly slice an onion and cook it in a little bit of water until very soft. Wrap the cooked onion in thin dishtowels, then apply to the chest for 20 minutes. Sometimes aromatherapy is anything but lavender-like!

■ Apricot Punch

Are you ready to try a centuries-old Chinese herbal remedy for coughs and colds? Ground apricot seeds contain potent chemicals that can help suppress dry, hacking coughs. You need only a little —a third of a gram—mixed into a cup of boiled water to make a therapeutic tea. Visit a Chinese herbalist to find ground apricot seeds if you are unable to find them in a general health food store. Otherwise, buy some apricots, break open the pit and grind the seeds on your own in a sturdy blender.

BRONCHITIS

■ Take It from a Skunk

How do herbalists spell relief for the spasms caused by a serious bronchial infection? Skunk cabbage—it's one of the best remedies for relaxing the muscles in the airways and the bronchial tree. Unfortunately, it can be hard to find. Contact an herbal pharmacy for assistance in tracking down a tincture of skunk cabbage. And truth be told, the aroma isn't all that bad.

■ Herbal Bronchial Remedy

Isatis root boasts natural antibacterial and antiviral properties for knocking out respiratory rattles caused by an infection. Take 35 drops of the tincture every few hours for a severe bronchial infection. *Helpful hint:* Since the isatis root tincture tastes very bitter, drop a little on your tongue and quickly chase the herbal remedy with a glass of juice to make the medicine go down easier.

■ Soothing Mustard Wrap

The best condiment for bronchitis is mustard. Whip up the following recipe for a deep-heat, decongesting treatment.

1 Add a teaspoon of mustard powder to a cup of flour.

2 Add enough hot water to the mixture to make a paste.

3 Put on an old T-shirt, then apply the paste onto the shirt in the chest area.

4 Cover the area with plastic wrap, and put a hot-water bottle on top. Then sit quietly for 15 minutes—maximum.

A few warnings: Do not put the mixture directly on your skin, as it can burn. Avoid applying the mixture near nipples, because it's too harsh for the sensitive area. And finally, if this treatment doesn't give relief after two applications, it's not going to do it.

■ Common Herbs, Uncommon Potency

A few drops of essential oils like eucalyptus or thyme in a bowl of hot water produce medicinal vapors that clear congestion and help calm bronchial coughs. Plus, herbalists and naturopaths say that both eucalyptus and thyme (which are widely available) have antimicrobial qualities that will help fight an infection. Even 5 to 10 minutes of breathing the vapors will bring results.

DRY, HACKING COUGH

■ An Acupressure Suppressant

If you've got a hacking cough, and the drugstore or herbal aids are letting you down, perhaps taming your muscles can help out. Try this two-thumb acupressure treatment, with a partner's help.

First, find the bump in the spine where the neck and shoulders meet. Apply pressure to points directly on either side of the bump, with the amount of time dependent upon the severity of the cough. This treatment can be repeated throughout the day.

■ A Homeopathic "Lesson"

Like standard drug therapy, homeopathic drugs often won't work if taken incorrectly—or inconsistently. For instance, when you have a dry cough that seems to take your breath away when you move too fast, make sure you stay with the medication for more than a day or two.

For this type of cough, homeopaths suggest Bryonia (6C), twice a day for four days.

■ The Oil Hanky Trick

When you have a hacking cough that robs you of breath several times a day, try this suggestion from a sage herbalist—simply place a few drops of essential oil of frankincense on a handkerchief (or tissue) and inhale every hour or so, or as needed.

Note: Shortness of breath associated with coughing could be a sign of asthma or other serious illnesses. See your doctor to be sure that you're okay.

■ A Very Cherry Cure

Wild cherry bark provides sweet relief for a scratchy throat and nagging cough. The syrup can be purchased at health food stores. Or look for herbal cough remedies containing wild cherry bark syrup. Naturopaths and others say taking a teaspoonful every few hours may help persistent coughs. They add, though, that simply flavoring a cough drop with the essence of cherry and sugar won't do the trick.

■ Weed Out Dry Coughs

Is a severe cough rattling your bones? Gumweed will work to get rid of the choking and painful spasms of a dry cough—and acts as an expectorant. *The prescription:* 10 drops of the tincture, or one to three capsules, three times a day until symptoms improve.

Look for gumweed tincture at a local health food store, or contact an herbalist for assistance in finding the uncommon remedy. Gumweed can be sipped in water or taken as an elixir blended with honey.

■ Horehound for Hoarse Throats

Hoarse? Hacking? It's horehound to the rescue. This herbal expectorant thins mucus in the lungs. Make a tea from 10 to 15 drops of horehound tincture in a cup of hot water. Drink up to three cups a day during an illness. Horehound lozenges are also available in health food stores.

"TICKLE" IN YOUR THROAT

■ Take It Lying Down

Not all coughs are alike—you knew that. So why do most people take the same medication for relief, when the symptoms are so varied? One of the more frustrating kinds of coughs occurs when you're going to bed, sliding into the sheets. Something about going horizontal kick-starts the cough—and you think you'll never get to sleep.

Homeopathic medicine offers a specific remedy for the "horizontal hack": Drosera (6C). Take it once an hour for up to five hours, when your symptoms have just started. Then, stay with it twice a day for four days.

■ A Slippery Lozenge

Slippery elm bark is the herbal prescription for taking a tickle out of your throat. Known for its soothing qualities, the herb, taken as a tea or lozenge, coats the throat and quiets coughing. Look for the lozenges at your local health food store. Or stir one teaspoon of powdered bark into hot water for cough relief.

DEPRESSION AND DEPRESSIVE DISORDERS

■ The Mood-Boosting Effects of Saint-John's-Wort

In Germany, where herbal medicine is held in rather high regard, doctors prescribe the herb Saint-John's-wort (hypericum) some seven times more frequently than they do the newer antidepressants (Prozac, Zoloft or other Selective Serotonin Re-uptake Inhibitors [SSRIs]) that are so popular in the US. A wild plant in Europe, Saint-John's-wort is said to be most effective in treating mild to moderate depression, general anxiety and depressed mood associated with menopause. This herb is rich in hypericin, a chemical that boosts production of norepinephrine, a neurotransmitter in the brain that elevates mood.

Like the other treatments for depression, though, the remedy won't work for everybody. Nor can it prevent future attacks of depression from occurring. Although Saint-John's-wort is generally well tolerated, it can conflict with standard antidepressant drugs, so the two should not be combined. Check with your MD or naturopath for dosage recommendations. Saint-John's-wort is widely available at health food stores and drugstores in the US.

■ Mustard Elevates Mood

It is far too simplistic to say that flower essences can *cure* depression or even extreme episodes of the blues, but mustard essence has been shown to lift the moods of many people who feel inexplicably sad or overtaken by malaise. Prepare a sun tea by leaving flowers and water in a glass bowl in the sun for a few hours. Mix this evenly with brandy. Then (similar to homeopathic medicine principles) take three drops of this "mother" essence and mix it with one ounce of water. Repeat, using three drops of this "stock," and mixing it with one ounce of water. You can make as many bottles as you'd like in this manner.

As for taking the essence, you can drop seven or eight drops under the tongue four times a day, or you can put a dropperful in the bathtub. Finally, you can put it in a misting bottle and spray it around the room. While some people feel mood lifts right away, most often the essences work more slowly, more subtly. And as with any kind of depressive disorder, consult a doctor.

Acupuncture Lifts Mood

The World Health Organization has officially recognized acupuncture as a successful treatment to lift depression. Physicians say that after an acupuncture session, the body increases production of endorphins and serotonin, which are suppressed when someone feels depressed. So what are some of the "happy" hot spots on the body that acupuncturists target? The elbow and ear.

■ *Mood-Food Connections*

Scientific study shows that there really are "comfort" foods that can affect your mood. For instance, bananas, tomatoes and walnuts help the body raise levels of serotonin, a neurotransmitter in the brain that regulates moods. So eating these foods truly does give you a lift. Depending on the severity of your depression, changes in diet may offer some relief and can also work well in conjunction with other treatments, such as antidepressants or psychotherapy.

■ *Go Cold Turkey*

When you're feeling a bit down in the dumps, turn to tryptophan. An amino acid located in proteins that increases production of serotonin, tryptophan can replace antidepressant medication in some cases of depression. Try adding tryptophan-rich foods to your diet, such as soy beans, dairy products and protein-rich chicken, turkey or eggs.

■ *A Breathy Way to Feel Better*

If you're having a bad day or a week full of the blues (as opposed to serious depression), consider changing the way you breathe. Nasal breathing—long espoused by yoga teachers and those who practice meditation as a step toward mastery—has now been tested in a lab and found to help lift moods.

A study at both the University of Denver and Stanford University tracked subjects who had varied moods, some of whom were told to breathe through the mouth only, some through the nose only, and some through both. *Results:* The nasal breathers' moods generally improved, while the mouth breathers' moods were rated a bit darker.

The theory: Inhaling through the nose, which cools blood running near the nasal passages, triggers positive changes in the way the brain regulates moods.

Aerobic Exercise as Medicine

Prescribing exercise instead of medication for depression may surprise some patients. Many patients and their family members would be alarmed if they thought professionals were not taking their condition seriously enough to prescribe a drug. But remember, in the field of cardiology it took 15 or more years for doctors and patients to acknowledge that exercise could indeed improve one's condition—that exercise can be medicine.

Well, science is not as advanced yet in relating aerobics to mood brightening, but it is getting closer. Aerobic exercise performed 30 minutes a day, five times a week, can have a marked effect on improving mood. It may take a few weeks to take effect, but the body can indeed alter the mind.

DIABETES

■ *A Fruity Way to Manage Diabetes*

Quite often around the world (but not very often in North America), people who have been diagnosed with diabetes—especially Type II or adult onset diabetes—turn to the unripened fruit of a bitter melon for help. Grown in many tropical lands, karela is commonly used in India, the West Indies and China to help diabetics improve their glucose tolerance.

Because information about this fruit is not widely known in the West, ask your doctor or health practitioner to check with an expert in Asian medicine about bitter melon and its side effects when planning your treatment program for diabetes.

■ Aid from a Bay Leaf

For diabetes patients who don't yet need daily shots of insulin, eating food that has been prepared with bay leaves can help boost the body's ability to use and control glucose in the blood. (When glucose or sugar levels in blood rise too high, symptoms worsen.) In some cases, the bay leaf effect can extend by months the amount of time diabetics can avoid insulin shots or it can minimize their reliance on insulin shots.

Bay leaf tea can be made by steeping several bay leaves in hot water. Two to three cups a day is the suggested dosage. A less-effective alternative is to add the leaves to sauces (such as pasta sauce) or soups.

A Biofeedback Adjunct to Standard Therapy

Biofeedback is gaining attention as a treatment for diabetes. Nobody is claiming that it can replace insulin as a treatment, and your doctor or endocrinologist must be aware if you plan to try it, but biofeedback—learning to monitor and relax the body—has been shown to help some diabetics improve their circulation and lower their dosage of insulin.

Many diabetics feel that they already spend enough time managing their disease, so why would they want to add another treatment to their time-consuming, blood-monitoring, insulin-injection regimens? The answer may be better long-term health. Biofeedback training to alter one's own blood flow and heart-rate responses does take up to 10 or 12 weeks to learn, and it may not be reimbursed by insurance companies, but at the least, proponents say, it is worth exploring.

Caution: Never eat bay leaves directly, as they can be poisonous. And don't rely on this or any other alternative treatment to replace prescribed medications for diabetes.

DIARRHEA
*See also **Digestive Disorders**, page 100*

■ Meals That Heal

The BRATT diet—bananas, rice, applesauce, toast and tea—provides surefire relief for a detestable case of diarrhea. Why? Bananas replenish the depleted supplies of potassium and sodium the body depends on for normal functioning. Rice and toast contain fiber. Applesauce provides pectin, a common ingredient in over-the-counter diarrhea remedies, which works with "good" intestinal bacteria to coat and soothe the irritated lining of the intestines. And the tannin found in tea reduces intestinal inflammation resulting from an infection. Physicians advise staying on the BRATT diet until diarrhea symptoms subside.

■ Water Aid

Failing to drink water and clear liquids during a bout of diarrhea can worsen the condition. Since you lose a lot of water as a result of the intestinal infection, limiting fluid consumption can cause serious dehydration. Try to drink as much water, broth or herbal tea (at least eight cups a day) to replenish fluids and restore your immune system so it can fight the infection.

■ A Two-Stage Plan of Action

First, some bad news. Physicians often tell patients that no matter how bad diarrhea may feel, it should not be treated for the first 12 hours or so. The body is actually trying to cleanse itself of the offending bacteria, virus or toxins—it needs to do its job before you bring in reinforcements.

After the 12-hour waiting period, activated charcoal capsules may be the best option. Taking two capsules each hour should bring quick relief, along with the temporary side effect of darkened stools.

Note: Charcoal is a wonderfully efficient absorbent—which means that it also will sop up other medications that have been taken recently. So, to be safe, if you have taken any other medication, wait at least one hour before taking charcoal capsules.

■ Eastern Wisdom Worth a Try

Macrobiotic practitioners often recommend brewing up a cup of Japanese kuzo-pickled plum paste tea for those suffering from painful stomachaches and/or diarrhea. Kuzo is a thickening ingredient, much like arrowroot, and acts as a binding agent. To make the tea, dissolve a teaspoon of kuzo in water to make a paste, then add a teaspoon of the plum paste to boiling water.

DIGESTIVE DISORDERS
See also **Diarrhea,** *page 99*

COLITIS

■ Acupuncture Has a Calming Influence

When colitis strikes, it can be a localized inflammation of the lower part of the large intestine or colon, or it may be more universal, causing inflammation and sores throughout the colon (ulcerative colitis). Although the cause of a colitis attack may be unknown, once food sensitivities and infections are ruled out, acupuncturists and naturopaths sometimes prescribe a course of acupuncture to calm the inflammation and hyperactive immune system that is in large part responsible for the condition. Acupuncture can bring considerable relief to symptoms of pain, diarrhea and cramping.

Homemade Remedy to Prevent Dehydration

When you suffer from diarrhea, make sure your body is taking in enough fluids to prevent dehydration. You can do this by drinking an oral rehydration solution. You can buy one premade (Gatorade, for instance) or you can make your own.

Add one-half teaspoon of salt to four cups of boiled water, then gradually stir in one to two cups of infant rice cereal. Drink 8 to 12 ounces of this rice drink after each watery stool. You may need to drink as much as three to six quarts over the next two to four hours to counteract dehydration.

If you're suffering from nausea as well, have small sips every few minutes. If you have more than three bouts of diarrhea per day, seek medical attention.

Treatments may continue for weeks or even months, depending upon the various imbalances identified.

■ *A Bark Eases the Bite*

For those who have inflammatory bowel diseases, such as ulcerative colitis, who are being treated with standard allopathic medicines (e.g., prednisone and/or sulfa drugs), slippery elm bark may help ease some symptoms during flare-ups of the conditions. It may also help soothe the digestive tracts of patients during remission. To take this remedy in liquid (decoction) form:

1 Combine one to three teaspoons of powdered bark (found in good natural food stores) with a cup of water.

2 Boil and simmer for about 15 minutes.

Some cinnamon or sugar may help the taste. Try drinking two or three cups daily.

■ *Unlikely Nicotine Aid*

It is not often that you hear positive things about the drug known as nicotine. But recent research has shown that for unexplained reasons, people who have ulcerative colitis, an inflammatory bowel disease causing diarrhea and intestinal upset, seem to respond well to nicotine. When nicotine patches were placed on subjects for weeks at a time, the colitis conditions improved noticeably. Now this early research is not meant to be a license for any afflicted person to start smoking, but in years to come, ingesting nicotine in some form may prove to be an option for some.

■ *Aloe Vera—For "Internal" Skin, Too*

The soothing, cooling properties of the aloe vera plant are not limited to sunburn, scrapes and abrasions. For some patients who have intermittent bouts of colitis, or inflammation of the colon, drinking one teaspoon of pure aloe juice (found in larger health food stores) after meals can have a lasting effect. They notice a lessening of intestinal upset and diarrhea.

Warning: At higher dosages, aloe vera juice can have a laxative effect—the last thing that colitis patients need.

Slow Down and Stop Chewing

Swallowing air can cause digestive problems, plus excessive belching. Eating and drinking too fast is one way to swallow too much air. Another less obvious offender is chewing gum. If this is a habit, stop for a few days to see if your symptoms subside.

■ *Herbal Aid for Crohn's Disease*

When diagnosed with Crohn's disease or ulcerative colitis, patients often are advised to take steroids and other drugs to help reduce inflammation of the intestines, the hallmark of both diseases. But these medications don't always effect a remission. Patients may continue to suffer from chronic intestinal cramping, diarrhea and sometimes fever.

In such stubborn cases, patients can try to soothe some of the symptoms with herbal remedies as adjunct therapy. One combination therapy your doctor may approve calls for a mixture of three herbs into a tea: Chamomile, meadowsweet and licorice, taken two or three times a day. An alternative is to mix or purchase the herbs in tincture form and take sequentially. These remedies contain soothing, anti-inflammatory essences that target the digestive tract.

■ *A Fishy Preventative*

The research may be preliminary, but it is great news for those afflicted with chronic, inflammatory bowel disorders such as Crohn's disease or ulcerative colitis: Fish oil may help keep the disorders at bay. A study from Italy published in the *New England Journal of Medicine* showed that those who took nine fish oil capsules a day were far less likely to suffer relapses of Crohn's than subjects who didn't. Experts suspect that omega-3 fatty acids in the fish oil aid the body's synthesis of helpful prostaglandins.

DIVERTICULITIS

■ *Weight Training Strengthens Intestines, Too*

File this item under those that don't often get discussed at the health club. Long-term, moderate weight training can speed up digestion by cutting the transit time of food as it moves through the intestines. That makes for healthier colons. Long transit times (28 hours, say, versus a more average 18) are associated with increased risk of diverticulitis, a kind of inflammation that results in intestinal-colon blockages. Weight training also builds the smooth muscles that guide the intestines along their daily missions, according to research at the University of Maryland, College Park.

INDIGESTION

■ *A Helpful Tea Combination*

Taken together in tea, three herbs can go a long way toward shortening your next bout of indigestion. Try this homemade anti-indigestion tea mixture:

■ Meadowsweet, used for heartburn and acid stomach.

■ Chamomile, a calming, soothing herb.

■ Fennel seed, used to relieve nausea (and even hiccups).

This fragrant, soothing blend may be sipped as frequently as you need it.

Nutritional Approaches to "Quiet" the Colon

Naturopaths and other holistic doctors often advise patients who have digestive disorders to stop drinking coffee, cola and other caffeinated beverages. People sometimes forget that caffeine is a drug—a stimulant. It just happens to be a legal drug in the US that tens of millions of people take once, twice or more times a day. But when patients with irritable bowel syndrome quit coffee, and increase their consumption of whole foods, noncaffeinated, soothing teas and fresh vegetables (which might be irritating to some), they tend to see improvement in their condition within weeks. That's not to claim that nutritional therapy is a cure, but it can be an effective treatment.

■ Take Five!

To help digest a large meal, lie down on your left side for a few minutes. This will increase the blood flow to your stomach, which is situated more toward the left side of the body. Not moving for a few minutes also ensures that blood isn't speeding to other organs and muscles while your stomach is busily processing food.

Don't Overlook Biofeedback

When someone asks you to clench your fist and biceps muscles, you can do it in an instant. Easy, right? This is the kind of approach a biofeedback practitioner might take toward treating irritable bowel syndrome (IBS). After all, the colon is controlled by a series of muscles—many of them under voluntary control. And many of them carry and send messages from and to the brain.

With practice, doctors say, patients who control their breathing and who use visualization skills can go a long way toward controlling the seemingly unpredictable spasms of the colon in cases of IBS. Ten sessions are usually enough to bring long-lasting relief from this hard-to-treat disorder.

■ Start the Day with Papaya

Enzymes from this sweet tropical fruit have been used in meat tenderizers for years for a reason. Start your day with half a papaya, or drink a glass of papaya juice, to give your digestive system a boost—or drink some any time you know you will be eating rich foods.

■ A Stomach Massage

Self-massage of the abdomen has been prescribed for chronic gastritis and constipation since the 1600s. Work any combination of five points from the top of the abdomen (below the ribs) to the lowest spot, about two inches below the navel. Two key middle points are the navel and halfway between the navel and sternum.

The basic technique is as follows:

1 Place the first three fingers of one hand on the first point, then cover them with the first three fingers of the other hand.

2 Press with both hands and gently knead the abdomen in clockwise circles.

3 Repeat on each pressure point, moving from top to bottom.

The top point should be kneaded for 36 clockwise circles, while the middle two points are massaged together for 18 circles each, before switching to 18 counterclockwise circles. The lowest point also calls for 18 circles in each direction.

Three Seasonings for Indigestion Relief

The spasms of a cranky digestive tract can be soothed with the essential oils of tarragon, rosemary and marjoram. Take one drop of each with a spoonful of honey. You can also try adding these common herbs (fresh or dried) to chicken, breads, fish, pasta and salads to help you digest dinner.

Ayurvedic Alternatives

Ayurvedic medicine, a body/mind discipline with roots in India, recognizes several body/personality types with their own tendencies. But there are some Ayurvedic remedies for stomach upset that work across the three main body types:

1 Boil one-half teaspoon of crushed or ground bay leaves in a cup of water for 10 minutes.

2 Strain the leaves from the liquid and add a pinch of cardamom.

3 Drink the tea after meals.

BBQ on the QT

Most of us associate charcoal with the outdoor grilling season. But natural healers like its active ingredients to quell digestion problems. To make your own charcoal liquid remedy:

1 Add two to three tablespoons of activated charcoal (available in health food stores) to a glass filled with a couple of inches of water.

2 Stir gently to prevent the charcoal from flying away.

3 Add water until the glass is full, then stir again.

4 Let the charcoal settle to the bottom of the glass before drinking (using a straw is helpful).

If you have no activated charcoal, you can get by with scrapings from burnt toast.

Juice Truce

Some health practitioners swear by onion juice as a digestive aid. Here is perhaps a more palatable drink. Juice the following ingredients together:

- A thick slice of ginger
- Half a handful of fresh mint
- One kiwifruit
- One-quarter of a pineapple (including the skin if your machine can handle it)

Taken twice daily, this concoction helps relieve chronic gas.

Juicy Kitchen Recipe

If you have overdone it at your own dinner party, here's a digestion remedy that can be made even while you are cleaning up. Add one teaspoon of lemon juice and one-half teaspoon of baking soda to a glass of cool water. Drink the mixture quickly.

A Peppermint Oil Solution

For indigestion, here is a fast-acting remedy: Three drops of peppermint oil added to a cup of warm water with a spoonful of honey. You can dab this potion onto your wrists or under the nose, or add it to a bath or vaporizer. It is also great for quelling nausea during pregnancy. A holistic pharmacy or health store will be well stocked with all kinds of essential oils.

■ Oregano Alternative

A healthy dose of oregano not only adds flavor to your favorite dishes but also stimulates the digestive system. Of course, oregano is not the seasoning to go with every meal, so when you're not feasting on Italian food, sip some oregano tea after your meal to kick-start digestion. Put a teaspoon of crushed dried oregano in a cup of hot water and let the mixture steep for about 15 minutes. Some may find oregano tea an acquired taste, but it's worth a try.

IRRITABLE BOWEL SYNDROME (IBS)

■ Healthy Start

Irritable bowel syndrome can cause gas, bloating, stomach cramps, diarrhea and constipation. A restricted diet and increasing dietary fiber can help ease all of these symptoms. Ground flaxseed, in particular, helps soothe inflamed intestinal walls. Add two tablespoons of ground flaxseed to eight ounces of juice or water, or stir them into your rice cereal.

Avoid beef and all cereal except rice and use soy-based products rather than milk or other dairy products.

Psych Yourself Out of IBS

Stress. Anxiety. Edginess. Mental anguish can really get you in the gut—not only causing butterflies in the stomach, but also exacerbating irritable bowel syndrome and perhaps even causing the illness. Psychotherapy eases your mind and your IBS. How? It gets to the bottom of mental and emotional issues that can provoke an outbreak of the disorder.

■ Minty Massage

Massaging your abdomen with peppermint oil feels refreshing and can help ease intestinal discomfort. Add 10 drops of peppermint essential oil to one ounce of almond oil, then place one-half to one teaspoonful of the oil mixture onto the abdomen and massage in a clockwise direction. Repeat two or three times daily.

■ Another Peppermint Plan

The misery of irritable bowel syndrome is curtailed for some people by a simple regimen: Three capsules of essence of peppermint oil per day, plus several cups of mint tea. The key is consistent dosing and making sure the peppermint oil is pure.

■ A Combination Herbal Tea Approach

A three-herb combination tea has worked effectively to calm some cases of constipation and irritable bowel that don't respond to simple, nutritional, calm-the-intestines approaches. The nutritional tea combines the familiar herb chamomile with marshmallow (the herb, not the candy) and yellow dock root, which is often recommended to relieve constipation. Mix the herbs in equal proportions.

■ *Power of Suggestion*

Research indicates that the relaxed state achieved by clinical hypnosis can neutralize irritable bowel syndrome in patients under 50. Most of us can fall into a deep calm through a guided imagery session using word-pictures suggesting such venues as placid lakes and serene mountaintops. Once learned, we can use these techniques at home. About 10% of the population needs more directed hypnosis to reach the relaxed state. For a referral, contact the American Society of Clinical Hypnosis, 140 N. Bloomingdale Rd., Bloomingdale, IL 60108; 630-980-4740, www.asch.net.

■ *Antidepressants Lift IBS Symptoms*

Strange but true: Research shows that antidepressants can help control the pain that some feel from irritable bowel syndrome. Plus, the drug therapy may battle the root cause of IBS, since physicians believe that the disorder may result in part from psychological problems, such as depression and severe anxiety.

LACTOSE SENSITIVITY, GAS, CRAMPS

■ *Problems with Milk Products*

If you have gas, cramping and diarrhea, and suspect that milk or milk products may be contributing to the condition, try a three-day "milk fast." Eliminate yogurt, cheese and even foods that may have dry milk solids in their ingredients, such as prepared baked goods (check ingredient labels carefully). If symptoms lessen or disappear, there's a good chance that you are lactose intolerant—a common condition in which your body cannot process the sugars in milk effectively. This is especially true if your symptoms recur when you reintroduce dairy products into your diet.

As a way to control the condition and still eat or drink milk products occasionally, enlist the aid of enzymes: Lactase tablets taken before you eat dairy products should calm your intestines. Also, consider switching to soy milk and soy-based products whenever possible.

DRY MOUTH

■ *Rain Forest Remedy*

While not a well-known plant throughout the US, jaborandi, or *Pilocarpus pennatifolius*, is used in other parts of the world, notably Central America (Belize), to treat the various causes of dry mouth. The leaves of jaborandi turn dry mouths moist after just a few minutes of chewing. Compounds in the plant seem to activate the salivary glands. How? Another secret of the rain forest, apparently. Check your herb shop for supplies.

EAR CONDITIONS

See also **Hearing Loss,** page 40

EARACHE AND EAR INFECTIONS

■ A Two-Step Echinacea Plan

Not just for bad colds, echinacea is gentle enough to treat earaches, from the inside out. Start the herbal treatment by taking up to one teaspoon of echinacea tincture orally, two or three times a day. The second step is to bend your head to one side and drop four to six drops of tincture directly into the ear, every two to three hours, while the pain persists. Since echinacea is such a popular herb, it is available in many forms in nearly all health food stores and drugstores.

■ Olive Oil to the Rescue

To soothe the pain of an earache for children or adults, warm some olive oil and apply it topically. Don't make it too hot—and consider this a temporary fix. The olive oil will not address any infection.

■ Golden Ears

Have you heard? Goldenseal, rich in berberine, a natural antibiotic, is an herbal earache aid. Relax with a cup of goldenseal tea, and give your body a chance to recuperate.

The recipe: Add one teaspoon of dried goldenseal to a cup of boiled water. Let the mix steep for 10 minutes and strain before drinking. You may safely sip up to three cups a day, herbalists say.

■ A Dairy Discovery for Your Ears

If your earache is caused by congestion, consider steering clear of milk, cheese and ice cream. Dairy products are thought by many alternative practitioners to be mucus-forming. Eliminating these foods from your diet during the course of the illness may make for a speedier recovery, especially for young children, who seem to be more susceptible to the effects of dairy products.

■ Onion Earmuffs

Although you may look a little like Princess Leia of *Star Wars* during the treatment, an onion poultice offers relief for throbbing, infected ears. First step? Place half an onion in a heated oven until it is warm, but not too hot, to the touch. Wrap the onion in an old T-shirt or piece of cheesecloth and hold it up to the sore ear. The chemicals in the onion help to increase circulation to the ear, flushing away infection and toxins.

■ Preventing Infections...Naturally

As soon as you feel that telltale popping in your ears, start popping the echinacea pills. Echinacea provides a jump start for your immune system that may prevent an ear infection from getting out of control. Take one to three echinacea capsules every two to three hours when you first experience any symptoms.

■ Warm Oils Soothe a Painful Ear

To treat ear infections, put two or three drops of warm mullein oil in each ear. Mullein acts as an anti-inflammatory and helps relieve pain.

Drops of warm garlic oil, calendula or Saint-John's-wort are also soothing for earaches. Since the oils last longer when refrigerated, warm them up on the stove first. Heating the oils makes them feel particularly soothing. If you suspect a punctured eardrum, however, don't use any of these oils.

As with any ailment, if pain persists, consult a doctor.

■ Top Carrot

What's up, doc? For an earache, carrots. Grind up a few and place the pulp in a piece of cheesecloth. Hold the pack against the infected ear for 15 minutes. The enzymes in the carrot help draw out the infection that's causing the pain. Repeat every few hours as necessary.

■ Garlic Eardrops

Not that popular in the US and Canada (yet), garlic mullein eardrops are a comforting cure for earaches, according to numerous herbalists. Garlic has antimicrobial properties, and mullein acts as a decongestant and also helps numb pain. Check your local health food store for these premixed drops. And don't forget to treat both ears, even if only one hurts. Infections often migrate from one ear to the other.

■ Healing Ears Homeopathically

Kali bichromicum may be a mouthful to say, but you only need to take a 30C potency once or twice a day for relief from an earache. According to experts, this homeopathic remedy works particularly well in clearing infected mucus from sinus passages and ear canals. Most health food stores and herb shops carry kali nowadays.

■ Natural Eardrops

Although Saint-John's-wort has made news in recent years for its remarkable effects on depression, herbalists have long known of its powers to help heal earaches. Once you've procured the oil (also sold as hypericum oil) from the herb shop or natural food store, warm it slightly, place just a few drops into the affected ear, then use a cotton ball to keep the oil from running out. Once a day for three days should bring relief.

FREQUENT FLYERS' EAR

■ The Little-Known Flight Attendants' Hot Towel Trick

If you're a frequent flyer, you may have seen, on occasion, an odd-looking sight in the seats around you: A seemingly normal person with Styrofoam coffee cups over his or her ears. Purportedly more effective than chewing wads of gum, this quirky remedy for earaches upon descent is catching on in first-class and other cabins worldwide. But it's not quite as simple as it looks.

Here is what's required:

1 Once the captain reminds you that it's time to turn off all electrical devices, ask a friendly flight attendant for two foam coffee cups and a couple of sturdy paper (or cotton) towels that have been doused in very hot water. *Caution:* Be *extra* careful here of excess hot water drips.

2 Place the towels snugly inside the cups.

3 While seated, place the mouths of the cups over your ears, forming a seal between the rims of the cups and your head. As the descent continues, you might want to close your eyes (to ignore nosy passengers), while breathing deeply and slowly to help unstuff your ears and sinuses. The steam-and-cup "compress" works more effectively than swallowing incessantly during the time it takes the plane to land.

■ *Chew Ginseng Gum*

To ease the pain and stuffiness of earaches while in flight, try chewing American ginseng gum as an alternative to regular old spearmint or cinnamon. Found in various urban China-towns, natural food shops or Asian-owned fruit and vegetable stands, the American ginseng gum called *Hatai* is made from white ginseng root and can be quite refreshing. It also increases your saliva production while you are sitting in an arid cabin as it helps unplug your ears.

■ *Take an OTC Decongestant*

Even if you don't feel congested, if you're prone to flight-induced earaches, over-the-counter decongestants can keep your eustachian tubes clear. A four-hour pill can be taken at the airport, an hour before the flight, and then again on the plane if you're flying for more than three hours. A 12-hour pill should be taken several hours before takeoff.

SWIMMER'S EAR

■ *Liquid Prevention*

You don't have to be an Olympic freestyler to contract a nasty case of swimmer's ear. Caused by bacteria or fungus invading the ear canal, the condition can cause itching, swelling and pain. (At times, antibiotics are required.) One way to prevent the ailment, if you or a family member is prone to it, is to use nonprescription ear drops—with alcohol—*before* you head to the lake or the beach. The key, ear experts say, is to prevent accumulated wetness.

TINNITUS: RINGING IN THE EARS

■ *Ginkgo Biloba Quiets Ringing*

Sometimes it's described as ringing, some-times as buzzing, but however it's described by those who have it, tinnitus is both frustrating and irritating. Often difficult to treat, it typical-ly afflicts those over age 55, but can strike at earlier ages when triggered by an infection of the inner ear. It is also frequently associated with excessive aspirin use or exposure to loud noises over a period of time.

In addition to watching your dose of aspirin, try using packaged formulations of ginkgo biloba to reduce the ringing. Ginkgo (as the product is known commercially) is reputed to improve blood circulation to the brain. It is available in health food stores and in many chain drugstores.

■ Down the Ringing

Cutting down on caffeine intake might work to turn down the ringing in your ears. Caffeine stimulates blood vessels in the ears, which can exacerbate tinnitus. Try eliminating coffee, colas and caffeinated teas from your diet for a couple of weeks to see if your condition begins to calm down. One soothing alternative is an Ayurvedic and antioxidant-rich coffee substitute called Raja's Cup, widely available in health food stores and natural food markets.

■ Music to Your Ears

For some sufferers of tinnitus, this treatment is literally music to their ears. It's a "music bath," recommended by specialists in ear disorders. Although most tinnitus sufferers crave silence over the high-pitched sounds they hear incessantly, listening to different kinds of music can help bring relief. An unlikely remedy, perhaps, but it's one that works for many. Experiment with all kinds of music to see what masks the tinnitus, or distracts the mind in a positive direction.

White noise machines can bring similar relief, by playing soothing sounds of nature or static noise. Find these machines at electronics stores. The Sharper Image sells Sound Soothers at www.sharperimage.com.

■ Outsmart It with Imagery

Frustration. That's the operative word many tinnitus sufferers use to describe the persistent ringing in their ears. One way to ease that frustration (though it does not reduce the perceived noise) is to practice guided imagery. Not hypnosis, not meditation, imagery involves simply imagining yourself in a tranquil setting and "escaping" to that setting at least a few times each day.

Close your eyes and imagine yourself on a perfect beach, the smell of salt air wafting around you. "Feel" the sun on your skin, "hear" the sound of the waves—and the seagulls. Offshore, you can see an island, where tinnitus mysteriously disappears. It's an image worth holding on to during the most frustrating times.

Time to Quit the Quinine

Of the many possible contributing factors to tinnitus, quinine may be one substance that is sneaking into your diet and causing or worsening the condition. Quit drinking quinine products for two weeks and notice if there's any change—if the ringing is quieter or gone altogether. The most popular beverage that contains quinine is tonic water, both flavored and unflavored.

■ Vitamins for Your Senses

If you're hearing a persistent dull roar or ringing, don't overlook a potential dietary link. Wheat and rice allergies, for example, are often linked to tinnitus.

Though the condition can be extremely frustrating, the good news is, vitamins may help. A number of naturopathic physicians believe that high doses of vitamin B3—commonly known as niacin—may remedy the condition. Because niacin in large amounts may be toxic to the liver, though, it's best to see a physician who will safely monitor this vitamin therapy. Another side effect to watch for is facial flushing or redness.

■ Antidepressant Solution

According to somewhat surprised physicians, recent research has shown that antidepressant medication has provided relief from tinnitus by acting on the nervous system in unexpected ways. In most instances, a short-term, low-dosage medication is effective. Check with your doctor to see if this is an appropriate "off-label" treatment for your condition. And rest easy—off-label uses for FDA-approved drugs are perfectly legal and, when properly monitored, are generally safe.

■ Hot-Feet Helper

Sometimes you can outsmart an ailment, especially one like tinnitus, where incessant ringing in the ears is related to blood flow and congestion. Some tinnitus sufferers report they have eased the ringing or buzzing (and the annoyance) by simply placing one heating pad on their feet, and another on their hands. This is apparently enough of a call to the circulatory system to reroute blood toward the arms and legs.

WAX BUILDUP

■ Baby Oil for You, Too

First things first. Most people don't need to clean inside their ears—with safety swabs or anything else. The ear does a good job of using the wax as a sort of safety seal—to keep dirt and bacteria out—and doesn't need pushing in on the wax. Plus, eventually, excess wax and oils push themselves into the outer ear canal, where you can easily reach them with a washcloth and a pinky finger.

If there is a heavy buildup of wax, and it is causing pain or affecting hearing, a home remedy of baby oil can help. Simply ease two or three drops of oil into the ear and let it do its work. It will soften the wax buildup, often overnight, making it easier to clean and safely remove (again, with a washcloth, not with an ear swab, in the outer ear canal). Some doctors prescribe "softening drops" for wax, but others say baby oil works as well and is less expensive.

EPILEPSY

■ "Pacemaker" for the Brain?

Despite significant advances in epilepsy medication in recent years, some epilepsy patients still suffer severe, uncontrolled, frightening seizures. (Nearly two million people in the US have the disease.) Now, they may be helped by a new, small, battery-powered implant that sends pulses to the brain, much as a pacemaker helps the heart beat on schedule. The vagus nerve stimulator, recently approved by the FDA, is implanted in the chest and sends low-voltage electrical signals to the brain on cue, every five minutes through the day and night. Apparently, these pulses help thwart signals that result in seizures.

For more information, contact The Epilepsy Foundation at 800-EFA-1000, or www.epilepsy foundation.org.

EYE CONDITIONS

See also **Eyes and Aging**, page 38, for Cataract Prevention and other aging-related disorders

EYE STRAIN

■ Five-Minute Massage for Computer Eyes

Admit it. You don't take that five-minute break every hour that computer users are advised to take for reasons of health and ergonomics. Maybe now, after repeated bouts of eyestrain and headaches, it's time to take "take five" seriously.

During those five minutes, try a relieving massage. While looking down, close your eyes. Then gently massage the tops of the eyeballs through your shuttered eyelids. Pay extra attention to tender areas—massaging in miniature circles.

Online Advice for Computer Eyestrain

If you spend more than a couple of hours at a computer each workday, it's worth taking a little time out for prevention. While you're online, check out Corporate Vision Consulting's Web site (www.cvconsulting.com) for detailed advice on preventing, recognizing and treating computer-related eyestrain. Then, be sure to take a break from your computer.

Get the Most from Eyedrops

Here's a handy idea about the tip of the trusty eyedrop bottle—and how to keep the medicine from running down your cheek. Whether you suffer from such benign conditions as tired or red eyes, or a more serious condition like glaucoma, before you next use your eyedrops, press gently with your finger between the corner of the eye and the nose (this creates a larger target). Apply the drops and close the eye—for two minutes! Ophthalmologists advise taking this much time to reduce tear drainage, and thus keep more medicine where it's needed.

■ Truck-Stop Help for Your Next Trip

It's not fancy, but it works. The next time you find yourself on the highway, driving with tired eyes and wishing your road trip were an hour or two shorter, pull off at the next rest stop. Grab a snack (fresh fruit, of course), then get a cup of ice. Also get eight or so bathroom paper towels (the heavy, scratchy kind), and head back to your car. Make a compress of sorts by folding in three ice cubes per paper towel (one trucker says four "gets all drippy"). Use these to dab your eyes and forehead as you head down the highway. Depending on the temperature, one ice cup should last quite a while.

See Straight, Thanks to a Surgical Solution

If you're nearsighted, there's a new type of surgery that could make contact lenses obsolete. A myopia lens—a type of permanent contact—is surgically implanted into the eye. It takes only a few days for vision to be normal. Ask your ophthalmologist if you're a candidate for this procedure, and make sure your surgeon is experienced performing it before going under the knife.

■ Ease the Eyes with Acupressure

This trick's a winner for eyestrain. Begin by placing your thumbs on the upper part of the eye socket—almost, but not quite pinching the bridge of your nose. Then, press upward and take deep, cleansing breaths for about a minute.

Follow up with a cheek press, of sorts. Using your index and middle fingers, press inward (with light pressure) in the center of the cheeks, beneath the cheekbone. Close your eyes, and take deep breaths, again for about a minute. The increased blood flow and circulation should bring quick relief.

FOREIGN OBJECT IN THE EYE

■ Flaxseed Relief

Your mother always said, "Don't rub your eye," when you had a speck of something in it. But she didn't always tell you what to do instead. Here's a simple, safe solution: Flaxseed. If you place a single flaxseed (available from any natural food market) just barely in the corner of your eye nearest the bridge of the nose, the tears and flaxseed oil will likely flush the foreign object right out. Of course, you need to be careful about putting *anything* in your eye (even partway). But in this particular instance, you are speeding along the eye's natural cleansing capabilities.

GLAUCOMA

◼ Eye Detox

This treatment may help draw toxins from the tissues around the eyes. Place one capsule of Nature's Way brand, Herbal Eyebright (available in health food stores) in one-third cup of boiled water. Steep for 30 minutes. Strain well through a cloth napkin into a dropper bottle, and apply two to three drops in each eye, three times a day. Use the drops for six days, then skip one day. Continue with the regimen, following this pattern, for a few months. While glaucoma is a serious condition that shouldn't solely be self-treated, this complementary treatment may also be administered by using a compress of the Eyebright liquid, then periodically laying that over the eyes.

STIES

◼ Potato Patch for the Eye

A sty is the bacterial infection of an eyelash follicle or the sebaceous gland at the margin of an eyelid. One home remedy works like this:

1 Scrape a small mound from inside a potato and wrap it in a piece of clean cheesecloth or similar thin cloth.

2 Place the minicompress on the sty, and hold it there for 5 to 10 minutes.

3 Repeat with fresh scrapings one or two more times during the next two hours.

The swelling should be much improved. If there are no potatoes in the house, try using a tea bag dampened in warm water. Apply it for half an hour a day for a week, or until the sty is gone.

TIRED, PUFFY, SWOLLEN EYES

◼ Hawaiian Eye Solution

Some naturopaths and facialists recommend fresh pineapple as a tasty remedy for puffy eyes. Because pineapple contains an enzyme, bromelain, that keeps skin from swelling after injury, it can also deliver an anti-inflammatory punch to the thin skin and tissues around the eyes. Bromelain can be taken in the familiar fruity slices and chunks—or in pure compound form, found in natural food stores. In this form, 400 to 500 mg is an effective dose when taken three times a day on an empty (or relatively empty) stomach.

◼ Shrink Puffiness with Oily Compress

Don't want to broadcast the evidence of your late night to your whole office? Try this quick method of reducing puffiness:

Soak cotton balls in a mixture of distilled water, vitamin E oil and a few drops of either chamomile oil, rose oil or lavender. Apply the soaked cotton balls to closed lids and leave on for 20 minutes.

The solution will nourish eye tissue and leave the entire area feeling cleansed and refreshed, while curtailing any swelling.

■ *A Double-Duty Catnap*

Lack of sleep is the most common cause of puffy eyes. To boost the efficiency of a catnap, go to bed with a cooling compress over your eyes. Apply a dampened spearmint or chamomile tea bag to each eye. Recline for half an hour, and even if you don't feel rejuvenated, you'll look it.

VISION PROBLEMS

■ *Eat Bilberries*

Hone your vision—particularly your ability to discern objects at night or in the dark—by sampling a few bilberries. Bilberry, a European relative of the North American blueberry, is known to strengthen capillaries and improve blood flow to the eye. If you can't find bilberries at the farmer's market, look for preserves in gourmet shops. Add a smear of jelly to your morning toast and look sharp.

■ *Exercises Replace Corrective Lenses?*

When most people think of eyes, they think of eyeballs, not muscles. But in fact there are six basic muscles attached to the eyes, and they can be trained to help improve vision. In brief, many behavioral optometrists and some ophthalmologists believe that eye muscles can become rigid before their time, and that you can retrain your eyes to see better by doing a series of relaxation exercises.

One such exercise is a blinking drill, especially suited to those who focus on computers or other objects up close for hours at a time. Try six or more "butterfly wing" blinks, then close the eyes for a few seconds. Over weeks and months, it is believed, this "focused resting" of the eyes can help delay the effects of aging on the eyes.

■ *What's Up Now, Doc?*

Surprise—it is not carrots. According to Harvard Medical School research, people who eat spinach or other dark, leafy greens, such as collard greens, at least twice each week have healthier retinas and thus better vision than those who don't. Eating greens up to six times a week shows even greater benefits, whether the vegetables are raw or cooked.

Scientists believe the benefit might come from lutein and zeaxanthin, pigments vital to vision that fade under light or with age. Unfortunately, carrots contain little of either substance though they are rich in beta-carotene and other healthy phytochemicals.

FATIGUE

■ *Reschedule Meals for More Energy*

When you eat can make a marked difference in your stress—and energy—level. One simple move is to shift your largest caloric intake to midday when, according to Ayurvedic wisdom, the digestive fires burn brightest. The typical American diet is based around eating the largest meal at night. Problem is, eating close to bedtime or going to sleep on a full stomach, when digestion is sluggish, often results in insomnia and can wreak havoc on your blood sugar levels and adrenal system.

■ *Soothing Isolation*

Unless you live near Utah's Great Salt Lake, you may want to seek out a flotation tank—not just to relax, but to restore energy too. Inside the oblong tanks, where light, sound, temperature change, touch and the effects of gravity are minimized, floaters quickly reach a state of complete relaxation. Studies have shown that floating from 45 minutes to an hour increases the body's production of endorphins, reduces its production of the stress-related chemicals adrenaline and cortisol, soothes headaches and improves athletic performance.

■ *Eight-Glasses-a-Day Energy*

Water plays a role in virtually every bodily function, yet many people are in a chronic state of dehydration. The average person needs at least eight (8-oz.) glasses of water a day. If you've found it difficult to drink a large amount of water at one sitting, try drinking four ounces of water every couple of hours instead. A couple of sips or a gulp will generally give you what you need. If you're exercising or it's unusually hot, increase your intake to four ounces every 15 minutes or so.

Suggestion: Just as weekend athletes or health club members now lug a bottle of water with them during their workouts, try keeping a bottle of spring water with you at your office— or in your car. You don't necessarily have to give up coffee breaks. Just add water breaks.

■ *Tap a Fresh Water Surge*

Making an effort to drink more water can at times work against you, especially if your tap water is not first-rate.

Check with your local water department to find out how your water is being treated, and how it rates in cleanliness. (Environmental reporters for local newspapers may also guide you to the latest findings.) In the meantime, drink bottled spring water, filtered or steam-distilled water. Your immune system might appreciate it, and you'll feel good about every sip.

Note: Not all the bottled waters are spring waters; some are even "bottled" tap water, so check the label for the source.

■ *Feeling Tired? Take a Breath Break*

Yoga and Ayurvedic practitioners believe shallow breathing (which most of us do without thinking about it) keeps a person in a kind of panic mode—hardly conducive to rest and relaxation. However, the average person takes 28,000 breaths a day, providing plenty of mini opportunities to offset fatigue.

Here is how to get more out of the air: Concentrate on taking most of your breaths through your nose, and inhale to a count of two. Exhale (now you may use your mouth) to a count of four. In minutes, your heart rate will slow down, your blood will become more fully oxygenated and you'll achieve a sense of calm.

■ *Instant Rosemary Refresher*

Instead of reaching for another cup of coffee during a mid-afternoon slump, take a whiff of rosemary. Keep a vial of the essential oil or a potted rosemary plant on your desk, or keep a vial in your car's glove compartment. When your energy flags, wave this vial or some crushed sprigs under your nose and inhale. The fragrant herb will stimulate your senses, may boost your circulation and should help keep you alert through that next late afternoon meeting. For a similar effect, add some of the essential oil to your bathwater.

■ Recharge with an "Almost Nap"

While you wouldn't want to spend as much time napping as your cat or dog does on an average day, a 10- to 15-minute mini-nap can help you dig yourself out of sleep debt. It also snuffs out fatigue. But if you're not able to take a short nap, simply getting horizontal for the same amount of time can be beneficial—on a stretching mat at the gym or health club at lunch, for instance. Just lie flat, close your eyes and breathe deeply. But don't read or watch TV during this downtime—the idea is to rest *all* of your senses.

■ Check Your Stride

Feeling inexplicably fatigued? Your gait may be draining you of vital energy. According to Hellerworkers (experts in body alignment also known as Hellerwork practitioners), most people tend to walk inefficiently, using only the outside of their foot or heel instead of the foot's full surface. This isn't just walking, it's work. To save and restore energy with each step, concentrate on taking even, measured steps, starting with the heel. Then, press down on both sides of the arch of your foot, and finally, push out through the toes.

Old World Coffee Wisdom

It almost goes without saying: Asking the dedicated coffee drinker to switch to tea is asking a lot. So, if you need that jolt and simply won't forgo the taste of coffee beans, switch to espresso. Relatively weak, American-style coffee may seem less stressful to your system than the thick, dark brew favored by Europeans, but it's not. According to nutritionists, the roasting and brewing process used to make espresso actually makes for a less acidic and less physically taxing cup of joe.

■ Magnesium for a Minor Boost

If you tend to feel dull and lackluster regardless of the amount of sleep you're getting, you could be magnesium-deficient. This often-overlooked mineral is crucial to your body's metabolism of fats and energy production, dietitians assert. Consider adding a magnesium supplement to your diet, or eat more dairy products, fish, tofu, leafy greens and grains (recommended daily amount is 400 mg, including that from food sources).

Note: Take supplements twice a day in smaller doses for better absorption.

■ Ginseng Zing

Different varieties of ginseng—Siberian, American, Asian and Suma, the Brazilian ginseng—are consumed around the globe to help boost up immunity and strengthen the body. Ginseng will help your body handle stress and utilize fatty acids more efficiently as an energy source.

In appearance, ginseng is either white or red, and will have different effects depending on the constitution of the person ingesting it. According to Chinese herbalists, if you are tall and thin, your constitution is probably "hot," and a cooling or white ginseng would be more appropriate to take. If you are stocky, your constitution is likely to be considered "cooler," and a warming, red ginseng is more suitable.

The Chinese ginseng, which comes in both red and white, is said to be the most stimulating of the ginseng varieties, and is especially suited for fighting periodic bouts of fatigue.

Antibiotic Antidotes

Prescription antibiotics may help you get rid of nasty infections, but they can also rob your body of the friendly bacteria it needs for proper digestion and nutrient uptake for your energy needs. If you can't avoid taking antibiotics, make sure to eat plenty of acidophilus-rich foods, such as yogurt and buttermilk, either several hours before or after, when your stomach is empty, to keep the bacteria in your colon varied. At the same time, stay away from sugars and complex carbohydrates—the favorite foods of *candida*, a fungus (yeast) that often fills the vacancy left by the good bacteria.

■ Posture Hint to Relieve Neck and Shoulder Fatigue

According to Hellerworkers, therapists who specialize in body alignment, the average person tends to hop up from the sitting position, putting undue stress on the neck and shoulders. The result of such habitual hopping is chronically tight neck and shoulder muscles, leading to premature fatigue.

So, before you get up from reading this, place one foot in front of the other, flat on the floor, and lean forward slightly to shift your weight forward, over your legs. Then, rise to a standing position. The idea is to recruit the powerful leg muscles and take the load off your neck.

■ An Ideal Pick-Me-Up

Chinese herbalists recommend drinking green tea on a regular basis for alertness without getting jangled. The tea is also used to combat viruses. Green tea is said to have a cooling effect, as opposed to the heating effect of coffee, which opens up the pores and causes energy *dispersion*. For those who can't live without caffeine, green tea contains some of the energizing drug (not nearly as much per cup as coffee). Plus, green tea is less acidic than coffee. Added benefits of drinking green tea include its ability to lower cholesterol and its potential as an aid in fighting cancer.

■ Potassium Power

Muscle weakness, irritability and general fatigue could be due to potassium deficiency. Dietitians say that this is more pronounced among the elderly but can apply to adults of any age. Next time your energy wanes, try increasing your intake of potassium-loaded foods, such as bananas, lean meats, whole grains, beans and sunflower seeds. *Note:* Juices or "smoothies" are a handy way to blend bananas and sunflower seeds into a tonic you can refrigerate and sip a couple of times a day.

■ The Five-Minute Hike Solution

Exercise has been proven to boost blood flow, relieve stress and help people sleep better. It can also perk you up in the middle of a long workday, and even a few minutes a day is beneficial. So when a mid-afternoon slump hits, or when the after-dinner ate-too-much lethargy sets in, take a quick walk around the block to get your circulation moving. The upshot is, better blood flow will boost your energy level for your next round of tasks.

■ Cut the Salt

It's not always the salt shaker's fault, yet excess salt could be sapping your energy. To relieve fatigue painlessly, refrain from eating canned products, including beans and spaghetti sauce, and cut back on restaurant meals whenever possible. (It's the salt you can't always taste that adds up in a hurry.) According to the nutritionists, not-so-obvious sources of sodium to watch out for include breads, bagels and prepared soups.

■ The Busy Bs

Nutritionists sometimes blame low energy levels on depleted stores of the B vitamins.

The antidote? Try to punch up your intake of vitamins B1, B2, B3, B5, B6 and B12. All are essential to energy production, blood formation, immunity, cell growth, circulation and the production of adrenal hormones.

The brief solution is to take a B-complex supplement, and make sure you include in your diet plenty of whole (unprocessed) foods, such as fruits, vegetables and whole grains.

Medical note: Be especially sure to take in a sufficient amount of vitamin B-rich foods if you are taking antibiotics or oral contraceptives.

■ Pause on Protein, Pass the Herb Tea

According to some alternative healers, many people who suffer from fatigue have slightly compromised kidney function, which contributes to a buildup of toxins in the bloodstream. To relieve kidney workload, nutritionists recommend taking a break from animal protein. At the same time, they recommend drinking a tea made from bearberry, or dried uva ursi, an herb believed to act as a urinary antiseptic and kidney toner.

■ A Dairy Link to Explore

One often-overlooked culprit that may be responsible for chronic fatigue is the lymph system. Over time a dairy-rich diet is thought to impair the lymphatic vessels, which normally filter proteins, bacteria, fats and dead cells. So do as many naturopaths suggest, and give your lymph system a break from dairy products. At the very least, cut out milk and ice cream, notorious sources of difficult-to-digest proteins that can tax your stomach, intestines and lymph system as well. Nutritionists give the okay to cheese, especially low-fat cheese—a cultured, and therefore less stressful, product to digest.

Unblock Your Energy

Too much energy held inside the body can add to fatigue. Emitting nonsyllabic vowel sounds, or toning, is one way to let that energy out. Buddhist and Benedictine monks are notable examples of people who have used voice for health for thousands of years (some traditions even believe that it is sound that holds the universe together). The classic *om* sound is said to create harmony in part because it unites the chanter with the multitude of sound waves circulating in the atmosphere. In the lab, studies have shown that toning synchronizes brain waves and works as a sort of internal massage to renew and invigorate the person vocalizing the sound.

Try the following exercise to combat fatigue through toning:

1 Sit or stand in a comfortable position. Make sure your back is straight and your feet are flat on the floor.

2 Listen to the silence for a few minutes, then take a few deep breaths.

3 Focus your attention on your throat.

4 Open your mouth and let the *om* (or other single syllable) sound out. Don't judge the tone you emit. Instead, sound out as long and as loud as you like. Repeat for 5 to 10 minutes, with breaks for breaths, of course.

Lavender Fights Brain Drain

Although it's controversial, some alternative practitioners believe that prolonged exposure to the electromagnetic field of a computer screen may be the reason you feel so drained after a day at the office. If you are unable to take regular breaks every hour or so, try dabbing your temples and wrists with organic lavender essential oil. In addition to promoting calm, lavender is thought by some herbalists to have shielding abilities against various kinds of toxins. *At-home extra:* Add the oil to your body lotion for all-over protection.

Garden-Variety Energy Booster

Add a teaspoon of royal jelly to your daily diet to help support an overworked adrenal system. Think of it as a low-tech hormone primer. The potent mix of honey and bee pollen in royal jelly is filled with vitamins, minerals and natural antibiotics, including pantothenic acid. Queen bees are fed an exclusive diet of royal jelly, and have 40 times the life span of worker bees. The spittle of bees, or bee pollen, is also a good source of B vitamins. Naturopaths sometimes advise patients to chew a teaspoonful of the yellow granules daily for an energy boost.

Note: Avoid bee products if you are allergic to bees—or pollen.

Color Therapy Boost

It may be that all you need to increase your energy level is a change of scenery or even a wardrobe update. According to Ayurvedic healers, different colors are thought to have specific vibrations that can help balance one's energy—or throw it out of whack. Some bodyworkers use color in conjunction with other modes of therapy to increase the healing effects of their work.

Too much or too little of a color surrounding you can affect your Eastern "chakras" system of energy flow. (In brief, chakras are the main energy pathways, thought to travel like electrical cords through the body, affecting body/mind states. These pathways can be influenced by healing massage and other modalities.) Shades of orange, for instance, are said to boost immunity, while yellow is thought to enhance mental clarity. Green helps balance heart and lungs, bodyworkers say, while blue helps the throat, and white is thought to help relieve pain.

To fight fatigue in an offbeat way, take a break from wearing your usual outfits, redecorate your space or simply buy a bouquet of flowers (with one or two "healing" colors dominant).

■ Co-Energizing

If you're looking for a natural way to erase the effects of occasional fatigue, you might try using CoQ-10 (sometimes called Coenzyme Q) to boost your energy by stimulating the action of enzymes in the bloodstream. As a coenzyme, CoQ-10 is not an enzyme by itself. It is a natural substance found in most foods, and in many B-complex vitamins. It is thought to energize the heart muscle a bit, and may thus help improve its capacity.

The result: Better blood flow and more energy. The usual dose is 30 to 100 mg per day. CoQ-10 is widely available in health food shops.

■ *Arousing Aromatherapy*

Scientific studies show that the nose knows: Scents work directly on the brain—and various odors can induce specific moods and emotions. To perk up sluggish senses, apply a few drops of citrus essential oils like lemon, tangerine, orange or lime onto a cotton ball, and take a whiff as needed throughout the day. Or arrange bundles of fresh rosemary on your desk for an invigorating aroma.

■ *Time to Retime Your Workouts*

Yes, working out provides an energy boost, in addition to the oft-mentioned heart and other health benefits. But most people who want to fight fatigue don't realize how working out at a particular time of day may be an antidote to lethargy. Even though millions of well-intentioned people work out in the morning, recent studies have shown that most people reach their athletic performance peak between 3:00 P.M. and 6:00 P.M.

So, even if you can't break away from work early, or take a late-late-"workout" lunch during the workweek, you may find that afternoon workouts on weekends give you the lift you've been looking for.

■ *An Energy Rainbow*

According to some spiritual healers, crystals possess vibrational properties that can help balance and fine-tune energy levels. For instance, purple amethyst is thought to be helpful for cleansing and energizing the body, and perhaps strengthening the immune system. Green aventurine, on the other hand, is said to have healing properties and may help reduce stress-related fatigue.

Try wearing a crystal, or placing one on your desk. Then gauge your energy level for the next few weeks. You might be pleasantly surprised.

FEVER

See also **Common Cold**, *page 85 and* **Flu**, *page 127*

99° TO 103° RANGE

■ *Elderberry for Fevers*

In addition to boosting the immune system (it is said to help fight the common cold), elderberry also works as a diaphoretic, meaning it promotes sweating. Because sweat evaporates and cools the skin, elderberry can reduce fevers. Naturopaths recommend the following concoction for fevers: Mix together elder, yarrow and peppermint for a tea. Use one tablespoon of the tea per pint of boiling water. Steep for 20 minutes. Drink four to six cups per day as needed.

Starve It—Sort Of

Although a fevered body is working double-time to kick out a virus or infection, nutritionists suggest keeping caloric intake down (under 1,000 to 1,200 calories a day for an average 150- to 175-pound person) until your fever subsides. Solid food may work to redirect energy toward your stomach, and your symptoms will linger. While your body sweats out or otherwise cleanses the impurities that are making you ill, drink plenty of fluids and trust that you'll be able to feast when your fever breaks.

Aspirin Alternative

It is worth remembering that fever is one of the body's natural healing responses. Uncomfortable as it may seem at times, low-grade to medium-grade fever is usually beneficial to the body. So, it isn't always wise to fight it with aspirin or anything else. Instead, let the fever run its course.

■ *Feed a Fever—Tea*

If you're feeling a little feverish, curl up with a cup of willow bark tea. Willow bark is loaded with salicylates, the active ingredient in aspirin. Add one teaspoon of dried willow bark to a cup of boiling water and let the tea steep for 5 to 10 minutes. Strain and sip while it's warm. During a cold, drink up to three cups a day.

■ *Eucalyptus for Fever Aid*

No one would suggest chewing on eucalyptus leaves—koala bears are the only mammals equipped to digest the tough fibers. However, the oil found in eucalyptus leaves has antiseptic and antiviral qualities. To make an infusion useful for treating fever, steep a teaspoon of crushed eucalyptus leaves in one cup boiled water for 15 minutes, then sip. Do not drink more than one or two cups a day, as it can upset your stomach. If you don't like the flavor, add some eucalyptus leaves or essential oil to your bathwater instead.

■ *Yarrow Tea for Cooler Foreheads*

Like ginger, yarrow works as a diaphoretic, promoting sweating. For a cooling tea during a fever (especially during the early stages), steep two teaspoons of the dried flower in hot water, and drink three or four times a day.

FIRST AID

BLISTERS

■ *Carrot Mash Works*

When blisters are at their most annoying, painful stage, head to the kitchen for a veggie solution—boiled carrots. Simply boil and mash a couple of carrots, then apply to the affected area. This carrot compress is perhaps best suited when a blister has been punctured and is irritated.

Better Bandage Removal

You don't have to zip adhesive bandages off in a hurry anymore. A better way to remove them from minor cuts and scrapes is to s-l-o-w down and get some help from baby oil. Simply soak a cotton ball in baby oil and dab around the edges of the bandage. Let soak for 10 minutes, which should soften up the adhesive. Now pull off and say, *Ahhhhh.*

CUTS AND SMALL WOUNDS

■ *Soothing Antibacterial Ointment*

Start by cleansing the cut or small wound with 10 drops of marigold flower (calendula) tincture diluted in eight ounces of already boiled and cooled water. Then soak a sterile gauze compress in the liquid and place over the injury to staunch the bleeding. A simpler, equally effective treatment is to apply health-food-store-bought calendula cream to the wound once it's been cleaned. With its antiseptic and blood-clotting properties, marigold is the essence of flower power.

■ *Take Your Sweet Time to Heal*

Not only is it inexpensive and abundant at home, but granulated sugar placed onto a clean cut or small wound can actually help reduce scar tissue. A couple of teaspoons of sugar should suffice, covered up with gauze. Clean and reapply sugar and bandage four times daily, less often as the wound heals. (This treatment also works for minor bite wounds from pets.)

Note: First aid experts note that you should wait until the wound has stopped bleeding before applying the sugar.

■ *Cheap and Greasy First Aid*

If you or a family member suffers a minor cut while away from home, and there is no antiseptic or antibiotic ointment handy, consider dabbing petroleum jelly on the wound. It can be just as effective as antibiotic cream in protecting the skin and in helping heal tissue, doctors say, and will save you money as well.

"Super Glue" Better than Stitches?

If a cut or minor surgery brings you to a hospital for suturing, you may not have to settle for old-fashioned stitches. Recent research has shown that in many cases doctors are able to bind lacerations more quickly and with less pain by using medical preparations and derivatives of the glue octylcyanoacrylate. (Don't try this at home—it's not the standard powerful household glue.)

The cuts apparently heal just as well as those with stitches, without requiring a follow-up visit for suture removal. The downside is that the glue "suture" is not suitable for wounds in "skin-stretchy" places, such as hands, feet, knees and elbows. The FDA approved Tisseel, the nation's first commercial surgical glue, in 1998.

■ Kitchen Cure for Kitchen Cuts

Bleeding caused by shaving mishaps, sport scrapes or superficial cuts from a kitchen knife can be stopped in seconds. How? Cayenne pepper. It's high in vitamin K, a nutrient that's essential for blood clotting. Just sprinkle a little bit of cayenne pepper on the scrape or minor cut, and the bleeding will stop almost instantaneously.

One warning: Don't try this trick on deeper cuts. If you do, you may feel a burn from the pepper, which will only add to the discomfort.

■ Honey—A Natural Salve

Using honey as first aid on a cut or scrape is something people outside the US do a lot more often than we do. According to a study in a British journal of plastic surgery, pasteurized honey has been found to reduce infection and promote wound healing. Yes, it can be messy, but honey also does its part to keep the wound moist while it heals.

Note: Only use pasteurized honey; the unpasteurized kind may contain disease-causing microbes.

INSECT BITES AND STINGS

■ Kitchen Concoction

Once you've been bitten by a mosquito, spider or other insect, fight back from the kitchen. Take a handful of vitamin C tablets, crush them using a mortar and pestle (or sturdy spoon and bowl) and mix with a dash of water. Apply the thick paste directly to the bite, and you should feel relief within minutes. The topical solution helps reduce inflammation.

■ Inexpensive Fizzy Solutions

After getting stung by a bee, especially if you're away from home, think fizzy for quick relief. First, attempt to gently scrape away the stinger with a credit card or dull knife. (Don't squeeze—it could release more venom!) Next, make a paste of baking soda and a little water, and rub it right onto the area of skin that got stung.

As an alternative, grab a tablet of Alka-Seltzer and moisten it just a bit before applying it to the sting. The fizz enables baking soda to dissolve from the tablet onto, and into, the sting. It helps relieve the pain markedly.

Tender Is the Bite

One homespun recipe for neutralizing a bee or wasp sting can be found in the pantry. It's not exactly a first-aid-kit staple, but Adolph's Meat Tenderizer can offset the swelling if you add a few drops of water and make it into a paste which you apply to the sting. Other meat tenderizers may work, provided the active ingredients include chymopapain, an enzyme that breaks down protein in meats—and in bee venom.

Fragrant, Oily Prevention

If you're the type of person that insects always seem to favor, consider using a natural, home-made repellent, especially if you're already recovering from stings or bites received earlier in the week. (This will also work in a pinch on vacation.) Using three parts almond oil as a base, add one part essential oil of either cit-ronella, eucalyptus or lavender. Since all have qualities that humans enjoy but bugs don't, choose the one that's most pleasing to you—and your skin.

PAPER CUTS

Cleansing Clove Does Double Duty

For something so seemingly small, a paper cut actually hurts a lot, even after the wound has been cleaned and dried. But before applying a bandage or other dressing, consider sprinkling a pinch or two of clove powder—right off the spice rack—onto the paper cut. It will act as both a cleansing agent and a painkiller. As a bonus, it will help prevent infection.

First Aid Online

If you're facing a minor first aid crisis and have access to the Internet, you can get excellent information from a number of Web sites in-cluding: www.webmd.com, www.mayoclinic.com and others. These sites have a search line to type in the kind of problem. You will get infor-mation to help you recognize the symptoms and tell you how to treat the condition.

SCRAPES AND OPEN CUTS

A Soothing Healer

Take a tip from pediatric nurses, who treat thousands of children's cuts and abrasions every day: Standard Band-Aids are fine for many cuts and scrapes, but more serious sores often respond better to the silicone Second Skin–type bandages. Usually made of thin, sheer, breathable and flexible materials, this new wave of stretchy skin coverings (that grew out of wound dressings used in hospitals) is clearly catching on. Plus, they don't hurt the skin around the cut when it's time for them to come off. If your local pharmacy doesn't carry them, check with a nearby medical supply house.

Wet or Dry?

Many doctors advise patients to keep wounds dry to avoid infection. But in a recent study of premature babies, cuts treated with a petroleum-based ointment (Aquaphor) healed quicker and were less likely to become infect-ed than those not treated. Researchers say the same treatment should also help wounds in adults.

SPLINTERS

■ *A Little Overnight Onion Magic*

Before you go digging around in a fingertip with a sewing needle you've just "sterilized" with a match, head to the kitchen instead. Preferably at bedtime, cut a small, postage-stamp-sized piece of fresh onion, place it on the padded part of an adhesive bandage, then wrap it around the splintered skin. By morning, your tweezer surgery should be ever so much easier —for the onion will have drawn the splinter to the surface.

■ *Plantain Power to the Rescue*

Here's a squishy way to help ease out a splinter before you hunt for the tweezers:

1 Mash up a few plantains until almost liquid.

2 Apply to the area with the splinter.

3 Cover with gauze and tape for a few hours at a time, as needed.

The oils in the plantain are quite skin-loving and will draw the splinter to the surface for much easier removal.

FLATULENCE

A FIVE-POINT PREVENTION PLAN

Among the causes of flatulence are poor digestion due to food allergies, eating too quickly, illness or stress. Here are five ways to reduce the gas and aid digestion:

1 *Drink a ginger aid*
Drink a cup of ginger tea after your evening meal instead of decaffeinated coffee. Ginger aids digestion of fats, easing the gas and cramps that come with poor digestion. To make your own tea, grate a teaspoon of fresh ginger root and simmer in hot water for 10 minutes.

2 *Eat fermented foods*
Boost your intake of acidophilus-rich foods, such as yogurt and buttermilk, which are known to aid in digestion.

3 *Stimulate with seeds*
Ayurvedic healers of India use anise, fennel and caraway seeds, as well as garlic to add flavor to meals and stimulate digestion.

4 *Soothe with spices*
Ayurvedic healers recommend use of coriander, cumin and ginger to flavor legumes and diminish gas.

5 *Hold the water—temporarily*
Put your water glass aside during meals—it dilutes (digestive) stomach acids.

■ Charcoal "Sponge"

If you are feeling the effects of excess gas and mild cramping, activated charcoal (from the health food store) can effectively absorb excess gas. Nutritionists recommend taking two capsules or a few tablespoons of powdered charcoal stirred into a glass of water. If you're still suffering from gas an hour after taking the charcoal, take another dose. However, do not take charcoal with other supplements or medicine, because it can absorb those, too.

FLU See also **Common Cold,** page 85 and **Fever,** page 122

■ Garlic as Flu Fighter

One way to ward off nasty flu bugs is to use garlic-oil nose drops. Garlic has been used for medicinal purposes for thousands of years because of its antibiotic properties. Nowadays the oil is available in health food stores and herb shops as preventive medicine. So, during the height of flu season, apply five drops of garlic tincture to each nostril—the first place you're likely to pick up a flu virus—every few hours for a few days. Make your own nose drops by mixing one clove of crushed garlic to 10 parts water.

Flu Recovery: Potassium as a Postflu Dietary Aid

If your last bout with the flu was accompanied by excessive vomiting and nausea, you could be depleted of potassium. Chances are, in the first few days of recovery you probably aren't up to eating full meals. As a bridge and nutritional aid, try whipping up something that's easy to keep down, like a banana-rich juice smoothie or banana-and-yogurt shake.

Herbal Flu Prevention

Naturopaths and herbalists list echinacea as one of the most powerful flu-fighting herbs around. The herb, derived from the purple coneflower, has antibiotic, antiviral and anti-inflammatory properties and is said to boost white blood cell production. Ingest 10 drops of echinacea tincture a few times a day, for five to seven days, to boost your immunity before cold and flu season hits. If you feel flu symptoms coming on, double that amount, but don't take it indefinitely: Your body will build up a tolerance, and the herb won't be effective when you really need it. Echinacea roots and leaves are sold in tablet, tincture or dried form.

Echinacea is especially powerful when taken in conjunction with goldenseal, a natural antibiotic. Experts also caution against taking goldenseal for extended amounts of time, because it will weaken the friendly bacteria present in the colon, much like the effects of synthetic antibiotics.

■ An Icy Foot Bath to Fight Flu

Most people are inclined to lie low when the flu strikes, although fast-moving blood and a strong circulation can help rid the body of contagions. One easy way to get your circulatory system moving is to plunge your feet in ice water for five minutes at a time. The cold will temporarily constrict blood flow to your feet, but when you remove them from the water, blood will rush back in and give a sluggish circulation a helpful jump start.

Rub Out the Flu

Oh, those aching muscles. When you're feeling sore in addition to the other full-blown symptoms, indulge in a massage. Not only does touch therapy relax and revive tired, sore muscles, but it has a medicinal effect as well. Massage stimulates your lymphatic system, which may help fight the flu virus. Plus, massage therapists say, it helps flush and carry away toxins that could be suppressing your immune system.

■ Vegetarian Soup Alternative

Whether or not you are a vegetarian, the next time flu strikes, try cooking up some shiitake mushroom broth or miso-garlic soup instead of grandma's chicken soup. Besides supplying needed fluids, both shiitake and garlic purportedly have antiviral and immune-boosting properties. These ingredients can easily be purchased at a greengrocer's. Be careful not to boil miso or you'll kill its beneficial ingredient—helpful bacteria for the digestive system.

Wave It Goodbye—With Magnetic Waves

Far more popular in Japan than in the US, magnetic therapy has been used increasingly in recent years to help fight flu—or at least keep it from becoming debilitating. At the first sign of flu symptoms, sufferers can place a wrap, or small pad, that has been studded with flat, flexible magnets, directly over their liver (located below the right front ribs).

Admittedly, clinical research will be needed to convince skeptics in the US that magnets are useful in fighting flu. In the meantime, you might give healing magnets a try. They are available at specialty back care stores and well-stocked health food stores, or through catalogs such as The Sharper Image, 800-344-4444, www.sharperimage.com.

■ Gimme Fever

When one comes down with flulike symptoms, it can actually be beneficial to induce a fever, which is one of the body's ways of fighting off viruses and bacteria. If you are feeling lousy—but otherwise are in good medical condition—a hot bath (as hot as you can take for as long as you can tolerate it) will help bring on the fever. Then wrap yourself in towels and blankets and drink fluids every half hour. Take some vitamin C (from two to four grams daily should suffice). Sleep it off.

If you don't feel better after a couple of days, it's time to call the doctor. *Note:* Naturopaths say that a runny stool indicates the bowels are no longer absorbing the vitamin C; you've taken too much.

■ Ginger Tea for Stomach Flu

Herbal tea is especially soothing to flu symptoms and helps keep you hydrated during times of fever. (For best results, alternate the varieties of tea according to your symptoms.) Ginger tea will warm you up and help quell a rebelling stomach. So, the next time you find yourself suffering from intestinal flu symptoms, grate a few teaspoons of the ginger into boiling water and steep for 10 minutes.

■ Boneset Tea for Achy Flu

Boneset, *Eupatorium perfoliatum,* offers quick relief, herbalists say, from the nagging, taxing aches and pains of flu. To prepare the tea, simply steep just a teaspoonful of the leaves of the dried herb in a cup of boiling water the next time you feel ill all over. Boneset is bitter, so add honey and lemon to help it go down. Within minutes, you should feel a sweat coming on. Drink throughout the day, or until your symptoms disappear.

Garlic for Long-Term Prevention

To boost your immune system throughout the year, add a few garlic cloves to your daily diet. (It's not as antisocial as it sounds.) Garlic is most effective when raw, although its healing properties won't be destroyed by cooking it lightly. If you're not fond of the taste, garlic is available in capsule, (odorless) tablet and extract form.

■ Green Tea and Yarrow—A Dynamic Duo

When flu symptoms include nausea, weakness and diarrhea, a one-two punch of herbal tea can help tame them. Chinese herbalists recommend drinking green tea to combat viruses. Then, enlist the aid of yarrow, which is both cooling and stimulating and works well to shrink mucous membranes and ease diarrhea. It can also be prepared as a tea.

■ Gargle with Tea Tree Oil

The oil from the Australian tea tree is believed to stimulate the immune system and fight infection. Aromatherapists believe that the scent is beneficial as a preventive measure against viruses. If your flu is accompanied by a raging sore throat, add a few drops of the oil to a saltwater gargle to relieve pain and speed up the healing process.

■ Homeopathic Flu Fighter

Oscillococcinum. It's a mouthful to say, but you only need a bit to stop the flu before it has a chance to put you flat on your back. A homeopathic treatment derived from duck livers, oscillococcinum must be taken as soon as you start to feel the twinges—chills, fever and aches—of the flu. If it's going to be effective, just one dose should do the trick. But be sure to check individual packages for dosage instructions. Look for oscillococcinum at health food stores or your local pharmacy.

■ Nature's Flu Remedy

Feeling feverish and think you're coming down with the flu? Swallow a tablespoon of sambucol extract every two hours as a good replacement for over-the-counter flu remedies. Sambucol, made from brightly colored elderberries, is loaded with bioflavonoids and vitamin C, which can help knock out the viral infection that causes the flu. You can buy it in most health food shops.

■ Chase Away Chills and Flu Symptoms with Osha Root

This herbal remedy stimulates the circulatory system, causing perspiration and breaking up mucus in sinuses and lungs. Plus, this herbal powerhouse soothes sore tissues. Take a teaspoonful of osha root tincture two to three times a day to remedy coughs, sore throats, chills and aches that often accompany the flu.

Reach for Isatis Root

Isatis root boasts natural antibacterial and antiviral properties which herbalists guarantee will quiet respiratory rattles that often come with the flu. Take 35 drops of the tincture every few hours for a severe infection. Note that this medicine is very bitter. Drop the tincture on your tongue and quickly chase the herbal remedy with a glass of sweet-tasting juice.

Soothing Steam

A few drops of essential oils like eucalyptus or thyme in a hot bowl of water produce medicinal vapors that clear congestion and calm coughs. Plus, both eucalyptus and thyme have antimicrobial qualities that fight infections.

Sage Solution

Used by Native Americans during purification rituals, white sage is also one of the best natural antibiotics to rub out infection and fight the flu. Make a white sage solution using 30 to 60 drops of tincture mixed with warm water. Either drink the brew as a tea or gargle with it.

FOOD ALLERGIES

*See also **Allergies**, page 55*

COMMON FOODS: WHEAT, GLUTEN (WHEAT PRODUCT), SHELLFISH

Can Urine Therapy Actually Help?

If it's good enough for the yogis... Drinking your own urine may seem like a disgusting and ridiculous way to fight food allergies—including those to shellfish and wheat products. But the yogis of India have on occasion (over the course of centuries) drunk their own urine for religious and health reasons. In fact, urine is sterile and contains vitamins, amino acids, antibodies and hormones.

Only a handful of doctors and health experts in the US go so far as to advocate this occasional practice as sound medicine. These allergists suggest a dosage of one cup a day for two weeks to lessen the severity of common food allergies. While natural, this self-made therapy will likely remain uncommon for years.

FOOD-BORNE ILLNESSES

A Spicy Remedy for Prevention

Certain spices act as powerful antibiotics, and cooking with them may help prevent food-related illnesses, including salmonella, according to recent research. A study of 4,578 recipes contained in 93 cookbooks from 36 countries found that the hotter the climate of a country, the greater the risk of food spoilage and the more spices used by cooks. In comparison, countries with colder climates, like Norway, often had bland food; and even when spices were used, they tended to be ones with low antibiotic properties.

Of the spices tested, garlic, onion, allspice and oregano effectively killed all the bacteria they were stacked up against, including salmonella and staphylococcus, while other spices killed between 50% and 75% of the harmful bacteria. The spice plants themselves use these chemicals to protect against parasites, which explains how they protect us.

FOOT PROBLEMS

ATHLETE'S FOOT

■ *Garlic Power Soak*

Garlic isn't just for dinner. This powerful herb has antifungal properties capable of wiping out a case of athlete's foot. Just steep six crushed garlic cloves in a basin of hot water for an hour, then soak your afflicted feet for 20 minutes. For an especially virulent case of athlete's foot, crush five or six garlic cloves and add to a small bottle of olive or sesame oil. Apply the oil to clean, dry feet as needed. But be careful—if the oil is too potent, it can burn your skin.

■ *Tea Tree Remedy*

If you don't want to smell like garlic, soak your feet in a basin filled with water and 8 to 10 drops of Australian tea tree oil. A natural cure for the itch and discomfort of athlete's foot, tea tree oil boasts antibacterial, antiseptic and antimicrobial properties.

You can also rub a small amount of the oil on your feet and between your toes to reduce redness, irritation and itching, as well as fight infection. Use at least twice a day on affected areas that have been cleaned and dried—preferably in the morning and evening—until rash disappears.

■ *Sole Ingredients*

Athlete's foot occurs when the skin environment between your toes loses its acidity. One fix is a vinegar and salt soak for your feet. The vinegar reintroduces the acidity, of course, while the sodium in salt dehydrates the topical skin cells to reduce itching.

■ *Fungus-Fighting Flower*

One little-known athlete's foot treatment combines a footbath with tincture of the bright yellow marigold flower, otherwise known as calendula. As it has antifungal and anti-inflammatory properties, marigold is well-suited for battling athlete's foot. Add one or two teaspoons of marigold tincture to a footbath bowl full of warm water and soak for 10 minutes.

Stop the Spread with Baking Soda

If you're feeling the first signs of athlete's foot—that late-in-the-day moist itch inside those shoes that don't breathe—use some baking soda when you get home to stop the fungus before it spreads. It's not that baking soda will cure a raging case of athlete's foot, but it will help keep those all-important crevices between the toes from becoming breeding grounds. Athletic and personal trainers sometimes suggest that clients use gauze or a handful of sterile bandages sprinkled with baking soda to swab the between-toes spaces.

■ *Shoe Sense*

Fungal infections thrive in moist, warm environments. To avoid athlete's foot or for fast relief, follow these rules:

■ Dry your feet carefully, paying close attention to the spaces between your toes.

■ Always wear (clean) socks with your shoes, and especially with sneakers (during a workout), to absorb moisture.

■ If you suffer from a bout of athlete's foot, wear shoes that can breathe so moisture is not trapped against your skin all day long. Avoid tight shoes and waterproof shoes. If possible, wear sandals or go barefoot, for speedier healing of fungal infections.

■ At the gym, wear flip-flops (rubber sandals) in community showers so you don't pick up an infection off the wet stall floor.

■ Always wash your hands after touching your feet to prevent spreading the fungus to your underarms or groin.

■ *Simple, Soothing Foot Freshener*

Keep foot odor and bacteria in check with germ-fighting essences of lemon. Add a few drops of lemon essential oil to a warm basin of water and give your feet a 20-minute soak daily. Dry well.

■ *Dry 'Em Off*

Protect your feet from stubborn athlete's foot infections by always drying your feet thoroughly after a bath or shower. Slipping moist feet into shoes and socks can create a breeding ground for fungi. For extra protection, sprinkle your feet with cornstarch or baby powder to absorb moisture during the day. Plus, make sure to keep some powder with you during the day and reapply at work or at the health club. Foot powder has to be handy to use it.

Check Between Your Toes...

Whether using a natural remedy, like tea tree oil, or an over-the-counter antifungal, like Micatin or Desenex, be sure to keep using the remedy until the infection is completely healed. Many times people will stop the treatment when the itching stops, which enables the fungus, the itching and the infection to recur. In other words, check carefully between your toes for days after the infection seems to have cleared up.

■ *Black Walnut for Fungus-Free Feet*

This potent antifungal treatment fights athlete's foot symptoms, including burning, itching and scaliness: Black walnut extract. You'll find the extract on the shelves of your local health food store. Just a few drops rubbed into the infected area and between the toes once or twice a day will clear up the fungus.

BUNIONS

■ *Stretch to Relieve Pain—Fast*

To combat bunion pain:

1 Start by taking a seat in a comfortable, hard-backed chair.

2 Cross the afflicted foot and leg over the opposite knee.

3 Twist the big toe down under the foot, pushing toward the center of the ball of the foot.

4 Hold the stretch for 10 to 20 seconds; release and repeat.

You should feel relief within a few stretches. Try the stretch for a week before resorting to more stringent measures, like surgery.

COLD FEET

■ *Hot Socks in a Hurry*

Here is an idea from a Rocky Mountain herbalist, who knows all about winter winds whipping up and down and inside those snow and ski boots. Step one is to put on a thin layer of socks. Step two is to grab a second, thicker pair of socks and put in some heat—specifically, one teaspoonful of cayenne pepper sprinkled into each thick sock. It may seem an odd way to fight winter, but your soles will appreciate the warmth.

CORNS

■ *Nighttime Lemon Aid*

Long before cosmetics companies discovered the power and efficacy of using fruit acids (or alphahydroxy acids, AHAs) to pump up their skin products, folk healers around the world were prescribing bits of fruit for various skin ailments. To relieve the pain and pressure of corns, apply a piece of fresh lemon peel—

rind side down—to the top of a corn, and affix with a small bandage. Leave it on overnight. Repeat for up to one week. Results should be apparent within a few days.

FLAT FEET—OR FALLEN ARCHES

■ *Workouts for Flat Feet*

Without properly formed foot arches, exercise can be painful. Chronic pain often arises in the feet first, then spreads up the ankles to the calves and elsewhere in the legs. (Sometimes it's not the lack of an arch, but weak muscles in the foot that mimic the effects of fallen arches.)

Here are two exercises to help you build strength and relieve pain, but note that the problem can be addressed by chiropractic care. (Often, structural problems in the foot cause the spine to take on added burdens.)

1 Standing in stockinged feet, rock heel to toe for three minutes, in rhythmic motion, daily.

2 While sitting, practice curling up your toes inside your shoes, forcing the sole of the foot to arch. Try this move 10 times, repeating often throughout the day.

FOOT ODOR

■ *Fruity Feet*

Spray apple cider vinegar on feet to stop the growth of bacteria that causes foot odor. The vinegar changes the pH of skin so bacteria won't spread. Buy the vinegar at your grocery store, then transfer it to a spray bottle. Store it in the refrigerator for extra refreshment.

Homemade Deodorant for the Toes

Aromatherapists have the right idea: You want your pleasant scents and essential oils to do double duty. Here's a homemade foot deodorant that gets right to the source of the trouble—bacteria. Add 40 drops of lavender, geranium or cypress essential oil (all have antibacterial properties; some other oils do, too) to four ounces of an unscented, light skin lotion. Apply twice a day, morning and evening, or after a workout and shower at midday.

Tea Party

Some recreational athletes make regular use of odor reducers for their favorite sports shoes. There are some people with feet that overheat (and sweat) during times of stress. A few tea bags boiled in a pint of water for 15 minutes, then poured into a foot bath with two quarts of cool water, can help eliminate foot odor. Dermatologists point to the tannic acid in tea as the neutralizer. Try this foot bath for chronic odor problems.

Freshen Up Your Feet

Your running sneakers have plenty of spring in their steps, but are they stinking up your gym locker? Don't despair, there's a natural alternative to the chemical-based absorbent insoles sold in drugstores. Try sprinkling a few drops of geranium essential oil directly into shoes, or put a couple of drops of lemon oil onto a cotton ball and leave it in the offending sneakers for a few hours.

FOOT PAIN

Drugstore Cure

Foot problems afflict more than 2 million Americans a year. A study of 236 newly diagnosed patients found that inexpensive, store-bought shoe inserts were more effective at reducing pain after two months than costly custom-made arch supports. All patients in the study also did exercises to stretch the Achilles tendon and the plantar fascia, the band of muscle that stretches from the ball of the foot to the heel.

HEEL SPURS (PLANTAR FASCITUS)

Keep Your Shoes On

Walking barefoot, especially in the summer, is wonderfully freeing, but it can exacerbate the formation of heel spurs, or *plantar fascitus*. For some, this is not a problem, but if you have had chronic foot ailments, you probably need all the support you can get. In general, wear supportive shoes or look into getting orthotics. At home, keep your sandals on.

Massage Your Feet

Your feet take more pounding than any other body part, yet typically receive little attention. Massage therapists recommend giving yourself a foot rub daily to keep your foot muscles supple and relaxed.

No-Brainer Stretching

Hate to spend time stretching? Physical therapists have come up with two helpful exercises that will aid in both prevention and healing of bone spurs. These exercises also require little conscious thought. While you watch TV or read, roll your foot over a golf ball. Do these stretches for a few minutes, a few times a day, to lengthen and relax the tight fascia in your foot.

Stretching Instead of Surgery

For many active adults, surgery has recently taken a backseat to alternative remedies to alleviate the pain of bone or heel spurs. In this ailment, commonly seen among runners and other exercisers, the main tendon connecting the heel and forefoot irritates the heel resting upon it. Over time, this friction results in bone irritation, or "spurs," near the fat part of the heel. For years, podiatric or orthopedic surgery was standard treatment over the long-term for heel spur sufferers, but not necessarily anymore.

Since the early 1990s, stretches, rest and acupuncture (a three-month course) or a combination of these therapies has gained favor. One helpful stretch goes like this:

1 Stand about one foot in front of a chair with your back to it.

2 Bend your knee and raise the injured foot behind you until the top of the foot is pressing against the seat of the chair.

3 Hold for several seconds, increasing the pressure, then release. Repeat three times, twice a day at first, over the course of eight weeks. Consult your doctor if pain persists.

SWEATY FEET

At-Home Antiperspirant

To keep clammy feet feelings at bay, make your own foot-freshening spray. Aluminum or aluminum sulfate (found in commercial deodorants and foot sprays) tightens pores, so sweat can't escape. Instead, mix a heaping teaspoon of alum (found in herb shops) with a cup of water and one-quarter cup alcohol. Store in an atomizer and spray on feet when needed.

TOENAIL FUNGUS

A Unique Fungus Fighter

First thought: Yuck. Second thought: What now? No one much likes to think or talk about toenail and fingernail fungus. But if you suffer through a case of this fungus related to athlete's foot, you will be wondering how to stop thinking about it. A physician might prescribe an expensive round of antibiotics that can take months to be effective. Alternative practitioners suggest applying tea tree oil to the affected area twice a day, which itself might require months to work. Grapefruit seed extract is another remedy if tea tree oil doesn't do the trick, but give it two months to clear the fungus.

GALLBLADDER PROBLEMS

■ Coffee Substitutes Can Ease the Pain

Your morning coffee may be giving you a needed jump start and keeping you sane, but it may also increase your risk of developing gallbladder problems. Naturopaths often suggest that patients who have digestive or gallbladder ills switch to herbal tea, or try a coffee substitute like Raja's Cup®, made from nut, kasmard, licorice and winter cherry. Another option is barley-based Yannoh® or Cafix®. If not available at your local health food store, the coffee substitutes can often be found at herb shops.

Cut Saturated Fat

First the biology: Bile helps digest fat. Now the reality: A typical American diet is heavy on fats and cholesterol from animal protein and hydrogenated oils, both of which tend to saturate bile—which is stored in the gallbladder. Over time, the excess cholesterol begins to calcify and form gallstones, which can become painful when they move through the small bile ducts going from the gallbladder.

If you've been showing signs of gallbladder disease or stones, the first step is to cut the fat from fried food and animal protein in your diet and eat a lot of fresh fruit and vegetables. Make sure you're getting enough protein from other sources, though, since protein aids in bile production (this is the part of the equation many people with gallbladder problems overlook).

■ Lecithin for Better Bile

According to some nutritionists and dietitians, taking lecithin—a natural fatlike substance—as a supplement can aid in gallbladder health. Lecithin is said to be effective at breaking down the fats that stress bile production. You can buy lecithin granules, or boost your intake of natural sources of lecithin, by eating or drinking soy products and beet juice.

Note: Consult your doctor before taking lecithin, which can raise your triglyceride level.

■ Peppermint Purifier

Peppermint has long been used as a soothing after-dinner drink, as this common herb aids digestion and helps increase bile production. These are just the things your body needs (after a rich meal) to prevent gallstone formation. Drink peppermint tea or add a few drops of peppermint oil to water.

■ Dandelion Is Fine

That bitter herb that most people know as a weed, dandelion, is especially effective in cleansing the liver and gallbladder, herbalists say. They often suggest adding young dandelion greens to salad, or drinking dandelion tea two or three times a day. Another way to ingest the herbal aid is by steaming the greens and serving them up in a bowl, not unlike spinach.

GALLSTONES

■ Olive Oil Aid

Not all fats are created equal. Nutritionists often recommend cutting back on foods like steak and fries, but they should also tout the virtues of olive oil, which actually promotes the passage of gallstones. So once you have cut the fat from your diet, and you're faced with a mound of greens instead of that favorite steak, take heart—it's okay to pour on a few tablespoons of olive oil.

Note: In general, gallbladder pain usually flares up after fatty meals.

■ Men Should Cut the Fat

As with so many ailments, consumption of lots of saturated fat and sugar coupled with a sedentary lifestyle dramatically increases chances of developing gallstones, according to a recent study at the University of Buffalo. The correlation between saturated fat intake and gallstones was significantly stronger for men than for women. *The good news:* A diet rich in monounsaturated fat and fiber can help prevent gallstones.

■ Go for the Crunch

Chinese medical doctors suggest eating crunchy fruits and vegetables to cleanse, or flush out, the gallbladder. Other nutritional options not often suggested by Western doctors include eating radishes between meals.

■ Another Reason to Eat Breakfast

If you're experiencing gallbladder pain after meals, try spreading your caloric intake out over the course of the day. Studies have shown that gallstones are more prevalent among those who skip breakfast. In addition, eating three or four lighter meals throughout the day is less stressful to the gallbladder.

Bonus: It is easier on other parts of the digestive system as well.

Acupuncture Relief for Gallstones

According to Chinese research, acupuncture may enable people with gallstones to pass them into the intestines, making surgery unnecessary.

GENITAL HERPES

■ Pass on the Peanuts

If you're in the middle of a full-blown attack of genital herpes, don't aggravate the condition by eating the wrong snacks. Nutritionists say that an amino acid known as arginine, found in certain foods, can exacerbate your symptoms. So, what foods contain the aggravating arginine?

Peanuts, sesame seeds, pumpkin seeds and squash, just to name a few.

At the same time, sufferers are encouraged to load up on another amino acid, lysine. The foods with the highest lysine to arginine ratio are margarine, yogurt and cheese.

■ The C Solution

During an outbreak of genital herpes, high doses of vitamin C may speed the healing of lesions and lessen the effects of any flulike symptoms. How? Vitamin C stimulates your immune system to fight the virus that causes the condition. Ask a physician for the correct dosage for your condition, which may range anywhere from 1,000 to 4,000 mg every day.

Controlling Stress Controls Symptoms

Stress compromises your immune system and, according to experts, may set the stage for an attack of genital herpes, which seems to flare up when the body's defenses are down. Biofeedback, massage, meditation and physical exercise are some solutions to keeping your stress levels down and, more important, your immune system up.

■ Nutritional Boosters

Copper, zinc and vitamins C and A—that's the vitamin and mineral combo of choice for keeping herpes outbreaks at bay. Not only will this nutritional therapy reduce the chances of another flare-up, but it may help clear up an existing outbreak. Talk to your physician or nutritionist about treating genital herpes with these supplements.

■ Fit to a Tea

Tarragon, because of its antiviral properties, is another herbal option for treating genital herpes. Make a tonic with a teaspoon of tarragon steeped in a cup of hot water. Drink the tea up to three times a day. If you don't like the taste of tarragon tea, steep a teaspoon of tarragon along with a lemon balm tea bag for a doubly strong, tastier remedy.

■ Beetlejuice

Cantharis soothes the burning and blistering bumps caused by the herpes virus from the inside out. Cantharis, a homeopathic remedy, is derived from—yikes—a beetle. But don't let that put you off this gentle treatment.

The prescription: A 30C preparation three times a day during an outbreak. But check with a homeopath before self-medicating to make sure cantharis is right for you.

GLANDULAR PROBLEMS

■ Herbal Detox to Reduce Swelling

Often a viral or other infection will cause the glands in the neck to swell. To pull toxins and microbes from the body, which will reduce swelling, treat the symptoms internally with this detoxing remedy: Take one teaspoon of echinacea and three goldenseal capsules three times a day for 10 days.

HAIR AND SCALP PROBLEMS

DANDRUFF AND DRY SCALP

■ Homemade Hot-Oil Treatment

This hot-oil treatment for parched hair also softens dry, cracked nails and cuticles.

1 Fill a one-ounce dropper bottle with avocado and jojoba oils.

2 Add 10 to 15 drops of any of the following oils: Lavender, rosemary, lemon, juniper, rosewood, sandalwood, geranium, orange or ylang-ylang.

3 Close the bottle and place it in a mug of freshly boiled water for several minutes.

4 Apply 2 to 3 dropperfuls of the hot oil to the hair and massage into scalp.

Leave the treatment in for 20 minutes, then shampoo out. For nails, massage one drop into each cuticle and over the nailbed.

■ Minty-Fresh Dandruff Remedy

You don't have to see white flakes on a black sweater to know you've got dandruff. You'll recognize the itchy, flaky scalp when you brush and style your hair as well. Instead of reaching for the dandruff shampoo, there's something else in the bathroom that can remedy this common problem—mouthwash!

Simply combine 1 part standard mouthwash with 10 parts tap water, and apply the mixture after shampooing. Massage it into your scalp, then leave it on. Your scalp will improve—and hair won't be left sticky.

■ It's About Time—Not Just Shampoo

You've seen the ads for the antidandruff shampoos. You've noticed the flakes on your shoulder. But here's a way to make the most out of whichever product you end up using (including, perhaps, the prescription shampoo Nizoral): Apply twice. The first application should last one to two minutes. Then rinse and re-lather. The key is the second application, which, dermatologists say should last three to five minutes. That's how long it will take to do its job properly.

Did You Know That...

Fashion may dictate that you hide those gray hairs, but repeated use of hair dye can lead to scalp dermatitis and hair loss. That's why dermatologists increasingly have advised patients to alternate chemical hair dye with vegetable-based dyes, such as henna.

■ A ("Dry") Martini Shampoo

Forget about the medicine cabinet—the solution to your scalp problems may lie in the liquor cabinet! The following treatment will help soothe an itchy, irritated scalp:

1 Mash a handful of fresh or dried peppermint leaves in a little vodka. Steep for one day.

2 The next day (or when you're ready to use it), shake the vodka mixture well, then add tap water until the solution becomes cloudy.

3 Apply the peppermint mixture to your scalp after shampooing and leave on.

■ Gentle Herbal Remedy

If you suffer from an itchy, flaky scalp, but prefer not to use conventional dandruff shampoos, try this sage-tea hair rinse. In addition to being gentle on the hair, it smells better than commercial dandruff shampoos. To prepare the rinse:

1 Add one tablespoon of dried sage leaf to one cup of boiled water.

2 Steep for 30 minutes, strain off leaves and let cool. If you have some antibacterial tea tree oil, you can add a few drops.

3 Pour through shampooed hair. Don't rinse.

DRY, DAMAGED HAIR

■ Spearmint Seal for Split Ends

Hair subjected to sun damage or daily blow-drying is especially susceptible to split ends. A hot cup of tea—poured into your hair—might be just what you need.

1 Place a few dried spearmint leaves in a cup of boiled water.

2 Steep the mixture for 30 minutes, then strain off leaves.

3 Allow the tea to cool, then pour it through your shampooed hair. Don't rinse afterward.

■ Sunny-Side Up Fix for Flyaways

Dry hair is often brittle and flyaway, and susceptible to split ends and static electricity. To rebalance, allow the hair and scalp to soak up some serious moisture. The following home-made treatment works wonders.

Start with one egg yolk and mix in enough vitamin E oil to create a creamy, mayonnaise-like mixture. Work the entire mixture through your hair (massaging it into your scalp), then cover your hair with plastic wrap. Leave it on for up to two hours, then shampoo. Your hair will look shiny and feel soft right away.

■ Kitchen Conditioner for Coarse Hair

For coarse, dry, frizzy hair, here's a super moisturizing treatment from the kitchen:

1 Melt one part butter and two parts olive oil together in a pot on low heat.

2 Immediately apply the warm (not too hot) melted mixture to your hair.

3 Cover your head with kitchen foil or plastic wrap and keep it on over the butter treatment for one hour before shampooing.

■ A Finer Oil Treatment

Cook up a rejuvenating hair mask for fine, dry hair: Mix one part olive oil with two parts glycerin. Immediately—before the mixture separates—apply the mixture to your hair, then cover your head with kitchen foil or plastic wrap for one hour. Shampoo out.

■ Wake Up Weak, Limp Hair

Your hair just may be reflecting what your scalp—and entire epidermis—is feeling. Perk up your head by sprinkling one to two drops of rosemary oil on your hairbrush or scalp before brushing. The invigorating essential oil will soothe and stimulate a tired scalp. Your hair will show the results.

■ Fragrant Oil for Brittle Hair

If your hair is brittle (or your scalp is dry and itchy), you may benefit from this moisturizing treatment. Warm a few tablespoons of jojoba oil and add a few drops of one of the following essential oils: Patchouli, lavender, juniper or bergamot. (All are stimulating and nourishing.)

Saturate your hair with the oil mixture, then cover it with plastic wrap and leave on 20 minutes before rinsing. *Hint:* To make rinsing out easier, apply a bit of shampoo to the hair before wetting it.

OILY HAIR

■ A Corny Cure for Greasy Hair

If your hair always seems greasy no matter how much you wash it (and this bothers you), you can find the solution in your kitchen cabinet.

Take a box of cornstarch and pour some onto your hands. Rub your hands together (like a gymnast applying chalk), and once you have a light, even dusting, massage the cornstarch into the roots of your hair. When you're through, be sure to comb out the powder.

While this is a safe, simple solution to chronically greasy hair, you should also pay attention to your diet. Avoid fried or greasy foods. And bear in mind that your hair is a barometer of what's happening inside your body. Extremely oily hair that persists over a long period of time could be a sign of more serious internal problems. So, if the problem doesn't go away, talk to your doctor.

■ Apple Astringent

Do you regularly use a toner on your face? If you have oily hair, you might want to try one on your locks. After you shampoo, rinse with two tablespoons of apple cider vinegar, diluted in one cup of water. (You can substitute lemon juice for the vinegar.) You should see a difference right away.

Be careful: Although this is a natural solution, it's still an astringent, so don't use it every day or you'll risk ruining your hair shaft.

HANGOVER

■ *Love Your Liver*

To rest and detoxify an overworked liver, take milk thistle for a few days after a big party. Milk thistle's active ingredient is silymarin, which naturopaths believe helps regenerate liver cells.

The Day After

To counteract the damage to your system of a night on the town, add some potassium to your morning meal. Bananas and sports recovery drinks, such as Gatorade, are loaded with the hangover-fighting mineral.

■ *Pepper Preventive*

It may be because of its sinus-clearing effects, or it may be because of its painkilling properties, or it may be for some yet-unknown reasons, but cayenne pepper can help minimize or prevent a hangover. In order to have a better morning after a tough night, take one-eighth teaspoonful of cayenne pepper in a cup of water just before bedtime. (Be careful with the measurement if you've had more than a few.)

■ *Acupressure Assistance*

An acupressure solution to hangover headaches may rest in your two hands. According to Chinese medicine practitioners, massaging each thumb, firmly and steadily, just below the knuckle toward the base of the thumb, should bring welcome relief. If it doesn't work at first, try again in a few minutes.

■ *A Homeopathic Hangover Remedy*

If you can think straight the night that you drink one too many, take a 30C potency of a homeopathic remedy known as *nux vomica* before going to sleep. It's derived from the poison nut, and will help relieve any upset stomach or queasy feelings you may experience the next morning.

HAY FEVER
See also **Allergies,** page 55

GENERAL SYMPTOMS

■ *Hang Up the Clothesline*

The smell of linens and towels dried outdoors is inviting for some. But for those with hay fever, line-drying laundry is asking for an allergy attack. While blowing in the wind, your clothes and sheets will be reeling in allergens and pollens, which can result in watery eyes and sneezing. Stick with the dryer so you won't exacerbate allergy symptoms.

■ *Honey's Helping Hand*

Natural health practitioners are busy as bees getting the word out: Honey can tame hay-fever symptoms in many cases. It has been reported not only to clear the sinuses but also to help control the puffy, red, itchy eyes that are the hallmark of hay-fever sufferers.

Though it's not yet medically confirmed, experts believe the reason honey works so well is that it contains traces of pollen. So each time honey is eaten or taken in tea, it has the effect of a miniature immunization. Homeopaths recommend a daily dose of honey from a hive close to where you live; the honey will contain a minute dose of the same pollen in your area that irritates nasal passages and eyes. Contact the American Beekeeping Federation at 912-427-4233 or www.abfnet.org to find out how to procure honey from a local hive.

Suggested: Three times a day in tea or on cereal.

■ Take the "Sting" out of Hay Fever

While many of us struggle through the ragweed and pollen seasons with extra boxes of tissues, help may be as close as the plants causing the trouble. Stinging nettle is believed to be effective in treating symptoms.

Freeze-dried extract of its leaves made into capsules (those from air-dried leaves aren't as potent) is the most effective form. Take one to two capsules every two to four hours, as needed. You can also try it in tea or tincture form.

■ Deep-Steam Sinus Relief

When suffering from stuffy sinuses resulting from seasonal hay fever, take a steam. Inhaling steam helps to drain and soothe swollen sinus passages. Place your face 10 to 12 inches away from a bowl of steamy—but not boiling—water. For even more soothing and decongesting power, add a few drops of eucalyptus essential oil to the steamy water.

■ Massage Your Face for Clearer Breathing

To relieve congestion caused by allergies, massage therapists suggest drawing your fingers in long strokes from your temporal mandibular joint (located just in front of your ear) on down your neck. To help clear clogged sinuses, massage your face by drawing your fingers along the top of your cheekbones. Each self-massage should last until you feel relief, or at least a few minutes.

■ Vitamin C Surge

When allergies attack, strike back with a super surge of vitamin C. A 500- or 1,000-mg tablet three to four times a day has an antihistamine effect, calming irritated sinuses and eyes. However, beware of C sickness: Many physicians believe that high doses of vitamin C can cause diarrhea and kidney stones—among other ailments—so take caution.

■ A Fruit-and-Flower-Based Answer

It may seem odd at first to hear that a flower-based remedy could help relieve hay-fever symptoms. But for people who don't appreciate the side effects (like drowsiness) of antihistamines, quercetin can provide fast relief. Made from derivatives of flowers and fruit plants, quercetin keeps the body from releasing histamines, thereby suppressing hay fever and cold symptoms. Found in most

Let the Sunshine In—Only

After a long winter cooped up indoors, the cool breezes of spring are a breath of fresh air. But people with allergies may not want to bring the outdoors—and high pollen levels—in. Installing special filters in open windows will trap irritants and allergens before they have a chance to blow inside and get into furniture, carpets and linens—and before causing sniffles and sneezes. Check local hardware stores or specialized allergy catalogs for window filters.

health food stores, typical dosage is 200 mg, taken just before eating.

Time to Avoid Sniffles

The ticket to a sniffle-free allergy season, nose and sinus experts say, is to travel during off-peak pollen hours. So avoid the hours between 5 am and 10 am, when pollen levels are at their highest. Plan workouts, weeding the garden path and walks around the block for times other than sunrise (noontime and later is better) for extra allergy protection.

■ Open Sinuses, Sesame

When allergy and hay fever season hits, do as the Ayurvedic healers of India do and try swabbing your nostrils daily with sesame oil. In particular, use raw, cold-pressed sesame oil. Often, dryness is an underlying cause of nasal congestion, and the sesame oil works to lubricate and clear your overworked sinuses. Be sure to keep your sesame oil refrigerated to prevent rancidity.

■ Easy Acupressure Antihistamine

When allergies attack, you can find relief with the touch of a finger. Acupressure stimulates qi (pronounced "chee," in Asian medicine, the body's healing energy), to relieve itching, sneezing and other hay-fever symptoms. You can perform the following treatment on yourself:

1 With the thumb and forefinger of your right hand, grab the meaty part of your left hand between the thumb and forefinger.

2 Apply very firm pressure for one minute, pushing toward the bones of the hand.

3 Repeat, switching hands.

■ Citrus Soup Solution

To relieve the symptoms of hay fever, try this tasty snack:

1 Fill a pot with the rind and white pith of lemons, grapefruit and oranges, and cover with water.

2 Add a few tablespoons of honey and a tablespoon of vegetable oil.

3 Heat to a boil, allowing the mixture to simmer until the rinds are soft.

4 Cool the mixture, then add a shot of vodka and stir.

Ingested, the pith and rind act as an antihistamine and decongestant. Eat a few pieces on the days when you're especially congested.

■ Jump for Relief

Feeling stuffed up, wheezy and itchy-eyed from hay fever? Movement of lymph fluid throughout the body is dependent upon healthy blood flow, breathing and muscle contraction. For jammed-up sinuses from hay fever, one drug-free trick is to jump up and down—for health! It's a fun, easy way to boost your lymph system, and alternative health practitioners have (quietly) suggested this remedy for years. So consider hitting a trampoline for a few minutes each day (if that's handy) or dusting off the old jump rope. Your sinuses may appreciate the bounce.

■ *A Sniffles–Digestion Link?*

Next time hay fever strikes, increase your fiber intake instead of automatically reaching for the antihistamines. Chinese medicine practitioners note that many hay fever sufferers have a tendency toward constipation or irregular bowel movements. Often when bowel function is addressed, the practitioners say, sinus problems clear up markedly. Try to eat three to four servings of fruit a day and/or take a fiber supplement. The results may be nothing to sneeze at.

■ *Steamy Solution*

For frustrating effects of hay fever, herbalists often suggest taking a steam to ease irritated sinuses. For a home version of a steam room, boil up a pot of water and add the juice of a lemon and a few drops of thyme oil. The lemon juice has antimicrobial properties, while the thyme works as an antispasmodic. Tent your head with a towel and lean over a steaming pot for 10 minutes or so. Be sure to keep your eyes closed, and your face at least 12 inches away from the pot.

■ *Flowery Solution*

A field of lilies in full bloom may send an allergy sufferer into an all-out attack. And yet homeopaths often suggest sabadilla, made from a plant in the lily family, as a surefire sneeze stopper. A 30C tablet, taken once or twice a day during allergy season, should soothe sinus passages and reduce other hay-fever symptoms.

ITCHY, IRRITATED EYES

■ *Shield Your Eyes*

Don't forget your sunglasses. A simple way to keep pollen and other allergens out of your eyes—avoiding runniness, itchiness and redness during hay-fever season—is to protect them with glasses or sunglasses. Simply slip on your favorite pair before going outdoors during allergy season.

■ *Contact Care*

During allergy season it can be difficult to wear contact lenses if you suffer eye discomfort. But contact lenses themselves may cause some of the irritation. According to some eye experts, lenses may act as a trap for allergens and irritants floating in the air. Be sure to follow your physician's recommendations for cleaning and caring for contact lenses. And at the first sign of irritation contact your ophthalmologist for assistance—or disposable lenses.

HEADACHE

■ *Acupressure—An Instant Painkiller*

Acupressure, like its ancient Chinese relative, acupuncture, promotes healing throughout the body by stimulating channels of energy known as meridians. But where acupuncture uses thin (sterile) needles, acupressure relies on fingertips to do the probing. For the general pain of headaches, here's a two-handed treatment:

1 With one hand, press the shallow indention in the back of the head at the base of the skull.

2 Simultaneously, with the thumb and forefinger of the other hand, press firmly into the upper hollows of the eye sockets, right where they straddle the bridge of the nose and meet the "T" of the eyebrow bridge. Press softly at first, then more firmly and hold.

Administer for three to five minutes (for an average headache). Repeat as needed throughout the day. At the least, this should provide relief until acetaminophen or other painkillers kick in.

Pain-Free Diet

Control headaches with foods that won't exacerbate a pounding, aching feeling. Avoid foods containing chemicals like nitrites and sulfites, which dilate capillaries in the brain, increasing blood flow and causing pain. What are some of the forbidden foods? Hot dogs and other processed meat products, red wine, caffeine and, unfortunately, chocolate.

■ A Drug-Free, Two-Step Treatment

This two-step method for relieving general headache pain is especially suited for those who suffer side effects from painkillers, or for pregnant women watching their drug intake:

1 Close your eyes and try to visualize yourself on a hot, sandy beach in the middle of a sunny afternoon. (A variation of biofeedback and visualization can actually raise your skin temperature, which in turn eases pain.)

2 Next is a breathing trick, in which you inhale slowly for four seconds, then exhale for four

seconds, keeping your beach scene in mind. The breathwork reduces tension, also associated with headache pain.

■ Pepper Pain Remedy

In recent years, holistic health practitioners have had great success in helping spread the word that chili pepper compounds can act as painkillers. In particular, the compound capsaicin, which is found in red peppers, is a powerful anesthetic and may even help keep blood vessels clear throughout the body. Capsaicin blocks substance P, a protein in the body that serves as a neurotransmitter of pain.

In a strange-but-true recent study, fully 75% of headache patients who rubbed capsaicin cream on their nose (in the form of Zostrix and other over-the-counter remedies containing capsaicin) said they felt pain relief. Or, massage it onto your temples or the base of your skull for relief from tension headaches.

But there's no proof that eating red peppers will deliver the same results.

Don't Have a Cow

Holistic physicians and health practitioners often ask one simple question of headache patients that is overlooked by mainstream doctors: Can you live without dairy products in your diet? If the answer is yes, then you might solve a migraine riddle without any strong prescription drugs. Some people react adversely to milk, butter, cheese and cream. On the other hand, yogurt and goat-milk dairy products are typically better tolerated. A similar dairy ban can help sinus patients, especially children.

Dentists Get to the Root of Headaches

If you experience frequent headaches, make an appointment with your dentist. According to experts, a tooth can set your whole jaw off-kilter, causing muscle tension in your face, head and neck, which results in pounding headaches. Your dentist—or a holistic practitioner—can examine your mouth for decayed or worn-down teeth that may not even hurt but are the cause of headache pain.

Press Away Pounding

Head pounding? Use your fingertips to push on the very top of your skull. According to massage therapists, using this technique will help to relieve pressure and pain associated with a tension headache. Press the area for 30 seconds, three times in a row, while breathing deeply.

Teatime Headache Relief

When the telltale throb of a tension headache begins in your temples, take a break and sip a hot cup of willow bark tea. Willow bark contains salicylic acid, the active ingredient in aspirin. Add one teaspoon of dried willow bark to a cup of boiling water, and let the tea steep for 5 to 10 minutes. Strain and sip while it's warm.

Just Say No?

Historically and all too frequently, headaches have been an excuse for not wanting to have sex. But for some individuals, sexual intercourse does cause headaches. A combination of vascular changes and muscle tension produces a pounding headache after an orgasm. The cure? No, it's not abstinence. Biofeedback. A technician will help these sufferers discover how to relax muscles in shoulders, neck and head so that they can apply these techniques during intercourse.

Caffeine Injections: No Joke to Some Patients

Dedicated coffee drinkers know a thing or two about pounding headaches—especially when they miss their daily fix. That's why some doctors, patients and anesthesiologists actually are ordering up intravenous (IV) infusions of caffeine for hospital patients who are not allowed to consume caffeine because of upcoming surgery. A Mayo Clinic study in Arizona even confirmed that giving coffee

addicts IV caffeine markedly reduced the incidence of postsurgical "withdrawal" headaches.

■ Hormones and Headaches

When menopause strikes, a woman's hormones may run wild, resulting in symptoms ranging from mood changes to sleep difficulties to hot flashes. Now, the experts report, headaches may also be spurred by the hormonal fluctuations a woman faces throughout her lifetime. Specifically, doctors believe that a decrease in the estrogen levels results in an aching head. Consult your physician to discuss the benefits and dangers of using patches or pills to maintain a more regular estrogen level.

Supplements Ease Caffeine Withdrawal

If you've decided to quit the coffee habit, or been advised to for health reasons, there are a few things you can try to help ease the transition to PSS—Post-Starbucks State. In addition to replacing coffee with roasted herb teas, some of which are also stimulating—dandelion, barley and chicory, to name three—get into the water-bottle habit. Try sipping six to eight glasses of filtered or mineral water while you're up and around, reminding yourself of the fact that this is liquid nourishment.

You may also want to take potassium bicarbonate tablets a few times during the day to help the body become more alkaline. This helps reduce withdrawal symptoms such as headaches or slight nausea. These tablets can be found in any drugstore. Follow package directions.

Finally, taking several grams of buffered vitamin C during the day can help ease the stress of caffeine deprivation.

■ Don't Take Two Aspirin

If you suffer headaches regularly, try to avoid using medications daily. It turns out that excess acetaminophen, aspirin, ibuprofen or other painkillers can actually cause a rebound effect—now called "daily headache syndrome." It's one more reason why some doctors are becoming more supportive of nondrug attempts at pain relief, including massage, acupressure, ice packs, biofeedback or relaxation therapy.

■ Minty Tension Headache Stopper

This drug-free headache remedy harks back to ancient Greece, where citizens were known to have pressed peppermint leaves to their temples to ease headache pain. Today, to get a similar effect, you can simply rub a 10% peppermint-oil solution into the forehead and temples.

And medical support for this remedy comes, a few millennia later, from the University of Kiel in Germany, where a team noticed that acetaminophen (as found in Tylenol) and peppermint oil were equally effective in easing the pain of tension headaches. Combining the two painkillers brought even faster relief. Time to head to the herb shop or natural food store for some oil.

"Ice Cream" Headache

If you've ever eaten a scoop of ice cream or frozen yogurt too fast, you know the feeling. It's as if the frozen concoction shot straight to the brain, pounding in the cranium, trying to get out. No, it's not as serious as a migraine, and this kind of headache usually vanishes on its own after a moment or two. But the better news is that you can have your ice cream cake and eat it too, without a headache at all. The trick, headache experts say, is to keep the ice cream (or other frozen dessert) away from the back of the roof of the mouth—the most sensitive part of the mouth, which quickly sends freezing pain signals to the brain.

MIGRAINE

■ Can Nose Drops Beat Standard Painkillers?

Though research is still preliminary, nose drops may be an effective way to deliver pain-killing drugs to long-time migraine sufferers. Recent research from a medical group in Southern California showed that lidocaine, a local anesthetic, had a significant effect on pain in more than 50% of subjects who took it in the form of nose drops. This is notable, considering that not even 25% of those who took placebo nose drops reported a marked decrease in pain. Though lidocaine nose drops bring quick relief, the effect may not last as long as that of standard migraine drugs such as sumitriptan (Imitrex).

■ Divert Blood Flow from Head to Toes

Lie down in a darkened room, and place an ice pack under the back of your neck and a hot-water bottle on top of your feet. Cooling the blood flow through your neck while warming your feet can sometimes halt the pain-causing dilation that's occurring in your head. Holding something warm in your hands or something very cold, like ice cubes, may also stimulate blood flow.

■ The Soothing Aroma of Mom's Apple Pie

While certain smells, ranging from general cooking odors to perfume, can bring about migraines, others may help relieve them, according to recent research. Many migraine sufferers report that eating certain foods helps reduce the length and severity of their headaches, and the aroma may have something to do with it.

In a recent study, migraine sufferers who had an affinity for the scent of green apples had less severe headache pain after inhaling the green apple odor. One theory is that the familiar scent brought back pleasant memories from childhood, relaxed them and enhanced their mood or, at the very least, distracted them from the pain.

Pay attention to which scents trigger feelings of comfort for you—and be sure to keep those foods handy.

■ Feverfew for Fewer Migraines

Over the past decade, interest in the feverfew plant as a migraine remedy has hit new heights, even though the herbal remedy has been around for millennia and has been used for other conditions (yes, including fevers). Recent research in Europe has shown that the feverfew leaves can bring relief to some migraine patients by reducing serotonin secretion and production of prostaglandin, an inflammatory agent, to help prevent the blood vessel dilation associated with migraines. What's more, it's been shown that feverfew can prevent future episodes.

The problem is, this is one natural medication that is far more effective in its raw form than in pills or tablets. So countless migraine sufferers have tried feverfew capsules and been left wanting—and in pain. Your best bet in this case is to track down the leaves, or a tincture made from fresh leaves (steeped in alcohol).

If you can't find the leaves (available from herb specialty stores and suppliers), look for prepared products that contain sufficient concentration (.2%) of the active ingredient, parthenolide. The national health organization of Canada has approved the feverfew leaf for migraine prevention, as long as products contain that level.

Dosage: At the first sign of a migraine, take one teaspoon of feverfew tincture mixed in a cup of water. If that's not available, take three or four 125-mg capsules or tablets. Repeat every four hours as needed.

■ A Sniff and a Cure

At the first sign of a migraine, dip the flattened end of a toothpick into cayenne pepper and sniff a little bit into each nostril. In addition to offering natural pain relief, cayenne pepper is a good source of magnesium (which helps ward off migraines).

Note: This may be a "painful pain remedy" at first. In some cases, adding cayenne pepper to foods may also help prevent future migraines.

■ Sharp Pain Relief

Both migraine and tension headache sufferers will find acupuncture may relieve their pain. Depending on your condition, an acupuncturist will target different parts of the body to correct energy imbalances that cause your aching head. For instance, the liver meridian, which runs up the leg and through the abdomen, may be targeted for tension headaches.

According to experts, you will feel relief immediately from the rush of endorphins—the body's natural painkiller—induced by acupuncture. But you may need to schedule as many as 15 treatments in order to treat the underlying problem causing your headaches.

■ *An Acupuncture Analgesic*

One of the odd things about acupuncture in the West is that many doctors who believe they're branching out by using it as a treatment are still unaware of the full benefits it can provide. As a treatment for migraine headaches, acupuncture works in many cases to control or block pain, but that's not the chief function of acupuncture in China and elsewhere in the East. There, the main goal of acupuncture is to rechannel energy in the body, with pain control as a side effect. So, migraine sufferers here who reduce their number of headaches and relieve their pain through acupuncture actually get an energy boost as a bonus.

It's in Your Head

Cranialosteopathy, a hands-on therapy that works to realign the bones of the skull, jaw and face, relieves tension and pressure that, in some instances, contribute to headaches. Depending on the frequency of your headaches, you may need to seek treatment from a trained cranialosteopath at least once a week until your condition begins to improve.

HEADACHE

See also **Digestive Disorders**, page 100

■ *Calm Upset Stomach with a Natural Approach*

Rather than blocking production of stomach acids, as most heartburn medications do, a licorice extract can help soothe the stomach upset caused by heartburn (and some ulcers) by making the digestive tract more resilient. The problem with many commercial heartburn drugs is that when stomach acid is "blocked," nutrient absorption may sometimes be blocked as well.

Deglycyrrhizinated licorice, or DGL, on the other hand, does not change the acid content of the stomach as much as it primes the body to process it painlessly. Recent studies have shown DGL to outperform the acid-blocking drugs, including the old standby Maalox®. Typical dosage is two 380-mg tablets, taken 20 minutes before meals. Chew the tablets slowly, or take a half-teaspoonful of DGL powder between meals. You might also try taking it before eating as a preventive measure.

Unfortunately, candy licorice won't help to calm your stomach.

■ *Drug-Free Enzyme Aid*

With all the new over-the-counter heartburn drugs that have come on the market in recent years—including the "acid blockers" Zantac, Tagamet and Pepcid—along with old standbys Tums, Rolaids and Maalox, you would think there's no need for another heartburn medication.

But now there's a drug-free product called, AbsorbAid, made from digestive enzymes, including cellulase and lactase. Instead of blocking actions, this product helps the body do what it normally does—digest food—but more efficiently. Take these capsules both during and after a meal. As an added bonus, when all is working well, the enzymes also help the body absorb more nutrients.

■ Baking Soda as Antacid

You probably have a quick remedy for heartburn sitting in your refrigerator. In addition to deodorizing your carpet, keeping your ice cubes tasting clean and polishing your teeth, regular old baking soda works great as an antacid.

To prepare your own antacid, mix a teaspoon of baking soda in four ounces of water, stirring until it is completely dissolved. Then, drink the whole glass. It won't taste great, but it's not entirely offensive.

Be sure not to exceed eight teaspoons in a 24-hour period (people over age 60 should not exceed four teaspoons a day, and children under 5 should not be given this at all unless approved by a physician). If you're on a low-sodium diet,

you might want to refrain from this particular use of baking soda (each teaspoon contains 476 mg of sodium). The Arm & Hammer baking soda box has complete instructions and warnings regarding the product's use as an antacid.

■ Squeeze In This Exercise

Yoga teachers will tell students with heartburn to perform a knee squeeze pose each day to gently massage the colon and encourage regularity.

1 Lie on your back on a firm surface, with arms at your sides and toes pointed slightly down.

2 Inhale slowly and deeply as you raise the right knee to your chest.

3 Hold the knee with both arms and gently pull it toward your chest for several seconds.

4 Exhale as you straighten the knee.

Repeat three times with each leg. To finish, bring both knees toward the chest while inhaling, hold for a few seconds, then straighten on the exhale.

■ Pre-Meal Plan

Eating Right Prevents Heartburn

There are some remedies to heartburn and indigestion that don't require a trip to the drugstore. First, try not to skip any meals. Doctors explain that skimping on breakfast and lunch causes many people to overeat at dinnertime, consequently overworking the digestive system. To make matters worse, people then go to bed or recline on a couch within two hours of eating, which can cause a backwash flow of acid into the esophagus. Better to eat more frequent and smaller meals, and keep consumption light in the two hours before bedtime. One more thing: Your mother was right—eat slowly. Doing so eases heartburn and belching.

While new over-the-counter drugs promote the idea of taking a pill before eating to protect against heartburn, there is a more natural way to soothe the esophagus before a meal. Drink a small cup of goldenseal or barberry tea, available in most health food stores. You might also try gentian root or Oregon grape root for variety.

What's Not on the Menu

It's no secret that spicy foods, alcohol and coffee (including decaf) can make your heartburn more turbulent. But there are some surprising items on the list of "Foods to Avoid," including dairy products, citrus fruits, tomatoes, onions, breath fresheners, soft drinks and mint herbal teas. Be aware of whether any of these items worsen the discomfort.

■ Semisweet Tea Soothes Discomfort

After the big meal, after the dessert and after the guilt sets in, but before the heartburn does, try a cup of meadowsweet tea. The name is sweeter than the actual petals of the flower, but its healing powers are well known in herbalism circles. For heartburn, add one to two teaspoons of dried meadowsweet flowers (available at herb shops) to one cup of boiling water. Steep for 8 to 10 minutes, then drain. Feel the burn dissipate as you sip it.

■ Make Your Own Acid Blocker

For heartburn and reflux, try stirring up this alternative kitchen remedy instead of using over-the-counter acid blockers. Mix a teaspoon of slippery elm root powder with a teaspoon of honey, and ingest. Both slippery elm root and honey will coat the digestive tract for soothing relief. You'll find slippery elm root powder at your local herbal pharmacy or health food store.

HEART DISEASE
*See also **Heart Disease Prevention**, page 40*

■ Hawthorn Fights Heart Disease

The red berries and flowers of hawthorn trees are used in 36 heart preparations that have been approved for mild cardiovascular disorders by German health authorities. Scientists there have researched the herb for more than 25 years, finding that it increases blood supply to the heart, tends to lower heart rate, regulates cardiac rhythms and increases the strength of contractions by the heart muscle.

Freeze-dried hawthorn in capsule form is widely available. The typical dose is one to two capsules, two to four times each day, depending on your condition and practitioner's orders. Be sure to check with your doctor before you try this herbal remedy.

■ Celery Seeds for a Healthy Heart

There's a kitchen cure for high cholesterol and blood pressure levels that promotes overall cardiovascular health—celery seeds. Make a medicinal brew by steeping a teaspoon of crushed seeds in a cup of hot water for 15 minutes. Drink a few cups a day—particularly if cholesterol and blood pressure are high.

Listen Up, and Heal

Becoming a better listener is one way to fend off cardiovascular problems. Duke University doctors have discovered that there is actually a Type-H person who has a four to seven times greater risk of developing a heart attack than a Type-A person. H stands for hostile. Typically, these individuals do not trust others, tend to interrupt, dominate conversation and always relate a discussion back to themselves. A pilot study at Duke, which is being followed up by a major study, shows that an instructed silence while others are talking has helped reduce blood pressure and stress-hormone levels.

■ A "Tea-Totaler's" Answer to Red Wine

According to a recent study, an antioxidant found in green tea is at least 100 times more effective than vitamin C and 25 times better than vitamin E at protecting cells and DNA from damage associated with cancer and heart disease. The antioxidant—called epigallocatechin gallate (EGCG)—carries twice the antioxidant punch of red wine's resveratrol.

EGCG is so potent in green tea because the leaves are steamed immediately after they are picked—preventing oxidation. Black and oolong tea are only about half as potent. Animal studies show that green tea inhibits tumor growth and metastasis. And in Japan, where green tea is a common beverage, the population has a lower incidence of cancer than in the US.

■ Check Out This Supplement

Saddled with a cumbersome name, coenzyme Q-10, or CoQ-10, is an increasingly popular vitaminlike nutrient that was identified in 1957. While an American pharmaceutical company first synthesized CoQ-10, the process was sold to Japanese manufacturers. Researchers there linked low CoQ-10 levels to heart failure, which is why the synthesized supplement is now one of the top five heart medications in Japan. It is also popular in Europe.

Those who have family histories of heart disease may want to consider taking the enzyme as a supplement starting in middle age. A protective dose (taken with meals or a bit of fat to promote absorption) is 10 to 30 mg per day. People with diagnosed disease are often instructed to increase the dose to 120 mg per day (or two 60 mg doses), under the watchful care of a physician. Be sure to check with your physician to see if this supplement is appropriate for your condition. You may also want to ask your doctor to measure the levels of CoQ-10 in your blood.

■ Tomatoes for Heart Health

Eating tomatoes helps prevent heart attack and stroke—as well as cancer. The yellow, jelly-like material that surrounds tomato seeds makes blood less "sticky," inhibiting the formation of dangerous blood clots that can trigger heart attack or stroke. Research is under way to develop a clot-busting drug containing P3—a compound found in the jelly-like material. Such medication could replace or supplement low-dose aspirin as a heart attack and stroke preventive. Until then, heart and stroke patients should eat two to four raw tomatoes a day.

Beware of Combination Treatments for Heart Health

Now that word is filtering out that garlic has the power to help thin the blood and prevent heart attacks, some heart patients—not surprisingly—believe that they can simply load up on garlic in addition to other preventive efforts. For many, garlic may be just the right medicine.

But another word has come in from the medical community: Garlic taken together with blood thinners may alter blood chemistry too much. This doesn't mean you can't cook with garlic or order the roasted garlic appetizer in a restaurant, but if you are taking these medications you should check with a doctor before using garlic medicinally.

■ *Vitamin E for Heart Attack Prevention*

Although vitamin E has numerous benefits, its advantage to the heart often goes overlooked. Recently, results of a three-year, peer-reviewed study showed that heart patients who took daily supplements of vitamin E, containing a natural form of the vitamin called alpha tocopheryl, recorded 75% fewer heart attacks than those who were taking a placebo. This substantial study involved more than 2,000 people with histories of heart trouble.

Absence Makes the Heart Grow...Weaker

What's the greatest risk factor for people living with coronary artery disease? Surprisingly, it's not a physical threat. It is emotional isolation. The stress of loneliness tends to put more strain on the body's systems than do physical ailments. Get involved in group activities or sessions for social interaction, conversation and regular contact with friends.

■ *New Drug to Thin the Blood*

It may not be as cheap and easy to obtain as aspirin, but clopidogrel, a blood-thinning drug tested on more than 19,000 people with clogged arteries or heart trouble, appears to prevent heart attacks and strokes more successfully than trusty aspirin. Clopidogrel seems best suited for those who have been diagnosed with heart disease or arterial disease. The FDA has approved the drug, which is to be taken daily as directed by a doctor.

■ *B Heart Smart*

The vitamin B family—including folic acid, B6 and B12—all help control homocysteine levels in the blood. The importance? Homocysteine, an amino acid, damages arterial walls. Include supplements in your diet to ensure that you are getting the recommended allowances of these vitamins. Or eat loads of whole grains, seafood and leafy green vegetables. If you have heart problems, you may want to increase amounts of these vitamins—some good target amounts are: 10 mg of B6, 1 mg of folic acid and .1 mg of B12. Discuss this vitamin dosage and any other heart-related supplements you may take with your doctor.

■ An Aspirin a Day

You don't have to have had a heart attack to qualify for this medicine cabinet staple in a healthy heart program. Aspirin as preventive treatment inhibits the production of chemicals known as prostaglandins, which increase the chance of forming blood clots. But consult your physician before starting to take low doses (sometimes children's doses) of aspirin daily to ensure that it's safe for you.

New Screening Scan Gets High Marks

It's quick. Painless. Noninvasive. Powerful. And it's too new to have reached all areas of the country. (It's also pricey.) Still, the Ultrafast CT scan, an offshoot of computerized X-ray machines that allow doctors to peer inside brains, is gaining favor in dozens of advanced cardio-screening centers in the US. Briefly, it allows doctors to check for calcium deposits in key coronary arteries. This indicates atherosclerosis, or blockages, that may need attention. (While calcium is good for teeth and bones, it doesn't belong inside coronary arteries.) Ultrafast CT scans provide nearly as much information to cardiologists as angiograms, which are invasive and require half a day's hospital stay. For more information, call 800-469-HEART.

ANGINA

■ Here's the Acupressure Point

Acupressure offers a remedy for angina, the pressing or gripping sensation in the chest that many patients control with nitroglycerin medication. If an attack occurs unexpectedly and no medication is available, try pressing the middle of your left wrist about two inches from the base of the hand. Press hard with the nail tip of the right thumb until pain subsides. Of course, seek medical attention immediately.

ATHEROSCLEROSIS

■ Psychotherapy for Strong Hearts

Cardiologists have shown that patients with atherosclerosis (arterial blockage) who participate in once-a-week psychotherapy sessions for one year in addition to diet and exercise regimen consistently show greater improvements than those who have bypass surgery or angioplasty. These sessions help patients reduce stress and increase the emotional well-being that is important to overall health. Your cardiologist or family practitioner can refer you to a psychotherapist or counseling organization.

■ An Apple a Day

What do apples, onions, red wine, teas, deeply colored berries and grapes have in common? They all contain flavonoids which help to reduce the buildup of cholesterol and plaque in the arteries. Adding these foods and drinks to your diet may prevent arterial damage or stop the buildup you already have from progressing.

CLOGGED ARTERIES, HIGH CHOLESTEROL

■ How a High-Fat Food Might Help

If you don't eat avocados because they're so high in fat, it's time to rethink that. While it is true that avocados are among the fruits with the highest fat content, recent research reports claim that subjects who ate a diet rich in avocados and olive oil had a drop in total cholesterol of more than 8% in less than two months. Of course, the olive oil may have contributed more to the cholesterol drop than the avocado, but remember: It's the tortilla chips that do more harm than the guacamole!

Unblock Arteries Without Going Under the Knife

Chelation is used by conventional physicians to detoxify the body from lead or other heavy metal poisonings. But now many alternative practitioners believe this treatment can help to get heart disease under control. In each session, a practitioner hooks you up to an IV that delivers a solution said to break down calcium deposits in the arteries.

While considered highly controversial and ineffective by most conventional physicians, many alternative practitioners believe that chelation therapy can reduce the amount of medication a patient needs. Both practitioners and patients like that it doesn't require surgery. For a full treatment, you'll need 20 sessions. Ask your physician for more information.

■ Eye on Carrots

Carrots have been widely associated with improved vision, and their beta-carotene content has been praised for preventing such illnesses as heart disease and cancer. But Scottish studies also show that over a period of three weeks, a daily snack of two medium carrots lowered subjects' cholesterol by 10% to 20%. The 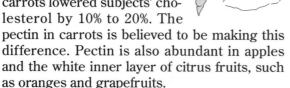 pectin in carrots is believed to be making this difference. Pectin is also abundant in apples and the white inner layer of citrus fruits, such as oranges and grapefruits.

■ Dental Floss Helps the Heart?

Can gum disease contribute to heart disease? A provocative thought—and one that researchers at Boston's VA Outpatient Clinic have been grappling with for well over a decade. In a long-term, well-designed study, they found a strong correlation between the overall heart attack rate and patients who had severe gum disease. Of course, bleeding gums didn't cause the heart attacks, but the bacterium P. gingivalis (as in gingivitis) has been traced to diseased carotid arteries of heart attack patients.

Conclusion: Bacteria that flourish in the mouth may contribute to heart attacks and serious conditions, including stroke. As studies continue, dentists' directives to "floss, floss, floss" will likely be taken to heart—or at least more seriously—in years to come.

■ An "Oil's Well" Approach to Better Health

Whenever you find a food, herb or ingredient that seems to provide multiple benefits, it's worth noting. That seems to be the case with safflower oil, which has been shown to help lower cholesterol, and to help lower the absorption of saturated fats as well. Recent research showed that in two months' time, subjects who switched to cooking with safflower oil cut their total cholesterol levels by some 10% to 15% while also reducing LDL (the bad cholesterol) readings by about the same amount.

■ Spice Up Your Dishes

Besides boasting antiviral properties, garlic also has been found to lower cholesterol levels in the blood. And high cholesterol is a leading risk factor for heart disease. In order to reap the benefits, you'll need to add the equivalent of four or five garlic cloves to your diet daily. Too hot to handle? Try two garlic tablets daily on a full stomach.

■ All Fats Are Not Created Equal

Unlike other fats that can clog arteries and raise cholesterol levels, a type of fat found in fish oil, known as omega-3 fatty acids, has a number of benefits for heart health. Physicians believe that omega-3 fatty acids reduce the chances of clots forming in the blood, raise good (high-density lipoprotein, or HDL) cholesterol and work to maintain a normal blood-pressure level. Although fish oil is available in capsules, experts say it's best to eat the fish itself. Salmon and mackerel are especially high in omega-3s.

■ Drink to Your Health

Moderate consumption of wine—such as a glass with dinner—has proven to reduce cholesterol levels. How? Chemicals known as polyphenols prevent harmful cholesterol known as low-density lipoproteins (LDLs) from damaging arterial walls and causing a buildup of plaque. Consult your physician before you begin raising your glass, because drinking has been proven to increase risks of other diseases, such as breast cancer. For those who choose to avoid alcoholic beverages entirely, look for capsules containing phenolics at health food stores.

■ Controlling Cholesterol

Adding servings of fiber to your daily diet is a simple step toward being heart smart. Why? Fiber helps to control levels of bad cholesterol by aiding the liver in removing cholesterol from the blood. As a result, the body excretes the potentially dangerous cholesterol before it has a chance to build up in the arteries. What should you eat? Fresh fruits, vegetables (especially broccoli and strawberries) and whole grains.

■ Exchange Dandelion Wine for Dandelion "Coffee"

The writer Ray Bradbury may have popularized dandelion wine, but cardiologists are hoping to spread the good word on dandelion coffee. Dandelions—yes, the weeds that grow in your lawn—have a twofold benefit for your health: Folks with high cholesterol can use dandelions to reduce cholesterol levels and kick a coffee habit.

You can make a healthful brew using dandelion roots and your trusty coffee grinder:

1 Get some dandelions, fresh from a pesticide-free field (or buy the roots at an herb shop). Then wash the roots thoroughly.

2 Dry and cut into inch-long pieces. Then, roast in the oven on low heat—250 degrees (like pumpkin seeds)—until they give off a coffeelike aroma.

3 Grind and steep one teaspoonful of the roasted dandelion in a mug of boiling water for about five minutes.

Have a mug of this every day instead of your morning coffee. In a few months' time, you'll feel great—and your cardiologist will be proud.

■ Grape Juice Aids Anticlotting

Now that heart patients most everywhere are aware of aspirin's ability to help keep blood flowing freely through arteries, it's time to add grape juice to the arsenal of blood thinners. Recent studies at the University of Wisconsin Medical School showed that drinking 8 to 10 ounces of purple grape juice daily reduced blood cells' ability to clot by more than 40%. That's about the same efficacy rate as aspirin when taken by heart patients in prescribed doses (very often one children's aspirin daily). Flavonoid compounds in the juice appear to help provide the anticlotting effects.

■ Exercise Your Options

Attention all couch potatoes: Aerobic exercise reduces blood pressure and cholesterol levels, strengthens the heart muscle and decreases your chances of dying from heart disease. Experts say that you should work up a sweat at least 30 minutes a day. It doesn't have to be a strenuous session. Brisk walking—even gardening— helps get your heart rate up and blood moving. However, if you have a heart condition, high blood pressure or another illness, contact your doctor before beginning an exercise regimen. A physician can assist you in choosing appropriate activities and levels of exertion that won't stress out a vulnerable cardiac or pulmonary system.

■ Stress Control

Still your beating heart—particularly if it's racing due to stress. According to the latest reputable studies, stress causes cholesterol levels in the blood to rise. So, make an attempt to catch your breath and calm yourself down. Take deep breaths, close your eyes and relive moments from your favorite vacation, or go for a quick walk around the block.

■ Mind Control

That's what experts say may be beneficial in controlling heart disease. Studies show that after biofeedback therapy, patients had stronger heart function and better blood-vessel dilation. Using electrodes to monitor breathing and pulse rates, a biofeedback technician (see pages 13–14) can assist a patient in learning how to increase blood flow to the heart and decrease overall mental and physical stress on the body. On average, some 15 sessions are necessary to learn biofeedback techniques.

HEMORRHOIDS

■ A Cool Treatment

For persistent pain and itching associated with hemorrhoids, aloe gel is an often overlooked but extremely effective ointment. The cooling effects of the pure gel act as an anesthetic, and the natural gel doesn't dry out as many commercial preparations do. It should be noted, however, that aloe gel by itself won't cure internal hemorrhoids, which are more serious and may result in rectal bleeding. Serious cases should be examined by a doctor.

■ Naturopathic Heat Treatment

Often used in treating gynecological disorders, sitz baths can also help treat and heal hemorrhoids. The inflamed blood vessels in and around the anus often respond well to the baths, in which the pelvis is immersed in hot water, while the torso, arms and legs are kept out of the water in a medium-to-deep basin. The heated water acts as a contrast of sorts, concentrating blood flow to the affected area. Ten to 15 minutes a day should be enough to see results in many cases.

Try Acupuncture Treatments

If you suffer from painful hemorrhoids, a few needles may hold the cure. Acupuncturists report that strategically inserting needles in the lower back relieves hemorrhoid symptoms. However, you will likely need at least 15 sessions in order to successfully treat the condition over the long term.

■ Eight Glasses for Relief

Instead of reaching for a drug or a pricey ointment, try treating hemorrhoids simply—to start. Some doctors and holistic healers suggest sufferers do little more than drink eight glasses of water or herbal tea daily, indefinitely. (Also, they often advise cutting back on dairy products and excess meat.) Most people who are constipated and most hemorrhoid patients drink far fewer than eight glasses of water a day, doctors say.

■ Witch Hazel Help

To relieve the pain of hemorrhoids, dab the afflicted area with a cotton compress soaked in witch hazel. This is especially helpful after each bowel movement. For best results, use a tincture of witch hazel that you can purchase in a health food store. Mix a few drops of witch hazel tincture in two cups of distilled water. For added relief throughout the day, place a compress coated with witch hazel inside your underwear for a few hours at a time. Its antiseptic and anti-inflammatory properties help reduce the inflammation and itching commonly associated with hemorrhoids.

■ Diet Watch

Most cases of hemorrhoids, doctors say, can be attributed to irregular bowel movements and poor eating habits. To ensure regularity, be sure to get enough fiber in your diet. Nutritionists say one method is to supplement your diet with psyllium husks (available at health food stores). Or take a mild natural laxative. Ingesting a couple of tablespoons of flaxseed or linseed oil daily will also help soften stools.

■ Eat an Orange—or Its Parts

Hemorrhoids occur when the walls of blood vessels near the anus weaken and swell, becoming painful and sometimes itchy. But relief can be found easily in an orange. The rind of citrus fruits contains rutin, a substance that strengthens capillary and blood vessel walls. Eat an orange a day—for safety's sake, you may want to go organic.

If the idea of eating the whole orange does not appeal, try boiling the rind and white pith of oranges in enough water to cover, adding a few tablespoons of honey and a tablespoon of vegetable oil. Boil the mixture until the rinds are soft. Let it cool before eating. Have a few pieces every day until symptoms begin to improve or subside.

Get into Circulation

Stimulating flow in the intestines can remedy constipation, a major contributor to hemorrhoids. Massage therapy is one approach for waking up the intestines. Here is a self-massage appropriate for hemorrhoid sufferers:

1 Lying on your back, bend and raise your knees, leaving your feet flat on the ground.

2 Starting on your left side, use your left hand and fingers or palm to make long, sweeping strokes from your lower ribs in the direction of your feet.

3 Stroke across your abdomen right to left.

4 Finish by pointing the fingers of your right hand at your right foot and stroking upward to the ribs on the right side.

Repeat this exercise three to six times daily.

Topical Topics

To reduce the pain, swelling and itching of external hemorrhoids, try dabbing pilewort ointment on the irritated area, several times a day. To make the ointment, warm seven ounces of petroleum jelly and two tablespoons of fresh or dried pilewort for 10 minutes. Allow the mixture to cool before using. Store the remainder in a closed container.

A Simple, Four-Point Plan of Attack

Most people who suffer from hemorrhoids do not realize that hemorrhoids are rarely triggered by just one thing—pregnancy, for example, or poor diet. Usually a combination of factors is responsible. As such, a combination of therapies proves most effective. Besides standard ointments, gastroenterologists and internists also recommend the following:

1 Drink at least 48 ounces of water and eat 30 grams of fiber daily.

2 Breathe regularly during bowel movements (do not hold your breath or strain).

3 Wipe with premoistened wipes instead of toilet paper during flare-ups.

4 Apply petroleum jelly, zinc oxide paste or cold compresses to the perineum (area between the anus and the genitals).

Weight Training to the Rescue

Probably more useful for prevention than for treatment, weight training nonetheless can help reduce recurrences of painful hemorrhoids. Research from the University of Maryland has shown that long-term weight training not only increases the strength of the arm, leg and shoulder muscles, but of the digestive tract, as well. Therefore, the intestines' wavelike contractions become stronger, leading to a faster passage of food through the small and large intestine. In the past, slower digestion time has been associated with hemorrhoids. That's one more reason to pump some iron in the name of prevention.

■ *Qigong Remedy*

Anal swelling and itching is literally an age-old problem. More than 1,200 years ago, the famous Chinese physician Sun Simiao first recorded the ancient qigong exercise remedy for hemorrhoids, which can be done standing, sitting or lying down:

1 Relax the body, but tuck the buttocks in and draw the thighs together with gentle force, as you inhale and touch the roof of your mouth with your tongue.

2 Next, clench the anal sphincter as if you were restraining yourself from defecating.

3 Hold the breath several counts, exhale, relax and repeat.

The movement encourages blood circulation to the area and should be performed for a few minutes each morning and evening for best results.

■ *Traditional Advice from the Chinese*

Some other worthy tips from traditional Chinese medicine:

■ Avoid taking too long on the toilet (don't make a habit of reading there).

■ Rinse the anus and perineum with warm water after each bowel movement.

■ Use hot compresses and light massage daily to further stimulate blood circulation.

RECTAL ITCHING

■ *An Overnight Soak of Sorts*

One nondrug way to combat the itching that accompanies hemorrhoid flare-ups is to soak a gauze bandage in apple cider vinegar and place in the anal area overnight. Use tight underwear or a sanitary pad to keep the gauze in place. Relief should be swift, unless the area is raw from scratching. Then, there may be burning at first. But this, too, shall pass.

■ *Soothing Oil Relief*

For hemorrhoid sufferers with persistent rectal itch, wheat germ oil can provide soothing relief—overnight. After washing the affected anal area with a mild soap, pat dry and apply wheat germ oil liberally. You might pull on some old underwear to keep the sheets dry and oil free.

Alternatively, you can dab the skin around the anus with olive oil to ease bowel movements and soften the inflamed tissues near the perineum.

■ *Essential Information*

Several essential oils provide hemorrhoid relief. About 20 drops each of lavender and juniper oils in a hot, shallow bath (about three inches deep) can be soothing. Soak for 10 minutes, then after gently drying off, apply two drops of lavender oil and one drop of geranium oil in roughly one ounce of a carrier oil, such as almond oil.

■ Another Soothing Bath

Try running a warm bath before bed, and pour into it a mixture of one cup of baking soda and 5 to 10 drops of chamomile oil. After a 15-minute soak, you'll feel much better.

A Laser-Lite Remedy

When hemorrhoids are severe or recurrent over years, many people believe that surgical excision is their only choice for quick relief. That used to be the case. In recent years, however, a new device that uses infrared light (not as intense as laser) can cause the hemorrhoids to shrink and recede, painlessly. At least that's how it's described by gastro-enterologists who have used the infrared coagulator. Most of their patients who've tried it say the same. There is no need for local anesthesia, and because there's no cutting involved, there's no bleeding to speak of either.

HICCUPS

■ Anise Works to Get Your Breath Back

At the first sign of hiccups, chew on this: Anise, or aniseed, is a parsley-like plant that aids digestion in a number of ways, including easing hiccups. Especially effective when taken in tea, anise soothes the throat and is said to thin mucous secretions as well.

Note: When taken in a form other than tea, follow the package directions closely, since anise is a strong herb.

■ Fennel for Your Hiccups

Herbalists say that fennel (which tastes like anise and licorice) is a helpful remedy for respiratory ills, queasy stomachs and even hiccups. The simplest way to treat the hiccups is to brew a cup of fennel seed tea and sip slowly. Make sure to inhale the aromatic steam as a bonus herbal aid. It's available packaged in tea bags.

■ Chew on This

Slowly chew a piece of dry or charred toast to make hiccups go away. Or chew charcoal tablets or chewable papaya enzymes, and continue taking tablets at least once an hour until the hiccups stop.

Another option: Mix two parts honey and one part castor oil, and ingest one teaspoonful.

■ Instant Acupressure Treatment

The lore associated with treating hiccups ranges far and wide, but many of the so-called cures—such as sipping a glass of water, slowly, through a paper towel—are not really practical if you're on the go or at the office. Here's a quick, easy acupressure solution you can perform anywhere: Simply place your fingers in the hollows behind each earlobe, pressing gently inward. Hold for 60 seconds (or as time allows between hiccups), and repeat until the hiccups stop.

Acupuncture Aid for Chronic Hiccups

Are you plagued by chronic hiccups? According to acupuncturists, you may be suffering from an energy imbalance. At times, excess energy rises through the body from the stomach, liver and spleen, and back up the digestive tract, causing hiccups. Acupuncture needles redirect the energy back down into the body—stopping the hiccups. While you may feel quick relief from the first acupuncture session, up to 15 may be necessary to correct the underlying cause of your condition.

■ Rub Hiccups Away

Time to take off your shoes and socks, and get serious. Acupuncture experts and reflexologists point out that the sole of the foot contains an acupressure point for hiccups. Try massaging the center of the instep with firm thumb pressure. It may take a few minutes to work, but it doesn't feel bad in the meantime.

■ Take a Ribbing

The right acupressure point and deep breathing might do the trick to control hiccups. Find the "Sp 16" points located at the base of your rib cage on the right and left sides, one-half inch inside the imaginary line running down from the nipples. With fingertips of both hands, firmly press both points while breathing deeply for several minutes. Closing the eyes is also helpful.

■ Bartender's Breakthrough

If hiccups persist over several days or occur repeatedly, then it's certainly time to visit the doctor. For temporary cases, the veteran bartender's trick of biting into a lemon wedge sprinkled with bitters usually works. Hiccups happen when nerve receptors in the diaphragm are irritated, usually from eating or drinking too fast. The irritation leads to muscle spasms, or hiccups, that transmit an ongoing neurological impulse between the diaphragm and your brain. Biting into the lemon introduces taste sensations (not all pleasant!) and swallowing, which break the pattern and relax the muscle.

■ A Spoonful of Sugar

The next time you have a nagging case of spasms of the diaphragm muscles—one serious case of the hiccups—try swallowing a teaspoonful of granulated white sugar, with no water to chase it. Sounds like a crazy confection, but it works. This remedy is even included in some medical textbooks.

HYPERTENSION (High Blood Pressure)

MODERATE TO SEVERE

■ Any Fish You Wish—But Not for Eating

One quirky, shockingly simple way to help control high blood pressure is to set up an in-home aquarium and watch it. Seriously. By following the movements of a fish (or two) around the aquarium, twice a day for 10 to 15 minutes, patients in research studies have witnessed beneficial drops in their blood-pressure readings.

This live-action biofeedback reduces the chances of suffering heart disease or a heart attack over time. It's too soon to say whether watching fish patterns on computer monitor screensavers could provide similar results.

Mind / Body Training Can Make a Difference

For people already on medication for high blood pressure or hypertension, cognitive-behavioral therapy is a complementary adjunct that can help bring blood-pressure readings down to a safer level. In experiments that taught patients how to practice stress management and relaxation, some 55% of subjects who brought their blood pressure down and kept it at a normal level by adopting a low-stress lifestyle, were able to cut their medication completely after a year. Only 30% of subjects in a control group that received a different therapy were able to be free of medication after one year. The key, heart experts believe, is that hypertensive patients respond best when they are able to reduce their feelings of stress, hostility and defensiveness.

■ The Blood Pressure–Banana Connection

Feel your blood pressure soaring after a run-in with your boss? Take a deep breath, and eat a banana. According to physicians, potassium helps lower blood pressure. If you have a normal blood pressure, potassium will help you maintain overall good health. Hypertensive patients can start lowering blood pressure by supplementing their diet with potassium-rich foods. What's on the menu besides bananas? Beans, avocados and whole grains.

■ Give Garlic a Try

Forget, for a moment, the jokes about bad breath. Heart problems are far more important—which is one reason millions of North Americans have discovered or rediscovered garlic, for their daily menus and in supplements. In both forms, garlic contains allicin and ajoene, chemicals that help lower blood pressure while reducing cholesterol—a nifty combination.

Some heart experts advise eating up to a clove of garlic every day to promote heart health. It's as helpful as aspirin, perhaps, with fewer side effects.

■ Relax with Marjoram Massage Oil

While it has been used in cooking for centuries, the use of marjoram to help ease the many effects of high blood pressure is relatively recent. Known by herbalists for dilating blood vessels, marjoram not only helps them open up a bit, but also may help keep them open. In this way, pressure drops, if modestly, throughout the circulatory system. The fact that it can be taken in through the skin in the form of a relaxing massage makes the treatment that much more pleasant.

Transcending Hypertension

Studies show you can use meditation and other relaxation techniques to improve hypertension. A research project at West Oakland Health Center in California showed that Transcendental Meditation (TM) practices reduced systolic blood pressure (pressure in the arteries when the heart pumps) by 10.4 points and diastolic blood pressure (pressure in the arteries when the heart is at rest) by 5.9 points in female subjects. The male subjects fared even better. (The TM method required practitioners to close their eyes and concentrate on a personally assigned mantra for two 20-minute sessions each day.)

The same study showed lesser but still significant decreases for subjects pursuing a progressive muscle-relaxation technique (a system of tensing and relaxing the muscles on specified counts).

■ Simple, Overlooked Exercise Solutions

Regular aerobic exercise for 30 minutes will provide a bundle of bodily benefits. But what about the millions of folks who don't adhere to that regimen and who have high blood pressure that could lead to more serious heart disease? What can they do daily? At least three things can help measurably:

■ When you're going to work or on an errand, intentionally park the car a few blocks away. It may not be aerobic, but it helps.

■ While at work or at a shopping mall, or if you live in a high-rise, take the stairs—at least for several flights—instead of taking elevators or escalators.

■ Get to know the sodium content of foods in the same way you've already learned to scan fat grams on labels. Adults need only 200 mg of salt each day; it's time to reach out for other spices. In cutting salt intake, substitute peppers or other vegetables for flavor. Better yet, grow your own and reap the exercise benefits of gardening.

■ DASH for This Diet

While lower consumption of sodium and alcohol along with increased physical activity are regularly prescribed for lowering blood pressure, a government study shows that eating a certain healthful low-fat diet can reduce mild hypertension without restricting sodium and alcohol, or introducing a new exercise program. The National Heart, Lung and Blood Institute has conducted research as part of its Dietary Approaches to Stop Hypertension (DASH) program. Subjects maintained the following dietary guidelines and significantly reduced blood pressure in eight weeks:

■ Less than 30% of daily calories from fat.

■ Eight to 10 servings of fruits and vegetables per day.

■ Seven to eight servings of grains per day.

■ Two to three daily servings of low-fat or non-fat dairy products.

■ No more than three ounces of lean meat, poultry or fish twice a day. Four to five servings of beans, nuts and seeds each week.

■ Here's the Rub

Chinese medicine practitioners believe that "disease at the upper should be treated from the lower." So it makes sense in this discipline to rub the arch of the foot for hypertension. Rub the center of the sole at a point between the two meaty sections of the ball of the foot. Work with both thumbs for about two minutes.

You can also rub the sole with the heel of your other foot. This practice needs to be done consistently to be effective.

■ Stalking a Solution

Though celery does contain some sodium (don't worry, not much), its overall chemical properties have a mild diuretic effect similar to some blood pressure medications. Besides munching on a few stalks, try a daily glass of celery juice cut with equal parts carrot juice and water.

HYPOGLYCEMIA

■ Food as Medicine

Low blood sugar is all about swings—and managing them. Diabetics—who know all about controlling the sugar levels in their blood—often suffer hypoglycemia when they skip meals or take too much insulin. As a result, their blood sugar levels can dip dangerously. For nondiabetics, the symptoms—sweating, weakness, tremors and headaches—are similar though generally milder, and severe reactions, such as coma, are extremely unlikely.

How, then, to control the swings? One way is through a seemingly odd dietary regimen: Cut out all sugar (even cereals that have it hidden). Instead, substitute protein and fresh fruits, vegetables and legumes. Many doctors also recommend having four to six small meals a day rather than three large ones.

■ Brewer's Yeast Controls Blood Sugar

When low blood sugar is a problem—as with many diabetics and others whose blood sugar levels may swing unpredictably—medical solutions, or even a strict diet, may not control the problem completely. Sometimes, though, the added effect of a mineral supplement—chromium—can make a noticeable difference. Many doctors will suggest foods that contain chromium (lean meats, whole-grain breads), but brewer's yeast is an even more valuable source.

Suggested dosage: Two teaspoons in juice or water, twice a day.

IMMUNE SYSTEM DISORDERS

■ Thrive Soup

An easy, nutritious recipe to follow even when you're not feeling well is for thrive soup. Next time you feel a bug coming on, stop at the grocery store and load up on as many green vegetables as are available—broccoli, kale, brussels sprouts, green beans and so on. Steam the vegetables until they're tender but not mushy, and puree in a blender or food processor. Add some chicken broth to thin out the mixture, or roll it in tortillas. It can be eaten as a soup or as a spread on breads.

Sensitive to the Difference

We know that common culprits such as nuts and shellfish can cause allergic reactions ranging from hives to anaphylactic shock in people who are allergic to them. And for about 30 million African Americans, among others, with lactose intolerance, milk sugars can cause indigestion and diarrhea.

But food sensitivities, which are much more subtle, can also wreak havoc on your immune system. The wrong food can cause any number of symptoms in different individuals, from head congestion to bloating to fatigue. If you are not feeling up to par, keep an informal food diary to determine your eating patterns. Dairy products and eggs are the most common sources of food sensitivities. Other foods include wheat products, kidney beans, soybeans and lentils. It doesn't mean you should not eat such healthful foods, but note if any of the items lead to atypical symptoms. Then you can talk to a physician or nutritionist about healthful ways to avoid trigger foods.

Herbal Help

For those who deal with regular bouts of fatigue and who repeatedly catch colds, suffer allergies, or have low-grade fevers or infections, immune deficiencies may be a culprit. Some alternative practitioners believe one way to shore up the immune system is to take 500 mg of astragalus, a Chinese herb, twice each day during the malaise or illness.

Colon Therapy to Improve Immune Function

The first thing to know about autointoxication is that it has nothing to do with hangovers. The second is that it has to do with internal body cleanliness. The third is that it is controversial.

Some alternative practitioners believe that immunity can be compromised by toxins that collect in and along the digestive tract, and that colon therapy may help cleanse the body of these waste materials. This is said to improve the quality of nutrient absorption, blood flow and immune response. One way to cleanse the digestive tract is through dietary and herbal means: Various herbs, psyllium seeds, pumice and certain types of clay are combined in pill form and taken over a period of a few days to two weeks. The lining of the intestines are, in effect, shed, and the buildup along the intestinal walls is just excreted. While undergoing an herbal cleansing, increased consumption of raw fruits and vegetables is advised. Be sure to check with your doctor or health practitioner before embarking on colon therapy.

Colon Irrigation—Not for the Squeamish

Colon irrigation is one form of colon therapy often used to methodically wash out the stubborn waste, said to be caused by years of eating processed, fatty and sugary foods.

More thorough and time-consuming than an enema, colon irrigation involves a 45- to 60-minute abdominal massage and flushing of the rectum and colon with purified water. Many doctors are not convinced of the health benefits of irrigation. Be sure you are comfortable with the practitioner you choose; and make certain that the instruments are sterilized, or request the use of new, disposable speculums and hoses.

■ *Picture This*

"Seeing" can be healing. Some research suggests that visualization can increase white blood cells, known as T4 cells, which boost the immune system and protect against disease and infection. Here's a sample exercise: Imagine a hot-air balloon in a meadow, held down by ropes attached to stakes. Then, put a problem in the balloon's basket, choosing a small, unimposing problem when first practicing this exercise. Finally, when you're ready, imagine yourself cutting the ropes. Visualize the problem floating up and away from your conscious mind. Build up to more serious problems.

INSOMNIA

■ *A Natural, Quick Compress*

After staring for too long at the ceiling, waiting for sleep to kick in, try a simple, quick fix: Head to the bathroom, soak a washcloth in cold water, then lie down and put the compress over your abdomen. Some naturopaths and Asian medicine healers believe that the cold compress pulls energy from the head to the torso, relieving much of the pent-up stress responsible for keeping you awake.

■ *Sensual Visualization Cure*

If you're not sleeping well, tapping the power of your mind may send you to better slumber soon. Imagine a restful setting as you lie in bed, maybe a gently swinging hammock on a quiet lakeshore or a lounge chair on a favorite beach. Mentally fill in the details of your surroundings and feel the comfort. Then, take it a step further: Instead of merely picturing a placid lake or beach, try to employ your other senses as well. Pretend your feet are in the hot sand or on the damp, grainy shore, heels digging as you walk. Hear the sounds of seagulls. Smell the suntan lotion baking into bodies alongside you as you stretch out on a soft terry cloth towel. The more vivid the images, sleep doctors say, the better chance you'll have of hitting the zzz's soon.

■ *Count on This Hint, Not Sheep*

One way to distract the bedtime mind from the day's troubles is to count backwards. This technique borrows from a standard relaxation warm-up for meditation classes. You can start with 100. Count slowly, mouthing the words to yourself. If you lose your place, do not be bothered. Start over at 100. This is about falling asleep, not counting.

■ *Valerian Dreams*

Not to be used every day because it is a natural mild depressant, valerian is a strong-smelling (some say foul) root that can induce drowsiness. A teaspoon of tincture with about two ounces of water is the suggested dose about a half-hour before bedtime. You might sample valerian tea products, too.

Another caution: It doesn't work for everyone. Valerian can make some people overly drowsy in the morning, and can become addictive if combined with alcohol (another depressant).

■ *Rest Those Bones*

There's plenty of good research about the bone-enhancing qualities of calcium, including age-related Recommended Dietary Allowances. But taking a calcium and magnesium supplement in a one-to-one ratio (400 mg each) about 45 minutes before retiring for the night is also an effective sleep inducer. Check with your doctor about magnesium, though, if you have heart problems.

■ *Breathe if You Pleazzz . . .*

Learning to relax at bedtime can actually be difficult for someone fretting about a bout with insomnia. Here is a simple breathing exercise that combines body relaxation and the repetition that makes for effective meditation:

1 Exhale completely through your mouth.

2 Inhale through the nose to a count of four.

3 Hold your breath for a count of four to eight, whatever is comfortable. The idea is to hesitate before exhaling.

4 Exhale through your nose for a count of eight.

Repeat three times or until sleepy.

■ *Relax Your Facial Muscles Before Bed*

Many people clench their jaw and face muscles at night. When you lie down to sleep, take a few minutes and concentrate on really relaxing each muscle in your face.

■ *Passionflower Dreams*

Simple, soothing, sleep-inducing—that's what fans of passionflower tea say about its anti-insomnia properties. About one hour before bedtime, simply pour boiling water into your favorite mug over one teaspoon of dried

Magnetic Therapy—An Attractive Remedy

These days, an increasing number of insomniacs are attracted to practitioners of magnetic therapy. Simply put, "medical" magnets and magnetic fields have numerous therapeutic uses, from alleviating some forms of arthritis pain to easing excess stress. But recently, with the advent of inexpensive blankets and (more expensive) mattresses with strategically sewn-in magnets, hundreds of US insomniacs have found the safe, low-frequency, brain-wave stimulation of the magnetic sleep aids surprisingly helpful.

The therapy is, of course, drug free. And starting at under $100 for a blanket that could give you restful sleep for years, it's a relative bargain. Insomniacs can also try lying on magnetic "wraps" or stretched-out seat covers to test the effect for a lot less cost than a mattress. For a low-priced, medically-approved and rated product information kit, contact The Bio-Electro-Magnetics Institute, Reno, Nevada, at 775-827-9099.

passionflower. Cover and let steep for 15 minutes before drinking. Pleasant dreams.

Note: Some herbalists suggest blending two parts valerian root with one part passionflower as a better bedtime remedy. But because passionflower is completely safe (whereas valerian root may have side effects), try the tastier, simpler tea first.

■ Light Up the Darkness

As odd as it might sound at first, adding light—extremely bright light as a tonic or therapy—can help you fall asleep earlier if you have trouble falling asleep before midnight. Researchers at the New York State Psychiatric Institute have found that people who sit in front of light boxes for an hour or so early in the morning reset their sleep clocks. Their bodies "think" the day has started earlier; thus, their usual 2:00 A.M. sleep time can shift to, say, 11:00 P.M. It's also a good technique for people who do shift work and don't keep regular sleeping hours.

■ Music Therapy Hits the Right Notes

Often, doctors advise people who can't fall asleep at night to avoid the stimulating effects of television, but that advice may not apply to the stereo. Recent research has shown that insomniacs who listened to two kinds of recorded music—New Age or Baroque—said they fell asleep faster and slept longer than when they didn't use any music as a sleep tonic. In fact, subjects reported that sleeplessness returned when the music was discontinued during the six-month study.

■ Siberian Ginseng Fosters Deeper Sleep

If you or a loved one are among those for whom sleeping pills seem too strong to battle stress-induced sleepless nights, try taking a teaspoon of Siberian ginseng extract before going to bed. It is considered by some to be more gentle than the prescription sleeping aids, as it eases one into a state of slumber by first quieting jangled nerves. *Note:* Siberian is one of the four main types of ginseng—Chinese, American and Tienchi are the other three.

JET LAG

■ Melatonin as First-Class Aid

Frequent flyers have, over the past several years, shared the good news about melatonin supplements: You can reduce jet lag by resetting your body clock, the circadian cycles that govern your sleep/wake cycles. In brief, melatonin is a naturally occurring hormone that may be involved in the aging process. We know it affects sleep cycles, but researchers suspect it may also affect length-of-life cycles.

For jet lag on trips that cross two or more time zones, proponents suggest taking up to 3 mg of melatonin before bedtime once you reach your destination. Keep taking the supplements for up to four nights, which should be sufficient to help you acclimate. Once you return home, you can help your internal clock readjust by taking up to 3 mg of melatonin again, before bedtime, until you're back on track.

Note: Melatonin should not be used regularly as a sleeping aid.

Preflight Preparation

Going overseas? Begin treating jet lag before you even get on the plane. For a few days before departure, drink little or no caffeinated or alcoholic beverages; they dehydrate the body. During the flight, drink at least one glass of water—no alcohol— every hour. Flying saps your body of water, which increases that sluggish feeling that frequently results from air travel.

■ Airplane Food

The in-air eating plan for long flights or the red-eye: Load up on carbohydrates—like pasta or bread with jam—at the beginning of the flight. These can help you relax and get some sleep. About an hour before landing, eat a protein-rich snack—peanut butter crackers or a small sandwich—to boost your energy.

■ Light Up Your Life

When you land early in the morning after an all-night flight, don't immediately crawl into bed with the shades drawn. Light helps to reset your body's clock and biological functions that are programmed to occur during a 24-hour period. A little dose of daylight might fool your system into thinking it's time to get up—when you're dying to get some sleep— and reduce the duration of jet-lag symptoms.

■ It Makes Scents

You can lull yourself to sleep or get a jump start on beating jet lag by using scents. Studies show that aromas directly affect the brain, and different odors have varying results. Bring along a favorite scent that you find soothing and relaxing, such as vanilla or lavender. Place a few drops of essential oil on a cotton ball and store in an old pill bottle. Take a few whiffs at the beginning of—and throughout—the flight to settle inner turbulence and let yourself get some rest. In preparation for landing, the stimulating aroma of pine, peppermint or a pungent citrus blend will clear your head and revive sleepy senses.

JOINT PAIN
See also **Arthritis,** page 30

GENERAL STIFFNESS AND SWELLING

■ Empathy from the Devil's Claw

One nonstandard way to combat general joint pain and stiffness is to take extract of devil's claw root, an anti-inflammatory herb that helps joints move together more freely after overuse or irritation. There are a number of commercial remedies available in health food or nutrition shops, usually prepared in 410-mg doses, which can be doubled on occasion when patients suffer more acute pain. In tincture form, one teaspoon taken twice a day can bring effective pain relief.

■ *The Buzz About Bee-Venom Therapy*

First the disclaimers: There have been no controlled scientific studies in the US to prove or disprove the curative powers of bee stings (though there have been a variety of studies in Europe). That said, it's worth looking at apitherapy, or bee-venom therapy, as an unconventional way to aid ailing joints. The theory has it—and this theory dates back millennia in Asia—that bee venom, properly applied, helps the body cure such conditions as arthritis, tendonitis and carpal tunnel syndrome.

The controlled, two- to six-sting sessions force the subjects' bodies to produce cortisol, an anti-inflammatory hormone, proponents say. The National Multiple Sclerosis Society has approved funds to research some of the claims of bee-venom practitioners. *Please note:* Although less than 1% of the population is allergic to bee stings, to these people a sting can be life-threatening.

For more information, contact The American Apitherapy Society, 1209 Post Rd., Scarsdale, NY 10583, 914-725-7944, www.apitherapy.org.

■ *Just the Flax*

Omega-3 oils found in fatty-type fish, such as salmon and mackerel, have been praised for protective cardiovascular benefits and anti-inflammatory actions that reduce joint pain. But vegetarians are not left out of the mix. Flaxseed oil may be an even better substitute. It is the richest vegetable source of omega-3. Herbalists recommend the Barlean's organic brand, which actually supplies other leading manufacturers. One to two tablespoons per day is the suggested dose, and it can be mixed in hot cereal or yogurt.

■ *Pull Down the Nightshades*

The research is not yet conclusive, but some studies indicate that you should avoid certain foods if you suffer from osteoarthritis. The so-called nightshade vegetables—tomatoes, potatoes, eggplants and peppers—contain high levels of alkaloids, which are thought to contribute to joint problems. An estimated two-thirds of individuals studied who avoided the nightshades reported some relief from joint pain.

Another possible trigger is aspartame, the artificial sweetener.

SWELLING, RECURRENT

■ *Embrace the Skin Compress*

It sure doesn't taste good going down, but castor oil doesn't have to be swallowed to be effective. Besides its well-known use as a laxative, castor oil could be used externally in a kitchen compress as a helpful overnight remedy for joint pain. Here's how it's done:

1 Start with two rectangles of flannel fabric (about the size of a magazine page) and fold them both in half.

2 Soak the fabric in castor oil for half an hour.

3 Wrap the compress around the joint, and cover it with a sheet of plastic wrap, securing everything with (loose) rubber bands.

By morning your joints will likely feel a lot better. Store the compress in a plastic bag, if you like, for reuse the next night, with a new dollop of oil on the cloth.

Note: Castor oil can, at times, aggravate rashes or other skin conditions.

KNEE PAIN

■ *Oddball Magnetic Therapy*

One uncommon way to relieve common complaints of knee pain and occasional creakiness is to use magnetic therapy. An alternative healer (and later you yourself) rolls small, squash-ball-size magnets (known as "Mag Boys") over the entire knee joint and the sides of the knee in a prescribed therapeutic pattern.

The "odd medicine"? Magnetic waves that are said to travel 17 inches reportedly stimulate joint fluids into a healing mode—a kind of non-hands-on massage. As a follow-up, magnetic "wraps" can be placed around the knees to help relax muscles. It might sound a bit odd, but in Japan, one in every eight families uses magnetic therapy of some sort, often as a preventive measure.

Check natural food stores and specialty back care stores for healing magnets. The Web site www.magneticideas.com sells inexpensive magnetic wraps for injury-prone parts of the body.

■ *A Quick, Seated Exercise*

Have a seat, and treat those tired, stiff knees. (Ironically, they may be stiff and tired from sitting for too long.)

1 While seated in a chair, extend your legs forward so that only the heels are in contact with the floor.

2 From this position, tighten the quadriceps muscles (the big muscles on the front of the thighs).

3 Hold the flex for a few seconds, then release and exhale fully.

Repeat four more times, to release a healthy amount of knee-joint lubrication, otherwise known as synovial fluid.

■ *Stronger Hamstrings Prevent Women's Knee Injuries*

As women have become more active in college, professional and amateur sports, they have also suffered an inordinate number of knee injuries compared with their male counterparts. Now University of Michigan research may indicate why this is so—women's knee joints are smaller than men's. If they perform the same movements as male athletes, there is

A Pilates Approach to Relieving Sore Knees

You've likely heard about runner's high, but not as many people know about runner's knee—even if they're suffering from it, and even if they're not a regular runner. Otherwise known as chondromalacia, the pain is usually described as a soreness or aching under or around the kneecap. It's aggravated by excessive walking or athletics, and often painkillers provide only temporary relief. Which is where the Pilates method comes in. This combination of rehabilitation, strength-building and postural exercise focuses first on the structural imbalance of the injured knee, before trying to build it back to its full strength.

The idea is to correct the imbalance in the joint, making sure the lateral (outer) and medial quadriceps muscles (the long muscles in the front of the thigh) share the load. Together, they enable the vulnerable knee joint to work through its entire, elongated range of motion. In chondromalacia, the joint is pulled to the side, which causes a crimped range of motion and eventually steady pain. The Pilates exercises are set up specifically to work on the joint's weakest link.

simply less room (in the knee) for a woman's anterior cruciate ligament (ACL) to "give" without tearing. That's the bad news.

The good news is that hamstring exercises, such as leg curls, can build the musculature around and behind the knee, protecting it from twists and turns during sports that women just didn't engage in (in droves) decades ago. Men typically ignore these exercises, but their anatomy apparently affords them a bit more cushion.

SHOULDER PROBLEMS

■ Expand Your Horizons

There's more than one way to unhunch stiff shoulders. Here's a yoga-based stretch that can be performed in an instant. It's called the chest expander.

1 While standing, bring your hands behind your back and clasp them together, interlocking the fingers, and letting the hands rest at the base of your spine.

2 Next, as you inhale (slowly, in always deliberate yoga time), raise your hands behind you as high as you can comfortably. Hold that position, feeling the stretch in the shoulder joints, for three full breaths. Then release.

Repeat a few times, but don't try to "climb" all the way up your back during the first few attempts at doing the chest expander. In time, you will limber up to it.

■ A Stress-Free, Simple Yoga Move

Even if you've never done a salute to the sun or any other yoga move, shoulder rotations are a quick and easy, yoga-based solution to stressed-out, sore and stiff shoulders (including those that have been hunched over keyboards for too many hours at a time).

1 Sit in a firm-backed chair, hands on knees.

2 Slowly rotate your shoulders forward in large circular motions making 5 to 10 (slow) circles.

3 Then, make backward circles the same size.

You should inhale as you raise the shoulders, and exhale (fully) as you lower them. This mini-yoga shoulder workout can be performed in three or four minutes.

KIDNEY STONES

■ Unlikely Use for Parsley

Unfortunately, kidney stones often don't announce themselves until they are large enough to cause irritation or obstruction in the urinary tract. Typically associated with diet, heredity and age, kidney stones are often made up of a hard accumulation of calcium and other materials. In addition to sometimes causing excruciating pain during urination, they can cause back pain, stomach pain, fever and nausea. Blood in the urine may also be present.

While strides have been made in standard treatment in recent years—relying less on surgery and more often on ultrasound and other means to "shatter" and flush the stones from the body—prevention is rarely discussed, at least before the first attack. One means of prevention, herbalists and some urologists say, is to eat parsley—up to six or more sprigs a day. It may not shrink kidney stones, but it can help prevent new ones from forming and retard the growth of those already formed. Plus, parsley is a natural diuretic, so it will help diminish any bloating.

Know Your Water

Doctors often advise people who have had kidney stones to make sure they drink lots of water. It's an easy way to keep the urinary system "lubricated," and anyone who's had a kidney stone will surely listen to advice on how to keep one from forming again. But recently, urologists have noticed a problem: Some patients who drink lots of water prefer mineral water—sparkling water—which gets its bubbles from limestone. Sure, it's natural, but the limestone deposits may have an unwanted effect. The calcium contained in some sparkling waters may be promoting the formation of future kidney stones. So stick to flat water, or drink seltzer or club soda which do not contain excess calcium.

LEG CRAMPS

■ Out on a Limb

Some people are bothered by mild cramping or a feeling of restlessness in the legs. Chinese doctors identify this condition as a disturbance or blockage in qi, which is the energy life force that acupuncture manipulates. The practitioners offer a subtle but effective maneuver to alleviate the cramping:

1 Lie down with legs and arms outstretched, keeping the heels apart and the toes touching one another.

2 Then extend the legs as far as possible maintaining toe-to-toe contact and heel separation.

Repeat this stretch 10 times, one to three times per day.

■ Root Cause—And Solution

If you frequently have leg cramps during the night, it is a good idea to have your physician check the circulation of your legs, especially if you are older. Depending on your doctor's advice, you may want to try ginkgo—an effective herb for what is known as "restless leg syndrome." It helps with circulation, though typically it takes a couple of months of treatment to begin working. Take two 40-mg tablets of standardized ginkgo extract three times per day.

■ Relief for Restless Leg Syndrome

Are restless legs and/or feet keeping you awake? Chinese herbalists suggest soaking your feet in a ginger bath before bed. Grate half a ginger root into a pot of steaming water. When it's cool enough, immerse your feet and soak for 10 minutes.

MOTION SICKNESS

See also **Nausea,** page 182; and **Vertigo,** page 219

■ Homeopathic Helper

If you're not a fan of Dramamine, but you are determined to get on that boat for the day, you might explore a homeopathic medicine that has the unfortunate name of nux vomica. A standard adult dosage, taken before you leave the dock, is three to five tablets of 24X (or 12C) strength. And by the way, the non-Latin name of nux vomica isn't much more appealing: Poison nut. Homeopaths, however, swear that it's both safe and effective in the appropriate dosages.

Substance-Free Remedies

Here's an instance where the mind can outsmart the body—rather quickly in fact: Refocusing the eyes. For those who suffer motion sickness and who can't or prefer not to take medication, doctors suggest that boat or train passengers focus their eyes on a small, stationary point on the horizon. At the same time, they should begin to breathe deeply, taking fresh air down in and to the bottom of the lungs.

■ *Why Some Passengers Prefer Ginger*

In ancient times, sailors from Asia used to chew ginger to prevent seasickness. Folklore, some might say. In modern times, as in the 1990s, a researcher at the American Phytotherapy Research Laboratory in Salt Lake City performed an experiment with 36 volunteers who tended to get motion sickness, giving them either ginger powder (940 mg) or Dramamine (100 mg) before setting them in motorized chairs that were designed to simulate choppy seas. (The subjects were instructed to stop the chair when they felt sick.) Those who took the ginger powder lasted some 57% longer than those who took the medication.

To keep things simple, try taking 1,000 mg of dried ginger 30 minutes before you set sail. Some unsteady sailors (safely) opt for a 2,000-mg dose. And bring along some gingerbread cookies and ginger ale for the ride.

■ *Ayurvedic Stomach Soother*

Ajuron, an Ayurvedic ginger compound, can alleviate the nausea and vomiting associated with motion sickness. Look for ready-made stomach remedies containing ajuron at your health food store (one is called Motion-Eze). The advantage of ajuron over other ginger remedies? You don't need to take as large a dose. Follow package instructions.

In a car, you can try reclining in your seat, slightly, with a pillow pressed behind your head and neck.

MUSCULAR CONCERNS

CRAMPS

■ *ER in A.D. 610*

The classic Chinese medical treatise by Chao Yuanfang, written more than 1,000 years ago, recommends immediately stretching out any cramped muscle. If necessary, you can press the leg or arm straight using a free hand. In any case, inhale deeply, then exhale forcefully in short, rapid bursts with the sound "heh, heh." Firmly tapping the affected area is also helpful.

Prolotherapy for Chronic Pain

When chronic pain from injuries refuses to respond to conventional therapies, a little-known injection treatment may offer real relief to many who have hurt for too long. It's called prolotherapy, and it delivers pain before it removes it. Some orthopaedic MDs use it; some osteopaths use it; so do some physiatrists (rehabilitation specialists).

In brief, the doctor injects an irritant (but safe) solution, such as glucose, directly into the area of the body where the pain is centered. Yes, it hurts at first. The theory is that the resulting inflammation helps collagen tissue to form, which then reduces pain as it strengthens the surrounding musculature. Over weeks, numerous patients say, the long-term benefits far outweigh the momentary injection pain.

Note: Anti-inflammatory drugs should not be taken during this therapy, as some inflammation is desired.

For information, call The American Association of Orthopaedic Medicine at 800-992-2063, or visit its Web site at www.aaomed.org.

■ Herbal Relaxant

Leg or back tied up in knots? Massaging a few drops of essential oil of Saint-John's-wort into the painful area can ease uncomfortable muscle cramps or spasms. Or swallow 15 to 20 drops of Saint-John's-wort tincture every few hours as needed. Saint-John's-wort is rich in hypericin, a chemical that affects mood and the nervous system.

■ A "Three-Course" Anticramp Menu

Ask anyone who suffers recurrent cramps, and they'll tell you, it's like being a prisoner—you feel locked up. Especially night cramps that sneak up on you in bed, when you think you can leave all your troubles behind. Here's a three-way plan to eat yourself to a cramp-free life (or at least less frequent spasms):

■ Increase your intake of vitamin D (from milk and fish, for example). Remember, though, your body can also produce vitamin D from sunlight.

■ Eat and drink more calcium-laden foods (milk products, dark leafy greens, tahini and other sesame products).

■ Try a daily vitamin E supplement of 300 to 400 IU—or add wheat germ, soybeans and parsley to your diet.

■ Wall Strrr...etch

Sometimes you don't have time to perform a self-massage or ask a running partner to knead your knotted calf muscle. Instead, head for the nearest wall, stand three feet or so away from it, facing it. Keeping your feet together, place your forearms (not hands!) flat on the wall and lean forward, with your heels flat on the ground. Try to feel the stretch in the back of the calves. To make the stretch more intense, increase your distance from the wall.

■ Preworkout Cramp Prevention

During or after exercise, a muscle cramp that sends you a sharp, painful warning is telling you there's too much lactic acid built up in there. One way of preventing these cramps that is too often overlooked is to stretch for 15 minutes before working out. Ever since sports medicine pros started spreading the word in the late 1980s that postworkout stretches are more important, millions of weekend athletes took that to mean, "Skip the preworkout stretch." Wrong. That's why cramps may seem to crop up so often—it's not (just) that you're getting older.

Note: Be sure to stretch the torso in addition to upper and lower body.

■ *Homeopathic Remedy to Loosen Muscle Knots*

Whether you're suffering from menstrual cramps or overdoing it in a weekend game of tennis, homeopaths suggest Mag Phos, a mineral and homeopathic remedy. It is believed to alleviate muscle spasms and cramps in a snap.

Dosage: 30C strength, as needed for pain relief.

MUSCLE PAIN

■ *Waves of Relief*

When muscles are sore and fatigued, and healing seems to be taking longer than usual, you might consider magnetic therapy—using small magnets to affect energy changes in the body. This has been shown to offer relief to many Japanese patients who have suffered repeated bouts of muscle pain and fatigue.

The common treatment consists of sleeping on a mattress with waferlike magnets stitched into the fabric. Or, flat, flexible shoe inserts with imbedded magnets can be worn throughout the day.

Healing magnets are available in some health food stores and back care specialty stores. Magnetic mattress pads can cost from $200 to more than $1,000. Try the Better Back Stores at 303-442-3998 or The Sharper Image catalog at 800-344-4444 or www.sharperimage.com for ordering information.

■ *Hot Shower/Cold Shower Relief*

Sore muscles, sore moves? Take a tip from the sports trainer's table and adapt it for use at home—an alternating hot-and-cold shower.

Start with hot water for two minutes; then change to cold, with sprays that focus primarily on the painful areas (but not exclusively on those areas). The theory is that the temperature swings force the blood vessels to open and close more frequently, which in turn forces lactic acid away from the muscle that hurts.

MUSCLE SPRAINS AND STRAINS

■ *RICE as in Ice*

For the garden-variety sprained ankle or wrist, the best remedy is still RICE—Rest, Ice, Compression, Elevation. This allows for proper healing more quickly. Sports team trainers prefer crushed ice for its ability to provide an even distribution of coldness to help reduce swelling. That's why an inexpensive bag of frozen peas is even better than a plastic bag filled with ice cubes the size of golf balls.

Intramuscular Stimulation (IMS) for Chronic Pain

Too much. Too often. That's what chronic sufferers say about their pain, whether it is from arthritis, fibromyalgia or migraine headaches. Of course, they want to get rid of the pain, but too often they can't—even with drugs or physical exercise. If other pain relief has failed, Intramuscular Stimulation (IMS) may help.

IMS, developed more than 20 years ago by Dr. C. Chan Gunn, a clinical professor at the University of Washington Pain Center, follows similar principles as traditional acupuncture, but it goes a step beyond. IMS uses acupuncture needles to target injured muscles which have shortened (tightened) due to distress. The stimulation of the needle causes deep muscle tissues to grasp the needle, in effect forcing the tightened muscles to release. The releasing of these formerly shortened muscles leads to pain relief.

IMS is particularly effective on pain without an apparent physical cause. Its effects increase with each subsequent treatment, until the pain is banished entirely. Some patients feel they require periodic maintenance treatments. The treatment is taught at many universities and pain centers around the world.

For more information about the method, visit the Institute for the Study and Treatment of Pain at www.istop.org.

■ Herbal Plaster Remedy

When people in Western societies hear the word plaster in regard to injury, they usually think cast or broken bone. There is another kind of medicinal plaster, however—made from herbs—that Chinese medicine practitioners often use to treat severe strains, sprains and sometimes fractures. Made with honeysuckle, Cape jasmine and a bundle of other assorted herbs, the so-called painkilling plaster is applied thickly, coating the entire afflicted joint. Relief is usually noticeable within a few hours. It is available in Chinatowns in larger cities.

■ Aromatherapy Aid

Sure, ice works well on a sprain, but after 15 minutes or so, the cold can be too much to take. (In rare instances, ice packs have caused frostbite.) For your next sprain, consider an alternative—a compress made with essential oils of sweet marjoram and rosemary. Herbalists say combining these oils can help reduce the inflammation and speed healing.

MUSCLE STIFFNESS

■ The Write Path

Chinese culture has provided a folk remedy for mild but chronic neck and shoulder pain for centuries. It instructs the afflicted person to "write" a Chinese character with his or her head. There are 14 movements (or strokes) that form the character for Phoenix, a mythical bird with great restorative powers. Here is how to trace the strokes:

1 Move the head down as if writing a J without too much hook on the tail.

2 Move the head horizontally from left to right, then do a similar backwards J.

3 Move the head four times as if writing a dash, comma, the number 1 and the number 7.

4 Move the head to write three dashes stacking on top of each other.

5 Move the head as if writing a 7 with the hook of a J.

6 Finish by moving the head to mark four successive periods.

■ *Relief for the Weekend Warrior*

It's not necessary to hobble around the office the day after a particularly active weekend. Instead of hitting the couch after your next long run or hike, seek out a cool-running stream or lake and wade up to your waist. The cold water will momentarily constrict the blood flow to your overworked limbs. When you get out, blood will rush back into your muscles, flushing away the lactic acid that causes pain the next day. The colder the temperature, the better, but go with what's comfortable. Likewise, though wading into cool water up to your waist is ideal, soaking just your feet offers benefits, too.

Electricity to Rescue Those Atrophied Muscles

There's more than one way to stimulate a painful muscle. As physical therapists and acupuncturists have found in recent years, muscle pain from underuse—due to injury or atrophy—responds well in many cases to electrotherapy, a way of juicing up "tired" musculature.

In brief, the therapist or acupuncturist uses a TENS machine (transcutaneous electric nerve stimulator) to dispense small pulses of electricity to various areas of the body. These pulses serve as wake-up calls to underused or stressed muscles and joints, and also help relieve pain. (Some theorize that the electricity works in much the same way as acupuncture.)

■ *Easy Aromatherapy Bath*

Far too often, folks who are sore and stiff from fatigue and sore muscles skip taking a soothing bath because "it takes too much time." So they hop in the shower, then proceed to extend the time they spend there, hoping the spray will hit each appendage and bring warm relief. Next thing they know, 15 minutes have passed. Why not plan a 20-minute, relaxing aromatherapy bath instead? After filling the tub with hot (not scalding) water, add eight or so drops of rosemary essential oil, diluted into a teaspoonful of witch hazel. Mix with your hand or your big toe and sink into it. After a short soak, although the relief may not steep all the way down into your bones, the essence and the warmth will make it feel as if it has.

NAILS

■ *Almond Oil or Jojoba Oil Buff*

One way to help fingernails that are brittle, dry and chipping is to apply almond oil or jojoba oil at the site of the frail nail. Dab on a good bit of oil while buffing, both morning and night, and look for results in six weeks.

Note: Brittle nails may indicate a nutritional deficiency.

■ *Herbs and Foods for Your Fingertips*

If your fingernails are bone dry and brittle, and you believe your diet is well balanced, you might try out one or all of the following herbs: Alfalfa, horsetail and parsley. Naturopaths might suggest eating more raw or steamed vegetables, including dandelion greens, seaweed, kale and asparagus.

■ *Moisturizing Manicure*

The aging process affects nails in the same way that it affects skin: Cellular turnover slows, and cells then shed in clumps. Possible results include nails that are weak or soft, or peel off in layers. Fortunately, you can reverse these symptoms with a little help from the cupboard.

Increase the flexibility of nails by coating the nail and cuticle every night with a thick, heavy emollient like Vaseline or Crisco.

Bonus: If you use an alphahydroxy acid, Retin-A or Renova on your face, rub a little bit into your nails for similar cell regeneration.

■ *Well-Oiled Nails*

Hands are often in and out of water, making nails brittle by robbing them of natural oils. Fighting back with serious moisturization can help. Try rubbing castor oil into nails and cuticles every night before bedtime to reduce cracking and brittleness.

If your nails grow slowly, try rubbing them with comfrey oil, from the leaf of the comfrey plant. A cell regenerator, it can help speed up the growth process giving you longer, stronger nails.

NAUSEA

See also **Motion Sickness**, *page 176*

■ *Acupressure Solution*

If you can monitor your pulse at the wrists, chances are you can give yourself some non-drug nausea relief through acupressure by stimulating a few nearby meridian points. (These are similar to the points probed by acupuncturists' needles.) Try this self-care treatment:

1 Raise your left arm slightly, fingers pointing upward.

2 Using your right hand, find the place in the center of the left forearm about three finger widths from the bottom of the wrist (where it flexes).

3 Use the thumb of the right hand to firmly press the flesh in that spot.

4 Hold until you feel relief, then repeat on the other arm.

If successful, you should start to feel relief within 10 to 15 minutes.

■ *Ginger for Upset Stomachs*

Ginger ale. Ginger tea. Candied ginger. Pick one for fast relief from nausea and an upset stomach. Ginger has been hailed for centuries as a digestive-disorder remedy. Choose from a slew of ginger treats to suit your taste. Twelve ounces of real ginger ale—not ginger-flavored soda—soothes upset stomachs. Chew on a hunk of candied ginger for sweet relief from nausea. Or sip a cup of ginger tea: Add a slice of fresh ginger to a cup of hot water. Let the brew steep for five minutes. Or take 1,250 to 1,500 mg of ginger capsules or tablets.

VOMITING

■ *Homeopathic Cure for Vomiting or Food Poisoning*

Nux vomica: It's an aptly named homeopathic remedy for nausea and vomiting. Homeopathy is based on the principle that just a minute amount of what causes an illness may, in fact, treat it. Nux vomica is made from a plant called poison nut, which is toxic in large doses. In infinitesimal or homeopathic doses, however, it is safe. Take this remedy for food poisoning or vomiting. Take one 6X tablet one to three times a day.

NECK PAIN

■ (Almost) Instant Shower Relief

A hot shower can be therapeutic as well as cleansing—if you know the right moves for your neck. Consider the "Head Rock," favored by chiropractors and others for relieving pain and releasing tension:

1 Begin by standing tall and erect under the spray of the shower, imagining your body is suspended by a cord running from the top of your head to a hook in the ceiling above you, elongating your spine. Drape a small towel along your shoulders to absorb the spray and distribute the heat along your neckline.

2 While keeping your head up and shoulders relaxed and (relatively) low, turn your head gently to the right as far as is comfortable.

3 Then, while turned to the max, lift your chin, slowly, until your eyes are staring at the imaginary hook in the ceiling.

4 After holding this position for a few seconds, lower your chin slowly until your eyes are staring down at your feet.

5 Gently raise your head back up to the starting position.

Repeat five times on the right side, then try the left side. The warmth will be with you.

NOSEBLEEDS

■ Acupressure Reduces Blood Flow

If the traditional way of stopping a nosebleed by applying pressure to the sides of your nose isn't working, think acupressure. For quick relief, press an index finger to the vein running under the gums between your two front teeth, while pinching your nostrils together. This will reduce the blood flowing to your head.

■ Bioflavonoids Prevent Nosebleeds

Bioflavonoids, including rutin and quercitin, help stabilize capillary walls, making them less likely to bleed. If you're prone to nosebleeds, try one of these supplements. And be sure to take the supplements with vitamin C to improve absorption.

■ Hydrate Nasal Membranes

If your nose is bleeding because your nasal membranes are dry, take one tablespoon of flaxseed oil daily and drink lots of water to improve hydration.

Note: Recurring nosebleeds may be a sign of a serious underlying problem, such as high blood pressure, a bleeding disorder or a tumor in the nose or sinuses—so be sure to check with your doctor.

■ How to Stop One...in a Pinch

When a bloody nose happens, follow the latest first-aid rules on how to stop it—safely.

1 First, although it may sound odd, blow your nose—gently—to remove any blood clots.

2 Next, sit upright (do not lie down) while pinching your nose closed halfway down the bridge, in the pliable spot where the bony septum stops and the bulb or tip begins, using your index and middle fingers (the thumb may apply too much pressure). Hold for five or so minutes which should slow the bleeding considerably or stop it.

Note: If the nosebleed was caused by a direct blow, pinch ever so gently at first.

If profuse bleeding continues, go to an emergency room at once to have the ruptured blood vessels checked or to see if your nose is broken.

OBESITY

■ Lifting Weight to Lose Weight

Sometimes you have to lift weight to lose it. Surprising findings have pointed to an apparently overlooked benefit of weight training: It helps curb cravings for fatty foods. Research at Brigham Young University showed that in a 12-week program of three-times-a-week weight lifting, subjects had voluntarily cut back their intake of fat by 30%, when compared with a group in the study that did stretching exercises instead of weight lifting. To get the full effects, the program should include about 10 exercises of 10 repetitions each, working up to four sets of these exercises after four to six weeks.

■ Safe, Mindful Appetite Suppressant

Some obese men and women snack and eat excessively out of anxiety, not hunger. (Many skinny folks do, too.) But a program at the famed Duke University weight-loss clinic has won praise for its two-part, drug-free approach to weight loss. Obese clients at the clinic first learn relaxation strategies, including deep breathing and visualization to quiet their minds. You could do the same in 5 to 10 minutes a day at home.

After clients master these relaxation techniques, the clinic then releases the scent of apricot oil every time they practice the technique, so that the scent and peaceful feelings become linked. When they leave the clinic, clients carry a vial of the oil with them—and take a sniff whenever anxiety sets in.

Note: You may do just as well with citrus-scented or other oils, as long as they don't promote hunger pangs.

■ Spicing Up a Weight-Loss Plan

Spice is nice. As an adjunct to structured weight-loss plans, try adding mustard seed, cayenne pepper or other fiery spices to your meals. There is evidence that the peppers speed metabolism, which makes your body burn more calories. Plus, you'll drink more water, which will help you feel sated faster so you'll eat less.

■ Sniffing Exercises to Slim Down

Based on recent research that showed inhaling food-based scents when hungry helped overweight people slim down, some doctors now advocate "sniffing" exercises to help control both appetite and weight. (It's a lot safer than some diet drugs.)

Here are two ways to smell more and eat less from the Smell & Taste Research and Treatment Foundation in Chicago:

1 Take time to smell your food before eating (inhale before each course, and again every five or so forkfuls—so the aromas reach the olfactory bulb).

2 Chew your food more thoroughly—this releases more aroma, especially if you're eating alone and can exhale slightly as you chew (no need to mind your manners), sending wafts of food scent toward your nostrils as you prepare to swallow.

These are not infallible ways to drop 20 pounds, but over the long term they may help you lose weight and keep it off.

■ Fill Up on Fiber

Forget diet pills and appetite suppressants. Psyllium, a seed high in fiber, helps create the sensation of fullness while slowing the digestion of carbohydrates. One teaspoon of powdered psyllium seed (found in health food stores) mixed into eight ounces of water may be consumed once a day. But use this remedy with caution: Too much psyllium can interfere with your digestive system.

■ Think—and See—Thin

Don't put fat pictures of yourself on the fridge as a reminder not to eat. And despite what you may have read, don't repeat "I'm such a pig, I can't eat another bite." According to modern obesity experts, those techniques are unsuccessful because they reinforce a negative body image. The best incentive to lose weight? Imagine yourself in the best shape you can be —in top physical form and emotionally healthy. These positive visualizations (along with other techniques) will help the body produce what you see in your mind's eye.

■ Mmmm...Chavanprash?

You'd kill for sugar—cookies, candy, anything. Well, don't despair. There is, finally, a healthful, sweet snack with which to indulge that sweet tooth: Chavanprash. What is it, you ask? A darkly colored, rich Ayurvedic jam made from Indian herbs like shatavari, gokshura and ash. People who love it actually suggest eating a spoonful straight from the jar when the sugar cravings strike. But some find it an acquired taste—definitely sweet but somewhat earthy. Try spreading it on whole-grain bread for a healthy snack. Available at some Asian-Indian markets or health food markets, or from the Ayurvedic suppliers like Maharishi Ayurveda at 800-345-8332.

Chromium to Quench Cravings

Too much is never enough. If that's your motto when it comes to sweets, consider chromium. This nutrient-mineral helps the body regulate sugar levels in the blood. Some nutritionists advocate taking 200 micrograms of chromium daily, as a way to help stop, or manage, the swings from sugar highs to energy lows.

A Different Type of Brew

Brewer's yeast, high in the B vitamins and chromium, can help curb sugar cravings naturally. You can find powdered brewer's yeast in most health food stores. Mix one tablespoon in one-half cup of warm water once a day to rein in longings for sweets. Some people enjoy the crunchy texture of a tablespoon of the powder sprinkled onto their salads. And don't worry: Brewer's yeast won't aggravate a preexisting condition like a yeast infection.

PERSPIRATION

Sage for Sweat Control

When a high-stress situation makes you sweat, kick back, relax and sip a tall, cool glass of sage tea. Sage helps regulate the flow of bodily fluids by affecting the sweat glands. Drink the tea iced or refrigerated, according to herbalists, to help slow an anxious, accelerated system.

Caution: Drinking the tea hot causes the sage to act as a diaphoretic, increasing perspiration. That might be a great way to treat a cold, but it isn't what you want when you're attempting to stay cool under pressure.

Homemade Antiperspirant

There are many natural antiperspirants on the market, but you can easily make your own. Alum (an aluminum compound sold in herb shops), or aluminum sulfate, tightens pores, so sweat can't escape. To create your own at home: Mix a heaping teaspoon of alum with one cup of water and one-quarter cup of alcohol. Store this mixture in an atomizer, and spray on when needed.

Caution: Some researchers believe long-term exposure to aluminum in foods, cookware and skin products can affect health adversely. Check with your doctor about the use of these forms of aluminum.

Surgical Solution to Excessive Sweat?

If you're chronically plagued by sweaty, clammy hands and skin, a relatively simple surgical procedure that's being studied may offer quick relief. Hyperhidrosis—the clinical term for excessive perspiration—is a malfunction of the sympathetic nervous system. Using long, thin needles charged with radio waves, a physician can zap nerve tissue near the shoulder blades that regulates the sweat glands. (Some doctors and dermatologists have begun using fiber-optic cables to view inside the body and sever certain sweat glands, and others administer Botox injections to deaden the sweat glands temporarily.)

POLYPS

BENIGN, COLON OR RECTAL

■ *Breakfast Table Treatment*

We've known for years that fiber is good for the digestive tract and for keeping cholesterol levels down, but recent findings suggest that wheat bran can go even further. Studies indicate that a daily bowl of wheat bran cereal reduces the level of potentially toxic substances in the intestines of patients who have colon polyps. While some polyps are completely harmless, some polyps can turn cancerous. The presence of certain types of polyps may indicate other lesions—even cancer—in different locations in the bowel.

It's too early to say whether wheat bran can actually prevent polyps from recurring, but the results so far are encouraging enough to suggest dietary changes among those who have family histories of colon cancer.

■ *Calcium for More than Strong Bones*

The anticancer properties of calcium have been building excitement in research circles since the late 1980s. Now, gastroenterologists recommend that patients who have colon polyps or other risk factors for colon cancer should consider getting some more calcium. Whether taken in the form of milk products, dark green leafy vegetables, sardines, salmon or supplements, calcium appears to reduce the development of polyps and cancerous growths.

Dosage: 1,000 to 2,000 mg of calcium daily in divided doses.

SEASONAL AFFECTIVE DISORDER (SAD)

■ *Sunny Side of the Season*

A lack of sunlight brings on a mild to moderate depression (with such symptoms as fatigue, loss of interest in normal activities, need to sleep more and cravings for sweets and starches) in some individuals during winter months, especially in northern locations. It is distinguished from clinical depression by its timing. The symptoms begin in late October and subside come March or April.

According to chronobiological research, getting outdoors during the winter months for 10 to 15 minutes between 6 A.M. and 8 A.M. is more effective in lifting a depressed mood than a similar excursion at noon. Also, scientists have discovered that allowing more light to enter your bedroom is helpful; closed eyelids still take in enough light to trigger the production of serotonin, the brain chemical that helps you feel more awake and less depressed.

■ *Light Therapy for Altering Mood*

It sounds very simple, but it works—light therapy for those afflicted with seasonal affective disorder, who fall into a sadness and funk each winter with the arrival of shortened days and longer nights. After taking a regular "dose" of bright light (ranging from 2,000 to 5,000 lux) from a light box for about one hour in the morning, sufferers report a distinct improvement in their moods.

Note that the bright light therapy of up to 5,000 lux is some 10 to 100 times stronger than standard office light, which typically ranges from 50 to 500 lux. Try using a light box for 30 minutes to two hours a day for about a week. A doctor can prescribe the light box; or you can contact the SunBox Company in Gaithersburg, MD, 800-548-3968, www.sunbox.com, for additional information. After about a week's worth of light exposure, you should start feeling chipper again.

■ An Herbal Pick-Me-Up

For those who suffer seasonal sadness almost on cue each winter, a natural antidepressant, Saint-John's-wort, may provide effective short-term relief. Already the most prescribed medication in Germany, where herbalism and homeopathy are far more common than in the US, Saint-John's-wort (hypericum) is widely felt to strengthen the nervous system.

Standard doses in prepackaged forms (available in most herbal and health food stores) work in many cases, but they may take three weeks or more to go into effect.

Caution: Do not use it in the case of severe depression. Instead, see a psychiatrist, psychologist or other mental health professional. And do not take Saint-John's-wort with conventional antidepressant drugs because they may interact.

SEXUAL CONCERNS

See also Sexual Matters, page 46

LOW LIBIDO

■ A Ginseng Way to Go

There are two different kinds of popular ginseng root (American and Oriental), plus myriad variations in quality and strength of formulation—which might explain why so many of the reports on herbal aphrodisiacs are sketchy. One of the reasons it is so difficult to measure herbal (and other) effects on sexuality is that sex is very subjective. What constitutes good, bad or so-so sex varies tremendously from person to person, and even day to day for the same person. Remembering that, and if you keep an open mind, there's a good chance you can increase your sexual energy with the aid of ginseng. Science has shown that ginseng increases a person's resistance to stress, and it affects hormone readings in both men and women. This indicates that age-old claims about ginseng's ability to boost sex drive may be valid.

Either purchase the prepackaged capsules or liquid tubes of ginseng, found in herb shops, natural food stores and now in many grocery stores, or prepare your own "love potion" as follows: Buy a few high-quality ginseng roots at a well-stocked herb shop, or at a Chinese grocery store if you live in a mid- to large-sized metropolitan area. Boil the roots in water to make a tea, and drink up.

The sexual charge from ginseng (in either form) may take from two weeks to two months to kick in.

Note: American ginseng may be labeled Panax quinquifolium, while Oriental ginseng may be labeled Panax ginseng.

Caution: People with high blood pressure are advised against taking ginseng, unless approved by a doctor.

Low Libido? Get a Checkup

If your sex drive has been in low gear for a few months, your troubles may be more serious than a sluggish libido. It could be a medical problem. Both thyroid conditions and diabetes affect hormonal balances within the body that can trigger a low libido. When the diseases are treated, an interest in sex normally returns. So, if your libido remains low, make an appointment with your doctor.

■ Take an Antidepressant Holiday

It's a catch-22. Lack of interest in sex may be a symptom of depression. Though antidepressants modulate your mood, they may dampen your libido as well as affect your ability to achieve orgasm.

Since some antidepressants don't take as long as others to enter—and exit—your system, psychiatrists may allow a patient to schedule time off from the medication. So, if antidepressants are at the root of your low libido, and your doctor approves, take a vacation (even if you don't leave the bedroom) and recharge your sex life.

"Coital Amnesia" Got You into Trouble?

Ever forget your lover's name? Blame it on neurons. If you've ever uttered the wrong name during sex, now you may be able to claim it's not really your fault.

A recent report in a leading journal of neurology stated that "transient global amnesia" may explain why people sometimes forget their lover's name during heated moments. It is not uncommon, the report adds, and may be linked with epilepsy or migraine headaches.

■ Sexercise

Feeling a little listless and uninterested in sex? Pick yourself up and walk —even run—around the block. What's the connection? Exercise raises the level of testosterone, a hormone that regulates sexual drive in both men and women. Try an exercise program for a few weeks and your low libido may get strengthened—along with your body.

■ Massage—A Slippery Solution

When sex has become a little too routine, one strategy is for partners to pay more attention to foreplay and touching, and less to sexual intercourse. As part of this strategy, couples may want to make the move to sensual massage and, in particular, to massage oil.

It's a trick long employed by sex therapists, but millions of couples still haven't tried it. Oil just makes it easier, more fun. Not body lotion, not moisturizing cream, but massage oil. It usually contains a subtle essence or two, like rosemary or lavender, and is made so as not to be easily absorbed by the skin. (That's why moisturizers don't kick up erotic effects as easily.)

After performing soothing neck and back massages on each other, partners can decide where to venture next.

Hint: Warm up a small dish of oil in the microwave just before starting the massage—for the heat and to release the essence. Or just rub some between your hands.

Psyched Out?

If a low libido has become a chronic problem, you might have a mental block against sex. Psychological issues—not necessarily related to depression—can interfere with emotional and physical desire. A sex therapist can help pinpoint the source of your anxiety, as well as outline a course of therapy. For a certified therapist near you, call the American Psychological Association, 800-964-2000, www.apa.org.

■ Sacred Sex Ritual

Sometimes when things aren't right in the bedroom, you've got to get out of the bedroom to fix them. Take a hint from Native American healers, who suggest using the wildness of nature to stir up libido in a flagging human body. They advise creating a kind of ritual of sacred sexuality, where you (and perhaps a partner) make a point of going outside and "connecting" with the earth.

There's no need to head for the mountains: Even a hike in a (relatively) remote urban space can be a way for you to connect—by walking on the earth's "skin." The point is to find a safe place, outdoors, where you feel no danger and can retreat to time and again, to make sensual connections—either in reality or in your mind. The flowers, trees, wind, water and assorted birds in these special places help make the experience sensual.

■ A Circular Exercise

If you feel inexplicably stuck in a sexual rut in an otherwise vibrant relationship, you might want to try a low-tech circle exercise. It involves pencil and paper instead of videos or gizmos, but sex therapists say it's surprisingly effective.

First, you and your partner draw three circles, separately, in which you list sexual behaviors that (1) you partake in and enjoy; (2) you don't perform but might wish to try sometime; and (3) you don't perform and have no interest in trying. If you'd like to, you can rate each list from 1 (low interest/enjoyment) to 5 (high interest/enjoyment).

Then comes the tough part: Exchange your lists at a prearranged time. After setting time aside for quiet contemplation, and after promising not to say, "That's disgusting," consider trading a few behaviors from each of your Circle 2s. Sex is often easier to write about than to talk about.

■ Healthful Hormone Hugs

Chances are you already know about endorphins and runner's high. But few people know about the potentially sex-enhancing hormone, oxytocin, which used to be thought of as a secondary hormone, limited mostly to female reproduction (childbirth) and breastfeeding. In recent years, it's been learned that the hormone is located in the brain and spinal cord of both men and women.

And now it appears that the hormone output can be triggered by sensual contact, such as holding, hugging and caressing. This contact need not be overtly sexual.

Researchers believe that the hormone can help stimulate feelings of intimacy and romance, which is a fine way to jump-start a stale

Watch Those Medications—Carefully

For many couples, it's tough enough to keep sex lively and fun over the years without battling unknown enemies of a healthy, vigorous sex life. In countless cases in recent years, women and men have complained to doctors and therapists about an unaccountable lack of desire for sex. Health professionals are now aware that many patients who take medication need to understand the possible side effects on their sex drive. At least five major classes of drugs can depress sexual desire markedly (in some people). They include:

- Ulcer and digestive drugs (including Tagamet and Zantac in large doses)

- Antianxiety drugs (including Valium and Xanax tranquilizers)

- Antidepressants (including tricyclics, Zoloft and Prozac)

- Diuretics (including Lasix and hydrochlorthiazide [HCTZ])

- Beta-blockers (including Tenormin and Inderal)

sex life. Holding and hugging, it turns out, may one day be prescribed by sex therapists as commonly as the classic foreplay exercises long espoused by Masters and Johnson.

SEXUALLY TRANSMITTED DISEASES (STDs)

■ Double-Protection Spermicide

People who used spermicide gels, foams and suppositories may have been gaining more benefit than just contraception. Nonoxynol 9, or N-9, in recent years was identified as a killer of the bacteria that cause chlamydia and gonorrhea as well as of sperm. It was even thought, perhaps, to kill HIV, the AIDS virus, but unfortunately that theory was recently disproven. Doctors recommend using N-9 in conjunction with condoms for the most powerful protection against STDs.

■ AIDS Prevention— A Milk-Based Future Spermicide?

There has been excitement in recent years over gains made with combination drug therapies (e.g., AZT, ddI and protease inhibitors) against AIDS. But a little-publicized study that used a natural-based product—whey from milk products—may soon get a lot more attention. When researchers at the New York Blood Center altered cells from bovine betalactoglobulin, which is found in whey, the cells prevented HIV (the virus that causes AIDS) from binding to human immune cells.

It should be pointed out that these were test-tube studies. It is not yet known whether this will be an effective treatment for humans. Still, the fact that a mild by-product had such an unusual effect on HIV/AIDS cells is a promising development that deserves close follow-up in the years to come.

SINUSITIS

■ Irrigation—A Different Kind of Nasal Spray

Sinusitis, the condition in which the nasal passages and hollow spaces in the skull become inflamed and/or infected, can be serious over time. Most cases, fortunately, are short-lived, albeit painful and more frustrating than a common cold. Symptoms include severe congestion, fever, cough and headaches. Following

diagnosis, the standard treatment for sinusitis is a 10- to 14-day course of antibiotics to cure the infection.

But there is another treatment—saline irrigation—that can relieve symptoms markedly and make the healing process a lot more pleasant. Naturopaths often prescribe this treatment.

1 In the morning, mix ¼ teaspoon of salt with 8 ounces of warm spring water and pour into a squirt bottle (a plastic bottle with a soft, narrow tip).

2 While leaning over a sink, squirt the saline solution into each nostril, alternating nostrils, until the bottle is empty.

3 Continue to lean over the sink as your nostrils drain.

You may already feel that the congestion has eased. Clean the bottle well before using it again.

Toe Massage for Relief

That cold that won't go away after two weeks of misery could be a sinus infection. Reflexologists work frequently to alleviate the drainage and congestion problems of sinusitis sufferers. These practitioners aggressively massage the toes, where they believe the sinuses' nerve endings reside. Gently pulling on each toe and then kneading all sides of the individual toes helps provide relief.

Another suggestion: Try eliminating dairy products from your diet for two months; some chronic sinus sufferers discover a significant decrease of symptoms.

Better Nose Blowing

They don't teach this in medical school—at least not yet—but allergists confirm that it's a wise and often-overlooked tip for sinusitis sufferers everywhere: Ease up when blowing your nose! Of course, this goes against many an afflicted person's instincts, but there is scientific reasoning for the allergists' advice.

Blowing your nose with too much force can send infected mucus back up into passages—which may trigger new rounds of infection and sniffling misery. And remember to keep your mouth open when blowing your nose.

SINUS PAIN

■ *Pungent Sinus Relief*

Sinus pain, due to pressure in the sinuses and caused by a buildup of thick mucus, can be relieved by draining the sinuses. Horseradish does just that by going right to the nose, making your eyes water and your nose run. Eat one-half teaspoonful of prepared horseradish by itself, or on a cracker.

■ *A Steamy Sinus Solution*

A steam inhalation of eucalyptus oil is easy to prepare and can help unclog sinuses. Simply place a pan of water on the stove and add one or two drops of eucalyptus oil (found in a health food or aromatherapy shop). Cover and bring the liquid to a boil. Remove the pot from the heat and let it sit for a few minutes.

Remove the lid. Using a towel, make a tent over your head and the pot. Inhale the steam.

SKIN CONDITIONS

See also **Skin Problems**, page 47

ACNE

■ Simple Herbal Astringent

You want to go easy on your face, even when treating acne. That's why herbalists and others often recommend a myrrh wash for acne prevention and treatment. All you need is a small, shallow dish of water and herbal myrrh tincture (from the health food store or herb shop). Add 20 to 30 drops of tincture, and mix. Dab a cotton swab in the dilution, then clean your face, using soft brush strokes, in the morning or evening.

New Prescription Lotion

Oil contributes to acne, but some lotions go overboard in their skin-drying effects. That's where sulfacetamide, or Klaron, comes into play in dermatology circles. It clears teenage and adult pimples by inhibiting the growth of acne-causing bacteria, and it doesn't dry the skin, according to doctors. While it doesn't claim overnight success, results are usually apparent within two weeks.

■ Tea Tree Oil for Adult Acne

Over-the-counter benzoyl peroxide formulations may dry out pimples, but many acne sufferers, especially adults, find the formulas too drying for sensitive skin. A drop of tea tree oil, with its antiseptic properties massaged into the blemish, is a potent but gentle alternative to commercial preparations. Look for 100% pure tea tree oil for the best results.

■ Fruitful Facial

Next time you have a nasty blemish, no need to go to the dermatologist. Go to the kitchen instead! An overnight "banana mask" will banish even the most stubborn blemish. The sugar and enzymes in the fruit will fight infection and draw out impurities. All you have to do is scrape the inside of a very ripe peel or mash up an overly ripe banana and apply to the affected area. Cover the banana mush with some surgical gauze and tape in place. In the morning, the dirt, oil and pus will be drawn to the surface. Gently wipe the area clean.

■ Sweet-Smelling Astringents

Oil elimination may not always be the best remedy for acne-prone skin. Essential oils of herbs, flowers and plants can be applied directly to a blemish to calm irritation and reduce redness without clogging pores. Try any of the following essential oils:

■ Geranium oil, which has properties similar to an astringent

■ Chamomile, containing azulene, an anti-inflammatory agent

■ Bergamot, an herb well known as having antiseptic properties

All are available at herb shops or large natural food stores.

◼ Cleaning Up Inside Out

Constipation and digestive ailments may contribute to a blotchy, blemish-prone complexion. Naturopaths and other holistic healers believe that poor elimination of body wastes and toxins in the normal fashion may cause them to build up and exit through the skin instead. It follows, then, that cleansing your colon may be the best way to clean up your skin. If you are troubled by frequent skin breakouts, add the following daily detox regimen to your diet for a month:

- Six barberry capsules

- Up to four cups of fennel tea (a digestive stimulant)

Your skin should be clear by the end of the month.

◼ Clear Mind, Clear Skin

Recent dermatological studies have shown that anxiety and stress can exacerbate skin conditions, including psoriasis, eczema and acne. In some cases, a visit to a trained mental health professional may help ease your acne problems by pinpointing, and eventually resolving, the sources of your anxiety. In addition, or if stress is mild and/or sporadic, you might try visualization techniques to ease your anxieties and improve your skin. Imagine yourself with a clear, bright complexion in a restful setting. Hold that thought.

◼ Food Allergies in Disguise?

Neither blackheads nor oil may be causing breakouts on your skin. Some alternative practitioners hypothesize that dairy products contribute to clogged up pores. Milk, cheese and other dairy foods tend to generate excess mucus in the body, which can hamper your circulatory system and irritate the skin. Reducing or eliminating dairy products from your diet for a few weeks is a way of testing to see whether they are contributing to your skin ailments.

◼ Wheat-Based Solution

Add azelaic acid to the arsenal of formulations—such as alphahydroxy (fruit acid-based) creams and vitamin A lotions—used to fight acne and improve your complexion. Azelaic acid, which is derived from wheat, helps to reduce inflammation, exfoliate and clear up acne-prone skin. See your dermatologist for a prescription cream containing this powerful, natural breakout solution.

◼ Purifying Tea

Brew up a pot of burdock-dandelion and red clover tea to offset acne outbreaks. Burdock, dandelion and red clover are thought to help purify the blood and detoxify the liver, which in turn affects the skin. To make your own tea:

1 Boil one chopped burdock root along with one chopped dandelion root in a pot of water for 20 minutes.

2 Remove from heat, and add a handful of red clover.

3 Cover and steep this mixture for 30 minutes, then run the brew through a sieve.

Drink a cup or two of tea every day for four or five days. Fresh roots ought to be available at a good herb shop. Off-season, dried roots and herbs will also work.

Laser Lessens Acne Scars

If acne scars are numerous or serious enough to damage your self-esteem, a relatively new treatment using a pulsed CO_2 laser is an option for many men and women who, years ago, would not have even considered a surgical solution. Shallow scars respond the most favorably to the laser "resurfacing," and research has recorded a reported 50% to 90% improvement in skin appearance.

The laser works by abrading and vaporizing the edges of a scar. When healed in one to two weeks' time, the scar looks noticeably smoother. (The amount of improvement is related to the depth of scarring and skin tone.) Depending on the extent of the treatment, procedures should cost from a few hundred dollars to less than $1,000. Be sure to find a dermatologist who has performed at least 50 such surgeries already.

■ Poison Ivy for Smooth Skin

Homeopathic acne treatments work from the inside out to clear up spotted skin. A favorite among homeopaths for treating an occasional blemish or breakout is rhus tox, derived from poison ivy. Based on the principle that a little of what causes symptoms can treat them, rhus tox helps get the redness and swelling out of bumps.

COMPLEXION CONCERNS

■ Strong, Quick Natural Cleanser

Here's a technique borrowed from professional facialists: As a way to loosen blackheads before cleansing, simply add one or two drops of eucalyptus oil to a bowl of hot (not scalding) water. Keeping your eyes closed (to avoid irritation), hold your face and head directly over the bowl so the heat rises up to and into your pores. Rinse after five minutes or so.

■ Egg Your Face—To Minimize Large Pores

Although you can't exactly open or close pores by applying an astringent, you can tighten up skin to temporarily reduce the appearance of your pores. A natural and effective pore minimizer can be made by mixing one organic fertilized egg with a few teaspoons of honey. Apply the sticky mixture to your face; let it work for 20 minutes. The treatment acts as an astringent, while the egg protein nourishes and tightens the skin.

■ Customized Steam Bath for Healthier Skin

The heat of steam will temporarily open pores and help release the built-up toxins. Customizing your steam bath with essential oils that suit your skin type makes the treatment benefits last longer.

■ For oily skin, add a few drops of cedarwood or lemongrass oil to a bowl of freshly boiled water.

■ If your skin is dry, steam with rosewood, lavender or rosemary essential oils.

Lower your face to the steam and cover your head and the bowl with a towel for 10 to 20 minutes.

Hint: Treat a pimple by applying lemongrass or cedarwood oil directly on the blemish.

■ Fruity Natural Toner

Keeping the skin's excess oil under control can prevent blemishes and blackheads. Try using a light carrier oil with astringent properties, like apricot or grape seed. Add to it a few drops of one of these other, mildly astringent essential oils: Bergamot, juniper or lavender. Apply this homemade astringent to your face after daily cleansing.

DRY FACIAL SKIN, UNEVEN TONE

■ Try a Fruit Peel Instead of a Chemical Peel

In Asian cultures, papaya isn't just for breakfast. In fact, one popular skin "moisturizer" is made from fresh papayas. Apply the flesh of the fruit directly to your face (keeping it away from the eyes) and leave on for about five minutes. Remove sooner if you feel any tingling or burning.

If you can't find the fruit in your produce store, you can purchase papaya pills from the heath food store. Crush a dozen or so pills, and mix with water to make a paste. The enzyme in the fruit is said to dissolve dead skin cells at the surface, providing a healthy, even-toned flush.

■ Simple, Self-Made Moisturizer

Rather than slathering the same $30-a-jar, "anti-aging" moisturizer on your face night after night, try using plant-based oils instead. They are said to penetrate the skin more easily than creams or lotions, which can clog pores.

One soothing homemade moisturizer is made by placing a drop of jojoba oil (it's light!)

into your palm, then adding a dollop of aloe vera gel. Mix with your finger, then apply the mixture to your face and at the hairline, keeping it away from the eyes. It's an inexpensive, light treat for your face!

■ Opportunity "Knox"

Of all the ways to help replenish moisture and oil to the skin, taking Knox® drinking gelatin is not the one you'd expect to hear from your doctor. But according to principles of Chinese medicine, gelatin is a blood tonic, and Knox will work just fine to plump up the skin and connective tissue (collagen).

■ The Soothing, Smoothing Delights of Carrot Seed Oil

In this era of costly bottles of elegant moisturizing lotion, unfortunately, essential-oil treatments for dry skin and minor rashes often get overlooked. Carrot seed oil, for one, contains vitamins A and beta-carotene, which help tone, smooth and moisturize the skin, as well as promote healing. Carrot seed oil can tame mild cases of dermatitis, and balance moisture in different parts of the body—when one region is too dry, another oily.

As for how much to use, the standard dilution guideline is 2% essential oil to 98% carrier oil, which may be cold-pressed sesame oil, grape seed oil or another oil of your choice. (Essential oils are almost always diluted, for safety.) Ask an aromatherapist at an herb shop to help match your skin type, preferences and carrier oil.

■ Oily Skin Needs Moisture, Too

You can moisturize oily skin without clogging pores and causing breakouts. Check your local health food store for squalene (derived from olive seeds) or hazelnut-based oils. Both are emollient enough to keep skin supple and young looking without clogging the pores. In fact, both have astringent properties as well. Add a few drops of lavender, sandalwood or tea tree oil for additional antiseptic benefits. If you have a combination of dry and oily skin, add roman chamomile to balance sebum oil production.

■ Just Add Crisco

Don't let the fact that it makes great pie crust fool you. Because it contains no preservatives, Crisco is an ideal moisturizer for many people who can't tolerate standard products. Slather it on: Its thick texture and fatty smoothness also make it ideal for tender skin right after laser surgery. But, not surprisingly, don't use it if your skin is oily or acne-prone.

■ Slough with Salt

Getting rid of the top layers of dead cells makes way for a fresher complexion. Mix a few tablespoons of a cold-pressed vegetable oil, like safflower or sunflower, with enough table salt to make up a gritty paste. If you like, add a few drops of your favorite essential oil.

In the shower, rub the paste in a circular motion on wet skin—on your face, hands, elbows—all over. Then rinse well.

Bonus: An oil mixture in the shower has the same moisturizing effect as a lotion.

Zapping Away Imperfections

More and more dermatologists and dermatological surgeons are using lasers to clear imperfections from patients' skin. Different kinds of lasers treat everything from spider veins to sun freckles, and laser centers are springing up to meet a growing demand for this procedure.

Most procedures are done on an outpatient basis. The length of the procedure varies. Getting rid of age spots on the back of your hand could take as little as five minutes. Usually, the pain of laser surgery for the skin is minimal—many patients liken it to that of a rubber band snapping the skin.

Keep in mind that after a laser treatment, your skin could look a lot worse before it looks better. Expect to wait several days before redness (and, in some cases, bruising) go away. Also, doctors who perform the procedure often urge candidates for laser surgery to inquire about the surgeon's training. For full skin resurfacing, the practitioner should have done at least 25 successful resurfacings.

Note: Using lasers on the legs (to treat stretch marks and spider veins) usually doesn't work as well as using it on the face (for age spots, freckling and discoloration).

DRY, CHAPPED SKIN

■ Avocado Salve

Avocados are for more than guacamole. Next time you're tossing the skins from the scooped-out fruit, consider using the hollowed-out peels as a skin conditioner and softener. Just sprinkle the almost-hollowed halves with a few drops of lemon juice and rub onto each elbow for 30 to 60 seconds. Sure, it will feel mushy at first; but isn't that a more pleasant sensation than dry scaly skin?

■ Don't Rinse to Prevent Dishpan Hands

It's not just for homemakers anymore. Often, those who work in professions that require them to handle chemicals or wash hands frequently will have dry, rough, raw hands. But this is a preventable condition.

Instead of washing, rub hands with Cetaphil nonsoap cleanser (available at drugstores). And don't rinse. Hands will get clean without being stripped of natural oils.

■ Soothe and Smooth Chapped Skin

Cold weather, wind and frequent exposure to water can leave skin raw, red and chapped. To soften and soothe the skin, add a few drops of sandalwood oil and vitamin E oil to an almond-base oil. Apply to hands, face or body once or twice a day, or as needed, and rub in well.

■ Salted Almond Oil Paste

Removing dead skin cells leaves skin looking younger and fresher, and can help speed up cell turnover. Try this grainy bath exfoliator: Mix a handful of sea salt with a few tablespoons of baking soda. Add enough almond oil to make a thick paste. In the bath or shower, rub this paste all over your body and rinse well.

ECZEMA

■ Skin-Cleansing Tea

Eczema, the irritating skin condition, shows up as red, itchy, scaly or bumpy patches. According to herbalists, the culprit that causes eczema may not be found on the skin but lies within the body. Red clover tea flushes eczema-causing irritants from the blood. Drink three to four cups of red clover tea a day for one month to cleanse the body of toxins, and your eczema may clear up as well.

Does Massage Help the Skin?

Perhaps it was coincidental, but when some eczema sufferers recently underwent massage therapy in addition to standard emollient or anti-inflammatory treatments, they reported less redness, scaling and hardness of the skin than did patients who underwent standard dermatological care.

Researchers have not yet been able to explain the surprising result, but because of the overwhelming frustration sufferers often experience, it is a safe, potentially helpful option to consider.

■ Gin Tonic

Here's an effective, herbal eczema remedy: A tincture of Oregon grape holly root. The secret ingredient is berberine, which soothes angry, red eczema patches.

To make the tincture: Put one teaspoon of chopped root (found in a well-stocked herbal store) in a pint of gin, and let the mixture sit for two weeks. Add a teaspoon of tincture to a mild, unscented lotion for a medicated skin cream. Apply the cream a few times a day to the affected area. (To simplify the treatment, you may be able to buy the tincture pre-made at herb shops.)

■ *Try an Oatmeal Bath*

Protein-rich and high in vitamin B, oatmeal is the natural choice when it comes to relieving the itching and dryness associated with rashes, eczema, stings and insect bites. While you can buy a prepackaged product in a drugstore, it is just as easy to make your own: In a blender or food processor, grind a cup of oatmeal (not the instant) into a powder. Stir the oatmeal into a warm bath—not hot, as it may exacerbate itching—and soak for 20 to 30 minutes.

Stress-Free Skin

According to some of the latest dermatological studies, stress can exacerbate skin conditions, including eczema. A visit to a psychotherapist or other counselor may help identify the source of stress that causes—or worsens—eczema patches. Also, try to relieve skin distress—and mental anxiety—using a relaxation technique: For about 10 minutes a day, close your eyes, take a deep breath and imagine a clear, itch-free complexion.

■ *Marigold Sun Tea*

This essential oil treatment is like sun tea for your skin. If you have dry skin or eczema, take a calendula (marigold) flower and chop it up. Add the flower pieces to one ounce of olive oil in a jelly jar, and steep in the sun (outside or on your windowsill) for three weeks. Then, strain the oil and discard the flowers.

Apply this fragrant oil straight to the skin after a bath. Add evening primrose oil, which is great for treating dry skin and eczema—or Saint-John's-wort oil, to soothe inflamed skin.

■ *Primrose Wildflower Offers Hope*

It's no secret to eczema sufferers that the condition is as stubborn as it can be unsightly. Over 8 to 12 weeks' time, the daily use of evening primrose oil capsules can reduce swelling, discoloration and itching. It is thought that the high concentration of essential fatty acids in the oil helps replace deficiencies often found in eczema patients.

The easiest way to take primrose is in capsules, which are widely available in herb shops and natural food stores. Follow package directions. Be sure to discuss the tablets with your dermatologist, too, especially if you are currently undergoing other types of treatment.

■ *Clean Clothes and Bare Fingernails*

Researchers at Battelle laboratories in Columbus, Ohio, recently determined that common household items such as new clothing, paints and finishes, wallpaper and fingernail polishes do emit substantial levels of formaldehyde. Long-term exposure to these toxic emissions may cause respiratory difficulty and eczema. In addition to avoiding acid-cured floor finishes (which ranked highest of non-pressed-wood products which are known for formaldehyde emissions), it would be wise to avoid using nail polish, and to wash all new clothing before wearing it. If it's impossible to avoid formaldehyde exposure, it's important to ensure good ventilation.

■ A Comfrey-Fresh Homemade Lotion

To ease the itching, swelling and redness often found about the knees, elbows and neck of eczema sufferers, try this homemade lotion: Mix a handful or two of fresh comfrey leaves (a common wild plant, or found in herb shops) with just enough distilled water to produce "juice" when blended. Then, strain the concoction into a cup. Apply freely. Since the lotion is only effective shortly after making it, use it right away and make it fresh, as needed.

■ Mineral Water Soothes

A very simple soother for red, itchy eczema patches is mineral water. Because soaps can be irritating, due to additives and perfumes, use plain mineral water to cleanse inflamed areas until the area is clear. If the case is serious, ask your dermatologist for a more potent cream or lotion to heal the skin problem.

HIVES

■ Red Clover Gets the Red Out

For relief from red, swollen hives, try treating them from the inside out. Red clover tea helps flush toxins out of the blood. The toxins may be escaping through the skin, resulting in hives and rashes. Drink three to four cups a day of red clover tea for a month to thoroughly rid your system of irritants.

MINOR INFLAMMATION

■ Flaxseed's Taming Effects

For a variety of skin disorders that cause reddening and inflammation, and that tend to reappear, flaxseed oil can help tame the outbreaks. Instead of applying flaxseed as a salve or balm, however, check with your naturopath or herbalist about taking it orally. One simple way to take it is to grind the seeds in a coffee grinder, then add a teaspoon or so to cereal or other breakfast foods daily.

■ Ginkgo Cleansers for Inflamed Skin

If it's time to treat your tired, itchy, inflamed skin right, but you don't have time for a bath, consider using some of the newer body cleansing products that have blended in extract of ginkgo. The theory is that ginkgo biloba increases oxygen delivery throughout the body, so it should apply to the exterior of the body—the skin—as well. Crabtree & Evelyn and Dr. D. Schwab, among other well-known manufacturers of skin care products, sell cleansers containing ginkgo.

POISON IVY, POISON OAK, POISON SUMAC

■ Prevent the Rash and Its Spread

Avoiding the outdoors and wearing long sleeves and long pants are not the only ways to prevent poison ivy, poison oak and poison sumac. Ivy Block, a lotion approved by the FDA, is the first preventive product of its kind on the market. Tested by forest rangers and others whose "offices" are in the wild, Ivy Block was discovered to be extremely effective. It works by binding to the oil from the poisonous leaves, which otherwise causes the characteristic itchy, blistering rashes.

■ Baking Soda Bath

You can't exactly undo poison ivy, but you can contain it after the fact. One of the best ways to do so is to hop in the tub as soon as you get home and soak in a baking soda-enriched bath. The action of the baking soda helps tone down the nastiness of the itch. Repeat the bath first thing in the morning.

■ Get into the Poison

Are you itching and uncomfortable from a bad case of poison ivy? How about a little more? A homeopathic remedy, derived from poison ivy, may cure your case. Take a 30C preparation of rhus tox three times a day until the rash, redness and irritation begin to clear.

Avoid Wrist and Neck Rash

Many women and men who break out after wearing jewelry or watches have an undiagnosed skin sensitivity to the metal nickel. Also present on belt buckles and blue-jeans rivets, nickel can cause discomfort wherever the metal contacts the skin. Allergy experts say some 6% of the US population has such a sensitivity: Tingling, redness, rash and itchiness typically follow.

The quick fix is to coat the offending piece with clear nail polish, which offers most people suitable short-term protection.

RASHES

■ Itching for Aromatherapy

If you suffer from an itchy, bothersome rash but don't want to smell like a commercial, mentholated, medicinal cream, try an essential oil mix instead. For sweet-smelling relief, massage into the skin one drop of lavender oil, a gentle first-aid remedy for rashes and stings. Or put a drop or two of chamomile oil, which contains the anti-inflammatory agent azulene, on the infected area.

■ Comfrey Comforts Irritated Skin

Comfrey is the comforting herbal remedy for inflamed, irritated rashes and related skin ailments. Packed with allantoin, a botanical chemical that has anti-inflammatory properties and helps to promote cell renewal, comfrey will reduce redness and speed healing. You can make your own herbal remedy using powdered comfrey root and water to form a paste.

Apply the paste to the infected area and cover with a bandage. Try this nightly, using fresh comfrey root, until the area heals. Found in most herb shops.

■ Calming Chamomile Cure

A chamomile compress is a calming cure for itchy, inflamed rashes. Chamomile contains azulene, an anti-inflammatory agent, for reducing the redness and swelling. To prepare this soothing compress:

1 Steep a few tablespoons of dried chamomile or dunk a tea bag into a cup or two of boiling water. Let the mixture cool.

2 Dip a cotton pad or small cloth into the brew.

3 Wash the rash with the cloth and repeat as often as needed.

You can refrigerate the mixture to use later that same day, but its potency wears off after about 24 hours.

RAZOR BUMPS

■ Avoid with Foam

Razor bumps on men's necks and women's legs or underarms are small, but painful and unsightly. With a little patience you can avoid them. After applying shaving cream, gel or foam, wait a full two minutes before you start shaving.

In the old days, a barber's steamed towel did the trick—which you can try in stubborn cases, before the lather goes on. Take another hint from the old-fashioned barber—use a sharp blade. It's well worth the extra dollars in new blades to have smoother, bump-free skin after a close shave.

ROSACEA

■ One Drug, Two Actions

The untimely flushing, redness and facial acne that occur with rosacea call for timely medical treatment. The sooner rosacea is treated, the better the results will be against this troubling skin condition. Often, the disorder seems to appear for no reason. It afflicts fair-skinned women the most and can have numerous triggers, including hot drinks, alcohol and even yogurt.

One successful treatment is the drug MetroGel, which has both anti-inflammatory and antibacterial properties. Often used for gynecological infections (under the brand name Flagyl), dermatologists

Which Witch Hazel Works Best?

Witch hazel, made from the leaves and bark of the *Hamamelis virginiana* plant, is commonly used as an astringent and antiseptic to soothe stings, cuts and rashes. However, in order to get the medicinal benefit (which comes from tannin), herbalists suggest making your own brew instead of dipping into commercial ones. Apparently, the antiseptic power of the drugstore brands comes from the high amount of alcohol they contain, not the tannin.

To make your own witch hazel, buy some witch hazel tincture (found in herb and health food stores) and dilute a few drops in two cups of distilled water or a mild lotion.

discovered its potential power more recently. As a gel it is best applied in a thin film over affected areas of the face twice daily, or as directed by a doctor.

SCARS

■ Erase with Vitamin E

Vitamin E can help erase the appearance of a scar—and keep one from forming altogether. But if you've sustained a large wound that required stitches, wait until they've been removed before you begin to massage the area with vitamin E. Otherwise, the vitamin E oil may soften the stitches before the wound has the chance to mend properly and may just increase the chances of the stitches breaking open. After these stitches dissolve or are removed, apply the contents of a 400-IU, vitamin-E oil capsule twice a day. Within six weeks you should see a change in skin texture and tone.

■ Essential Scar Healing

Herbal ingredients can help repair scars and broken capillaries, and have even been used to heal postoperative scars. Add 48 drops of either carrot seed oil or everlasting essential oil to four ounces of a carrier oil. Apply daily to affected area until damage fades.

WAXING IRRITATION

■ Oil Before and After

If the pain keeps you from having your legs waxed as often as you'd like, take a tip from the Aussies. Try using Australian tea tree oil on the legs (and bikini line) both before and after the procedure. It blunts the sting from having the hairs pulled right out of their follicles, and provides a soothing coating on the most sensitive skin.

SMOKING CESSATION PROBLEMS

■ Stay Off Cigarettes with Hypnosis

It's hypnosis—not hocus-pocus. Some practitioners believe that hypnosis offers a successful way to stop smoking. A trained practitioner helps you reach a relaxed state in which you can better identify the psychological need for cigarettes and helps you overcome the craving. Plus, the practitioner will provide relaxation techniques

---

Vitamin E Pre-Op

Going under the knife—or even the laser? Skin experts say that taking vitamin E daily before any surgical procedure may help your body mend before scars have a chance to form. According to holistic dermatologists, you must get started supplementing your diet with a 400-IU vitamin-E oil capsule at least a few months before the procedure in order to see results. *Special note:* Vitamin E acts as a blood thinner, so speak to your doctor before a surgical procedure if you plan to take—or have been taking—these supplements.

that you can use to reduce stress, instead of relying on a cigarette. You may need more than 10 or 15 sessions to stop smoking.

■ *Lung Power to Quit Smoking*

Although there is a diversity of smoking-cessation products on the market, from gum to nicotine patches, one inexpensive and uncommon technique may catch on in coming years: Breathwork. A short series of deep breathing sessions, based on meditation and yoga principles, can train smokers to replace cigarettes with reliance on their own lung power for stress relief and instant feelings of calm.

Obviously, it won't change a longtime smoker's habits overnight. But replacing a few cigarettes a day with "breathwork breaks" can help reverse the smoke cycle.

SNORING

■ *Weight Reduction Reduces the Snores*

If your incessant snoring keeps your loved one up at night, the problem may not be all in your head—and neck. It may be in your stomach. A recent well-designed study found that male subjects who lost about one pound a month over a six-month period cut their snores per hour nearly in half. Those who gained weight during the study snored even more than before the study began. So, if you're looking into special pillows or surgical options, it's worth considering the diet route first.

SORE THROAT

See also Common Cold, page 85, and Cough, page 92

■ *Marigold Tea Does the Trick*

You thought it was merely a tickle in your throat, but then it became scratchy. Then, downright painful with every swallow. Now, it's tea time: Steep one teaspoon of dried marigold (calendula) into a cup of boiling water, and drink while hot. Herb and tea shops will have freshly dried leaves. If you prefer, the tincture of the marigold flower can be used as a mouthwash or gargle to quash soreness and inflammation in the throat and mouth.

■ *Marjoram Gargle*

From easing common colds to relieving the pain of bronchitis, marjoram can be a powerful remedy for a basketful of respiratory symptoms. The herb is said to have antibacterial and painkilling properties, which is why it is often recommended for use in a gargle for acute, garden-variety sore throats. You'll note the pungent flavor—unfortunately, closer to oregano than cinnamon. But you'll probably appreciate the results.

Healing, the Chinese Medicine Way

When it comes to a lost voice or sore throat, Chinese healers probe deeper to look for the cause. Rather than viewing laryngitis or a sore throat as caused by a virus or bacteria in the throat, Chinese medical practitioners believe that heat and poison in the lungs are at fault. As a remedy, they recommend licorice, peppermint teas and, sometimes, honeysuckle flowers. The exact combination depends on your constitution and symptoms—and on the healer.

■ Essential Oil Gargle Help

You don't find many over-the-counter remedies for laryngitis that simultaneously soothe your throat and fight infection. That's why aromatherapists and naturopaths prefer to combine a few essential oils for an aromatherapy remedy. Try adding one drop each of lavender and sandalwood oils to four ounces of warm water for a basic gargle; add two drops of peppermint essential oil to the mix if you know an infection is at work.

■ Give Sore Throats the Slip

For minor sore throats and cough relief, slippery elm root is one of the all-time favorite herbal remedies. The root coats and protects inflamed, sensitive throats. Suck on slippery elm root lozenges, available at most health food stores. Or sip tea made from one teaspoon of powdered root (available in herb shops or larger health food stores), mixed with one cup of very hot water.

■ Sweet 'n' Spicy Remedy

The ultimate sore throat solution is sweet and spicy. *To prepare it:*

1 Mix one-eighth teaspoon of each of the following spices—clove powder, ginger powder and cayenne pepper—in eight ounces of hot water. (The fresher the spices or herbs, the better.)

2 Pour an ice cold glass of pineapple juice and set it aside.

3 Take a swig of the spicy mix and gargle.

4 Gargle with the pineapple juice.

The hot and cold fluids will feel soothing to a scratchy throat. And the spices and bromelain, an enzyme in the pineapple, will loosen and pull irritating mucus from the throat. Repeat three times a day.

■ *S'more Solutions*

Marshmallow root puts out the fire in red, raging throats. This herb (yes, it's the same one that is heavily doctored into candy) has anti-inflammatory properties for calming and coating tickly and tender tonsils. Put a teaspoon of powdered root into a teaspoon of honey, or add 10 drops of tincture into a cup of boiling water to make a tea. Herbalists recommend taking either the honey or tea mixture three times a day.

■ *Acid Wash*

It may not be the first sore throat remedy you think of, but if you're tired of commercial medicines (or out of them), apple cider vinegar kills infection and calms an inflamed sore throat. Gargle three times a day with one-half cup of vinegar when you have a scratchy or sore throat. Dilute the vinegar with a little water if you can't stand it straight.

Be advised: The stronger the solution, the better it will relieve the symptoms.

■ *A Spoonful of Honey*

Grandma was right, she just didn't know the whole story about honey as a cough and sore throat fighter. It melts in your mouth and has medicinal effects to boot. Astringent and antiseptic, honey will coat and clear sensitive throats. Take a teaspoon every few hours to relieve scratchiness, or stir a dollop into your favorite herbal tea.

SCALDED THROAT

■ *Condiment Coating*

If you sipped a hot drink too quickly, or tasted the soup too soon, take two teaspoons of olive oil for instant, soothing, safe relief. This is one of those times when you don't need to worry about counting the fat grams.

STRESS
See also **Anxiety**, page 60

■ *Stress-Busting Oil*

Natural fatty acids can be calming, but they don't get much credit for the medicinal role they play. It's time they did. Borage oil, made from borage plant seeds, contains an ample amount of gamma-linolenic acid (GLA), a fatty acid recently linked with a calming effect on research subjects who had reason to be riled. They took nine capsules a day for one month and were noticeably at ease when encountering a stressful event.

Multi-Symptom Stress Reliever

Stress. Anxiety. Tossing and turning from insomnia. A treatment for all three of these symptoms, which often accompany one another, is Ignatia. This homeopathic remedy will lift your spirits and help you sleep. Take a 30C preparation of Ignatia during the day to relieve tension, and another before you go to bed if you feel restless.

Stress-Taming Thoughts

One of the least-publicized effects of stress is on memory and the brain. Over years, excess cortisol hormone (a result of stress) can cause part of the brain that directs memory to deteriorate. As an antidote, try rethinking how you react to stress. You can't always control events, but you can control your reaction to them.

Two tricks for better mental health: Try reframing frustrations as "challenges." Ask yourself, when in a jam, "What is the best response I can make to the challenge?"

Similarly, instead of using a word like "worry," rephrase it in your mind—and speech—so that it is a calming word, such as "concern." Even words that have motivational overtones (e.g., "reassure" someone; "complete" tasks) can have calming effects.

Stress Relief

Scenic driving routes lower the stress of the drive. Commuting on a scenic route can be worthwhile even if it takes longer than the most direct route. Natural scenery calms anger and stress, making tension and aggressive driving less likely.

Hug Therapy

Hugs make life less stressful. A brief hug and 10 minutes of hand-holding with a romantic partner keep heart rate and blood pressure down in stressful situations.

A Passion for Anxiety

Although not yet common as a stress reliever in the US, passionflower extract is popular in Great Britain and throughout Europe as a general antidote to stress and stress-related conditions. The extract is said to help reduce blood pressure, have a slight tranquilizing effect and boost sleep time without your waking up groggy. Taking the extract in tea form is often helpful; twice a day, especially in the evening before bedtime, is most effective, herbalists say.

Calming Breathwork at Work

Take five, but in a new way. When work pressures are relentless, instead of going the espresso route, look within yourself for a short, calming respite that starts in the lungs. Instructors of meditation and, more recently, breathwork classes, can teach clients to change their poor breathing patterns—shallow breathing with pauses—into deep, fuller inhalations that calm the mind and promote better health.

Scientific research may be scarce, but take it from those who get to know their diaphragms: When you are extremely stressed, chances are your fight-or-flight response is on and you are breathing up in your chest (that is, shallow). Try simply placing one hand over your navel, the other hand on top of it, and notice whether your belly flattens as you exhale. Make a point of making it flatten…by continuing the exhale longer than you normally would. Then keep on breathing out. Feel the belly go in!

Taking a full, complete breath can teach you a lot about yourself. Try it a couple of times a day, even if you've never made it to yoga class. It's a quick, caffeine-free time-out from tension.

■ Natural, Sweet Method for Managing Severe Stress

Stress, in the medical sense, goes beyond merely feeling anxious. It involves longer-range physical effects, often contributing to allergies, depressed immunity, even depression. One way to combat recurrent stress is to take licorice root. It has been shown to relieve effects of stress by acting on the adrenal glands, which manufacture adrenaline and are at the core of the body's response to stress. Packaged capsules can be taken safely for two weeks at a time; because large doses can act as a laxative, follow package instructions.

■ Additional Benefit of Oats

You know all about the benefits of fiber in oats, but most people—doctors included—are not aware of the positive effects oats have on the nervous system, and on stress in general. Whether eaten in hot or cold cereal form (be wary of sugared varieties), oats can be a safe, long-term, food-based aid both to the nervous system and to help fight stress-related conditions.

Herbalists note that there is a connection between oats and the adrenal glands (which manufacture adrenaline) that eventually may affect the immune system. Under times of stress and fatigue, the adrenals need all the help they can get. Oatmeal is a too-often overlooked ally.

STROKE

MODERATE TO SEVERE

■ Aspirin as Emergency First Aid

For some time now, heart patients and those with high cholesterol have heard doctors' advice to take low doses of aspirin to help thin the blood and prevent clotting and heart attacks. Not receiving as much attention in the medical and consumer press is the idea that similar benefits may accrue to people at high risk for stroke.

When you consider that a stroke—a circulatory disorder of the brain caused by insufficient blood flow—is often caused by obstructions in arteries, it makes sense that a substance that thins the blood ever so slightly could prevent a frightening blockage of the brain's blood vessels much as it does with those of the heart. But, there is a theoretical risk that aspirin therapy could increase the chance of the less common form of stroke—hemorrhagic. In this type of stroke, thinning the blood could actually worsen the damage. Ask your doctor about the relative risk of preventive aspirin therapy and about dosage—every day or every other day, perhaps.

Prevent Stroke Side Effects

If you or someone you know suffers from a stroke, there's an emergency medication that may help prevent or minimize resulting disabilities, such as speech difficulties and paralysis. Tissue plasminogen activator (TPA), an anticoagulant, is a heart attack treatment that is now also used against strokes that occur as a result of a blood clot in the brain. To be effective, however, TPA must be taken within three hours of a stroke. Because some strokes are caused by a rupture of an artery in the brain and can actually be made worse by TPA, it is necessary to get a CT scan of the head or other tests to determine the cause of the stroke before instituting therapy.

Because time is of the essence, it's important to recognize the symptoms of a stroke. If you develop slurred speech; numbness or weakness in the lips, fingertips, face, arms or legs; loss of or blurred vision, call 911 or get to an emergency room immediately.

■ Oxygen Chamber May Help Recovery

Even moderate strokes can be dangerous and deadly. After all, they are a result of the brain being starved of oxygen temporarily. In recent years, however, tantalizing experiments have shown that stroke patients who are placed in hyperbaric oxygen chambers as soon as possible suffer less brain damage, on average, than those who don't have access to the egg-shaped, podlike chambers.

These pressurized oxygen tanks, long used to help deep-sea divers recover from the bends, have more recently been employed by professional sports teams to help their athletes recover more quickly from muscle bruising and sprains. Oxygen under pressure speeds the healing of certain tissues, and now emergency room doctors and cardiologists are finding that benefits accrue to stroke patients as well. In the future, the hyperbaric chambers may help prevent stroke-related paralysis, some experts assert.

For information, contact the American Heart Association at 800-242-8721, www.american heart.org.

SUNBURN

■ Aloe Alternatives

Once you're through feeling guilty for overdoing the sun or underdoing the SPF-25 sunscreen, hop in a cool shower or bath. Then, as an alternative to ever-popular aloe, consider applying lavender oil over the burned area. As an alternative to lavender, some health practitioners recommend using the contents of vitamin E gel caps, which you pierce with a needle and empty into a small container or large ladle or cooking spoon. Often, the vitamin E mixed into aloe creams is such a small dose that it just won't be as helpful.

■ A New Body Brew

A long day at the beach does not have to result in a sleepless night. To take the sting out of a sunburn, add a pot of strong, black tea to your bath water. For localized burns, soak a cotton cloth in the undiluted tea to make a poultice, and apply it to your skin throughout the day.

Better Sunscreen-Cover Tip

Here's a way to reduce frustration at the beach and to apply sunscreen like you mean it—completely covering the back. If you don't have a friend or partner handy, take a cotton rag (or T-shirt swatch), and rubber-band it around a back scratcher or ruler (preferably 18 inches long); then, apply SPF-15 (or higher) sunscreen. Liberally. Your back will thank you.

Note: To make it easier, you can order an applicator from a surgical supply store.

■ Stew the Burn

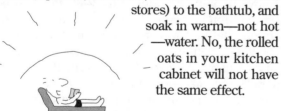

To add a thin, soothing layer of protection to sensitive sunburned skin, add two cups of colloidal (liquefied) oatmeal (available in natural food stores) to the bathtub, and soak in warm—not hot —water. No, the rolled oats in your kitchen cabinet will not have the same effect.

Using Aloe Effectively

While aloe vera is hailed elsewhere in these pages as a multifaceted healer, it is often misused by those who think they are right on track when it comes to treating sunburn or other mild burns. The problem is that applied by itself, aloe vera can be drying. That's why herbalists and aromatherapists often advise sunburned clients to mix aloe with vitamin E oil, the herb calendula or a few drops of Roman or German chamomile before applying to burned skin.

■ Three-in-One Cooling Salve

Because you can't always predict when you're going to get sunburned, it helps to know how to use things you've always got at home. For instance, if you apply witch hazel in a compress to sunburned areas, you'll get relief. But it will feel so much better, if you (or better yet, a partner) apply a kitchen salve made of witch hazel, a spoonful of honey and a beaten egg white. You don't want to rub anything on a sunburn; you want to smooth it on. That's where the honey and egg help out.

■ Cool as a Cucumber When Your Skin's in a Pickle

This is about as simple as you can get: When your sunburn rages, head to the fridge and grab a cucumber. After cutting it into thin, flexible disks, wipe the cool "medicinal" vegetable slices over the sensitive areas, using circular motions and a light touch. (This works especially well for people who don't appreciate the slithery-thick feel of aloe gel.) By the way, it's not just the coolness that helps: Cucumbers contain antiswelling compounds.

TEETH AND GUM CONDITIONS

See also **Bad Breath**, page 74

MINOR GUM INFECTION

■ Soothing Sesame Rinse

To prevent or alleviate gum disease, rinse your mouth with raw, cold-pressed sesame oil once a day. India's Ayurvedic healers often suggest swishing a splash of the oil around in your mouth first thing in the morning. Sesame oil is loaded with vitamin E, calcium, essential fatty acids and other minerals that will help nourish and heal the gums.

■ Vitamin E Rinse

If you suffer from the effects of gum disease, such as bleeding, irritation and swelling at the point where teeth meet the gums, try a vitamin E potion. Especially suited for those who have an aversion to sesame oil, a topical application of vitamin E oil can soothe and alleviate gum soreness in a matter of minutes.

Antibiotics Fight Gum Disease

Without proper care, your gums can become infected, inflamed, sore and prone to bleeding. What's the cause? Bacteria known as *P. gingivalis*. If a daily regimen of flossing and brushing doesn't seem to control the condition, speak to your dentist or physician about a short course of antibiotics that can successfully fight a severe condition.

■ Fruit-Based Rinse Helps Control Infection

One of the lesser-known remedies for minor mouth infections is a mouthwash, or rinse of sorts, made from peach pit tea. The fruit-based solution won't irritate the gums when they are infected; and apparently it helps control the spread. As a rinse, the tea is mild enough to use a few times each day.

Note: This is a palliative, not a cure. Infections should always be examined by a dentist.

■ Cold Relief for Ailing Teeth and Gums

Goldenseal, with natural antibiotic properties, can destroy bacteria plaguing teeth and gums. And echinacea will strengthen and stimulate the immune system so that the body may better fight off bacteria that can cause periodontal diseases—and even painful dental surgery. The prescription? One to three capsules of echinacea as soon as symptoms begin, and one-half to one teaspoon of goldenseal tincture twice a day.

An Uncommon Implant that May Catch On

The next time you go in for a cleaning, ask your dentist about the new "treated dental fiber" method of combating gumline infections. In brief, it works like this: After the hygienist has cleaned the teeth, the dentist places (or implants) a few thin medicated strips of flosslike fiber between irritated teeth and gums. The antibiotic-laced fiber should remain comfortably in place, even after brushing, for 48 to 72 hours. The theory is that the implant releases the medicine gradually, and in safe doses. And although the procedure may still be in experimental stages, it is worth following—or trying—because of its safety and the potential for savings and avoiding pain.

■ Try Tea Tree Oil for Tender Spots

With antiseptic properties, a dab of tea tree oil placed directly on the sore area in your mouth can help fight infection that's causing toothaches or red, inflamed gums. Apply tea tree oil once or twice a day until the area heals.

■ Natural Extract Soothes Teeth and Gums

Grapefruit seed extract, which has antibacterial properties, can kill microorganisms that may be eating away at the tooth and gums, causing painful infection. Using a cotton swab, dab a drop or two onto the infected area, two or three times a day as needed.

Be advised: This treatment is to hold you over only until you can get to the dentist for a more thorough treatment of a sore tooth.

■ Make a Medicated Mouthwash

Goldenseal tea, boasting natural antibiotic properties, is a soothing solution for infected gums. Brew a tea from a teaspoon of dried goldenseal and a cup of hot water. Strain and chill. Use as a mouth rinse three to four times a day until the area is healed. If your gums continue to bleed, remain red or swollen, see your dentist.

TOOTHACHE

■ Homeopathic Help for the Mouth

When you have a toothache that has more shooting than throbbing pain, the homeopathic remedy Coffea Cruda may provide lasting relief. The medicine is made from unroasted coffee beans (berries, technically). The remedy is also helpful to some for general headache pain.

Typical strength: 6C.

■ Oral Argument for Salt

There is almost nothing more distracting than a toothache. To nip one in the bud, at the first sign of pain, apply a pinch of salt to the affected area. It helps soothe your ache and calm down a sensitivity.

You can keep salting to relieve the pain, but remember that continuous discomfort is most likely an indication of an infection that needs attention from your dentist.

■ Chew on Cloves

Depending on the severity of tooth and gum pain, or how sensitive the tissue around the tooth happens to be, chewing whole cloves can reduce the pain and also act as an antiseptic. Purchase fresh cloves at an herb shop or well-stocked gourmet store. The good news is, you don't need to chew the cloves with the side of the mouth that's in pain.

Pain-Free Dentistry

Pain is no longer an excuse for avoiding having that cavity filled. Transcutaneous electrical nerve stimulation, otherwise known as TENS, uses electric impulses to block pain neurotransmitters. The dentist (and more are being trained in the technique each year) applies sensors to the area that's being worked on—and the patient doesn't feel a thing. If your dentist doesn't use TENS, dental schools in major cities may offer the technique—and you don't have to be treated by a student!

■ Spicy Sore Tooth Treatment

In a pinch, clove or allspice oil will tide you over until you can get to the dentist to fix a decayed, sore tooth. Although some naturopaths don't believe in using clove oil, proponents of aromatherapy believe it should not be overlooked as an effective painkiller.

Be careful: Dab the oil only on the tooth that's tender, and use just a touch. If you swallow a mouthful of clove oil, it could make you sick to your stomach. Look for clove and allspice oil at your local health food store.

■ New Use for Tea Bags

When you're hurting from a toothache and waiting for tomorrow's (or the next day's) dental appointment, try applying moistened comfrey tea bags directly on the afflicted tooth and gum. In many cases, the moist comfrey will reduce pain and swelling noticeably.

■ Icy Toothache Cure

Can't find a thing to calm a painful tooth? Try an ice cold compress...on your hand. That's right. The meaty part of your hand, between thumb and forefinger, is known as the "hoku point," which can be pressed to relieve a tension headache, for instance. But, say massage therapists, placing a cube of ice or compress on the hoku point can lessen the pain of a toothache. Hold the ice pack on the area for five minutes as is necessary throughout the day.

TOOTH AND GUM CARE

■ Massage Between Meals

We have long been told to brush between meals, but for those on the go who are caught without a toothbrush, a little preventive care for the gums can ease dental guilt while promoting gum health. Some dentists (and periodontists) now advise patients to massage the gums along the gumline with their fingertips daily.

You can also stimulate the gums gently with a toothpick, or a slim, metal-handled, rubber-tipped prod (like the one your dentist uses), just slightly under the gumline. Most chain drugstores now carry these dental tools, priced under $10.

Not the Same Needles

Instead of the prick of a needle filled with novocaine, holistic dentists are turning to acupuncture needles to relieve problems ranging from toothaches to jaw pain. According to acupuncture experts, energy imbalances throughout the body can cause dental difficulties. And, they add, problems in other parts of the body—the foot, for example—may be related to residual, or referred, pain in the mouth. Where are some of the acupuncture "hot spots" for the teeth? Energy meridians that run from the inner thigh up to the head.

Postsurgical Tea Bag

If you experience excessive bleeding after having a tooth pulled—or after an accident that knocks a tooth out—try the following kitchen remedy. Roll a tea bag into a tight cylinder and wedge it into the gap left by the absent tooth. The natural astringent properties of the tea work to coagulate the blood. Saliva only adds to the healing process of the mucosa, dentists and MDs report.

■ Brush Up on Your Technique

Are you overbrushing? Although a thorough cleansing helps to rid teeth of bacteria, plaque and tartar, scrubbing can, at times, do more harm than good. According to many dentists, overbrushing can erode tooth enamel and result in sensitive teeth. It can also cause gums to recede prematurely. Be gentle—use sweeping motions with soft bristles—and, if you need to brush up on good oral hygiene, ask your dentist or hygienist for specific pointers. *Here's another:* Change your toothbrush every month! It's an inexpensive way to commit to better dental health.

■ Sugar-Free Teeth and Gums

If your teeth and gums don't look their healthy best, revisit some advice from your parents: Don't eat so many sweets. Or at least plan when you eat them: The evening hours (before bedtime brushing) are best, because over time, sugar raises acidity levels in the mouth, causing tooth decay. And after a midday sweet snack, brush your teeth as soon as possible so acid levels don't have a chance to soar. Even rinsing with water immediately after eating can help.

■ Herbal Mouth Rinse

Minty, it's not. But goldenseal, an herb that has disinfectant as well as immune-enhancing properties, makes a great tooth and gum rinse, according to natural healing practitioners. Here's the formula: Mix one cup of warm water, one-quarter teaspoon salt, and one-half teaspoon goldenseal powder (the amount in one store-bought capsule). Rinse twice a day.

YELLOWING TEETH

■ Naturally Shiny

Look to the sea to soon see whiter teeth in the mirror. You can make a quick, at-home whitening paste using sea salt, lemon juice and baking soda. *Here's how:* In a shallow cup filled with equal parts sea salt and baking soda, pour in lemon juice. Dip your toothbrush in the paste. Then, concentrating on the face of the teeth and avoiding the gums, use gentle downward strokes with this once-a-day paste. Rinse well. Not only will your teeth look brighter, they'll feel fresher, too.

Treat Your Teeth to High Tea

Many types of tea are potent in fluoride and have antibacterial properties, which makes tea the perfect drink for the pearly whites. While both black and green tea boast these properties, black tea can stain teeth.

TEMPOROMANDIBULAR JOINT SYNDROME (TMJ)

■ Fix Your Fillings

It's time for a checkup if you've got jaw pain or TMJ. Check not just your teeth—but also your fillings. A raised or improperly placed filling can slowly, methodically, realign your bite, putting stress on your jaw—and even neck and shoulders. A dentist can identify faulty fillings that may be the root of your problems; it's worth asking about before you sign up for more extensive TMJ treatment.

The Biofeedback Approach to Fighting TMJ

People who suffer from temporomandibular joint syndrome (TMJ) are stressed, even if they may not be aware of it. The mysterious malady is often caused by nighttime teeth-grinding or other habits that force the masseter muscle and joints of the jaws to become inflamed, painful and misaligned.

Biofeedback training, in addition to or in place of dental methods (e.g., bedtime bite plates), can unlock much of the hidden stress that causes TMJ, its related headaches and chronic pain. In brief, biofeedback technicians (who might be dentists or psychologists) measure the tension in the jaws' masseter muscles, or in other parts of the body, then work with patients to learn to lower the tension. In time, usually within 8 to 10 sessions, patients are able to get the same results at home, without the aid of the therapist.

Cranialosteopathy Can Eliminate Grinding

Cranialosteopathy, a therapeutic massage technique that works to realign the bones of the skull, jaw and face, relieves tension and pressure that at times contribute to teeth grinding, jaw pain and temporomandibular joint syndrome. Depending on the severity of the condition, you may need to seek treatment from a trained cranialosteopath at least once a week until your condition begins to improve.

■ Acupressure Relief for TMJ Pain

If you can't get to the acupuncturist, there's a do-it-yourself acupressure technique that offers temporary relief from the pain and pressure associated with TMJ. Use your forefinger to find the point at the base of your jaw where the muscles protrude when you bite down hard. Apply pressure to those points on both sides of your jaw for about a minute. Repeat up to three times a day.

TEETH GRINDING AND TMJ

■ Stop the Nightly Grind—Inexpensively

If you suffer from bruxism, or nightly gnashing of your teeth while you sleep, you need to be treated for the condition. And most often, dentists will recommend a pricey, customized bite plate.

Here's a money-saving tip from athletic trainers of pro hockey teams: Buy a sports mouth guard and mold it to your teeth yourself. It may not be dentist certified, but many sports mouth guards are inexpensive (under $15) and have incredible staying power.

According to package directions, the mouth guard is boiled until soft, then cooled a bit before you bite down into it. Minutes later, you have a mouth guard that does double duty: It protects your bite and saves you several hundred dollars.

THYROID CONDITIONS

HYPERTHYROIDISM

■ *Chinese Medicine Tames Hormones*

You do not notice it much, until it is out of whack. But when the thyroid gland is hyperactive, so much can go wrong: Increased appetite, sweating, weight loss, even tremors. That is because the thyroid hormone is powerful. It regulates metabolism.

In addition to doctors' or endocrinologists' standard counsel, you might want to explore a two-pronged Chinese medicine remedy: Acupuncture and/or a dietary regimen with plenty of seaweed and other sea plants and sea vegetables (all iodine rich). In the moderate cases of hyperthyroidism, these may do enough to control the condition to enable you to avoid surgery or prescription drugs.

HYPOTHYROIDISM

■ *Natural Solutions*

If the thyroid gland becomes underactive, called hypothyroidism, one of the first things patients notice is lethargy. The next is weight gain. That's because the thyroid is underperforming, and metabolism is running sluggish.

Helpful natural solutions include:

■ Eating iodine-rich foods such as seafood, shellfish, seaweed and other sea vegetables.

■ Taking supplements of tyrosine, an amino acid (suggested dose: 250 mg a day).

■ Increased intake of foods rich in vitamins A, C, E, niacin and zinc.

■ Avoid peanuts, cabbage, soybeans and mustard—all foods that inhibit the body's use of iodine.

Easy, At-Home Diagnosis

If you're inexplicably extremely sluggish and wondering if your thyroid is to blame, you may be able to help diagnose hypothyroidism. Take your temperature at the same time for three consecutive mornings. If it reads below 97.6° each of those days, contact your doctor. Hypothyroidism could be to blame.

Note: The absence of a low temperature does not rule out hypothyroidism. See your doctor if you're experiencing unusual symptoms.

TONSILLITIS

■ *Herbal Remedies for Swollen Tonsils*

As the tonsils are part of the immune and lymph system, herbal remedies can help to decrease the frequency of tonsil infections. Besides echinacea, a basic immune strengthener, tonsil sufferers might try myrrh, Oregon grape and poke root (available at herb shops and natural food stores)—all of which naturopaths believe have antimicrobial properties and serve as tonics for the lymphatic system.

ULCERS

■ *Helpful Root for Occasional Pain*

Now that gastroenterologists realize that many ulcers are caused by bacteria, a number of holistic-oriented doctors have directed ulcer patients to use licorice root to help quell the associated pain and digestive unease. Licorice root (but not the sweetened candy—rarely made from the root) contains active substances that attack the bacteria that cause ulcers.

As an adjunct to treatment, or if you can't take antibiotics, stir licorice root into hot tea to get the medicinal effect. Or add licorice root extract to hot drinks, in part as herbal medicine, in part as a sweetener.

■ *A Carrot a Day*

According to top nutritionists, a daily six- or eight-ounce glass of fresh carrot juice—rich in beta-carotene—may soothe an ulcerated stomach lining. (Check with your physician for a diagnosis, though, before taking carrot juice as the sole treatment for a stomach discomfort that might indicate an ulcer.) Other complementary therapies, along with a short course of antibiotics, may be necessary to successfully treat a persistent stomach ulcer.

■ *Go Green*

It's the natural tonic for an ulcer: Chlorophyll, the green photosynthetic matter that gives plants their color. Some alternative practitioners believe chlorophyll is very effective in cleansing the intestinal lining and reducing irritation associated with a pre-ulcerous or ulcerous condition. Take a teaspoon of liquid chlorophyll—available at most health food stores—every day. Or try a daily eight-ounce glass of "green" juices that are high in chlorophyll, such as parsley or spinach juice.

Did You Know...

The latest studies indicate that a bacterial infection—not just excess acid as previously thought—is at the root of many stomach and duodenal ulcers. Specifically, the stubborn *helicobacter pylori* causes infection of the intestinal lining. A short course of antibiotics often rids the body of the bacteria and offers long-term relief from ulcers. Check with your doctor to see if this treatment is appropriate for you.

■ *Watch What You Eat*

If you suffer from a pre-ulcerous or ulcerous condition, you can avoid aggravating the area further by shunning irritating foods. What's on the forbidden food list? Besides the regulars, such as highly acidic fruits and spicy items, the list includes rough or scratchy snacks—for example, nuts and popcorn, which can scrape the intestinal lining.

■ *Aloe Vera Inside Out*

Aloe isn't just for sunburn anymore. Aloe vera gel is a time-honored favorite for taking the sting out of burns, cuts and scrapes. According to the experts, it's true for tissues inside as well as outside the body. And it's safe. Taken internally, aloe vera gel will soothe sore, ulcerated spots in the stomach. Take one teaspoonful twice a day. Look for aloe vera juice in the health food store. (Follow dosage directions carefully.)

■ Cabbage Fix

Whether you prefer cole slaw or a cup of juice, cabbage is a common kitchen fix for an ulcerated stomach lining. Why? It's rich in vitamins and amino acids that help heal the mucosa that lines the intestines. Eat a wedge of raw cabbage daily, drink an eight-ounce glass of cabbage juice, or add about one cup of cabbage slices to a tossed salad. Make it a habit. No matter which suits your taste, be sure the cabbage is fresh. That's the key to getting good results with this crunchy therapy.

■ Try an Anti-Ulcer Tea

Only recently have doctors agreed that a bacterial infection causes many more ulcers than stress does. Yet for decades, herbalists have recommended calendula tea to ulcer sufferers because of its immune-stimulating properties. (They didn't know calendula's antibacterial properties would come in handy as well.)

Four or five teaspoons of calendula flowers, brewed in a lemon-spiced tea, can often calm burning ulcer symptoms in a matter of minutes. Calendula, also known as pot marigold, is also available in tincture form.

■ Natural Antibiotics Soothe Ulcers

Dioxychlor, a hydrogen-peroxide-like liquid with antibiotic properties, can fight the bacteria that cause stomach and duodenal ulcers. The tonic is taken orally—a teaspoonful every day. Look for dioxychlor at your health food store or herbal pharmacy.

Make sure to get a diagnosis before beginning this antibiotic course to be sure that an infection is the cause of your ulcer.

VARICOSE VEINS

■ Two-Step Spider Vein Prevention

Sometimes ginkgo can't go it alone. When it comes to preventing spider veins and larger varicose veins—which form after vein walls become weak and expand under pressure—herbalists and naturopaths recommend taking a combination of ginkgo biloba and gotu kola extracts. Together, these herbs help strengthen circulation, which over time should reduce the formation of new varicose veins—during pregnancies and at other times in your life. Exercise helps too.

Suggested dose: One dropperful of a ginkgo-gotu kola extract three times a day. An herb shop can mix it for you, or you can combine them into a dropper bottle yourself. Allow a few months to gauge results.

■ Horse Chestnut Helps Drain Veins

Germany's version of the Food and Drug Administration, known as Commission E, has gone on record supporting the use of horse chestnut extract to treat varicose veins. It's believed that horse chestnut works by strengthening the cells of the capillaries.

Horse chestnut extracts, at least standardized ones, are not yet widely available in North America. And the herb is too strong to leave the dosage to chance. To find the standardized extract, try a specialty herb shop, or remember to stop off at a pharmacy on your next jaunt to Europe.

Reduce Salt for Slender Legs

Are you suffering from pain and swelling along with unsightly varicose veins? There's a simple dietary measure that may control the symptoms associated with blue, bulging veins: Stay away from the salt shaker when you sit down to a meal. Salt increases puffiness and swelling in the legs, which in turn causes tenderness.

■ Boost Your Circulatory System

Do you have aches and pains from varicose veins? A homeopathic circulatory medicine helps push blood that has pooled in defective varicose veins, thus reducing swelling and tenderness. The prescription? A 30C potency of pulsatilla, otherwise known as windflower, up to three times a day, until symptoms disappear.

■ "C" Results

Vitamin C strengthens skin and underlying vessels by increasing collagen production. Some alternative practitioners believe high doses of vitamin C every day can fortify the weakened walls of varicose veins.

Warning: Check with a doctor to identify a safe dosage.

■ Better Bowel Behavior Can Make a Difference

Varicose veins are damaged blood vessels that cannot push blood from the legs back up to the heart. What exacerbates the condition? Constipation. This condition causes strain and pressure on the lower half of the body, which may result in further stress on vessels in the legs. In related fashion, when the colon is full, it presses on abdominal veins, which impedes blood flow from the leg veins.

A high-fiber diet can relieve your constipation and give your varicose veins a break.

■ Lose Weight and Erase Those Veins

While it may not be a quick fix, losing weight will relieve pain, swelling and other symptoms associated with varicose veins. Extra weight puts pressure on your circulatory system and causes or exacerbates varicose veins. A consultation with your physician can put you on a healthy course of diet and exercise that will take off the pounds.

VERTIGO
See also **Motion Sickness,** page 176

■ A Settling Herb

When you feel as if you're spinning out of control, ginger brings you back to earth. Sit down and sip a cup of ginger tea in order to lessen the symptoms of vertigo.

The recipe: Stir a teaspoon of ground or crushed ginger into a cup of warm water to make a spicy tea. Drink one cup every day in order to get a handle on the disorder.

Get Your Balance Back with Ginkgo

Vertigo, caused by a dysfunction of the inner ear, results in sensations of dizziness or spinning around. Fortunately, there's a powerful natural remedy that can restore a sense of balance and calm: Ginkgo biloba. Take 120 mg every day in order to keep symptoms under control. Look for capsules in your health food store or pharmacy.

Ginkgo for Better Blood Flow

Of all the medicinal uses that have been cataloged for the ancient ginkgo tree, the one that mystifies herbalists even today is that it can cure dizziness in a matter of minutes. Theory has it that because ginkgo biloba helps speed blood flow throughout the body, the brain gets a fresh blood boost as well. This would, again in theory, nourish the parts of the brain that are temporarily short on oxygen. Packaged formulations are simplest to take—and to find.

Strawberry Solution

When someone feels dizzy, but not to the point of feeling faint, it may be related to the body's energy flow—something that often goes ignored. Not so in Chinese medical circles, where the concept of yin and yang energy is a basis for treating ailments both common and uncommon. And strawberries, say Chinese medicine practitioners, can help relieve or head off dizzy spells. This is because of the fruit's impact on the body's energy flow, they believe, not necessarily because of the vitamins or complex carbohydrates the fruit has to offer.

If yin can be thought of as oil that keeps a car engine cool and running smoothly, yang can be thought of as the gas that fuels the engine. Strawberries, it is said, address the body's shortage of yang energy. So, pack a quart (carefully) of strawberries in your backpack before hiking up to high altitudes.

Chinese Medicine to Relieve Dizziness

Time to spell those dizzy spells. If you or a family member is prone to dizziness and your doctor has not yet found the right treatment, a Chinese patent remedy could help you in the meantime.

Blood Pressure Repressing tablets, which combine the herbs coptis and scutellaria, are believed to be strong enough to remedy dizzy spells without causing the side effects of stronger drugs. The tablets can be obtained at Chinese medicine pharmacies in most major cities. Check with your physician before you begin treatment.

WARTS

■ Herbal Wart Treatment

For a natural wart remedy, naturopathic physicians recommend a cream containing the herb thuja. Apply the cream to the affected area twice a day.

Be forewarned: You will need to treat the wart religiously for up to six months. Warts, caused by a virus, have "roots" beneath the surface of the skin. Unless you kill the virus beneath the skin, the wart may reappear.

■ Ulcer Drugs Cure Warts

According to recent studies, acid-blocking drugs (specifically Tagamet), typically used to treat ulcers, have proven to thwart the virus that causes warts. Although you can get acid-blocking drugs over the counter, it's best to speak to your doctor or dermatologist before you begin any self-treatment for your warts. Depending on the severity of your condition, you may need a prescription-strength drug or another type of therapy for best results.

■ Oil Away Warts with Vitamin E

Vitamin E is known as a skin soother. And it might also erase that stubborn wart. Take 400 international units (IU) in pill form, or apply the contents of an oil-filled capsule onto the area. It will take a few months before you start to see the effects.

■ Banana Peel's Appeal

Long before there were dermatologists and laser treatments, folk healers treated warts with banana peels. They still do—and rather effectively at times. Before bedtime, take an extremely ripe (blackened) banana; remove a small, square section of peel; place it on the wart; cover with gauze and tape; repeat the next night and the next. Some warts vanish in a week; others are more stubborn.

■ Garlic Aid

You won't find this treatment in any standard dermatology textbook, but many warts respond to garlic oil. For a wart on the hand or foot:

1 Spread vitamin E oil around the wart, to protect the surrounding skin.

2 Then apply a clove of freshly-crushed garlic directly onto the wart, covering it with an elastic bandage.

Your first sign of progress will be a tingle or slight burn, then

Laser Treatments

If you've tried every wart treatment under the sun and the stubborn thing keeps popping up in the same spot, zap it off—with a laser. A CO2-pulsed laser removes the entire bump and some skin underneath to ensure that the infected area has been completely obliterated.

Or a technician can use a vascular laser which blasts the blood vessels that nourish the wart, so that it's left without a "food" source. These treatments cost a few hundred dollars to remove a wart or two.

Contact the American Society for Dermatologic Surgery to find a licensed physician in your area: 800-441-2737 or www.asds-net.org.

you will notice, often within a few days, the formation of a blister. Keep applying vitamin E oil to soften the skin and aid the healing process.

PLANTAR WARTS

■ Aspirin to the Rescue

Painful plantar warts on the soles of the feet are among the most stubborn to remove. They grow in, not on, your skin. Yet a simple and often successful solution is not widely known: Aspirin. Here's how to apply it: Crush half an aspirin tablet, drop the pinchful of powder directly onto the wart and cover with medical or adhesive tape. Leave on for one or two days, enabling salicylic acid from the aspirin to irritate the skin. This then triggers the immune system to heal the wart and surrounding skin. More common (and more expensive) over-the-counter wart medicines also contain salicylic acid.

WHIPLASH

■ Beyond Bones-and-Muscle Treatment

Unlike many of the maladies that are discussed elsewhere in this book, whiplash is a modern condition. Caused most often by rear-end auto collisions in which one's head snaps back violently, the resulting injury afflicts muscles, bones and the myofascial tissue that connects them—and more.

One uncommon way to treat the condition is to move beyond rest, braces, muscle massage and pain relievers, to try craniosacral therapy. The soft massage of membranes and tissues that connect the cranial and spinal column can help relieve severe, intractable pain over time. Many physical therapists, in fact, have trained in the practice of craniosacral therapy, an adjunct to many treatments that attempt to root out the cause of bodily trauma. Treatments typically last 12 to 16 weeks, and often help relieve psychological wounds from an injury as well.

CHAPTER 3

Especially for Women

ASTHMA

*See also **Asthma**, page 64*

■ *Birth Control Pills Bring Relief to Some*

After consultation with an allergist or primary care doctor, some female asthma patients may find that taking birth control pills helps improve lung function. Recent research from Scotland's University of Dundee found that of two groups of asthmatic women whose hormone levels tended to change dramatically before menstruation, those who took the Pill could breathe easier than those who didn't.

BALDING

■ *Female Hair Loss Remedy*

A prescription drug commonly used for a swollen prostate may help with female balding. Hormonal alterations associated with menopause can sometimes trigger hair loss in women. Finasteride, a drug that helps keep the testosterone levels high and other male hormone levels low, can also keep balding in check. Ask your doctor for more information about treating female balding with this drug.

Note: Finasteride should be avoided by men contemplating fatherhood. (Women should also avoid it before and during pregnancy.)

BLADDER PROBLEMS

URINARY TRACT INFECTION

■ *A Naturopathic Path*

For those whose doctors or health professionals shy away from antibiotics, herbal echinacea has been used to good effect to battle urinary tract infections (UTI), both in the US and throughout Europe. It may not work in all cases, or by itself, so be sure to consult a physician. But echinacea is an ally worth considering if you suffer occasional bouts of UTI. In tincture form, 20 to 30 drops four times a day is a commonly suggested dose.

■ *The Last Word on Cranberry Juice*

People have argued for years about the purported value of cranberry juice in fighting minor urinary tract infections. Folklore or fact? The fact is that cranberries are an antiseptic for the urinary tract. Plus, they contain a substance that makes it tough for bacteria to adhere to the bladder itself. So, if you drink a lot of the juice, you can help fight the infection, if not cure it outright.

To make the fruity dose stronger than you'd get by drinking sweetened juice, use cranberry juice concentrate from the health food store, mixed with plain or sparkling water (less sugar, more power). Meantime, increase your intake of water during the day and cut your intake of caffeine, a potential irritant.

■ *Tea Tonic*

Tired of people pushing cranberry juice on you? The next time you're faced with a urinary tract infection, try bearberry tea. With antiseptic properties, the tea can cleanse your bladder of the bacteria that causes the burning and discomfort associated with UTIs. Drink three cups a day until you begin to feel better. But if symptoms persist for more than three days, call your doctor.

■ *UTI? Take C*

At the first sign of a urinary tract infection, head for your kitchen or medicine cabinet for a super surge of vitamin C. The body cannot store excess vitamin C, so any extra in your system will be excreted from the body in the urine. And because vitamin C offers antimicrobial properties, the bladder and urinary tract will be cleansed in the process.

What amount do you really need? A dose of 2,000 to 3,000 mg of vitamin C per day is often suggested, until you begin to feel relief.

Bladder Infection Self-Defense:

Drink eight to 16 ounces of water every 15 minutes after you first feel burning when urinating. Do this for one to three hours. That amount effectively washes away many toxins—even troublesome bacteria. *Also:* Avoid acidic foods and drinks such as tomato sauce, coffee and carbonated beverages. They can make the irritation worse. Avoid cranberry juice. It can help *prevent* infections—but when symptoms are present, it may also make the irritation worse. *Caution:* Drinking water may provide relief, but if your symptoms have not resolved within 12 to 24 hours, you should contact your doctor to see whether additional treatment is needed.

Warning: Too much vitamin C in the system for long periods can cause kidney stones. (If you have kidney stones, check with your physician before beginning to treat a UTI with vitamin C.) Even without kidney problems, don't take high doses of vitamin C for extended periods.

■ Bladder Infections

Serious bladder infections usually require antibiotic therapy, but complementary approaches may cure mild infections and aid antibiotics in clearing up more serious ones. Persistent symptoms—or more worrisome ones, such as high fever or low back pain—should prompt a visit to a doctor sooner rather than later.

■ Get Your Greens

Parsley, boasting diuretic properties, can help clean out an infected bladder and flush out infection. Look for parsley capsules in your health food store and follow package instructions.

Or sample some parsley tea when battling bladder problems: Add a teaspoon of dried parsley to a cup of hot water and let the mixture steep for 10 minutes. Strain before drinking. Drink at least three cups daily throughout the course of a bladder infection.

■ Lemon Aid

For fast relief from a bladder infection, check your refrigerator. All you need is a lemon to create an acidic alternative to the time-honored remedy—cranberry juice.

Add the juice of one-half of a medium-sized lemon to a cup of warm water. Drink at least five cups of the lemon-water mixture a day during the course of an infection until symptoms subside.

■ Bee Better

Crushed bee—that's what apis, a homeopathic remedy for bladder infection, is made from. Take three 30C tablets every two hours at the first sign of discomfort, particularly burning and stinging.

One warning: If apis doesn't cure what ails you after three doses, it's not going to work, and you'll need to find another treatment.

■ Homeopathic Infection Fighter

Do you feel like you need to urinate every five minutes? That's one of the most irritating symptoms of a bladder infection. And one that may be cured by *mercurius corrosivus*, a homeopathic remedy. Take three 30C pills at the first sign of these symptoms. Repeat the dosage every two to three hours. You should notice an improvement after three doses. Otherwise, discontinue the use of mercurius corrosivus.

Sexual Strategies for Curing Bladder Infection

Holistic gynecologists report that unprotected intercourse can also cause or aggravate a bladder infection. Why? Seminal fluid raises the pH level of the vagina, creating an environment that invites the growth of bacteria which can then make their way into the urethra during intercourse. If you're prone to bladder infections, have your partner use a condom and avoid intercourse at the first indication of symptoms until they clear up. Urinating after intercourse flushes bacteria from the urethra, helping prevent infection.

■ Soothing Sarsaparilla

To alleviate the burning associated with bladder infections, swallow some sarsaparilla. Otherwise known as wild licorice, a homeopathic dose of three 30C pills every two to three hours should clear up the symptoms—and clean out the infection. If you don't notice a change in your condition after three doses, don't continue the treatment. Check with your physician regarding another type of remedy.

■ Herbal Detox

Ready for detox? Take the following herbal cocktail for relief from a current bladder infection three times a day for 10 days. It will provide an overall "detox" cleansing that could also prevent future infections from occurring.

- 1 teaspoon echinacea

- 3 capsules of Nature's Way KB (a kidney-bladder formula rich in juniper and parsley)

- 3 capsules of goldenseal root

- 3 capsules of cranberry

- 3 garlic tablets or a couple of cloves of garlic

Warning: If you're pregnant, you may follow this protocol but omit the goldenseal and KB formula, which contains herbs that should be avoided.

■ Relief for Honeymoon Cystitis

Searching for a homeopathic remedy for bladder infections induced by sexual intercourse? Staphysagria. Take three 30C pills every two hours at the first hint of any infection. According to experts, if a homeopathic remedy is going to improve a bladder infection, you have to begin treatment as soon as you can and you will see results within three doses. If you don't feel better, then discontinue the treatment and ask your physician for another form of treatment.

■ Bladder Infections Fly Away

If the main symptom of your bladder infection is a bothersome burning sensation, then cantharis (otherwise known as Spanish fly) is the homeopathic remedy of choice. Take three 30C pills every two hours as soon as you notice the signs of infection. If you don't feel any better after three doses of cantharis, then this medicine won't do the trick for your infection and another remedy will be necessary.

■ Corn Silk Tea—Safe, Sweet Solution

Finally, someone has figured out what to do with those thin, pale yellow strands that are found in the rows of fresh corn. Dry the corn silk (between paper towels), and use it to brew tea. Then, sip the corn-infused tea when you have a bladder infection, especially when pregnant, as you'll want to minimize your use of drugs. (It turns out the starches in corn silk are helpful diuretics.)

As you'd expect, corn silk from organic corn is favored by naturopaths over commercially grown corn; the sweeter and more aromatic the corn, the better for your bladder.

■ *Saw Palmetto, for Women, Too*

Although saw palmetto has received a lot of attention in recent years as an herbal aid for men's prostate problems, women with urinary tract problems have been using it for decades. In truth, saw palmetto berries, in tincture or tablet form, have an antiseptic effect on both men's and women's urinary tracts. Bladder infections (cystitis) and more serious kidney infections are simply more common among women.

As for dosage, 20 to 40 drops of the tincture in water should be taken three times a day. Saw palmetto is also increasingly available in prepackaged form.

■ *Healthy Bladder Tea*

The following tea acts as a mild diuretic. Goldenseal has an antibiotic effect which helps to prevent bladder infections, and the ginger enhances circulation to the bladder by relaxing and dilating blood vessels.

To make healthy bladder tea:

1 Bring four cups of water to a boil.

2 Stir in one teaspoon parsley, one teaspoon grated, fresh ginger root, one teaspoon uva ursi and one teaspoon goldenseal.

3 Simmer for 15 minutes on low heat.

4 Serve, adding honey and lemon juice if you desire.

Acupuncture Relief for IC

Although interstitial cystitis (IC) is a newly recognized condition, a centuries-old remedy can help reduce pain in and around the bladder—acupuncture.

Inflammation of the bladder and lining leads to some of the worst pain. Acupuncture treatments for IC attempt to do two things: Stimulate the production of painkilling endorphins, and drain excess energy, or qi, from the bladder area. Once-a-week sessions—aimed at the SP-6 acupuncture point—have shown positive results, but they may need to be more frequent during particularly painful episodes.

INTERSTITIAL CYSTITIS

■ *Nutritional Therapy May Reduce Pain*

Women who suffer from interstitial cystitis (IC) say that the pain is worse than everyday bladder infections—women liken it to having a persistent charley horse in the bladder, or worse. And the urge to void is relentless. In severe cases, women have to go to the bathroom 50 times a day. This disorder is recently recognized by the National Institutes of Health (with research grants of nearly $10 million awarded in the past few years to determine the cause). Treatments vary widely. Often, women are incorrectly diagnosed and treated for urinary tract infections.

One way IC sufferers have found relief is by dietary means: They avoid foods that are considered acidic, including grapefruit and orange juices, hot peppers, vinegar and berries.

Typically, patients will have to try several types of treatments before finding one that works.

■ FDA-Reviewed Drug Offers Hope

One moderately successful treatment for IC is Elmiron, an FDA-approved drug. When it works, it may take as long as three to six months to bring relief. In government studies, 37% of IC patients responded to Elmiron, which is among the most successful medications prescribed to IC sufferers to date.

BREAST CANCER

■ Freezing Treatment Fights Cancer

Cryosurgery, a treatment that freezes tissue and has been used for years to "burn" off warts and other skin growths, has now been tested successfully in a small number of breast cancer cases. Researchers at Rush-Presbyterian-St. Luke's Medical Center in Chicago, with the aid of ultrasound pictures, eliminated small breast cancer tumors after freezing them for seven-and-one-half minutes each. Three months later, the tumors had not returned. While long-term follow-up is certainly required before the procedure can be termed a cure, this experimental treatment is nonetheless exciting for breast cancer patients.

■ Go Fish!

Oncologists believe that omega-3 fatty acids found in fish oils may offer protection against breast and other types of cancer by reducing the production of some hormones. Although there are numerous beneficial fish-oil capsules on the market, physicians do suggest eating fish at least twice a week. Good choices include salmon, tuna, whitefish and anchovies.

■ Don't Go It Alone

For women living with breast cancer, group therapy has been shown to be a crucial component of treatment. According to the researchers, women with advanced breast cancer who attended group therapy sessions with other patients lived 18 months longer than those who did not incorporate psychotherapy into their treatment. Ask your doctor about groups and therapists that may be able to help you.

Stress and Cancer Recovery

Recent studies of breast cancer patients undergoing treatment revealed that the stress of the diagnosis and the treatment compromised their immune system function. Activities (in addition to exercise) that provide an outlet for stress and anxiety are an important aid to recovery. And relaxation therapies (including yoga) can help a patient learn how to control and cope with anxiety associated with battling an illness—so that your body can be at its best.

ADVANCED CASES

■ Alternatives in Drug Therapy

Taxol, a drug derived from the Pacific yew tree, has been one of the most exciting drugs to fight advanced cases of cancer in the past decade. Officially known as paclitaxel, this chemotherapy is expensive as well as rare and often effective.

Taxol is not to be confused with tamoxifen, however, which is a first-line hormone therapy often used in premenopausal patients. Tamoxifen has also gained favor as a preventative drug; Taxol treatment follows diagnoses of cancer.

Current guidelines recommend Taxol for patients who have advanced breast and ovarian cancer. Ask your doctor or oncologist if it is appropriate in your case.

BREAST-FEEDING PROBLEMS

ENGORGED BREASTS AND BLOCKED MILK DUCTS

■ Hydrotherapy Relieves Soreness and Swelling

After giving birth, many women find that their breasts become engorged as the body produces more milk than needed. But there's a soothing, simple solution: Fill a sink halfway with warm water. Lean over and place breasts into water. As you massage breasts from the ribs to the nipple, milk should flow out into the water. This will relieve some of the pain and discomfort associated with an oversupply of milk. Repeat as necessary.

■ Warm Herbal Poultice Eases Pain

Comfrey is the staple for treating cuts, scrapes and skin conditions. But according to herbalists, a comfrey poultice will relieve pain and irritation from blocked milk ducts, as well as reduce soreness from engorged breasts.

Modern Mammograms—At the Mall

It began as an attempt to reach women who were avoiding mammograms because they were fearful of coming to a clinical setting. Evanston Northwestern Healthcare opened the Breast Health Program at Nordstrom/Old Orchard in the northern suburbs of Chicago in 1995. Initial response was so favorable that doctors decided to expand the program to include screening for osteoporosis. For information on the project, call 888-ENH-6400. For general breast cancer screening information, contact the Susan G. Komen Foundation at 800-462-9273, or at www.komen.org/bci.

To prepare a soothing poultice:

1 Take one handful of fresh or dried comfrey leaves, place in a piece of cheesecloth or a cloth diaper, and tie with a piece of string or twine.

2 Place the packet in a small pot of simmering water for 10 to 15 minutes.

3 Remove the packet of herbs and allow it to drain and cool for a few minutes before applying it to the affected breast.

If both breasts are showing symptoms of infection or blockage, prepare two comfrey packs. Do not reuse the herbs. Repeat four to five times a day as symptoms persist.

■ *A Hot, Herbal Compress*

A soothing parsley compress may help flush blocked breast ducts and reduce inflammation. Place a handful of fresh or dried parsley in a piece of cheesecloth or cloth diaper and tie securely with string. Place the parsley bundle in a small pot of simmering water for 10 minutes. Remove and let the pack cool and drain for a few minutes before placing on the tender part of your breast. If both breasts are sore or infected, prepare two parsley bundles.

Note: Be sure to throw out the packs after you've used them, say herbalists, because they absorb toxins from the breast tissue.

■ *Marshmallow Root Makes a Soothing Soak*

Marshmallow root is an herbal remedy for all types of ailments that result in sore, inflamed breasts and nipples after giving birth, including mastitis, blocked ducts and an oversupply of milk.

1 Add two ounces of dried marshmallow root to one-half gallon of boiling water that has been removed from the stove.

2 Let the mixture sit overnight to fully infuse.

3 In the morning, reheat the solution until comfortably warm.

4 Pour the mixture into a large bowl or fill a sink halfway.

5 Lean over and place breasts into the herbal infusion and soak until the solution cools.

Repeat soaking in the heated infusion four or five times a day. *And be forewarned:* This mixture will feel a bit slimy to the touch.

■ *Potato Packs a Punch*

A cold potato poultice not only relieves mastitis and reduces inflammation, but also can help clear up blocked tubes and ducts in the breast tissue. To prepare:

1 Grate one or two large raw potatoes.

2 Apply the grated potato to completely cover one or both of your breasts as needed.

3 Cover the area with a towel or cloth and let sit for 10 or 15 minutes.

Repeat four to five times a day as long as symptoms remain.

MILK DEFICIENCY

■ *Tea with Milk?*

It may smell like licorice, but to many new moms aniseed is better than candy. Tea from the aniseed herb is a baby-safe, mother-safe way to help boost the production of mother's milk for as long as the child nurses. Long touted by herbalists as a digestive aid, aniseed has been catching on among nurse-midwives and new mothers-in-the-know in recent years.

To prepare, pour one cup of boiling water over one teaspoon of the dried herb, and let steep for 10 minutes. Commercial preparations such as Mother's Milk tea from Traditional Medicinals are also available. Within a few hours of drinking the tea, you'll feel the results.

■ Alfalfa—A Calcium Booster

Alfalfa is high in silica, which can help stimulate lactation if you're having trouble breast-feeding. As an alternative to capsules, which may be taken according to package instructions, you can prepare a tea with dried alfalfa. Put one teaspoonful into a cup of warm water and allow the herb to infuse for 15 minutes. Strain the mixture before drinking.

■ Raspberry Remedy for Lactation Problems

Raspberry leaf tea, because of its uterine toning properties, is often recommended to pregnant women. But don't stop drinking raspberry leaf tea after giving birth. This tea has tonic properties for stimulating glands responsible for the production of milk. Drink up to three cups a day.

To prepare, steep one teaspoon of dried leaves in a cup of hot water for 10 to 15 minutes. Strain and sip.

■ Milk Thistle Lives Up to Its Name

Just like expectant mothers, new mothers often worry about the foods and drinks they ingest—and what effect those foods will have on the baby. New moms can rest easy in the case of milk thistle, which can be sipped in tea throughout the months of breast-feeding to promote milk production. Prepackaged preparations of milk thistle are available, but midwives often recommend the tea, as it lends itself more to a routine for both mother and baby.

■ Let Goat's Rue Work for You

Goat's rue, an herbal extract from Austria, has been reported to increase both a mother's production of milk solids and the volume of milk during her breast-feeding months. It may not be widely available in raw herb form, but goat's rue extract can be found in well-stocked herb stores. One teaspoon of the extract taken three times a day in water, tea or milk can make breast-feeding a lot more comfortable— especially for those who need to pump "for later" or during workdays away from baby.

SORE NIPPLES

■ Oil Relief

Nursing mothers often suffer from sore nipples, but must be careful not to use treatments that could be harmful to the baby. Here are two simple but worthwhile remedies that are also baby-safe:

■ Apply vitamin E oil to the area daily, or as needed.

■ Try a castor oil compress: Dip a washcloth in castor oil and apply to the breast, covering with a hot-water bottle, for one half hour at a time. (Check with your doctor first.)

■ Ease Sore Nipples

Nursing mothers can treat sore nipples with this baby-safe hot compress. Try dipping a towel or washcloth in warm water with a few drops of an antiseptic, but soothing, essential oil, such as lavender. Apply to the breast for half an hour at a time. Or look for a beeswax (not petroleum)-based salve with nourishing herbs like yarrow and sage.

BREAST PAIN AND TENDERNESS

■ Make Fitness More Comfortable

It's a very common complaint of modern, fit women: Bra straps that chafe and slide at the gym or during running workouts. One athlete-savvy solution is to switch to a T-strap style of sports bra, which tends to be more comfortable than it may appear to someone who has never tried one. A second solution (for those who don't need a lot of support) might be to wear one tight cotton sport top over another, as some top athletes and dancers do.

■ Slippery Solution to Nipple Irritation

For women who suffer repeated bouts of nipple irritation during workouts or other sporting activities, sex may be about the last thing on their minds. But it shouldn't be. One way to ease or end the irritation is to use a sexual lubricant, like AstroGlide or Body Glide, on the inside of your sports bra. And make sure your sports bras have seamless cups!

■ Herbal Salves

During pregnancy and after giving birth, nipples can become very sore, dry and even cracked. Herbalists suggest these soothing natural remedies for their moisturizing and cell-renewing benefits: Comfrey root ointment, burdock salve, vitamin E oil and aloe vera gel. All can be found in health food stores. Use according to package instructions; however, ask your doctor about using these remedies while breast-feeding, as they may pose a danger if your baby ingests them.

■ Midwives' Parsley Remedy

Though there are many causes of breast pain and tenderness, sometimes bloating and water retention are responsible, spurred on by a number of hormone changes. To combat this naturally, try chewing chopped, fresh parsley at least twice a day.

One of the properties not widely known about parsley is that it is a diuretic. It helps flush excess liquid out of your breasts and the rest of your body. Nurse-midwives may be more supportive of this treatment than MDs are, but that shouldn't keep you from trying it.

■ *A Fragrant Massage*

This treatment is especially good for large-breasted women who wear restrictive bras. Perform a self-massage on breasts, using a mild concentration of rosemary, bay laurel or basil essential oils in a carrier oil. These oils will help stimulate local circulation and move blood out of the area.

Note: This type of massage is also effective on swollen lymph nodes in the neck or groin.

■ *Lymph Massage for Tender Breasts*

Drawing out liquids (away from the breasts) and increasing circulation can reduce tenderness. While you conduct your monthly breast self-exam for lumps, give yourself a lymphatic drainage massage.

Apply a 1% essential-oil mixture, using a few drops of cypress or juniper oil (both diuretics) in a carrier oil. With your thumbs in your underarms, cup breasts with your palms and rub slowly, toward the heart.

FIBROCYSTIC (LUMPY) BREASTS

■ *Naturopathic, Dietary Treatment to Help*

Although fibrocystic, or lumpy, breasts are said to occur in more than three-fourths of all premenopausal women, they still cause pain, tenderness and alarm to varying degrees in many of the women who have the condition. Sometimes the lumps, or cysts, are so small and short-lived that they can't be felt at all. Often they are noticeable just before the onset of a woman's menstrual period.

Dietary changes can serve as a remedy, including:

■ Cutting caffeine intake considerably.

■ Lowering the intake of carbohydrates and refined sugar.

■ Increasing the intake of vegetables and other fibrous foods.

■ Taking (packaged) herbal supplements of dong quai, Vitex or sarsaparilla. The herbal preparations may be mixed or taken alone, on the advice of a health practitioner.

■ *Oils Can Make a Lasting Difference*

In addition to dietary changes (see above listing), women can help ease the formation and effects of breast cysts by taking packaged omega-3 and omega-6 fatty acid supplements (or consuming plenty of salmon or tuna). You might also consider flaxseed or black currant oils, both of which can help decrease the inflammatory process and help the liver in cleansing the system. The oils can be found in herb shops. Follow package directions.

■ *Vitamin E Eases Painful Problem*

Vitamin E has been shown to be beneficial for some women who have fibrocystic breasts. Between 400 and 600 international units (IU) of vitamin E taken orally every day may help to reduce the pain associated with these recurring cysts and lumps. However, see your doctor before you begin vitamin E therapy to discuss the safety of vitamin E and to be sure that these lumps are fibrocystic and not related to another condition.

■ *A Diet for Pain-Free Breasts*

High doses of a selection of vitamins may reduce the pain and symptoms of fibrocystic breasts. What's the secret combination? After confirming this treatment with your doctor, take the following daily:

- 25,000 international units (IU) beta-carotene
- 150 micrograms iodine
- 600 IU vitamin E
- 100 milligrams (mg) B6

But there are several caveats: There is no iodine supplement on the market. Iodine suitable for ingestion is different from the solution you might find on drugstore shelves. You must get iodine from foods like fish.

And don't take the 100 mg of B6 all at once because it can be very harsh on your system. Instead, divide the amount into two or three doses over the course of the day.

■ *Root Out the Problem*

Poke root can be an effective treatment for lumpy, fibrocystic breasts. The cysts are usually harmless but can be frightening to women because the cysts can feel hard to the touch and because they often recur every month. (Some gynecologists hope to do away with the term "fibrocystic" because they think it sounds too technical and scary.)

A solution is to use a tincture of poke root: Add one-fourth to one-half ounce of warm tincture to a flannel cloth or soft hand towel, then place it on the breast overnight (or for at least four hours). Check with your herb shop about availability of poke root and tincture.

CELLULITE

■ *Tighten Up to Fight Cellulite*

It's genetic, so if you've got it, thank your parents. Although there are no true preventions or cures, you can temporarily improve the appearance of cellulite. Fill up your bathtub and add two drops each of the following essential oils: Juniper, grapefruit, cypress and mandarin. Swish them around in the water before climbing in. Their mildly astringent effect will temporarily tighten your skin, improving the appearance of cellulite.

If you have dry skin, try premixing the oils in one teaspoon of a carrier oil, along with one-quarter cup milk or one tablespoon of honey or glycerin, for added moisturizing benefits.

CERVICAL HEALTH

■ *Vitamins for a Healthy Cervix*

Changes in the cellular structure of the cervix, according to research, may contribute to the onset of cervical cancer. Specifically, when older cells aren't sloughed off they disrupt the growth of new cell layers. This condition is known as cervical dysplasia and may raise your risk of cancer.

Vitamin therapy can maintain the health of your cervix or heal it. Here's what you should take every day:

- 25,000 IU of beta-carotene
- 400 micrograms of folic acid
- 100 IU of vitamin E
- 500 mg of vitamin C

Check with your doctor before beginning this treatment, as high doses of vitamins can be toxic if you have certain health conditions.

ENDOMETRIOSIS

■ Prevent Endometriosis

High doses of beta-carotene, folic acid and other B vitamins, as well as vitamins C and E, can help decrease the risks of endometriosis, a condition in which the mucous-membrane lining of the uterus begins to grow in other places. High doses of certain vitamins and minerals can be toxic and cause health problems, so seek advice from your physician for correct dosages and supervised treatment.

Estrogen-Free Diet

According to physicians, endometriosis may be caused by elevated estrogen levels. How do you bring them down? In some cases, it may be as simple as watching what you eat. Avoid eating animal fats, including red meats, pork and chicken, as well as foods that have been fried in animal lard. Talk to your doctor to determine if this type of nutritional therapy suits your individual case of endometriosis.

■ Fortify with Vitex

Symptoms of endometriosis include heavy bleeding, lower back soreness, pain with intercourse, nausea, heavy periods, constipation and difficulty conceiving. Vitex, an herb that fortifies a woman's reproductive system, can help control endometriosis and alleviate some of its side effects. Take Vitex under the supervision of a physician in order to ensure the safety of the treatment.

■ Balance Hormones Naturally

Endometriosis may be the result of a progesterone imbalance. And progesterone, a hormone associated with ovulation, may be regulated with prescription drugs. But holistic physicians suggest controlling progesterone levels with wild yam.

Look for this natural hormone therapy in herbal pharmacies and health food stores. For the correct dosage to treat your individual case, ask your physician.

■ Nourish Your System

As an alternative to drug therapy to control endometrial tissue growth, try eating foods that are naturally high in plant estrogens. A serving of soy beans, tofu, tempeh or soy milk—all rich in phytoestrogens—can provide a necessary boost.

Talk to your doctor about the severity of the condition and the possibility of using nutritional therapy with or instead of prescription drugs.

■ Herbal Options

Siberian ginseng can be used to treat some cases of endometriosis. Look for capsules, tablets or an extract in an herbal pharmacy or health food store, and use according to package instructions. Or make a tea using one-half teaspoon of the Siberian ginseng powder stirred into one cup of hot water. Drink a cup or two every day. Be sure to get a diagnosis and discuss this treatment with your physician.

■ *Pain Relief Tea*

This tea is particularly good for menstrual cramping, digestive problems, fibroids and symptoms associated with endometriosis. It contains raspberry leaves, which help relax the uterus and prevent diarrhea. Ginger helps relieve pain and nausea. To prepare:

1 Bring two cups of water to a boil.

2 Add one teaspoon of fresh, grated ginger root and one teaspoon of raspberry leaves to the water and stir.

3 Simmer for 15 minutes on low heat.

If you want, strain and add honey.

ENDOMETRIAL CANCER

■ *Soy and Other Legumes May Lower Risk*

Consuming soy products such as tofu and legumes, including peas and beans, may lower a woman's risk of endometrial cancer, according to a recent study. Women who ate the most soy beans and other legumes were 54% less

likely, on average, to develop endometrial cancer than women who ate the least. Soy has an anti-estrogen effect, say researchers, which is important because high levels of estrogen have been linked to this and other cancers.

GENITAL WARTS

HUMAN PAPILLOMA VIRUS (HPV), FEMALE

■ *Naturopathic Procedure Restores Cervical Health*

Standard OB/GYN care, including cryotherapy (freezing), is not the only way to rid the female genitals of the stubborn (and sometimes dangerous) warts caused by human papilloma virus (HPV), a sexually transmitted disease. Naturopaths, who are now licensed in some states and Puerto Rico, also perform a less common procedure called escharotic treatment, which can be quite effective over a period of time.

After a patient presents with an abnormal Pap smear, a naturopath performs a follow-up gynecological exam and inserts an antiviral suppository in the womb against the cervix. Depending on the practitioner and the severity of the HPV, the suppository may contain lomation, white cedar (*thuja*), other herbs or a combination of these herbal preparations. Echinacea and goldenseal may also be added.

Treatments—which typically rotate suppositories for varying lengths of time—can last up to three months. And because of the potential harm of HPV, patients should feel comfortable asking for a referral to an obstetrician or gynecologist at any time during the naturopathic treatment.

INFERTILITY

FEMALE FACTOR

■ *A Tea Worth Trying*

Calendula, from the marigold family, when dried and taken in tea, may help clear blocked passages in fallopian tubes. In related fashion, the herbal remedy is said to ease the swelling of cystic ovaries—another factor that may contribute to infertility. Try three cups per day, but as with any treatment for infertility, results may be months, not weeks, away.

■ *Hit the Streets to Prolong Fertility*

Want to do something in your twenties that could impact your ability to have a child in your thirties? Get walking. Regular brisk walks keep a woman's reproductive system "grounded," her menstrual cycles regular and the pelvic region strong and toned. All of these add up to a healthy, energetic body that may have fewer problems conceiving.

Diagnosing the Cause of Infertility

A new, relatively simple surgical procedure may be able to quickly pinpoint the reason you're having trouble conceiving. Using falloscopy, a physician makes a tiny incision (in the lower abdomen) and feeds a miniature camera inside the fallopian tubes, which carry the eggs from the ovaries to the uterus. If a problem inside the tubes is hindering regular ovulation, a doctor can diagnose it right away. *Best of all:* It's an outpatient procedure that takes only a half hour.

Analyze Hair, Have Baby

Although not generally accepted by conventional doctors, some alternative practitioners believe a new, nutritional analysis of a few strands of your hair can reveal if you're getting enough vitamins and minerals, drinking too much caffeine or taking too much aspirin. The results can help determine the supplements and lifestyle changes that are needed to strengthen your body and system in order to increase the odds of conceiving.

■ *The Stress-Reduction Plan*

If you're not having luck getting pregnant, don't stress out about it. Stress, in fact, can affect your ability to conceive just as it has been shown to weaken your immune system. Whatever the source of your stress, try to find an outlet like exercise or massage or consider counseling to help pinpoint the sources of your anxiety and learn how to banish them.

■ *Skip Wine with Dinner*

It's strongly advised that women avoid alcohol during pregnancy and while breast-feeding. Drinking can also diminish the fertility of both men and women. Alcohol's toxicity can affect sperm production in males and hormonal balances in women. The more you drink, the greater the problems.

■ *Women, Weight and Infertility*

Having trouble becoming pregnant? Check your weight. Physicians report a link between weight problems and estrogen levels, which can contribute to ovulation irregularities. This

relates only to women who are seriously over-weight or underweight. Talk to your doctor about appropriate exercise and diet plans that can help you get into a healthy weight range.

Fertility Tests for Your Tongue

There's a new type of at-home pregnancy test on the market. Unlike others on drugstore shelves, this one doesn't reveal if you're pregnant, but whether you might get pregnant. What is it? Ovu-Tec, a small microscope that lets you monitor changes in your saliva. Apparently, saliva reveals crucial details about ovulation and the stages of a woman's menstrual cycle. Just put a little saliva on a slide, place it under the scope and look for bubbles (nonfertile) or lines (fertile).

For more information, http://domus.ws/ovu-tec.

Hands-Off Healing

Want to get your fertile energy flowing, but fear the acupuncture needle? Reiki, a hands-off approach to energy balancing, may be the thing for you. During a session, a practitioner holds her hands above the body to redirect and order the energy that surrounds and runs through the body. With a freer energy flow, so the theory goes, you're more likely to get pregnant.

Get in the Flow

Acupuncture works on the meridians of the body, through which energy flows, and corrects imbalances and blockages that may be hindering the body from functioning normally. And, according to reputable acupuncturists, these imbalances can cause infertility. Depending on the cause, a few well-placed needles may fix fertility problems within several—or in some instances more than 10—sessions.

■ Strawberry Aid

Chinese medicine practitioners in Asia and in the West say that eating strawberries may help increase fertility—female and male. The recommendation to eat strawberries regularly, not just occasionally, stems from the belief that yin and yang energy balance is necessary for fertility. In Chinese medical belief, yin is considered "cooling"; yang is considered "heating." Strawberry consumption can remedy a shortage of yang energy.

■ The Fingernail Test

Having trouble having a baby? Check your fingernails. Do you have a half moon at the base of each nail? If not, it's a sign that your life-force energy—or *qi*, as the Chinese call it—is likely on the decline. The moons usually disappear from pinkie fingers first and fade progressively toward the thumb. What's the connection? Waning energy causes organ weakness and hormonal imbalances that can lead to infertility. A gynecologist may recommend herbs like Vitex to boost energy and overall health for a woman in her reproductive years.

■ Super Shatavari

Shatavari, an Ayurvedic herb, is known for its restorative and soothing properties in regard to the female reproductive organs. Try one teaspoon of shatavari extract or powder with a little milk or honey every day. Look for shatavari at an herbal pharmacy or a local health food store. Or ask an Ayurvedic practitioner where you can purchase it if you have trouble finding it in your area.

Treat Depression to Bolster Fertility

While years of infertility may lead to depression, improving one's mood may increase a woman's odds of conceiving, especially if she has been severely depressed, according to a recent study. After a group of women who had been trying to conceive, on average, for three years participated in a 10-week stress-management program, their depression diminished. Within six months, 60% of the women who had been the most depressed became pregnant, 35% of those who had been moderately depressed conceived, while 24% of the women who had been mildly blue became pregnant.

The Food–Fertility Link

Before considering things to take to improve your odds of getting pregnant, think about what you can do without—such as sugary or starch-filled foods. Doctors and midwives point out that healthy vaginal fluid is somewhat acidic. But poor dietary habits (lots of sweets and starches) can make the vaginal fluid alkaline instead of acidic—which lowers the chances of conception. In fact, dietary changes should be discussed early on when meeting an obstetrician or gynecologist for the first time prior to pregnancy.

■ All-Purpose Aloe Vera

Aloe vera is a favorite soother and stimulator for skin. But many holistic physicians suggest that women take the gel or extract as a tonic for infertility. Take one tablespoonful once a day to nourish and cleanse the reproductive system. Be sure to check the label to be sure that the aloe vera is suitable for ingestion.

■ Homeopathic Pill for Prolactin Imbalance

Infertility may result from a hormonal imbalance, particularly that of prolactin, a chemical produced by the pituitary gland that induces lactation. A homeopathic remedy—a 30C preparation of Thorzine—helps to normalize the function of the pituitary gland, regulate hormonal imbalance and improve a woman's overall energy levels. Follow package—and a physician's—instructions.

■ Redecorate the Bedroom for Optimal Fertility

Feng shui (pronounced fung-shway) is the ancient Chinese art of organizing interior and exterior spaces to create and control the flow of *qi*, or life-force energy. A feng shui consultant can perform a fertility ritual in the home—rearranging furniture or adding a splash of color—to remove any energy obstacles that might be blocking your ability to become pregnant.

Also, there are a few things you can do by yourself to increase positive energy: Make sure your bed is facing the entry into the room, but not directly opposite it. Move the bed from underneath an overhead beam, which can obstruct the flow of energy, and make sure there's equal space on both sides of the bed—a sign that the relationship is in balance.

ENDOMETRIOSIS-RELATED INFERTILITY

■ An Often-Overlooked Surgical Option

For women having trouble getting pregnant, and who also have endometriosis—a gynecological condition that causes painful menstruation and severe cramping—minimally invasive surgery can help boost the odds of conception.

The latest research indicates that surgical removal of overgrown uterine (endometrial) tissue (using thin laparoscopes and incisions so small they can be covered with Band-Aids) can result in many pregnancies that would not otherwise have occurred. In one Canadian study of 341 infertile women with endometriosis, some 31% of those who had endometrial surgery later became pregnant, while only 18% of those who did not opt for the procedure got pregnant. Doctors warn, though, that no surgery should be taken lightly, despite the promising results.

LOW LIBIDO

■ The Pill Problem

Isn't it ironic? You go on the Pill and immediately feel completely uninterested in sex. The effect of birth control pills on hormones may result in an imbalance that causes your libido to plummet. Choosing another type of birth control pill may be the answer to your problem; there are a handful from which to choose. Or, alternately, your hormones may regulate themselves within a few months. Check with your doctor for the appropriate option in your individual case.

If You Have to Have a Hysterectomy

A complete hysterectomy causes hormone levels to plummet, resulting in a less than lively libido. While there are hormone replacement therapies that can get the body back in balance, ask your gynecologist about a revised surgical option. Instead of removing both ovaries, sometimes surgeons can leave one in place. This will reduce the severity of hormonal changes as well as changes in libido.

MENOPAUSE

GENERAL SYMPTOMS

■ Midlife Exercise Eases Menopause

Want to make menopause a more pleasant experience? Get moving, say experts. Exercise strengthens the vascular system which, during menopause, is involved in hot flashes. But it's best to get started before the menopausal years in order to adequately build a strong cardiovascular system.

When to Stop Taking Iron

Iron is an important part of a woman's dietary supplement before and during menopause, replenishing minerals lost during years of menstrual periods. But, experts say, once menopause has passed, you must be sure to stop taking iron supplements. Research suggests that the iron no longer needed can be stored in the heart muscle, which may contribute to cardiovascular disease.

■ The Joy of Soy

A naturally occurring form of estrogen known as phytoestrogens may supplement low levels of hormones that occur during menopause. Besides adding tofu and soybeans to your diet, try substituting soy milk for cow's milk. And try to have at least one or two servings a day.

■ Balance Hormones Naturally

Squaw vine has a tonic effect on the uterus, strengthening it during pregnancy and reducing cramping throughout the PMS years, but is also a powerful hormone regulator, lessening symptoms of menopause, such as hot flashes and night sweats.

The prescription? Take 20 drops of squaw vine extract orally two to three times a day—preferably when menopausal symptoms begin. Continue this herbal therapy throughout the course of menopause if symptoms persist.

■ Birth Control for Better Postmenopausal Health

If taking progesterone after menopause causes too many side effects, there is another, underused way to obtain this essential hormone. Progestasert, an IUD filled with progesterone, is commonly used for birth control. But it can also be used to deliver progesterone to the uterus in postmenopausal women, often without the side effects of pills. And it's easy. The IUD is replaced just once a year. Talk to your gynecologist about this option if other methods don't work for you.

Note: There are other side effects associated with IUDs.

HOT FLASHES

■ Cooling Flower Remedy

For those who favor floral remedies for hot flashes, linden flower may provide both mildly sedative and cooling effects. Even though linden

provides an inner chill of sorts, herbalists recommend that women take a pinch of the dried flower in a cupful of boiling water—after meals.

A Milder Menu = Milder Menopause

Hot and spicy foods—like those laden with cayenne pepper—cause blood vessels to dilate and may trigger a hot flash among menopausal women. *Best bet:* If you are going through menopause, stick with a milder menu, in general, in order to protect against flushing and flashes.

■ Handling Hot Flashes on the Go

Active menopausal women might want to try this herbalists' trick: To combat hot flashes during a busy day or week, try aromatherapy-to-go. Just carry a bottle of peppermint oil essence with you, and, as needed throughout the day, sprinkle a few drops on a handkerchief and inhale slowly and deeply. As peppermint is known to have cooling effects, it's a portable way to head off hot flashes.

■ Use Soy to Ease the Unease

Sometimes simple solutions work best. For some women, especially those who have elected to avoid estrogen therapy, adding two to three teaspoons of soy protein to their daily diet can ease the discomfort and debilitating feelings of hot flashes. Soy protein (found at the health food store) can be added to breakfast cereal or mixed with beverages. It may provide relief for those who aren't ready to start estrogen replacement therapy or replacement therapy with "natural" hormone compounds.

■ Vitamin Therapy

Suffering from hormonal hot flashes? Taking 400 to 600 IU of vitamin E orally every day may ease this menopausal problem by lessening the effects of the drop in estrogen production. However, don't expect immediate results. It takes two to four weeks to feel the effects.

■ Waiting to Exhale

It seems too simple to be effective, but paced respiration can be a cool idea for any woman experiencing hot flashes in the active phase of menopause. Slow, deep breathing can reduce the frequency and intensity of hot flashes.

Whenever symptoms arise, control your breathing to allow only five inhale-exhale sequences during each minute. Focus on making your breathing come from the abdomen (shallower breathing stems from the chest). Follow this technique 15 minutes per day until symptoms subside.

■ A Ginseng-Twice-a-Day Remedy

The tonic effects of ginseng may help to decrease the occurrence and severity of hot flashes. Take one 500-mg capsule twice a day, once in the morning and again in the early evening. According to nutritionists, Chinese ginseng and Korean ginseng offer the best results. Look for capsules and tablets in your health food store.

■ Get Fruits and Berries

Good news from the orange grove and berry patch: Bioflavonoids, found in citrus fruits and berries, have been shown to reduce some of the

New Benefit of Estrogen Therapy

You already know that estrogen therapy after menopause helps prevent bone loss and osteoporosis in later life. But it is not nearly as well known that hormone replacement therapy (HRT) can also help women keep more of their original teeth into their late sixties, seventies and beyond.

When more than 500 women in the landmark Framingham Heart Study in Massachusetts were surveyed about their medical habits and dental hygiene, researchers found that those who were on HRT had retained more of their teeth than those who never took hormone supplements after menopause. In addition, the longer the women took HRT, the fewer teeth they lost. Still, due to the risk of side effects, HRT is not advised for most women—ask your doctor about your situation.

center of the brain to simulate the effects of estrogen.

A recent study found that black cohosh improved or eliminated menopausal symptoms; overall, women taking the herb felt better than others taking estrogen. Improvements are generally seen in four to eight weeks. Look for the standardized form of the extract.

NIGHT SWEATS

■ A Dry Drink

A glass of cool or iced sage tea three times a day can help regulate night sweats, which keep some menopausal women from getting a good night of sleep. In Germany, sage tea actually is licensed as a medicinal tea for night sweats. Don't drink it hot: It could increase perspiration, which might kick off a hot flash.

Another warning: Sage tea can provoke or exacerbate vaginal dryness, another symptom of menopause.

symptoms associated with menopause—including hot flashes. These vibrant pigments, which give fruits their color, increase fatty acids in your system, which lessen swelling in muscle tissues. But get started as soon as you can—even before menopause begins, if possible—so that your body has a chance to build up the vitamin levels.

■ Prescription Help

For some women, hot flashes can be a debilitating aspect of menopause, causing heavy sweats that interrupt both work and sleep. A drug used in treating high blood pressure—methyldopa—has also been recommended to treat hot flashes because it affects the circulatory system. Ask your physician about methyldopa if you're experiencing severe hot flashes.

■ Natural Estrogen Replacement Therapy

Black cohosh, a relative of the buttercup, effectively treats mood swings, sleep disturbances, hot flashes, vaginal dryness, loss of libido and other menopausal symptoms by affecting the hypothalamus and thermoregulatory

RECURRENT PAIN, DEPRESSED MOOD

■ Powerful Root-Based Remedy

Naturopaths, herbalists and other holistic practitioners speak glowingly of black cohosh when treating women for menopausal symptoms including dark moods. Its pain-relieving properties are well known in natural medicine circles, but patients don't often realize how powerful a remedy black cohosh can be.

It should only be taken in small doses, and although it is a good, natural painkiller, it should not be used during pregnancy.

Note: Remifemin, a packaged product containing compounds from the black cohosh plant, is now available in the US. It costs approximately $30 for a one-month supply. It has been sold in Europe for years.

MENSTRUAL TROUBLES

IRREGULAR PERIODS

■ *An Herb that Balances Hormones*

If you have irregular menstrual periods, where you miss a period one month and get it the next, a safe herb to help regulate your cycle is Vitex. By affecting the part of the brain that controls the release of the hormones estrogen and progesterone, Vitex helps keep these two hormones in balance.

Take one or two teaspoons of Vitex per day. If your menstrual cycle doesn't become regular, see your physician to rule out a thyroid problem, pregnancy and other possible causes.

■ *Marjoram for Regular Menses*

As a flavoring aid to many Mediterranean dishes, marjoram is an herb with a distinctive, pungent aroma. Sparking the senses with its pleasing, exotic taste and smell, marjoram may also spark the menses in some women. Those who have irregular menstrual patterns and who wish to stabilize them (without resorting to birth control pills or other hormonal treatments) can try aromatherapy treatments with marjoram massage oil. The oil, which can be blended at an herb shop, is massaged onto the lower abdomen at regular intervals, as a kind of hormone helper. Many users notice a mild sedative effect as well.

Surgical Solution to Excessive Bleeding

For women who have suffered for years with unusually heavy bleeding during menstruation, and who have considered a hysterectomy to treat the condition, an experimental treatment involving balloons may provide unusual relief.

At more than a dozen medical centers across the US, doctors have treated excessive bleeding in the following manner: First, a thick balloon is inserted into the uterus. Then it's filled with heated water, which in turn destroys the uterine lining in a controlled manner. This alternative to hysterectomy results in less blood flow during menstruation, or a cessation of menstrual flow altogether. It is said to be 25% to 50% as costly as a hysterectomy, and purportedly has fewer side effects.

■ *The Case for Dong Quai*

For women who have difficult periods and who are battling through menopause, the Chinese root *dong quai* may offer steady, lasting relief. Herbalists consider it a general female tonic, as it not only eases symptoms of irregular menstruation (and PMS), but also appears to help women feel more energetic.

Those who benefit from it will notice its effects within a month or two. Extract of dong quai can be found most often in capsule form. Typical dosage is one or two capsules twice a day, depending on the formulation.

New Menstrual Migraine Medication

For women who have severe migraines tied to their menstrual cycle, unlikely aid has come from the world of Parkinson's disease treatment. In a recent study, bromocriptine, a drug used to treat Parkinson's symptoms, such as tremor and muscular rigidity, helped three out of four women afflicted with menstrual migraines. They took the drug for one year, in addition to their regular medication, and found it quite effective. Ask your doctor about possibly prescribing this medication to treat migraines.

■ Irregular Periods and Your Diet

It is rather common for female athletes to experience irregular periods or to stop menstruating altogether. But even nonathletes can have irregular menstrual cycles. The most common cause is hormonal, but weight also may be a factor. If you're underweight, you're likely to miss a period now and then.

On the other hand, many overweight women experience what's called polycystic ovarian disease, where the protective cyst that carries the egg fails to rupture, therefore halting ovulation. It's not certain whether women experience polycystic ovarian disease because they're overweight, or if the disease is somehow responsible for weight gain. But losing weight seems to solve the problem for most women.

In addition to exercising and drinking *plenty* of water, women who skip periods may want to try taking 50 mg a day of vitamin B6. As for water consumption, experts recommend from six or eight glasses to one gallon daily. If this seems excessive for you, check your urine. It should be the color of very pale lemonade, or even clear. If it isn't, try increasing your water intake and watch for results. Keep in mind, if your period continues on its erratic schedule, you may be noticing effects of a different health issue, such as menopause.

PAIN AND CRAMPS

■ Ovulation Pain

Despite the silly-sounding name, mittelschmerz—or ovulation pain—causes problems for many women each month. This discomfort, which can occur for three or four days during the middle of a woman's cycle, is different from the cramps some women get the first or second day of their period.

Each month, the ovary forms a fluid-filled cyst to protect the egg as it drops into the uterus. Most women don't feel this at all, but not every woman's ovaries are in the exact same place. Occasionally one or both of a woman's ovaries rest against nerve endings, which can be triggered when the cyst forms. And if a woman's uterus is twisted, she might experience the pain every other month (ovulation usually switches sides each month).

If you experience mittelschmerz, you'll probably feel better just because you read this section. Most women don't realize that if the pain lasts for only three or four days and isn't severe, it's perfectly normal.

But since it can still be uncomfortable and annoying, you might want to take a look at your lifestyle. If you're not exercising at least three or four times a week, the pain will probably persist. Also, most remedies that work on menstrual pain will also alleviate ovulation pain.

Natural Energizing Snack

Feeling sluggish and fatigued during the week before your period? Forget caffeine or the chocolate bar. A dark-colored, rich Ayurvedic jam made from Indian herbs is a surefire pick-me-up. Known as chavanprash, it's a sweet but earthy jam that's perfect for a mid-afternoon boost of energy.

Try spreading it on whole grain bread—or eat a spoonful straight from the jar. Look for the jam at your local health food store or contact an Ayurvedic expert for help in finding chavanprash. One source to try: Maharishi Ayurveda at 800-345-8332.

■ Alcohol for Menstrual Pain Prevention

It may be hard to fathom that up until the late 1970s, many midwives and doctors administered alcohol to women who entered premature labor. When researchers uncovered the risks associated with drinking and pregnancy, this practice came to an abrupt end.

Unfortunately, though, some women who aren't pregnant shun alcohol completely now, even though it seems to have many beneficial effects, including lowering risk of heart disease and relaxing the uterus. For the latter reason, many midwives recommend a glass of wine or a beer for patients who experience painful periods—that is, pain that lasts beyond the normal one- or two-day bout of cramps.

Keep in mind, however, that one drink works as well as five, and drinking five can cause other problems, so don't overindulge. Also, red wine apparently is not the magic cure—even though winegrowers would like you to think it is. A shot of whiskey appears to have the same effect on the uterus and the heart.

■ Feverfew Relief

In addition to reducing fevers (true to its name), this herb, taken from the leaves and flowers of the *Tanacetum parthenium* (formerly known as *chrysanthemum partheni-um*), also appears to ease dysmenorrhea (menstrual pain). To benefit from the pain relief of feverfew, it's important to take an extract that contains the chemical parthenolide—not all feverfew products have it. Take about 125 mg of feverfew daily (with a minimum of 0.2% parthenolide) in the form of a capsule or tincture. *Migraine sufferers take note:* Feverfew also works to inhibit histamines and serotonin in the brain, which are partly responsible for those agonizing headaches.

■ Valerian Soothes

Chances are, if you're suffering from painful periods (dysmenorrhea), you're not about to leave your bed, let alone go out and do hard labor. But if you want to enjoy the relaxing effects of valerian, make sure your plans for the day don't require mental alertness.

Valerian, most often taken in capsule form because the liquid has a strong smell, is a natural sedative. The normal dose is around 100 to 200 mg, with about 1% valerenic acid. But remember, while valerian is probably safer than Valium, its effects are similar.

■ An Acupressure Time-out

Give painful period cramps the thumbs down—literally. With a partner's help, try a two-minute acupressure solution. While lying face down on a firm floor or (padded) bench, expose your rear end and lower back so that your partner can apply skin-to-skin pressure. Using the flats of his or her thumbs, and starting at the tailbone (or coccyx), your partner should press down just to the left and right of the spinal column, in a straight line north to the small of the back. The pressure should end at waist level; one minute on each side may well bring relief.

■ *Caraway Cure*

Caraway seeds are not just for rye bread anymore. If you suffer from painful cramps on a regular basis, try this concoction:

1 Using a mortar and pestle, crush one ounce of fresh caraway seeds and pour into a glass jar.

2 Add 20 ounces of cold water to the jar and let steep overnight.

3 The next morning, strain the mixture.

Take one or two tablespoons of the liquid as needed throughout the day for the duration of the cramps. As long as it's refrigerated, the liquid will be potent for several days.

■ *Chamomile-Based Concoction*

This combination herbal approach is a bit stronger than some other herbal remedies for cramping:

1 Heat a cup of water to boiling in a small pot and remove from heat.

2 Add one tablespoon of chamomile and a pinch or so of grated ginger root.

3 Steep the mixture like a tea.

4 Pour the mixture into a coffee mug and drink the entire cup.

The combination of herbs is both soothing and restorative.

■ *Fish Oil as an Adjunct*

It may not allow you to forego conventional pain medication altogether, but fish oil taken in capsule form throughout your period has a noticeable effect on many women who have painful cramps every month.

Based on recent research among women who cramp often, those who took fish oil capsules needed only half as many ibuprofen pills (5) to cope with their cramps as those who took only ibuprofen (10). However, doctors caution women with a tendency to bleed easily against taking fish oil supplements.

PREMENSTRUAL SYNDROME (PMS)— GENERAL SYMPTOMS

■ *Evening Primrose Oil Works for You*

The problem with most remedies for PMS is that symptoms vary so much from woman to woman. But natural science is catching up. Many researchers now believe that deficiencies in essential fatty acids are associated with severe PMS symptoms, such as breast tenderness, pain and irritability.

By taking supplements of evening primrose oil (made from seeds) at mealtimes, women can replace some essential fatty acids at a critical time of the month. Typical dosages range from three to six capsules a day and should only be taken at that time of the month.

PMS Help Rated by Women

When women with premenstrual syndrome were asked to name the treatments they found most helpful, the women cited dietary changes, evening primrose oil, exercise and vitamins, including B6, most often.

■ *Cooking Wisely*

Although doctors still don't know precisely how to treat or explain PMS, they now believe it is directly affected by hormonal changes, including monthly fluctuations in progesterone, a powerful female hormone.

One way to counteract PMS-related hormonal changes is to use specific cooking oils during—or before—the premenstrual phase. Corn, safflower and canola oils all contain substances that influence the body's production of prostaglandin, and in turn help relieve PMS symptoms.

A Mood Menu

Feeling blue? Whether from PMS or menopausal hormonal fluctuations, certain snacks can boost your mood. Bananas, tomatoes, walnuts and carbohydrates, such as bread with jam, help the body raise levels of serotonin, a neurotransmitter in the brain that regulates mood. Depending on the severity of your depression, changes in diet may offer some relief and can also work well in conjunction with other remedies, such as antidepressants or therapy.

■ *Some Relief with Black Cohosh Root*

Used much more frequently in Europe than in the US, black cohosh root is approved in Germany to aid women who have PMS as well as those who are going through menopause (especially those who are experiencing hot flashes).

The reason it works is not yet fully understood, but part of this plant's root has been shown to have estrogen-like effects. It may work as an estrogen mimic, which may explain why it is so helpful to some women—and also why the German government restricts the course of treatment to six months or less. Powerful stuff, perhaps. Typical daily dosages are 40 to 200 mg of the root in capsule form. Tinctures can also be taken.

■ *Homeopathic Help*

Pulsatilla is the multipurpose homeopathic remedy for menstrual discomfort and PMS. Also known as windflower, homeopaths believe pulsatilla can control irregular periods, as well as water retention or emotional "blues" resulting from PMS. A 30C strength three times a day when necessary balances a woman's body.

PMS-RELATED MOOD CHANGES

■ *Homeopathic Remedy Brightens Moods*

When serious mood swings strike during a bout of PMS, accompanied by excessive feelings of hopelessness or despair, homeopaths might suggest using pulsatilla. Choose the 30C potency, and drop 10 pills into a liter bottle of spring water. Keep it with you at home, the office, on the road, and sip it all day long—between meals, not during them. It's best taken when it does not have to compete with other substances in your system.

■ *Homeopathic Pellets*

Can't bear the thought of yet another cup of chamomile tea? Instead, you might try the homeopathic version of chamomile to aid relaxation during PMS. Follow package instructions—but standard treatment is usually 30C three times a day.

■ "B" in a Better Mood

According to a growing number of dietitians and nutritionists, vitamin B6 works within the body to help patients overcome irritability, feelings of anxiousness and even depressed moods. Recent studies suggest that many women suffering from these types of emotional problems actually have a B6 vitamin deficiency.

What's the link? This vitamin helps the body synthesize amino acids into serotonin, a neurotransmitter that regulates mood. Consider trying 25 to 50 mg of B6 as a supplement, in addition to eating wisely.

■ Nutritional Rescue

When your hormones are on a roller-coaster ride, you may occasionally—or quite regularly and predictably—feel down in the dumps. Tryptophan-rich foods (such as soy beans, dairy products and protein like chicken, turkey or eggs) can sometimes ease cases of mild, episodic depression. How does it work? It stimulates the production of serotonin, a neurotransmitter in the brain that regulates mood.

■ PMS Relief Tea

This tea recipe offers PMS relief. It contains ginger, which helps counter mood swings, fatigue and nausea. Dandelion root acts as a mild diuretic to help reduce bloating and water retention and is rich in minerals that help prevent PMS.

To make the tea:

1 Bring two cups of water to a boil.

2 Stir in one and one-half teaspoons of fresh, grated ginger root and one-half teaspoon dandelion root.

3 Simmer for 15 minutes on low heat.

4 Serve and sip, adding honey if desired.

PREMENSTRUAL WATER RETENTION

■ Natural, Three-Step Plan

If you suffer from premenstrual bloating each month, enlist this three-step plan to help beat the bloat:

1 Beginning in the second half of your menstrual cycle, make celery part of your daily diet for a week to 10 days. (It's a mild diuretic.)

2 Increase your intake of potassium-rich foods (e.g., bananas) and water, which may reduce fluid retention.

3 Take vitamin B6, up to 100 mg a day, as a supplement. (It's also a natural diuretic.) Again, beginning in the second half of your cycle, take 50 mg in the morning and 50 mg in the afternoon.

You'll find B6 tablets or capsules in your drugstore, grocery store or health food store. Check the ingredients of your multivitamin before you begin taking extra B6. If B6 is already included in your multivitamin, check with your doctor about possible side effects of excess B6.

■ A Dandy Diuretic

Dandelion leaves, which are potassium rich, work within the body to regulate out-of-whack water levels. Steep a teaspoon of dried dandelion leaves in a cup of hot water for a bloat-busting tea. As an alternative, sauté the leaves in olive oil to tone down some of the bitterness, and serve as a side dish. Or mix dandelion leaves with other types of greens for a PMS-symptom-soothing salad.

OSTEOPOROSIS

■ The Lifelong Calcium Connection

Mother's milk is only the beginning. According to dietitians and doctors, girls and women should incorporate foods rich in calcium throughout their lifetime to protect themselves from osteoporosis.

Why? Because excess calcium in your body is stored in the bones, strengthening them decades before osteoporosis concerns set in. (*Note:* Men suffer from osteoporosis, too, but in lesser numbers.) If you don't get enough calcium in young adulthood, then you put your bones—and overall health—at risk unnecessarily.

How much do you need? Nutritionists suggest 1,000–1,500 mg a day. Calcium is found in ample quantities in milk, yogurt, leafy green vegetables and low-fat cheeses. Supplements can also be incorporated into your diet.

■ Take Calcium Correctly

When it comes to maintaining healthy bones, make all the right moves in your efforts to battle osteoporosis. In order for calcium to be metabolized properly in the body—and ultimately to build up your bones—you should also take 350 mg of magnesium and 400 IU of vitamin E. *And remember:* Dietitians suggest 1,500 mg of calcium from dairy and leafy green vegetables daily.

■ Calcium Maintenance Plan

A diet high in protein and sodium can cause calcium loss from the body, which may put a woman at risk for osteoporosis. Follow a low-sodium diet. To determine how much protein you actually need, follow this simple equation: Multiply your weight in pounds by 0.36 to calculate how many grams of protein you should eat every day. (If you are 20% over the ideal body weight for your height and build, talk to your doctor about a nutritional plan. This formula can

---

Antibiotics for Osteoporosis Sufferers

There's promising news for those with osteoporosis—and those who worry that they're at risk. Recently, researchers have studied the effects of minocycline, an antibiotic, in treating osteoporosis patients. It's an unlikely remedy, but may be more common soon.

According to the studies, this antibiotic not only increases bone density but actually prevents bone loss. In high doses, however, physicians warn that minocycline can be toxic to the liver. Discuss with your physician whether this treatment—or prevention plan—is right for you.

overestimate the safe level of protein for over-weight people.)

■ *Dairy-Free Calcium Drink*

Are you concerned about osteoporosis and trying to add more calcium to your diet, but want to avoid dairy products? Look for calcium tea in your local health food store. This dairy-free alternative can be an important addition to your daily diet to ensure that your bones stay strong. Follow package instructions for best results in taking calcium tea.

OVARIAN HEALTH

CANCER PREVENTION

■ *How Birth Control Pills Boost Ovaries' Health*

More than 10 million US women take birth control pills each year, but only a small minority have learned how to alter their dosage to possibly protect their long-term ovarian health. Some leading OB/GYNs (including David Grimes, MD, of Family Health International, Research Triangle Park, North Carolina) have advocated extending use of the Pill past its normal three-week-on, one-week-off cycle in order to help women control, or "time-shift," their periods. Sometimes women extend their Pill cycles to 10 to 12 weeks in a row, or even six months to a year, without taking time out for menstruation. (Those who suffer from endometriosis may benefit from this schedule.)

Although extended use of the Pill under a doctor's supervision is considered by the FDA to be an "off-label" use of the medication, it is not illegal. And in fact, some researchers believe the fewer periods a woman has during her lifetime, the less risk she will face for developing ovarian cancer. This is a potentially exciting finding, sure to be followed over the next few years. To find out more information, call the Ovarian Cancer National Alliance at 202-331-1332 or www.ovariancancer.org.

PREGNANCY

DELIVERY

■ *Guided Therapy for a Healthy Delivery*

Afraid of giving birth? Guided therapy is the ticket to fear-free delivery. A trained therapist can lead you through relaxing, thought-provoking sessions. During these meetings you discover the source of your anxiety and learn how to cope with these issues before the baby arrives. The number of sessions different women need varies—so do not wait until the week before your due date.

Pregnancy and Natural Therapies

Warning: Ask your doctor before starting any alternative or natural therapy if you are pregnant. Just because it's natural, doesn't mean a remedy is 100% safe and without side effects. In fact, for pregnant women and their growing fetuses, herbs, plants, massage and other complementary therapies may be toxic and could pose health dangers.

■ *Midwives Aid in Natural, Intimate Delivery*

Cold hospitals, distant doctors and an increasing desire for a closer relationship with the person delivering the baby are fueling a boom in nurse-midwifery. Qualified nurse-midwives have nearly doubled in number since 1990, to about 7,000, according to the American College of Nurse-Midwives.

Studies have not indicated that the services of a midwife lead to easier pregnancies and deliveries, but in deliveries using midwives, cesarean and epidural rates are nearly half the national average. And a national study in 1991 found that infant mortality rates for births attended by a nurse-midwife were half the national average (4.1 to 8.6 per 1,000, respectively). Meanwhile, 90% of all midwife-attended births are performed at hospitals.

Costs for a nurse-midwife can vary widely. Expect a bill amounting to about the same costs as a physician's. *Rationale:* Certified nurse-midwives, in particular, provide all the basic services provided by the typical OB/GYN office.

More and more, health insurance—and managed-care plans—cover the services of a midwife, so be sure to check with your carrier. Thirty-one states mandate private-insurance reimbursement of midwives. All states mandate Medicaid reimbursement.

■ *Herbs Help Expel the Placenta*

There aren't numerous scientific studies to prove the connection, but midwives who have seen it in action are believers already: Basil tea taken during delivery somehow helps expel the placenta after birthing.

One clue to its effectiveness might be that essential oil of basil, when used in massage on the belly, helps ease muscle spasms of the intestines. The antispasmodic effects may be strong, so it's wise to use basil moderately.

Note: Some herbalists suggest blue and black cohosh tea as alternatives.

Using the Pill to Prevent Ectopic Pregnancy

A recent study found that the rate of ectopic (tubal) pregnancy is 500 times lower in women who use birth control pills than in women who use no contraception whatsoever. If further studies replicate this finding, this will be an exciting development in preventing an often dangerous condition.

Types of Midwives

To be fully informed when choosing a midwife, you should understand a few terms. There are three types of midwives:

■ *Lay midwives* provide prenatal and delivery care but don't offer other routine gynecological services, such as Pap smears. And although they are qualified to oversee the delivery of a baby, they learn via apprenticeships, not in school programs, and thus lack certification from an accredited school.

■ *Direct-entry midwives* are a small but growing group of certified midwives without a nursing degree. In fact, the first school to offer such certification opened in New York City in 1995.

■ *Certified nurse-midwives*, or nurses trained and certified by an accredited school, are most common. Typically, certified midwives perform all of the routine services done in an OB/GYN's office.

A common thread among the services of all midwives is an emphasis on developing a more personal, longer-lasting relationship with the client.

For assurance when selecting a nurse-midwife, check references and ask about training. To find a midwife, call the American College of Nurse-Midwives at 202-728-9860, or see the Web site at www.midwife.org.

GESTATIONAL DIABETES

■ *Control Through Diet and Exercise*

Gestational diabetes is usually a temporary condition in which the body does not produce enough insulin to handle the increased blood sugar of pregnancy. If controlled, it's usually not serious, but it must be monitored by a doctor. Signs of the ailment include sugar in the urine, unusual thirst, frequent and copious urination and fatigue.

Babies born to mothers with gestational diabetes tend to be large, but serious problems can occur when excessive sugar is allowed to circulate in the mother's blood and enter the fetal circulation. Blood sugar abnormalities disappear after delivery in about 97% of women. While some women need to take insulin, others are able to control blood sugar levels through diet and exercise.

Your diet should be planned by your doctor or a nutritionist. Women with gestational diabetes might benefit from a chromium supplement of 500 micrograms per day. Chromium helps regulate insulin and prevent high blood pressure.

PREGNANCY

"Walking Epidurals" May Ease Pain and Distress

Although many a painful birth has been eased by using an epidural anesthetic, the large needle inserted into the spine often has stirred as much fear as relief in the delivery room. Enter a new kind of birthing aid, the "walking epidural," which seemed promising when tested at Rush-Presbyterian-St. Luke's Hospital in Chicago.

In brief, the walking epidural uses injections that contain less anesthetic and more painkiller than traditional epidurals. In fact, typically, regular epidurals don't contain painkillers, which is why so much anesthetic is traditionally needed. Then, when the lower half of the body is "numbed" during delivery, the mother is not able to push or help with the final stages of birth. The walking epidurals enable women to sit up, get out of bed, if necessary, and help use gravity for the final moments before birth.

■ Tincture Aid

While noting the potential severity of gestational diabetes, some naturopaths and nutritionists recommend supplementing your obstetrician's plan with regular, small sips of gentian (root) tincture before meals. *Suggested dosage:* One-half teaspoonful.

Note: Gentian is considered to be one of the best-known bitter tonics in herbalism today. Interestingly, bitter vegetables, such as endive and radicchio, are also recommended to gestational diabetes patients.

HEMORRHOIDS—PREGNANCY-SAFE REMEDIES
See also Hemorrhoids, page 159

■ Tea to the Rescue

Raspberry leaf tea is a favorite herbal tonic for strengthening the uterus. But herbalists also recommend the brew for gentle hemorrhoid relief during pregnancy. Unfortunately, the treatment doesn't call for drinking the tea.

Instead? A raspberry leaf tea enema will help tone the walls of the rectum and reduce the swelling. An herbalist can help you administer this treatment. Or if you decide to go it alone, repeat the procedure daily as necessary.

■ Sit in a Sitz

A comforting sitz bath containing soothing herbs is a risk-free hemorrhoidal treatment during pregnancy. Add three ounces of dried witch hazel leaves, comfrey leaves and oak bark to enough warm water to cover your lower body. Sit in the bath for 15 minutes with your legs resting on the side of the tub. For a severe condition, take two sitz baths a day until symptoms improve.

■ Comforting Comfrey

For relieving the itch and pain associated with hemorrhoids, apply comfrey ointment externally. Comfrey is high in allantoin, which is known for its cell-renewing and healing properties. Premixed, comfrey ointment or salve is available at your health food store. Follow package instructions, and, to be on the safe side, check with your doctor before using this herbal salve.

LABOR PAINS

Mineral Oil for Smooth Delivery

Many obstetricians perform episiotomies as a routine matter to make delivery easier. But midwives have long relied on mineral oil to lubricate and soften the vaginal opening, allowing for a smooth and more natural delivery. Using mineral oil instead of scissors not only makes the delivery less painful, but will also speed healing time.

Music to Give Birth By

Music therapy, now being used during childbirth, helps ease labor pain naturally and often without drugs. Many couples who want to incorporate music therapy into the birthing process will begin classes during the third trimester.

The goal is to train couples to use music to relax during the early stages of labor, and to give the women the drive and focus to push when need be and to elevate their natural endorphins to block pain. Couples choose a variety of music (from relaxing to energizing) that appeals to them and evokes positive feelings. Many patients who opt for the therapy don't need anesthesia.

For more information, contact the American Music Therapy Association at 301-589-3300, www.musictherapy.org.

■ Arnica Oil Softens Tissues

Because arnica oil can reduce bruising and swelling, midwives (and some doctors) often use arnica as the oil of choice for softening vaginal tissues prior to childbirth. There are no known negative effects from using this natural lubricant during childbirth, and most doctors will use it on request (although you might have to supply it yourself if you wait until the last minute to ask).

■ Evening Primrose Oil—Start Early

To prepare the cervix for labor and childbirth, many midwives recommend evening primrose oil to mothers-to-be. By modifying chemicals known as prostaglandins, evening primrose oil ripens the cervix, making it softer

and thinner. The body easily processes evening primrose oil, but for it to work, women need to start taking it in the final three or four weeks of pregnancy. A capsule a day of evening primrose oil can also decrease breast tenderness. Be sure to consult your doctor or midwife before using this treatment.

■ Hot Tub Cure-All

When you're having labor pains, a hot bath can go a long way. In the late stages of labor, when the walking and position changes cease to provide relief from the pain, midwives often tell women to descend into the Jacuzzi. The warm water relaxes muscles and also facilitates flow of blood. The latter also means that soaking in a hot tub can be a great way to promote healing, in addition to easing aches and pains.

LEG AND BACK PAIN

■ Back Hurts? Check Your Kidneys

Oh, your aching back. If you're pregnant, that pain could be from the fetus pressing up against your kidneys, causing stress and strain. Check with your doctor to ensure that you don't have a full-blown kidney infection. But as long as it's simply stress on your system, drink the juice of half a lemon in a cup of warm water several times a day to cleanse toxins from the kidneys. Or instead of lemon water, try a nettle tea tonic. Infuse one teaspoon of dried nettles in one cup of hot water for 10 minutes, and strain.

MISCARRIAGE PREVENTION

■ A Five-Herb Combination Approach

This may sound like a lot of "medicine" for someone with concerns about a possible miscarriage, but Chinese medicine practitioners say that An Tai Wan, a five-herb combination, can calm a fetus, relax tightened muscles, reduce premature contractions and counter pain. In brief, all these herbs are said to nourish the blood. In particular, the uterus is said to be "warmed" by increased circulation. Check with your doctor or midwife before trying any herbal remedies; but typically the suggested dosage is seven pills, three times a day.

■ Astragalus for Lower-Body Strength

To help maintain strength in the abdominal and pelvic region, especially when fears of miscarriage are present, pregnant women may want to explore astragalus capsules. This herb is often prescribed in Chinese medicine circles to boost energy following illness and exhaustion, and is said to prevent weakness in the lower body, including the legs.

Astragalus is available in herb shops (fresh and in capsule form) and Chinese markets, and can be made into a tea. Toss a handful of the herb into a quart of water; simmer for 30 to 45 minutes. Typical dosage is three cups a day.

■ Natural Miscarriage Prevention

If you have suffered repeated miscarriages, there are a few herbal remedies that might help future pregnancies. According to herbalists, extracts of both false unicorn root and black haw root tone and strengthen the uterus. However, these tonics must be taken under the guidance of a professional—and are difficult to find on one's own. Ask an herbalist or holistic gynecologist for more information.

■ European Approach Gains Favor

To some mothers-to-be, taking any kind of medication while pregnant seems risky. But to those women who have had one or more miscarriages, and who are at risk for another, a recent study in England offers real hope for a healthy pregnancy.

In the study, 90 pregnant women at risk for miscarriage took low-dose aspirin alone or along with an anticoagulant drug, heparin, through 34 weeks of pregnancy. As a result, those who used both drugs had a markedly higher chance of giving birth, compared with those who took aspirin alone or no drugs. The belief is that the drugs help reduce blood clotting (as with heart patients), which might otherwise lead to miscarriage.

Immune-System Treatments

In order not to reject a growing fetus during a normal pregnancy, the mother's immune system essentially turns off the rejection reaction in the uterus, letting the fetus develop. Studies have also shown that this natural shutdown sometimes just fails to kick in, allowing the immune system to attack the developing fetus. When this happens, the pregnancy does not "take," resulting in miscarriage.

As a result of this research, several doctors are now looking to immunology to solve infertility problems. Many couples have been successful in conceiving after receiving immune-system treatments such as IVIg, a gamma-globulin preparation typically given to pregnant women who are Rh negative. Using IVIg in this way to help prevent miscarriage is a nontraditional use of the drug.

Other immune treatments may be used instead of IVIg. If you have had two miscarriages, multiple failures using in vitro fertilization (IVF) or previous immune problems such as lupus or rheumatoid arthritis, you may be a candidate for this immune-system treatment.

MORNING SICKNESS

A Chinese Medicine Tea

As an alternative to pregnancy pillows or your mother's soda-cracker remedies, you might take a tip from Chinese mothers-to-be, who brew fresh ginger tea to treat waves of morning sickness naturally.

Simply place a few slices of raw ginger in a cup, and steep in hot water. This is among the safest of effective herbal remedies, so you need not worry about side effects as you might with stronger herbs.

Raspberry Leaf Tea

Raspberry leaf tea is not the same as raspberry tea. Often, commercial preparations of the tea are fruit-flavored, sweetened beverages that don't contain the healing powers of the plant.

For years, pregnant women have observed the easing of morning-sickness symptoms when they drink raspberry leaf tea regularly. (Some even claim it helps to ease childbirth.) The purported benefits of the leaf, as well as peppermint tea, are that they help to relax muscles of the uterus, and thus ease waves of nausea.

Resources for Reproductive Immunology

The InterNational Council on Infertility Information Dissemination (INCIID; pronounced "inside") is an on-line resource for infertility information that covers cutting-edge technologies and treatments. Visitors can participate in chats and read articles on hot topics.

■ INCIID, www.inciid.org or 703-379-9178

Dr. Alan Beers established the Reproductive Medicine Program at Finch University of Health Sciences/Chicago Medical School in 1987. The Web site includes research results and information on reproductive immunology. You can also visit the discussion board where Dr. Beers answers questions daily. Dr. Beers is professor of obstetrics and gynecology and professor of microbiology and immunology at the Chicago Medical School.

■ Reproductive Medicine Program, www.repro-med.net or 408-356-9500

■ Fennel Seed's Calming Influence

Known to be a strong, yet gentle natural medicine, fennel seeds can help calm the waves of morning sickness that appear on their own particular schedule. Among the most handy of remedies, fresh fennel seeds can be kept in a small plastic bag for periodic munching—no need to steep into a tea. As a bonus, you can use the extra seeds when morning sickness fades, as the herb also helps promote the milk flow of nursing mothers.

The Nose Knows

If the smell of coffee or the thought of pancakes makes you feel queasy, listen to your body. According to homeopaths, a pregnant woman has a natural aversion to those foods she shouldn't eat. In fact, morning sickness is a signal your body is sending to stay away from certain foods because digesting them puts too much stress on your system.

■ Acupressure Relief

This acupressure treatment for morning sickness really hits the spot. Place your right index and middle finger in the hollow between your collarbones. Press fingers against the ball of the right clavicle, using firm pressure. Continue to apply pressure for a minute or so and repeat as needed when nausea hits.

■ Sepia Settles the Stomach

Sepia, otherwise known as cuttlefish ink, is a popular homeopathic remedy for morning sickness—particularly the type where the thought, smell or sight of food makes you nauseated. Dissolve a 30C or 60C tablet in your mouth when you feel sick to your stomach. Make sure that your stomach is empty or that you have not eaten within the last 30 minutes before taking the tablet. You may repeat the dose every hour as needed. After four doses, if no improvement is noticed, you need to look for another treatment or homeopathic solution.

Eating Right?

Women plagued by nausea and bouts of morning sickness should seek advice from a nutritionist on changing their diet. According to the experts, this symptom could, in fact, be a result of something that you ate (e.g., fried foods)—or are not eating. A few alterations to your diet—including eating smaller "mini-meals" every two to three hours and drinking liquids between (not with) meals—may put an end to this pregnancy plague.

■ Meadow Saffron Tempers Morning Sickness

Are you in the early months of your pregnancy? Do you wake up in the morning and can't bear to be near food? Take a 30C tablet of colchicum, derived from meadow saffron, every two to three hours until the stomach settles. If three doses of colchicum doesn't put a stop to nausea or vomiting, try another morning sickness remedy instead.

Nux Vomica Knocks Out Nausea

No more nausea, thanks to nux vomica. Derived from the poison nut, nux vomica is a homeopathic remedy for all types of stomach ailments, and it is gentle enough for morning sickness. Take a 30C tablet every two to three hours. As with other homeopathic remedies, if there's no marked improvement in your condition after three doses, seek an alternative treatment.

Herbs to Avoid When Pregnant

What are some common herbs that should be avoided during pregnancy? Barberry, goldenseal, juniper, sage and thuja. Herbalists recommend that pregnant women avoid any external or internal treatment including teas, creams and capsules that include these herbs. And for more information on other herbs and botanical remedies that pose potential danger, speak to your physician, an herbalist or other health care professional.

Tiny Dose of Ipecac Calms Queasiness

For ages, ipecac syrup has been swallowed to induce vomiting. But according to homeopathic principles, a minute dose of something that causes your symptoms may relieve them. That's why ipecacuanha, a tiny dose of the toxic ipecac root, will soothe an unsettled stomach and morning sickness.

According to homeopaths, ipecacuanha is very effective for women who suffer from severe nausea and vomiting. Take a 30C or 60C tablet every hour as symptoms persist. You may take up to four doses. Be sure your stomach is empty before dissolving the pill in your mouth.

A Sour Morning Remedy

Try this natural remedy for morning sickness. As soon as you wake up in the morning, drink one cup of warm water mixed with one teaspoon of apple cider vinegar. You'll be able to tell pretty quickly whether this trick works for you.

Control Morning Sickness with Biofeedback

Biofeedback is an unusual treatment to combat morning sickness, but it has proven successful for some women. Electrodes attached to your body will measure breathing rates, blood pressure and perspiration levels. These sensors feed into the computer monitor which allows you to watch your stress levels rise and fall. After 5 to 10 treatments, you can learn to relax and control breathing rates, among other body functions, so that nausea subsides.

POSTPARTUM DEPRESSION

Homeopathic Treatments Can Help

An abrupt drop in two hormones, estrogen and progesterone, has a lot to do with the postpartum depression experienced by many mothers after giving birth—not to mention the added stress of suddenly having a new baby in the house and life never being the same again.

To treat postpartum depression, eat foods high in vitamin B6, such as blackstrap molasses, brewer's yeast, wheat bran, soybeans, brown rice, veal, lamb, salmon, tomatoes and bananas. For additional protection, take supplemental magnesium and up to 50 mg daily of vitamin B6.

Various homeopathic remedies may also help:

■ For mild depression, unpredictable moods and weepiness, use pulsatilla.

■ If you're irritable, tired and weak, try Kali carbonicum.

■ Use ignatia if you're weepy and sighing.

■ Try natrum mur if you want to be alone and feel like crying all the time.

■ Start off with sepia if you're feeling weak, tired, sad, hungry, indifferent and have brownish facial discoloration.

With any of these homeopathic remedies, take two doses of a 6C or 30C potency every 10 minutes to one hour, depending on your symptoms. Follow the instructions on the label.

■ Other Mild Antidepressants

Nerve tonics evena and oat straw act as mild antidepressants, will help ease anxiety and soothe body and mind, and are safe for breastfeeding mothers. Take two or three teaspoons of tincture per day, or three to six capsules. You might also try licorice or Siberian ginseng, both of which target the adrenal glands—often stressed during pregnancy and childbirth. Both herbs help energize. Either drink several cups of one of these herbal teas daily, or take two or three teaspoons of a tincture of one daily. Remember to eat nutritionally sound foods and continue with your prenatal vitamins.

■ Arnica Eases Aches and Pains After Childbirth

Whether you've chosen natural childbirth or had a C-section, you're probably experiencing a fair amount of pain after the delivery of your baby. A homeopathic dose of arnica can help alleviate soreness resulting from the birth. But check with your doctor before taking a homeopathic pellet—particularly if you are breastfeeding—for dosage instructions and to make sure it's safe.

PREMATURE LABOR

■ Herb Slows Contractions

Among its many uses, valerian in capsule form can be used as a sedative to slow premature contractions during pregnancy, or if you simply need more time to get to the hospital or wait for the midwife and birthing coach to arrive in your home.

Herbalists, naturopaths and others attest to the fact that valerian can soothe the nerves of the uterus, while reducing the pace of uterine contractions. Typical suggested dosage is two capsules, but check with your health professional well ahead of the due date to make sure valerian would be appropriate for you in this instance.

SKIN SPLOTCHES

■ A Two-Step Hint: Medicine and Mushrooms

The common but nagging skin splotches (called melasma) that occur during pregnancy don't always disappear after childbirth. In recent years, dermatologists have recommended a prescription of Retin-A, along with a skin-bleaching cream that contains hydroquinone. Together, these medications have worked rather well, although using bleaching creams at home can be tricky, and can sometimes make dark spots worse.

But kojic acid, a new, perhaps gentler and safer bleaching agent made from mushrooms, has begun to gain favor among dermatologists and patients who have used it so far. It won't replace the Retin-A part of the treatment; but it appears to be safer to use than hydroquinone, as it won't bleach normal skin tone by mistake. As a bonus, it is antibacterial. Have your doctor check into it if it hasn't been recommended for your condition.

STRETCH MARKS

■ Citrus Solution of Sorts

A good way to prevent or minimize stretch marks during and after pregnancy is to use orange blossom essential oil as a soothing massage. When you add a few drops of orange blossom oil to a pint of sunflower oil, you've made a handy massage oil that can be spread, gently, directly onto the belly. It should help keep your skin supple and firm.

■ Fighting Back Against Stretch Marks

Until recently, the only advice dermatologists could give about stretch marks was to prevent them by moisturizing well, especially during pregnancy. However, if you had stretch marks already, there wasn't much you could do—until now. Anecdotal evidence suggests that vitamin A derivative Retin-A (an antiwrinkle and anti-acne prescription product) may be able to remove stretch marks.

Important: Do not use if you are pregnant.

SWOLLEN ANKLES

■ Salt? For Swelling?

A minute dose of the homeopathic remedy *natrum muriaticum* (sodium chloride or salt) will relieve swelling and water retention in puffy ankles. Take 30C every few hours as needed. Pregnant women can rely on this treatment for shrinking swollen ankles and lower legs. Begin the therapy during the third month, but don't take the tablets after your eighth month. And double-check with your doctor before taking any alternative remedy.

SLEEP DISTURBANCES
See also **Insomnia**, page 169

■ The Hormonal Link

After having sleepless nights, women may well wonder how hormones affect the female sleep pattern. Ever-fluctuating levels of progesterone can throw a woman from nights of insomnia to days when she just can't keep her eyes open. Why? Progesterone is the hormone that readies the endometrium, the mucous-membrane lining of the uterus, for a fertilized egg. Plus, it's a hormone that induces sleep.

During ovulation, progesterone levels rise, then they decline around the time of your period, causing some restless, sleepless nights. What can you do? Limit alcohol and caffeine, get plenty of exercise and try to get to bed at the same time each night to make sure your internal sleep clock doesn't get off kilter.

UTERINE FIBROIDS

■ Surgical Update

A cutting-edge procedure is good news for women with uterine fibroids. Using a catheter, a physician inserts small plastic balls into the vessel that feeds the fibroid, cutting off the flow of blood. Within weeks, the fibroid shrinks significantly—or altogether. The best part? This surgery doesn't require heavy sedation, a large incision or stitches. Ask your doctor about this procedure for treating fibroids.

■ Alternative Treatment

Instead of surgery, a doctor may prescribe drug therapy for keeping uterine fibroids in check. Leuprolide, a hormone-balancing drug approved for treating prostate cancer, has been used in some instances to treat uterine fibroids. For more information on this type of treatment, ask your gynecologist or family physician.

VAGINAL DRYNESS

■ Sexual Healing

Recent gynecological research has shown that sexual activity stimulates secretion of moisture and mucus from vaginal walls regardless of a woman's age. (The amount of moisture may decrease over time, however.) Some gynecologists and naturopaths will sometimes suggest that, instead of using prescription or other creams, menopausal women try to have more sex—with a partner or through masturbation.

Bottom line: Blood flow to the pelvis from rigorous activity (sex or exercise) aids the production of moisture in and around the vagina.

■ Herbal Remedy

Call it a naturopath's secret. Calendula cream applied to the vaginal opening alleviates vaginal dryness and any accompanying irritation. This herbal salve is available prepackaged at most health food stores. Follow directions on the label for safe use.

■ Opt for Soothing Vitamin E

If the onset of menopause has caused vaginal dryness, a cure may be as close as your cabinet. Vitamin E oil is a safe, natural remedy for dryness and irritation. Apply the contents of a 400-IU capsule to the vaginal opening and inside the vagina once or twice a day.

■ Avoid Dehydrating Drinks

To ease the discomfort of vaginal dryness, avoid drinking alcohol, caffeine and sage tea (a therapy for hot flashes); they all sap moisture from your system.

■ Using Lubricants and Creams in Nonstandard Ways

For women who experience vaginal dryness that adversely affects their sex lives, a trip to the doctor often results in a prescription for estrogen cream and possibly advice to try a lubricant. What many doctors don't tell their patients, or perhaps don't realize themselves, is that women may be applying the cream too deeply to bring them the most benefit. There is no health reason why creams shouldn't be applied to the labia—it's a matter of trial and error—or in many cases…trial and success!

VAGINAL YEAST INFECTION

OCCASIONAL INFECTION

■ Herbal Suppositories Can Help

It's not a well-publicized part of naturopathic medicine, but often naturopaths provide gynecological treatments, especially when the conditions are not deemed dangerous. Such is the case with many yeast infections, which may occur occasionally and which can be successfully treated with a natural herbal suppository.

The suppository consists of a base of powdered boric acid, combined with antifungal herbs such as calendula and barberry (also used for bladder infections). Whether this should be an adjunct treatment or a substitute for a conventional antifungal treatment is a question for your doctor to answer.

■ Internal Herbal Aid

For some of the same reasons people take goldenseal to fight off colds and flu, goldenseal tincture (or tea) can be used in helping the immune system battle yeast infections. One of the compounds in goldenseal is berberine, a natural antibiotic. According to naturopaths and herbalists, yeast is one of the microorganisms particularly vulnerable to berberine.

For tea, brew one heaping teaspoon of the dried herb in a cup of water. Drink twice a day.

RECURRENT INFECTIONS

■ *Dietary Changes Can Make a Difference*

The good news first: Millions of women are now able to treat their vaginal yeast infections at home, using over-the-counter medicines that formerly were available by prescription only.

Now, the bad news: Millions *more* women are suffering from the itching, pain and discharge associated with yeast infections than were afflicted with the condition in the 1960s and 1970s. In large part, the overuse of antibiotics has led to long-term changes in women's bodies that make them more receptive to the infection. Dietary regimens can go a long way toward reducing recurrent infections (check with your doctor or a naturopath to see if dietary changes would be appropriate for you).

The hallmarks of an anti-yeast diet are: A very low-sugar, yeast-free regimen (hardly any breads) and very few fermented foods. Also, increased intake of yogurt and garlic are recommended, as well as a possible nutritional supplement of acidophilus (a friendly bacteria).

■ *Echinacea Keeps Recurrences at Bay*

Evidence of echinacea's efficacy increases year by year. Recently, a European study of women with recurrent yeast infections showed that when subjects combined traditional antifungal medications with the echinacea, they reported far better results than with the antifungal treatment alone.

In tincture form, or in prepackaged bottles, use 20 to 30 drops in a full glass of water, three times a day (check with your health care professional for how long to take this treatment).

■ *Cardamom's the Word*

More often recommended by herbalists as a chew-the-seeds breath freshener and indigestion aid, cardamom (essential) oil may bring marked relief to those suffering from yeastlike overgrowth and inflammation of the vagina.

One possible remedy is to soak a tampon in a half-cup of yogurt, to which two or three drops of cardamom oil have been added. Insert the tampon overnight; repeat for up to six nights. Tea tree oil can be used in place of the cardamom oil as well.

CHAPTER 4

Especially for Men

BALDNESS

■ *Herbs for Hair*

Saw palmetto berries are widely recognized for their potential to diminish an enlarged prostate gland, say studies at major medical institutions such as the University of Chicago. But saw palmetto may also help prevent baldness by blocking the body's production of dihydrotestosterone (DHT), a substance that deadens hair follicles.

Adding licorice extract (which also reduces the body's amount of DHT) to your shampoo helps do the same thing. For additional benefits, regular scalp massage can increase blood circulation to the head.

■ *Three Drugs May Do the Trick*

In the 1980s, doctors and patients found out that the drug minoxidil does help grow—and regrow—hair. It just didn't work predictably well for many of those who tried it. Ten years and countless trials later, some dermatologists think that a three-drug regimen may be more successful in battling baldness.

This less common regimen involves mixing Rogaine (minoxidil), now available over the counter, with Proscar (finasteride), originally a medication for prostate enlargement, and thyroid hormone. The application method is similar to what is suggested on the packages of minoxidil: Rub it into the scalp every day. Of course, this combination treatment will cost more—but early results are promising.

Note: Finasteride should be avoided by men contemplating fatherhood. (Women should also avoid it before and during pregnancy.)

■ *Sunny-Side Up*

"Male pattern baldness" is a form of hormone-related hair loss. But of more concern to many men and women afflicted with hair loss is alopecia areata, a lesser-known disorder that causes hair loss in nearly 4 million Americans.

Typically, hair grows in cycles of two to six years, after which hair lies dormant, and then falls out. On a normal head, some hair is at the beginning of the cycle while some is further along in the growth cycle. With alopecia areata, some or all of the hair follicles stop growing at the same time, leaving tiny bald spots or complete baldness. Normally, hair will grow back in anywhere from six months to a year. But for those afflicted, the wait can be devastating.

However, research shows that alopecia areata may be an autoimmune disease, and this information has opened the door for a new treatment. Many doctors use ultraviolet light to prevent the body's immune system from attacking hair follicles. In what may be one of the few cases when a slight sunburn is a good thing, psoralen, a medicine that increases sun sensitivity, is rubbed onto the affected area. Then, the doctor shines a UV light on the scalp until the bald area shows some redness or irritation.

Figuratively speaking, the body's immune cells start worrying about the irritation caused by the sunburn, and stop worrying about the hair follicle, which really never meant the body any harm in the first place!

Blocking DHT to Prevent Hair Loss

The male hormone DHT is responsible for more than just hair loss. It can also cause the prostate gland to enlarge in middle-aged or older men. To mitigate this effect, doctors often prescribe Proscar, a DHT blocker. Proscar also seems to prevent hair loss, although it was not originally developed for this purpose. (Across a wide population, the drug may work better for controlling prostate swelling than it does for ending hair loss.)

For preventing hair loss, low doses of Proscar (sold under the name Propecia) appear to work better than Rogaine and other vasodilators. Although large-scale, FDA-sanctioned tests have not been completed, there does not seem to be a problem using Rogaine and Proscar together, as many patients do. As with any prescription medication, it is essential to discuss the possible effects with your doctor prior to using it.

GENITAL HERPES

■ *For Men Only*

Zinc oxide applied directly to genital herpes lesions helps relieve pain and burning sensations, as well as clear up blisters. Look for a cream or ointment containing zinc oxide at your local drugstore or health food store.

Be advised: Zinc oxide is for external use only. It should never be applied to mucous membranes.

Testosterone Treatment for Chronic Cases

There is no male menopause, many urologists claim. Yet, they are paying attention to recent research (at St. Louis University and elsewhere) showing that about one third of men over 50 have a deficiency of testosterone, the hormone that fuels a man's sex drive. Since women sometimes take estrogen supplements after menopause to replace what their ovaries no longer produce, it might make sense for men to take replacement doses of testosterone after age 50. Not so fast, the experts say.

The fact is that it's not easy to measure testosterone levels in the blood, and figure out the dosage of supplements you'll need to reach a level you used to be at in your 30s, when erections came more easily.
There is concern that hormone supplements might contribute to some cancers—especially prostate cancer. There is simply not enough information yet on the effects of testosterone supplements on men's entire bodies.

Yes, there are cases in which men (and sometimes women) are clearly deficient in testosterone—and where monthly injections of up to 200 milligrams (mg) will spark libido and improve sex lives. But the details are still being worked out.

IMPOTENCE

■ A Way to Delay the Inevitable

In middle age, impotence is a lot more common than even knowledgeable men realize. A recent federally funded study found that nearly half of American men over age 40 have experienced impotence—a failure to achieve an erection sufficient for intercourse—to some degree. Fewer than half of those same American men went to a doctor or therapist to see how they might correct the problems they were experiencing. That amounts to millions of untreated conditions that could seriously affect relationships.

In the instance of common, moderate impotence, quitting smoking and starting an aerobic exercise routine under a doctor's supervision can keep erection problems at bay, or at least delay them. After all, when blood vessels of the penis are partially clogged, erections don't always happen on cue. The cause may be a lack of fitness, not a lack of virility. Then, too, merely being aware that impotence occurs to most men on occasion, may prevent an emotional overreaction.

■ Herbal Roto-Rooter

Better erections don't grow on trees. Or do they? In a recent German study, some 50% of the subjects who consumed extracts from leaves of the ginkgo tree regained the sexual potency that they previously had lost.

Two points to note: First, the subjects had circulatory problems going into the study; second, the study stretched over six months. That's a lot of ginkgo leaf. But in the end, not a bad alternative at all for middle-aged men who are willing to experiment.

Ginkgo extract has been tested by some physicians who have discovered positive results with 60 to 240 milligrams (mg) per day. Doses higher than these can lead to diarrhea, restlessness and irritability. Be sure to use the ginkgo that comes in the form of a standardized extract, which should be indicated on the

bottle or box. And be sure to run this treatment alternative by your doctor.

The Vacuum Effect for Organic Impotence

For many men, the most dreaded pillow talk is summed up in just four words: "It happens to everyone." Indeed, occasional impotence—brought on by performance anxiety or other stress—is often more embarrassing than anything else. But for most men who experience impotence more than occasionally, the cause is not psychological. Approximately 87% of all cases of impotence have a physical cause, at least in part. Organic impotence is a vascular problem, and often accompanies diseases such as diabetes and chronic heart disease.

The vacuum device, a minimally invasive solution to impotence, helps draw blood into the penis, causing it to become erect. How does it work? The man places the tube around his penis and against his lower abdomen, then presses a button, creating a vacuum that draws the blood into the penis. At the base of the penis, a rubber ring acts as a tourniquet, allowing the penis to stay erect for up to 25 minutes. The drawback of this apparatus? It doesn't really allow for spontaneity and can be a bit embarrassing. Furthermore, the clock is ticking. Typically, it's recommended only for older, married patients.

■ Better Erections Through Better Nutrition

Size does matter. Because the penis is so much smaller than the heart (let's be honest), its blood vessels in middle-aged and older men are more prone to blockage than are those of the heart. But this fact is not commonly known. As a result, there is a lot more erectile dysfunction and impotence than doctors are aware of. Millions of cases go unreported and untreated.

The good news is the preventive treatments are simple and important for general wellness: The antioxidant nutrients recommended for promoting general health (see page 30) might also prevent erection problems.

In addition, urologists recommend fish oil supplements to help keep blood running freely *throughout* your body. In particular, EPA (eicosapentainic acid) from fish oil works well in concert with vitamins C, E and beta-carotene to help reduce "stickiness" of blood through vessels. So, grilled fish, with perhaps a side of steamed spinach or carrots, could actually make for a very romantic dinner.

■ Full of Beans?

The fava bean is regarded in some naturalist circles as the food of choice for any man struggling with erection problems. It contains significant amounts of L-dopa, which is used to treat Parkinson's disease. L-dopa can be toxic in large doses, but a plate of beans won't contain anywhere near toxic levels and might, in fact, be enough to improve blood flow where it is desired most.

■ Anyone for...Viagra Lite?

A number of sex and marital therapists are beginning to discuss how certain men might use one of the drugs to treat impotence —Viagra, Levitra or Cialis—recreationally and safely, rather than as a treatment for clinical impotence. For middle-aged and older men who are looking to improve their sexual performance, a tactic involves obtaining a prescription (legally), and then cutting the pills in half. You might call it a compromise—between safety and sparked sexuality—but as always, package inserts and doctor's orders must be followed to guard against side effects.

■ A Shot in the...

For most people, getting a shot is no fun, and giving one to yourself is practically out of the question. But the drug Caverject works as a vasodilator and muscle relaxant and is now easy to administer with small needles.

Caverject, which is about 75% effective in treating impotence, must be injected directly into the penis, which may scare some men. But it's virtually painless, convenient and takes just 10 minutes to work.

■ Impotence and the Muse

Muse may be one of the few erectile dysfunction treatments a couple can incorporate into foreplay. Muse, a drug developed by Vivus, Inc., and approved in early 1997 by the FDA, is a mini-suppository filled with the drug alprostadil. Alprostadil increases blood flow into the penis, and patients use a tiny applicator to insert the suppository—which is smaller than a grain of rice—into the urethra where it is absorbed so it will spread into surrounding

tissues. Like Caverject, Muse takes about 10 minutes to start working. And the best part is that in order to help the suppository melt, a man should roll his penis between his hands (back and forth—like a pencil). There's nothing in the warning label that says his partner can't do this for him.

INCONTINENCE

■ Pulsed Magnetic Therapy

In this newest method, a mild magnetic current flows through the seat of a special chair called the "NeoControl" chair. The current stimulates contraction of pelvic floor muscles. No device is inserted into the body. Individuals remain clothed during treatment.

Therapy usually involves two 20-minute sessions each week for eight weeks. After treatment, muscles are strengthened and Kegels are done more effectively. For more information on the NeoControl chair, visit www.neocontrol.com/index.htm or call 877-636-2668 or 800-895-4298.

■ Think "Dry"

Bladder training, in which people adopt a variety of techniques to control the urge to urinate, can be used to treat urge and stress incontinence in both men and women. One common method is distraction—where sufferers simply think about things other than their bladder. An alternative is to void the bladder on a schedule, gradually increasing the time between bathroom visits.

Keeping a bladder diary—taking note of leaks, urges and bathroom visits, as well as which liquids were consumed beforehand, and what you were doing (sitting, running, driving) during episodes of incontinence—may help to pinpoint patterns that can be corrected.

INFERTILITY

EARLY STAGE, MALE

■ *Organic Produce May Produce More Sperm*

There are lots of reasons why Americans eat organic foods, but until recently, boosting male fertility wasn't one of them. However, new information indicates that men who follow organic diets have, on average, higher sperm counts than those who eat more conventional foods. A study from Denmark comparing the sperm counts of organic farmers with those of men who worked for an airline, showed that the farmers, whose diets were laden with organically grown fruits and vegetables, produced 43% more sperm in their semen than their study counterparts. (Admittedly, factors other than lack of pesticides may have come into play.) Until more research is completed, you might consider "going organic" during times of planned conception.

■ *Strawberry Aid*

In a developing country with more than 1 billion people, infertility would not seem to be the first priority of doctors. Even so, Chinese medicine practitioners in Asia and in the West say that eating strawberries is a way to help boost fertility—male and female.

This decidedly low-tech approach to conceiving babies does not work by itself, meaning that a regimen of a certain number of strawberries a day won't bring immediate results. But Chinese medical experts say that yin and yang energy balance does relate to fertility, and that eating strawberries regularly can remedy a shortage of yang energy. *FYI:* Yin is considered "cooling"; yang is considered "heating."

■ *Recognize the Zinc Link*

If you know or suspect that poor sperm quality may be contributing to an infertility problem, consider zinc. In many cases of male infertility, a zinc deficiency has been detected. It may not be the cause, per se, but over a span of a few months up to two years, men who have taken standard doses (400 mg a day) of zinc supplements have exhibited a noted improvement in semen quality.

Note: Seminal fluid, prostatic fluid and sperm together make up semen.

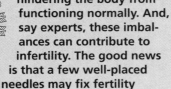

Removing Energy Blockages

Acupuncture works on the meridians of the body, through which energy flows, according to Asian medicine principles. It also corrects imbalances and blockages that may be hindering the body from functioning normally. And, say experts, these imbalances can contribute to infertility. The good news is that a few well-placed needles may fix fertility problems within a few—or, in some instances, more than 10—sessions.

Forget About Cigarettes and Sex

Not long ago, in a respected urology journal, researchers reported that sperm cells of men who regularly smoked cigarettes couldn't swim as efficiently as those of nonsmokers. What's more, it turned out that smokers' sperm cells didn't perform as well on tests that gauge the ability of the sperm to penetrate the outer shell of a female's egg. This suggests that couples trying to conceive make certain that the father-to-be, as well as the prospective mother, quit smoking early on in their family planning.

■ Vitamin C for Healthy Sperm

Agglutination could very well be the cause of your infertility problems. What is it? It's a condition in which sperm clump together and become sluggish.

Fortunately, there's a natural, nutritional treatment: A high dose (1,000 mg) of vitamin C daily for one month.

■ Trying to Conceive? No Vino for You

If you and your partner are trying to conceive a baby, then lower that glass. Alcohol can diminish fertility in both men and women. Its toxicity can affect sperm production in males and hormonal balances in women. There is a direct link between the quantity of alcohol consumed and its effect on fertility.

JOCK ITCH

■ Garlic Aid

Jock itch can take the enjoyment out of any exercise—or any day. The itching is caused by fungus, which tends to thrive in dark, moist areas. One possible cause is health club towels washed with water not hot enough to sterilize.

If you get a case, nutrition therapy calls for the addition of raw garlic to your meals for its antifungal properties. You can give supplements a try if you can't tolerate the garlic cloves, though research is scarce on deodorized products.

Also, cut down on or eliminate yeast sources, such as bread, baked goods and alcohol (be sure to check ingredients of processed foods). Some alternative healers believe that yeast can predispose some people to fungal infections, such as jock itch and athlete's foot.

OSTEOPOROSIS

■ Finding Tough-to-Find Medication

Most people believe that osteoporosis is a woman's disease. But it affects millions of men, too, although many of them develop it later in life than their female counterparts. In addition to recommending regular weight-bearing exercise and calcium supplements (and calcium-rich diets), some doctors prescribe testosterone supplements (via injection, gel or adhesive patch) to help build up men's bones, in the same way gynecologists often prescribe estrogen for women.

While totally legal, this use of testosterone supplements hasn't yet been approved by the FDA because they haven't been studied over the long term. As an alternative, men might ask their doctor about some of the other, newer osteoporosis drugs for women. Might they be applicable—even if they haven't been studied for men? Such off-label uses of drugs occur quite often in medicine, sometimes with good results, though the risk of unanticipated side effects is greater.

PEYRONIE'S DISEASE

■ Curved Erection Has Cure

Developing a curved erection in adulthood is not only embarrassing, it is considered a deformity by some men who have it. And quite often, sex is so uncomfortable and frustrating that it is avoided altogether. Peyronie's disease, caused by scar tissue that develops on one side of the penis, is usually treated (and cured) with surgery. But most men who go to see a doctor for the problem are not aware that *as many as one-third* of all cases of Peyronie's disease heal by themselves within one year to 18 months, without any medical intervention.

Besides so-called "watchful waiting," 400 IU of vitamin E daily is frequently suggested.

PRIAPISM

■ Water for Painful Erections

While priapism—prolonged, painful erection of the penis—may appear to be the opposite of impotence, it is often a precursor. In a patient who suffers from priapism, prolonged erection often occurs regardless of sexual stimulation (although intercourse or masturbation can trigger it as well) and can last for hours, even days. The condition is common in boys with sickle cell anemia. Unfortunately, treatment for priapism is often unsuccessful, and most severe cases eventually require surgery.

Secondary priapism—which can be caused by underlying illnesses such as urinary tract infections, venereal disease or prostatitis—generally disappears once the primary malady is treated. Acute priapism is usually difficult to treat, and erections can last for weeks, accompanied by moderate to severe pain.

In cases that don't require surgery, the pain and duration of a sudden attack sometimes can be mitigated by urinating, drinking water, then taking a warm bath immediately after the erection begins.

PROSTATE TROUBLES

PROSTATE CANCER

■ Cut the Fat

Low-fat eating has gotten another boost. Researchers at the Harvard School of Public Health have found that men who eat higher-fat diets have higher rates of prostate cancer. And the suspected reason? A link between fat and testosterone production. And urologists know that testosterone fuels the growth of prostate tissue, including cancerous prostate tissue. As is often the case, more research is needed to confirm the findings, but a low-fat diet provides so many other benefits, a healthier prostate may be but a bonus.

One-Stop Shopping

Whether you are looking for information on common conditions such as enlargement of the prostate, known as benign prostate hyperplasia (BPH), inflammation or infection of the prostate (prostatitis) or prostate cancer, contact the American Foundation for Urologic Disease, 1000 Corporate Blvd., Suite 410, Linthicum, MD 21090, 800-828-7866, www.afud.org.

■ Ultrasound for a Better Exam

For decades men have complained about the digital rectal exam, saying it is a crude way to examine the health of the prostate gland. Recently, an ultrasound probe—a kinder and gentler approach than a doctor's gloved finger—has been developed to aid diagnosis. At your next checkup, ask your doctor if he has ultrasound available, although it is new enough that most urologists have not used it for this purpose.

Ultrasound can detect growths that doctors can't feel; however, the probe may not be able to distinguish between malignant and benign growths. That is one reason why ultrasound may at times be considered "excessive treatment" (by insurance companies) for many men under 45 who exhibit no prostate problems and have no family history of prostate cancer.

■ Ejaculation as Prevention

When the results were tallied, the findings were surprising. A recent study in England showed that men who had ejaculated five times a week or more had a significantly lower incidence of prostate cancer than those who were markedly less sexually active. It's too soon to say that there is a definitive relationship between the two phenomena—but it is not too soon to speculate or, male health experts believe, to test the hypothesis.

■ Support Groups Ease Emotional Pain

In the spirit of support groups founded by breast cancer patients in the 1980s, such as Y-Me, two national groups for prostate cancer survivors arrived on the scene in the 1990s: Us Too!, based in the Chicago area, and the Man-to-Man program, organized by the American Cancer Society. In both groups, members share first-hand information about doctors and treatments. Testimonials can be powerful and extremely helpful. (In some Man-to-Man meetings, members wear coded badges to identify the type of treatment they have undergone: Surgery, radiation, hormonal, etc.)

■ Us Too! International, Inc., 5003 Fairview Ave., Downers Grove, IL 60515, 800-808-7866, www.ustoo.org

■ Man-to-Man, c/o American Cancer Society, 800-ACS-2345, www.cancer.org

No Sex Please, Before the Blood Test

Urologists recently reported a significant finding regarding PSA testing and the male prostate gland: In order to provide an accurate measure of PSA—prostate specific antigen—in the bloodstream, men should refrain from having sex 24 to 48 hours before the test. The proteins found in PSA, which are known to become more abundant after ejaculation, are made by both healthy and cancerous cells. By restricting sex before testing, doctors have a better chance of getting an accurate PSA reading.

■ The Truth About PSA Tests

The PSA blood test, for middle-aged and older men, helps doctors gauge the state of prostate health by measuring the density of a substance in the blood, prostate specific antigen (PSA). Typical readings range from 2.0 to over 15 ng/ml (and occasionally over 100). Most men, if they know a bit about PSA, believe that as long as it's under 4.0, you're okay. Not always.

The new thinking in urology is that the change in PSA levels over time is more important than a mere number. Some men have a PSA of 3.2 and have cancer cells in the prostate, whereas other men may have a PSA of 14 (due to other conditions) without any detectable cancer whatsoever.

Bottom line: Beginning in your forties or fifties (based on your doctor's assessment of your personal prostate cancer risk), get a digital rectal exam and the results of your PSA so you can have a baseline score.

■ Green Tea Cancer Cure

Recent laboratory research conducted by the Mayo Clinic reveals that a plant substance in green tea is a powerful inhibitor of prostate cancer cells. Although clinical tests haven't yet been conducted on humans, prostate cancer is much less common in Asian males—who consume more plant products—than in the West.

Since the cancer-fighting component in green tea is structurally like the components found in red wine and some vegetables, future research will concentrate on these substances.

PROSTATITIS

■ Stream of Consciousness

Prostatitis is the benign inflammation of the prostate gland usually triggered by an infection. The symptoms (which more often afflict younger men) include pain during urination and ejaculation, and frequent urination. It can be a difficult condition to treat because circulation is poor in the gland. Here are options beyond prescription antibiotics:

■ Drink lots of water to cleanse the system.

■ Avoid irritants such as alcohol, tobacco and caffeine.

■ Beware of physical activities that require prolonged sitting, such as riding a bike, motorcycle or horse.

■ Relax in a very warm, waist-high sitz bath 20 minutes a day.

■ Visualize healing energy flowing to your prostate gland (just below the bladder) to help increase circulation to the area.

■ Adjust your frequency of ejaculation. Too much or too little can affect prostatitis, urologists say. Some doctors even prescribe ejaculation exercises to relieve the condition.

Hypnotherapeutic Healing

Hypnotherapeutic help: Its time has apparently come—to men's health. After a diagnosis of prostate cancer and before surgery, it may be worthwhile to examine hypnotherapy as an adjunct to treatment, according to doctors at Columbia-Presbyterian Medical Center in New York City. Since 1995, the Complementary Care Center at the hospital has been offering hypnosis and relaxation tapes to men scheduled for prostate surgery to help quiet the mind, ease anxiety and promote the healing process. *Expected bonus:* A decreased perception of pain during recovery and an enhanced sense of well-being.

■ Hands-On Approach to Reduce Prostate Inflammation

While decidedly not for the squeamish, prostate massage can be helpful in relieving the pain and "congestion" of fluid in the gland that is associated with prostatitis. Gently insert a manicured, lubricated and gloved finger in the rectum and exert light pressure on the prostate gland for a few seconds each day. Better yet, have a loving, understanding partner perform it. The brief massage is said to aid the prostate in draining and increases (helpful) blood flow through it.

■ Herbal Method Reduces Inflammation

Maybe you've heard the ads on rush-hour news radio, or seen the ads in health food stores claiming that saw palmetto relieves prostate troubles. As the population ages, millions of men in their forties, fifties and sixties are beginning to notice that they must get up during the night to urinate. *The cause:* Aging-related enlargement of the prostate gland that impedes the flow of urine from the bladder.

While many men are helped by prescription drugs, such as Proscar, it turns out that extract from berries of the saw palmetto tree is often an equally effective, natural remedy. In brief, it works by helping shrink the prostate, thus easing urination.

Note: Not all formulations are effective. If possible, have your doctor or pharmacist obtain a pharmaceutical-grade extract. An often suggested dosage is 160 mg of the extract, twice a day, but be sure to check with your doctor first.

■ Mineral Treatment

Sometimes the numbing, nagging feeling of nighttime or daytime bladder pressure—related to age-associated prostate trouble—can be eased rather simply. Open-minded urologists and other holistic doctors sometimes suggest that men take 60 milligrams (mg) of zinc picolinate once a day until symptoms subside. Then, reduce the dosage to 30 mg to prevent recurrence. This can be taken in addition to other treatments, and the lower dosage can be taken indefinitely. Relief can occur within a few weeks.

■ The Great Pumpkin Prostate Aid

Happy Halloween—and pleasant dreams! There's new evidence that extract of pumpkin-seed powder (oil), combined with saw palmetto and a handful of other herbs and nutrients, may ease the nagging pain of enlarged prostate glands. Plus, anecdotal evidence indicates that men who have mild to moderate cases of prostatitis can sleep through the night more often without having to rise to urinate.

One such product—The Prostate Supplement—is manufactured by Real Health Laboratories in San Diego and sold with a guarantee over the counter at health food stores nationwide. Most likely, it won't be long until a homemade version of prostate/pumpkin-seed-oil nutrient is circulating in health food circles. Ask your herbalist.

Prostatitis and Benign Prostatic Hyperplasia (BPH): What's the Difference?

If you own a prostate, chances are you're going to have trouble with it at some point. Right now, prostatitis and BPH are the most likely (and treatable) prostate villains you will face. Simply put, prostatitis means inflammation of the prostate gland. Some forms of prostatitis are caused by bacteria, but most cases are something of a mystery. About one-third of all men will experience prostatitis in their lifetime. Prostatitis sufferers tend to be younger than those who have BPH.

BPH, however, is even more prevalent. It is caused in part by age-related hormone changes and afflicts about 60% of those between the ages of 40 and 59 and even greater numbers of older men. It is characterized by frequent and/or difficult urination, usually at night. As the prostate becomes enlarged, it squeezes the urethra. In particular, BPH seems to be related to increased concentrations of dihydrotestosterone (DHT), a male sex hormone also believed to play a part in male-pattern baldness.

■ Bark with a Bite

Pygeum africanum—the bark of an African evergreen tree—works equally well on prostatitis and BPH. This herb limits the production of DHT, which increases oil in the glands, makes your hair fall out, and enlarges the prostate.

Also, pygeum africanum has a mild antibiotic effect, which makes it particularly effective against bacteria-induced prostatitis. Typical dosage is 50 to 100 mg in extract form twice a day. Studies have shown that the herb is effective,

with few side effects other than occasional stomach irritation. Research also shows that this herb increases the efficacy of saw palmetto, another prostate-friendly herb.

■ *Nutritional Aid for a Strong Prostate*

You say "tomato," prostate researchers say "lycopene." According to one Harvard Medical School study, men may want to favor a diet that is low in fat, high in red-orange vegetables and high in lycopene, an antioxidant found in tomatoes and tomato sauces. (The study found that men who ate more than 10 servings a week of tomato-based foods had a 45% lower risk of prostate cancer than other men in the study.)

BENIGN PROSTATIC HYPERPLASIA (BPH)

■ *A Less Invasive Surgical Alternative*

By the time they reach age 50, more than half of all men have an enlarged prostate. That doesn't mean they will develop cancer; it just means that the plum-shaped gland surrounding their urethra has grown extra tissue over the years, possibly slowing down urination or causing other urinary symptoms, including dribbling and numerous stop-start feelings beneath the bladder when voiding. Unlike prostatitis, this disorder is not caused by infection.

Sometimes standard drug therapy helps. At other times, surgery is called for, in which doctors chip away or otherwise trim the excess tissue. A less invasive technique appears to offer relief to some BPH sufferers: Trans-urethral needle ablation, otherwise known as TUNA. In this procedure, a urologist uses a catheter (the unpleasant part) and radio waves to heat and destroy extra prostate tissue, leaving most of the gland intact. Healing time is cut markedly in this outpatient procedure, and side effects are reduced.

Another Surgical Alternative

After age 50, a man who is otherwise in good health may notice minor prostate or urinary problems for the first time. But if standard drug therapy doesn't work, and if the patient is not ready to try standard surgical removal of the tissue, he might opt for another procedure—new and less invasive than prostate removal—called transurethral microwave thermotherapy (TUMT).

In this treatment, microwaves heat up and destroy excess tissue of the prostate gland that has been crimping the urethra (and thus, urine flow). And while it is not exactly surgery, it does involve threading a thin microwave wand through the urethra and into the inner recesses of the male reproductive cavity.

■ A (Sort of) Sweet Treatment

Glycyrrhizic acid, the active ingredient in licorice root, helps thwart some of the effects of testosterone and helps reduce enlargement of the prostate gland. That means fewer trips to the bathroom for many men who have enlarged prostates, and less urgency related to urination.

You can add licorice root extract to hot drinks to get the medicinal effects. Or, stir a cup of tea with a piece of licorice root, which will steep into the hot liquid. Unfortunately, eating licorice candy won't do the trick.

■ A Zinc-Plus Combo Approach

While most nuts are high in fat, they are also high in zinc—so eating like a squirrel could help combat prostate trouble. Zinc—also found in many seeds, such as sunflower and pumpkin seeds—is believed to shrink the prostate and reduce the symptoms of benign prostatic hyperplasia (BPH). When taken with vitamin B6, zinc also helps keep DHT (dihydrotestosterone) production in check, further reducing the risk and/or effects of BPH. Suggested dosage is 30 to 60 mg of zinc a day, along with 100 mg of B6.

While munching trail mix may be a more appealing way to get zinc, you may be better off with a supplement. After all, too much fat could counteract some of the good the zinc can do.

SKIN CONDITIONS

RAZOR BURN

■ Liquid Soap Lubricant

As a quick way to prevent the redness and irritation that too often follow a close shave, consider a little prep work. Some of the new moisturizing pump-bottle soaps are surprisingly pure and scent free. (Ask a cosmetics professional at a department store for suggestions.)

By spreading a thin layer of liquid soap on your face *before* applying shaving cream, you'll notice your razor slides more smoothly around the nooks and crannies of the cheekbones, chin and jawline. It is also a lot less expensive than applying some of the new aftershave lotions.

■ Morning Tea Time

Besides its purported immune-boosting properties, chamomile can make a soothing, instant aftershave compress. Here's how to perform the "facial first-aid" first thing in the morning: Wet and chill three or four chamomile tea bags, then hold them against the inflamed skin of the face and neck (your neck will want to drink them up). The azulene oil in the tea helps keep the pain and redness down. As a minor bonus, chamomile is believed to have antibacterial, anti-infection properties.

SHAVING NICKS AND CUTS

■ A Sweet Styptic

Take it from a traveling salesman: If you find yourself in a hotel one morning without a styptic pencil and dabbing at a cut with toilet tissue, make uncommon use of a common convenience in hotel rooms these days—sugar packets for morning coffee. Try dabbing sugar directly onto the cut once it's been cleaned. It may not have that characteristic styptic sting, but as an old herbalist's first-aid trick, it will work in a pinch. (Sugar is also said to reduce scar-tissue buildup.)

Note: If you find yourself bleeding more easily than in prior years, or bleeding more excessively from small razor cuts, notify your doctor; vitamin deficiency, liver problem or another condition could be the cause.

■ A Quick Remedy for Excessive Bleeding

The diluted juice of a lemon works well as an alternative styptic to treat shaving or other small cuts. The juice can be applied directly with gauze or the pad of a sterile bandage, whichever is more handy at the time. Think of it as a natural, cleansing sting. Then pat dry.

TESTICULAR CANCER

■ Simple Self-Exam

Of all the self-exams men should perform until middle age, testicular self-exams to detect cancer are the most critical, leading urologists say. With improvements in therapy, testicular cancer, which most often strikes younger men, has a 90% cure rate.

The problem is that millions of men don't see doctors often enough to catch the disease in its earliest stages. Thus, the real need for a quick, monthly self-exam that, unfortunately, most men fail to perform.

After a warm shower:

1 Hold each testicle between your thumb and first two fingers (thumb closest to the body).

2 Gently run your fingers around the surface, feeling for either lumps or hard spots. The testicle should feel like a small, firm plum, only smaller.

Note: As you move to the back of each testicle, toward your thumb, you may feel a lump (the epididymis), but the rest of the surface should be smooth.

CHAPTER 5

Money-Wise Ways to Wellness

DENTAL INSURANCE

■ *Three Features to Look For*

Grin and bear it! Managed care has reached the mouth. Now that consumers have gotten to know a bit about managed medical care for their bodies, it's time to use that knowledge in the dental arena. So the next time you're looking to buy or change your dental health insurance (or evaluating the plan you now have), keep these three points firmly in mind:

■ Does the plan have a toll-free phone number for claims information or to answer questions about the plan? If not, that could mean an extra $15 to $50 a year in phone charges.

■ Does the plan cover your initial visit? That could mean $75 or more out of your pocket.

■ Does the plan provide benefits nationwide? *Remember:* Teeth don't always chip and caps don't always fall off in your hometown. Most people don't ask about this regarding their dental plan, even though they may when shopping for their main medical insurance.

■ *Allow for Preexisting Conditions*

Like managed-care medical plans, health plans for dental coverage go to great lengths to describe and define preexisting conditions. They do so for business reasons: To reduce their liability for potential high reimbursements and surprising future charges. Unfortunately, many dental patients don't spend enough time reading the fine print about these conditions when they sign up for dental coverage through their employer's plan or an independent policy.

Preexisting conditions, when excluded or limited from dental plans, can render a plan much less valuable to a patient. A little bit of research in this area, however, could save you a lot of money. You must ask, specifically, about cases of gum infections, gingivitis, periodontal disease (and treatment!) and even capped teeth. Also, ask about oral surgery, should that become necessary.

It may make sense to split your coverage— one company for medical coverage, another (perhaps with a higher deductible) for dental— even though it may seem more convenient at times to have a single, umbrella company.

HEALTH CARE

■ *Boost Your Health Care IQ*

Money matters, but your health matters more. Now that hundreds of thousands of procedures are performed in outpatient or "ambulatory" operating rooms, it's crucial to know all you can about the doctor's place of business.

So, before you sign up for eye surgery, minor plastic surgery or even biopsies related to urological or gynecological care, try to verify that the outpatient operating room has been certified— recently. One way is to contact a California agency, the Institute for Medical Quality (IMQ), which rates and accredits such facilities. The nonprofit IMQ measures not only cleanliness and support services, but also whether patients are receiving enough pre- and postoperation information about their procedures.

■ Institute for Medical Quality, 415-882-5151, www.imq.org

How to Find a Clinical Trial

With state and federal governments, universities and pharmaceutical companies all doing cutting-edge medical research, finding information on the latest clinical trials could appear to be a daunting task. But no longer. One of the easiest places to locate clinical trials looking for subjects is the Internet.

Two excellent Internet resources are the Web sites of the National Institutes of Health and a private company called CenterWatch. Both Web sites offer continuously updated coverage of thousands of clinical trials taking place around the country. All you have to do is type in a medical condition, and every clinical trial tracked or sponsored by these organizations is listed. Or join an e-mail list, and when a new trial comes up looking for participants with a certain condition, you will be notified. Both organizations also have "snail mail" newsletters available.

■ CenterWatch: www.centerwatch.com; or 617-856-5900

■ National Institutes of Health, www.cc.nih.gov; or 800-411-1222

■ *Cheap, Advanced Care*

Clinical trials are experimental and should not be the first stop in shopping for solutions to medical conditions. But for those facing chronic or even life-threatening conditions, participating in a clinical trial may offer an answer, or at least hope.

Clinical trials are almost always free—paid for by the project's sponsors. And almost every metropolitan area, especially those with teaching hospitals, has a host of programs under way at any given time. Keep in mind, though, that some participants receive a placebo.

Remember: Clinical trials are experiments. And if the trial is not free, most insurance companies will not pay for it, even if the alternative is certain death. Some managed care plans actually refuse to allow patients to participate in clinical trials because they fear complications from the trials.

■ Health Care Fairs

Used to be, the only way to keep up with what was truly going on in the business of natural healing was to ask your holistic healer or an MD interested in holistic healing about what he or she learned at the last alternative medicine convention. Meetings held by groups such as the Society for Behavioral Medicine, the American Medical Women's Association or Natural Products Expos serve as forums for some of the latest products, ideas and wellness tips. Unfortunately, the meetings are limited to doctors, healers or those "in the trade." These days, however, you can attend consumer versions of some of these shows, often sponsored by magazines that cover the news in natural healing and offering all sorts of product samples.

INSURANCE PLANS

EVALUATING PLANS

■ Know How Your HMO Ranks

Saving money is not always the primary factor in choosing your health care. That's why many—but not nearly enough—savvy consumers contact the National Committee for Quality Assurance (NCQA) to check out the accreditation of their current (or proposed) HMO or other health insurers. Before giving accreditation, NCQA measures the variety of services offered, the range of coverage and the ways in which health care firms respond to complaints. (The complaint factor is something you won't find in the plan's brochures, or in the materials your company may provide.)

■ Call NCQA at 888-275-7585; or visit its Web site at www.ncqa.org

■ Don't Overlook Your Doctor's Advice

Doctors are smart, in more ways than one. In addition to a large amount of medical information, they've acquired some financial savvy in recent years that could help you. One recent survey found that primary care doctors today belong to an average of 10 managed-care health plans. Besides rewriting the ways modern doctors get paid, this arrangement has also enabled doctors to watch

Are Teaching Hospitals Truly Better?

Teaching hospitals may be better for your health than local community hospitals. That's according to a new study from Case Western Reserve University School of Medicine in Cleveland, Ohio.

Researchers found that the death rate was 19% lower at teaching hospitals. They also found that the length of the stay was usually 10% shorter. The findings are based on a review of nearly 90,000 patients in the Cleveland area who were treated at both teaching and nonteaching hospitals for stroke, heart attack, pneumonia and other conditions.

and track how generous, or miserly, certain health insurance providers tend to be toward reimbursing the doctors—and their patients.

So, if and when you are shifting insurance coverage, ask the doctor you're closest to for a recommendation. Even better, ask (or fax) the office manager of the doctor you've had the most dealings with in the past two years. He or she could help you save thousands of dollars in years to come in the space of a one-page faxed answer.

Savvy Consumer Information

There are dozens of ways to judge an HMO or other health care provider, but one handy source is the federal government's Web site, www.consumer.gov. This site offers valuable information that can help you choose the plan that offers the best quality for you and your family. It also includes information on how health plans work and how to effectively use the benefits they provide. Visit its Web site or call 800-688-9889.

■ Your Union with a Union

Never thought you'd be a union supporter? Over the past few years, tens of thousands of Americans have recast their votes and joined unions, largely due to rising health care costs and the pressures of managed care. The National Writers' Union, for one, invites various scribes to join its guild and subscribe to its health plan— you don't even have to be a published novelist...yet. In some cases, former executives-turned-freelance writers have found themselves allied with former factory workers, all in the name of obtaining better health care coverage.

Other unions or organizations that have seen spikes in membership roles include the Federation of Nurses and Health Professionals and the Jewish social organization, B'nai B'rith.

■ National Writers Union, 113 University Place, 6th floor, New York, NY 10003, 212-254-0279, www.nwu.org

■ AFT Healthcare, 555 New Jersey Ave. NW, Washington, DC 20001, 202-879-4491, www.aft.org/healthcare

■ B'nai B'rith International, 2020 K St. NW, Washington, DC 20006, 800-723-2624

■ Location, Location, Location

As in real estate, the value of health care is related to how convenient it is to you—and how well you are treated compared with other plans in your city or town. For instance, is your coverage going to be concentrated at or near one major medical center—or are the options available to you more widespread? *Health Pages*, an Internet-based review of health care options in many major newspaper markets (including those served by *New York Newsday, Seattle Times, Los Angeles Times* and Denver's *Rocky Mountain News*), lays it all out clearly and succinctly. You can access this information for free (for now at least), through the newspapers' Internet sites. For additional information:

■ Visit its Web site at http://thehealthpages.com

MONEY-SAVING TIPS

■ When Two Plans Are Better than One

If you and a spouse or partner both have access to a benefits package at work, it may make financial sense to split up—split up health care plans, that is. One of you might consider choosing an HMO (health maintenance organization) or PPO (preferred provider organization) for general, wide-ranging insurance coverage for illness and injury, while the second partner picks a different kind of coverage—such as indemnity or FFS (fee for service) plan.

By splitting coverage this way, you and your partner or family have more options in case of severe injury or catastrophic illness—which could help you save thousands of dollars in the long run, or allow you to choose a specific doctor and still get reimbursed from your insurer. In many cases, people tend to gravitate toward the least expensive plans, especially when they are young and healthy. But then they find out they have less freedom to choose doctors or "manage" their illnesses than they would have had if they had signed up for at least one indemnity or FFS plan.

Note: In exchange for freedom of choice, the indemnity or FFS plans usually don't cover 100% of doctor or surgical costs. Plus, they have a deductible that must be paid by the insured before benefits accrue. But up-front costs are not a large concern when a serious illness strikes. The best care—and substantial reimbursement—matters more.

■ An Underused Option for Singles

Since the mid-1990s, millions of single Americans reluctantly have signed up with HMOs or other managed-care health plans to save money, even though they would have preferred to choose their own doctors (and still be reimbursed). One uncommon alternative some health care experts advocate is to sign up for a plan that allows consumers to choose their doctors—an indemnity or fee-for-service plan—even though these plans usually require the patients to pay a large deductible, say $1,000 or more, per year.

But, if consumers also open up an Archer Medical Savings Account (MSA)—a relatively new, tax-advantaged option—they can draw from it to pay health care costs with tax-free dollars. When you consider that even the cost of parking at the doctor's office or hospital can be paid for with tax-free money, the high deductibles don't seem quite as high anymore. Also, the cost of things such as eyeglasses or dental care—which may not count toward your deductible—can be paid for out of your Archer MSA. Many insurance companies now offer Archer MSAs, which are funded by payroll deductions to further soften the out-of-pocket blow.

■ Two Ways to Save with a Preexisting Condition

If you have hypertension, allergies or another illness that requires regular treatment, be sure to check how your current and any future health insurance plans will cover such preexisting conditions. Often, you may be accepted for insurance, but must face a three-month waiting period before reimbursement for such conditions—and the appropriate medications—kicks in.

In addition, you may need a referral to an in-plan specialist. If you already have an appointment to see your primary-care physician, ask him or her for that referral even before you are covered; that will save both time and an additional fee from the referring doctor.

If you require regular treatment and are planning a job or insurance change, you may save money by buying a temporary insurance policy or making sure that your doctor treats you until the very last day your current coverage remains active.

■ How Sharp Shoppers Buy Insurance

Nobody will say it's fun, but it may save you thousands of dollars. When shopping for a new health insurance plan, don't settle for the glossy brochure and 16-page summary often distributed by health care companies. Instead, do what state health insurance professionals do: Ask for the "certificate of coverage" or "evidence of coverage" statements. These lengthy documents are the actual contracts filed with the states in which the firms practice. They detail the coverage provided, especially in the tricky area of preexisting conditions.

If you have asthma, depression or other recurring disorders, careful reading (stay with it!) of the coverage statements could be the best financial step you'll take over the next few years, in regard to your own or your family's health care.

■ Family vs. Individual Plans

What might not be a loving thought may actually be smart consumer advice. Sometimes married couples should maintain their individual health insurance plans to save money rather than switch to a family plan. The reason—divorce. Should a split occur, any preexisting conditions from the family days will be carried over, leading to higher premiums for both partners.

Another reason to go it alone: Keeping an individual policy may also save money when chronic conditions, such as asthma or diabetes, exist.

Remember: Making the jump from one policy to another brings the insurance game—and the examination of medical records—back to square one.

■ End-of-Year Doctor Visits

Can the time of year help you save money on your health bills? Yes, it can. Most health insurance plans allow for one reimbursed routine evaluation per year. For women, it could be more. If your plan does not have an exam built in, and you've already paid your deductible for the year, let your insurance company pay for that routine visit before January 1.

RESOLVING REIMBURSEMENT PROBLEMS

■ What to Do if Your Reimbursement Doesn't Come Through

Of course health insurance companies make mistakes. When they do, it could cost you plenty. One step to take is to enlist the aid of your doctor (or the office manager). If you've been denied coverage by your insurance company, write or fax a short note to the doctor, asking the office to please review the charges for services that were provided, but were not initially covered by your plan.

■ HMO Medication Reimbursement Trick

Now that HMOs have gotten tough on reimbursement for many popular drugs by writing 30- or 60-day limitation clauses into policies, it's time to explore your options. If you're facing a 30-day limit and you know you'll be taking a prescription drug for more than 60 or 90 days, ask your doctor to write the prescription to be taken "as needed" instead of for a specific time period. This may enable you to obtain more medication for your dollar, as the insurance company will have a tougher time tracking pills.

Note: Be sure, though, to write on the label the correct time frame for your prescription—30, 60, 90 days or more, for safety's sake.

■ How to Challenge an HMO

If your initial request for reimbursement for treatment—physical therapy or nonstandard cancer therapy, say—is denied, don't hesitate to go beyond the normal channels in search of remedy. But be aware that appealing insurance decisions will take time.

Meanwhile, write or fax your state insurance commission (record the full names of those who help you) "warning" the commission of possible suffering by future residents of the state in predicaments similar to yours. In your communications, send copies of actual bills and rejections. Then, let your insurance company know of the action you took.

Finally, send a letter to the editor of your local newspaper, sounding a reasoned alarm at the potential for other citizens to

be similarly shortchanged at the health care window. Send or fax a copy of that letter to the insurance company, too. You may not get all the coverage you were searching for, but you will get noticed. And you just might get a fair(er) shake.

Refinancing Hospital Bills

Sometimes the surgery may seem less painful than the bills. A knee operation alone can cost thousands of dollars, even with insurance coverage. Needless to say, hospital debts can wreak financial havoc on a person. But a little negotiation can ease some of the burden. Most hospitals recognize that it's better to get something than nothing and are often willing to negotiate monthly payments and even the total bill.

Hospital case workers assigned to collect your money can seem unapproachable. But a phone call and a little charm could go a long way toward healing those financial wounds.

■ The Power of Attorney's Paper

"The power of letterhead." That's how one consumer advocate organization justifies the recommendation to hire an attorney when you are having trouble getting an insurance company to reimburse you.

A half-day of legal work, several hundred dollars—and the right letterhead—might be worth the investment if an insurance company balks on a big check or sticks you with an unjustified bill. Insurers are bottom line–driven businesses. Getting bogged down in litigation might cost more than what's owed to you. So playing a little legal hardball at the right time might make the problem go away.

■ Look for free legal information online at www.nolo.com. Legal encyclopedia, law dictionary, research center, forms and advice are available at this site. 800-728-3555.

MEDICAL INFORMATION RESOURCES

■ *A Valuable Internet Database*

Our tax dollars—finally—at work. A huge medical database, including summaries of journal articles published in the US and around the globe, is now available to the public through the National Institutes of Health. Formerly, this information was available only to doctors, or others, for a hefty fee. MedlinePlus is run by the National Library of Medicine. So unlike many sites on the Internet, you can trust its medical veracity going into your search.

■ Look for MedlinePlus at www.nlm.nih.gov

■ *Research Services*

If you're low on time or energy—and don't mind paying for medical information—consider using a research service. For a fee of $150 to $400, such services will scan huge medical databases and assemble a bound report containing copies of relevant articles.

Reputable research services include...

■ The Health Resource, 933 Faulkner, Conway, AR 72034. 800-949-0090, www.thehealthresource.com.

■ Institute for Health and Healing Library, 2040 Webster St., San Francisco 94115. 415-600-3681.

■ Schine Online, 39 Brenton Ave., Providence, RI 02906. 800-346-3287, www.findcure.com.

■ *An AAA-Type Patient-Driven Service*

"Today's doctors have given up their ability to advocate for the patient," said Dr. Vincent Riccardi. So what did the 57-year-old doctor do?

In 1994, Riccardi started American Medical Consumers, Inc., a patient advocacy organization, modeled on the operating methods of one of America's most popular crisis management groups, the Automobile Association of America (AAA).

Riccardi calls the organization's mission "utilization review." *Translation:* A full-time, phone-call-away service that not only offers a guiding hand for patients caught in the medical bureaucracy, but an advocate who will always be there in times of financial (health-related) need. As Riccardi says, a good doctor is necessary not only for prevention and cure, but also as a medical advocate to work the same wonders on a bottom line.

The for-profit American Medical Consumers, Inc., offers several types of memberships and services.

■ Contact the American Medical Consumers at 818-957-3508, or visit its Web site at http://medconsumer.com

Information on Genetic Testing

The Genetic Alliance serves as a national resource for information on genetic diseases and issues surrounding genetic testing. The organization consists of consumers and health professionals and, in addition to providing information, reviews genetics policies, initiates education programs for health care professionals and coordinates several regional support networks.

While the Alliance does not recommend specific doctors or labs, it can help you locate regional support groups and genetic counselors who specialize in certain diseases (counselors often help coordinate physician care and other treatments for you, but they usually do not provide medical care). The Alliance can also provide information on ongoing clinical trials which you may want to access.

Genetic Alliance, 4301 Connecticut Ave. NW, Suite 404, Washington, DC 20008, 800-336-GENE, www.geneticalliance.org

ALTERNATIVE MEDICINE RESOURCES

■ Wellness Directory Assistance

Frequently described as an alternative *Yellow Pages*, the *International Association of Healthcare Practitioners Directory* lists 50,000 acupuncturists, bodyworkers, occupational therapists, naturopathic physicians, and speech and language therapists, among others. It also lists academic degrees and phone numbers for the healers listed. *Cost:* $10. Order a copy by phone: 800-311-9204. Alternatively, its Web site lists all member practitioners for free: www.iahp.com.

MEDICAL RECORDS

■ Know Your History

Last year, more than 200,000 people contacted the Boston–based Medical Information Bureau (MIB) to check the accuracy of their medical files. *The result:* 6,000 reports had inaccurate information. Those inaccuracies could mean higher premiums or even difficulty in obtaining coverage. Unpaid gas or phone bills can send a credit report into a tailspin, keeping many from getting a loan or credit card. But did you know that the ghosts of delinquent medical bills and former insurance policies could keep you from getting insurance?

The MIB is a century-old, for-profit concern funded by more than 600 health insurance companies. By tracking more than 200 categories ranging from unpaid bills to individual EKGs and cholesterol histories, MIB is able to keep tabs on more than 15 million people flagged with "questionable" medical–financial histories. It even notes disappointing driving records and people who participate in hazardous activities, like skydiving.

Only one out of six requests by individuals turns up a report. But, for people dubbed dubious, the result can alert an insurance company and leave them with no coverage. Consumer advocates and MIB suggest checking with the bureau periodically to see if a record is being kept on you and, more important, if it's accurate. Write or call Medical Information Bureau, 160 University Ave., Westwood, MA 02090, 781-329-4500. Access its Web site at www.mib.com.

A call to MIB will lead to a recorded message asking for a name and address. If the bureau has a report on you, you'll get the report by mail in about a week, along with a $9.00 bill.

MIB will investigate if a file is disputed and will delete any mistakes. Otherwise a "statement of dispute" will be put in the file and passed along when the next insurer comes looking for information.

■ *The Truth About Confidentiality*

Traditional belief holds that medical records are confidential, bound by a sacred doctor–patient relationship. But that's not always the rule—or law. Guidelines for the release of patient information vary state to state. Typically, disclosures to government agencies are required when gunshot wounds, communicable diseases or child abuse are involved.

If a physician determines that physical injury to the patient or others is imminent, or there is immediate mental or emotional injury to the patient, records can be released to government or law-enforcement authorities.

And be careful about signing anything. Often life and health insurance policy examinations allow a company to circulate the findings to other organizations. As one insurance executive said, "It's tough work to be a careful consumer. And it's getting tougher."

■ *Medical Mistakes*

Recording notes into a tape recorder about a patient's symptoms, treatment and progress is standard operating procedure in today's health care delivery system. And, according to Pat Forbis, associate executive director at the American Association for Medical Transcription (AAMT), "Mistakes are made." Often, the job of transcribing those somewhat muddled and medical lingo-laden tapes falls on a handful of trained professionals.

Why is this important? Transcripts are used in case reviews by insurance companies or other organizations that have access to your medical history. Often, decisions about future delivery of care or insurability—of you and others—are based on these reviews.

Bottom line: Mistakes in transcripts can be costly, according to Forbis. So, be sure your doctor checks your records before they are passed along to prying eyes.

If you suspect an error in your medical records, ask your physician to check the report or get in touch with your local medical society for assistance.

■ *Picking Up the Medical Tab*

Sometimes paying for a doctor's bill out of pocket is the cheaper deal.

If a particular treatment might not look so good on your medical record—and you can afford to pay for it yourself—it may be to your advantage if you *don't* file for reimbursement from insurers. Preexisting or chronic conditions (made evident by certain treatments) could bump up your premium when your policy is reviewed or switched.

And, even though your health plan may be tied in with your employer, there is no guarantee a personal problem won't be discovered. For instance, some insurers may ask your psychiatrist to submit detailed therapy notes to justify reimbursement.

Picking up the medical tab in some circumstances might seem overly cautious, but as one clinical psychologist and attorney said, "That's not paranoid. It's pragmatic."

■ Know Your Doctor

Keeping a condition off the record may not be so easy. Always interview potential doctors, particularly mental health practitioners, asking what their policy is in regard to reporting medical conditions and treatment to managed-care companies and employers. While many will concede to keep the treatment off the books, some won't.

Online Shopping for Alternative Medicine Specialists

When you'd like to try an alternative medical remedy, but aren't sure there's a qualified expert in your area, consider an online referral service. Healthy Alternatives is a resource center and referral service combined at one site. It contains a directory of practitioners throughout the US who do acupuncture, Rolfing, naturopathy, hypnotherapy, Reiki and much more—and provides coupons for some. The site also includes a glossary, has articles about alternative and complementary therapies, and provides grids to help you determine which therapy may help you.

Remember, though, that online doesn't necessarily mean authoritative—or certified. In some ways online sites and listings are little more than computerized *Yellow Pages* listings. So use the site (and other similar sites) with the same care and caveats as you would if you were picking a doctor out of a phone book. Still, it's a good first step in researching and adding to your personal health care team. You can find the site at http://health-alt.com.

MEDICAL SUPPLIES

■ Shaving Postsurgical Recovery Costs

When you or a family member has non-emergency or outpatient surgery, don't overlook the cost of recovery—and what you can do to cut it.

Oftentimes, orthopedic bandages, wraps, physical therapy devices and even nonprescription remedies can be purchased at a deep discount in medical supply houses. While these businesses don't advertise much and are typically found only in larger cities, it may be worth your while to investigate them a week or two before planned surgery. If you do, you will be prepared when the unreimbursed expenses start streaming in. Though you probably won't be able to head off all the charges of recovery, you may be able to make a sizable dent in them.

Beyond the *Yellow Pages,* your local pharmacist most likely can point you in the right direction.

■ Saving Money on Medication

There's no such thing as a free lunch, but there may be free prescription pills in your future. Whenever a new drug is introduced on the market, doctors are deluged with free samples from the manufacturer. Frequently these drugs go unused. And while a pharmaceutical company could be introducing one kind of medication, sales reps may drop off samples of two or three medications already on the market. These bonus samples can really come in handy.

Ask your doctor or the nursing staff or office manager about the samples on hand. You may receive a week's supply or more for free.

Note: Always check the expiration dates on any samples!

■ Unadvertised Pharmacy Price "Cuts"

If you or a family member has a chronic illness that requires medication, and your health plan is rather stingy on drug reimbursement, there are ways to stretch your medication dollar. Some people opt for mail-order drug delivery to cut costs, although these customers lose the benefit of interacting with a pharmacist who can answer questions or warn of side effects.

But if you're going to be buying a certain drug or drugs for a few years, why not do a little phone research first? When you reach the pharmacists, ask if they can match any of the mail-order prices for certain drugs. Sometimes they will—especially an independent drugstore looking to firm up a relationship. You've got little to lose, and a professional's service to gain—in addition to your monetary savings.

If you do go the mail-order route, a reputable supplier is:

■ Prescription Resources, 800-374-2762

■ More Vitamins, Less Cost

Now that you've finally got your vitamin and nutrient regimen all figured out, it's time to find out how to stock up much more cheaply. Consider a vitamin discount house. They don't advertise much, but that means more savings for you and your family. One reputable source—PIA Discount Vitamins— offers you Bach, TwinLab, Natrol and Kyolic,

among other reputable brands, and sells them at 20% or more off the retail price. They also have a free catalog.

■ Contact PIA Discount Vitamins, 800-662-8144 or www.eventoutpost.com/piavitamins

■ Doctor's Orders

Let your doctor know that price is an issue for you if you need to take prescription drugs. Find out if there's a generic alternative to brand-name medications—or if there is an entirely different, less costly medication that might work just as well for your condition. You can also ask your doctor to prescribe medication in large quantities. Some pharmacies will offer discounts to patients who purchase more than 100 pills at a time.

■ Medical Supplies by Mail

Mail order beats hospital pharmacies for extended recoveries. After (or during) a hospital stay or emergency room visit, consider using a mail-order medical supply house for bandages, wraps, arthritis and repetitive stress injury aids and other assorted healing devices. Some medical houses have free (or inexpensive) catalogs; or ask your doctor for a catalog from last season. Savings can reach up to 60% on particular products, while others are not discounted at all.

■ Dry Goods

The best way to keep pills potent? Take them out of the medicine cabinet. Humidity causes drugs to decompose more quickly. So keep medications in a cool, dry place—where your children can't get to them.

EYE CARE SUPPLIES

■ Hold Eyeglass Costs Down

The eyes have it—better than ever. A growing number of optical shops have opened mail-order and catalog operations in recent years, offering top-name frames and prescription lenses at 30% to 70% off what you'd pay at the mall. The same goes for bifocal, trifocal and polycarbonate lenses. One top source is Prism Optical, which offers a free catalog.

■ Prism Optical, 10992 NW 7th Ave., North Miami, FL 33168, 800-637-4104; fax: 800-617-5367; www.prismoptical.qpg.com

■ Contact Lenses for Less

See the difference in cost, not acuity. Once you've been examined by an optometrist or ophthalmologist and had corrective lenses prescribed and fitted, consider choosing a mail-order optical supply house when it is time for replacement of lenses. One reputable firm that provides soft, hard and gas-permeable contact lenses (including bifocals) at a discount is Contact Lens Replacement Center, P.O. Box 615, Wheatly Heights, NY 11798, 800-779-2654.

■ Buying Club for Name-Brand Lenses

If you're thinking of "trading up" your contact lenses, but the cost has you down, consider joining a lens users' buying club. 1-800-CONTACTS is one club that offers big savings off the list prices of lenses. The average customer saves $20 to $50 per year. Membership is free.

■ 1-800-CONTACTS; www.1800contacts.com

TRAVEL HEALTH

■ Safe Shots

Ask anyone who has contracted malaria or hepatitis A while traveling, and you'll hear the same story: Diseases that are rare in the US flourish elsewhere. Research on inoculations and medications is an important early step in planning a trip abroad.

But many of these preventive measures have side effects. Further, some can't be taken with other medications. Still others may no longer be effective. Getting the vaccine lowdown is a good, healthy idea, and it's easy to do. The National Vaccine Information Center in Virginia researches and catalogs information and provides a monthly newsletter of updates. The Centers for Disease Control in Atlanta also can give you useful information.

■ National Vaccine Information Center, 703-938-DPT3 or www.909shot.com

■ Centers for Disease Control and Prevention, 877-394-8747 or www.cdc.gov

TRAVEL INSURANCE

■ *Is Travel Insurance Worth Buying?*

Two questions need to be asked. First, are you already covered? If you already have a major health policy, you probably don't need any travel insurance. Many major American insurance companies will reimburse you for medical expenses due to an injury or illness during an international excursion. But coverage varies widely, so check with your carrier before you hit the road.

Second, where are you going? Reimbursement doesn't mean much when you've just been trampled by a water buffalo in the backcountry of Vietnam. Some adventurous travelers may be trekking where insurance as a concept doesn't even exist. Do you need a policy that will cover the cost of a $10,000 air evacuation? Maybe. Well, most normal policies won't pick up that tab, whereas travel insurers often do. (And the water buffalo story actually happened.)

But keep in mind: Reimbursement doesn't mean much when a hospital in Asia or Africa wants payment right away. If you're without the means to pay immediately—cash or a credit card—travel insurance might be necessary.

■ *Traveling with a Chronic Condition*

If you have a chronic disease that demands special medication, such as insulin for diabetes, adventures to remote locations can seem a bit risky. Even a simple vacation to the Caribbean can turn into a nightmare if the luggage with the medicine is lost. Several groups around the world offer insurance for such a predicament by making arrangements to get medicine to their clients. Ask your regular insurer or your travel-health insurer if this is an option in its plan.

Keep Your Doctor Close

If an injury or illness lands you in a foreign hospital, a long-distance telephone call to your primary-care physician may actually save you money.

Primary-care physicians play two critical roles in today's health care climate: Not only are they the first ones to turn to in case of health troubles, but they are also the gateway into the health care maze—and its bureaucracy. Your primary physician's sign-off on medical services being performed abroad, particularly if you are in a managed-care plan, can determine whether that foreign bill will be reimbursed.

So, when traveling abroad, be sure to pack your primary-care physician's telephone number.

■ *Medicare Shortfalls*

For seniors, crossing the border can be a risky endeavor. Medicare plans, for all their wide coverage, don't cover expenses incurred from international illnesses or injuries. That's why buying travel health insurance is a good idea if you're over 65 and traveling overseas. (Some agents would say it's a "must have.")

■ *Getting Reimbursed for Foreign Health Care*

One of the more frequent occurrences of insurance fraud today is in the area of claims submitted by foreign hospitals to American insurance companies. So, when treated overseas, it is imperative to get copies of the foreign medical reports from your doctor(s) before you return home. (If you're in a rural, undeveloped land, ask for handwritten notations—they will be helpful.)

Also, to get proper reimbursement, the cost of those foreign services needs to be converted from foreign currency to US dollars. If the bill is in another language, it must be translated. You'll need to pay for those translation costs out of your own pocket.

How Much Is Enough?

Most travel insurance companies offer a host of plans that include coverage for people interested in a two-week excursion or a two-year, expatriate adventure. But, for the most part, solid protection can be secured for about $150 to $270 for a two- to three-week trip. For that relatively modest amount, travelers can expect about $10,000 in medical coverage and $20,000 to $50,000 for air evacuation or another major emergency.

Other available coverage is car insurance, accidental death, an escort to accompany children and even coverage to, well, return a body to the US. To find the best deal, figure out what you could need, depending on where you are going, then shop around. A great place to reel in company names and view policies is on the Internet. A good starting point is www.utravelpro.com or 800-694-4311.

Online Resources

The World Wide Web now provides a world of opportunity for people who want to educate themselves about their conditions and keep informed about the very latest medical findings in every corner of the globe. The downside to this accessibility and flood of information is that there is no filter. Not only are consumers buying unregulated formulations and medications online, but medical lore and shaky science is sometimes passed off as fact; and it's easy to confuse advertisements with endorsements.

This is a frontier that's changing daily. The following list—which is by no means comprehensive—includes the Web sites of established, accredited organizations specializing in alternative healing that we've found particularly useful and reliable:

Acupuncture.com
www.acupuncture.com. Information and resources on alternative medicine. It has a provider directory, provides answers to frequently asked questions, and allows you to call on its experts to answer more specific questions.

Alternative Health News Online
www.altmedicine.com. Links to excellent sources of information on the Web about alternative health issues. Also provides a digest of new information in the field.

Alternative Medicine Homepage
www.pitt.edu/~cbw/altm.html. A jumpstation for sources of information on unconventional, unorthodox, unproven or alternative, complementary, innovative, integrative therapies.

American Academy of Medical Acupuncture
www.medicalacupuncture.org. General information and the latest research on medical acupuncture and the licensed doctors who are changing the way illness is treated. Also lets you search for an acupuncturist near you.

American Association of Naturopathic Physicians
http://naturopathic.org. A national database of naturopathic doctors, message boards, articles and recipes.

American Botanical Council
www.herbalgram.org. Educates the public on the use of medicinal plants, provides an herb reference guide including common uses and appropriate dosages.

American Chiropractic Association
www.acatoday.com. Nationwide directory of chiropractors.

American Dietetic Association
www.eatright.org. Offers information on general healthy eating with up-to-the minute reports on findings and research relating to food and nutrition.

Bottom Line Secrets
www.bottomlinesecrets.com. Excellent source of nonbiased health information. The Bottom Line experts also clue you in on secrets of money management, people skills, leisure activities and business planning.

CSPI (Center for Science in the Public Interest)
www.cspinet.org. Engaging health newsletter, covering food information and news, provides information about food safety, additives and other health and diet information.

A Dictionary of Alternative Medicine Methods
www.canoe.ca/AltmedDictionary/home.html. A glossary and bibliography of alternative treatment terms and methods.

Health & Beauty Resources
www.health-library.com/index.html. Links to a wide variety of health, fitness, nutrition and sexuality sites, with a section on alternative medicine.

Herb Research Foundation
www.herbs.org. Detailed resources about herbs and their uses. Includes timely news articles, other documents for sale, a gallery of botanical photos and more.

International Chiropractors Association
www.chiropractic.org. In addition to its professional resources, this site answers common questions and helps you locate a chiropractor in your area.

International Food Information Council
www.ific.org. Answers questions about food allergies, general nutrition, food additives and more. Helps you avoid food-related health problems.

MayoClinic.com
www.mayoclinic.com. Health news, links to other sites for specific conditions, quizzes, glossary and ask the doctor.

MedWeb
www.medweb.emory.edu. A directory of health-related Web sites, maintained by Emory University.

MotherNature.com
www.mothernature.com. In addition to its main commerce area, this site provides a wealth of information, an encyclopedia of natural health topics, expert advice and an archive of articles on a range of subjects.

National Center for Complementary and Alternative Medicine (NCCAM)
http://nccam.nih.gov. The NCCAM is a department of the National Institutes of Health whose purpose is to evaluate the effectiveness of alternative treatments. The site includes news, events and information about research grants.

National Center for Homeopathy
www.homeopathic.org. All about homeopathy.

National Institutes of Health
www.nih.gov. A wide variety of health resources with links to new research results, publications and hotlines.

National Women's Health Information Center
www.4women.gov. Sponsored by The Office of Women's Health, U.S. Department of Health and Human Services. Provides current health news and glossaries.

WebMD
www.webmd.com. A comprehensive health site that includes information on herbs, alternative medical practices and more.

U.S. National Library of Medicine
www.nlm.nih.gov. Comprehensive health library with links to extensive health information.

Pain.com
www.pain.com. Resources about pain studies, links to other pain-control sites, etc.

Sources

CHAPTER 1: American Acupuncture Association
• American College of Obstetricians and Gynecologists
• *American Journal of Clinical Nutrition* • American Society of Dermatologic Surgery • American Society of Plastic and Reconstructive Surgeons • *Bottom Line/Health* • *Bottom Line/Personal* • Andrea Candee, herbalist, board member, Holistic Resource Network, Inc. • Kim Cook, MD • Michael Davidson, MD • Jocelyn Eberstein, D.Ac. • Richard Ellenbogen, MD • Ken Goldberg, MD • Jeannette Graf, MD • Herb Research Foundation • Hospital for Special Surgery, New York City • *Journal of the American Medical Association* • Michael Kaminer, MD • Richard Kavner, OD • Doug Kennedy, DC• Steven Lamm, MD • *The Lancet* • Barbara Levine, RD, PhD • Randall E. McNally, MD • National Institute on Aging, Baltimore • Marion Nestle, PhD • *The New England Journal of Medicine* • Nancy Rao, ND • William Regelson, MD • Richard Restak, MD • Rush-Presbyterian-St. Luke's Hospital, Chicago • Philip Sutton, PhD • Donald Teig, OD • Dana Ullman, M.P.H. • University of Colorado–Boulder Museum • U.S. Dept. of Agriculture, Human Nutrition Center, Grand Forks, ND • Paul Venger, MD • Roy L. Walford, MD • Bernie Zilbergeld, PhD • and Frania Zins, Physical Therapy Arts.

CHAPTER 2: Acupressure Institute of America
• Adler School of Professional Psychology • *Alternative Therapies* • American Academy of Otolaryngology • American Academy of Anti-Aging Medicine (A4M) • American Association of Sex Educators, Counselors and Therapists • American Botanical Council • American College of Obstetricians and Gynecologists • American Heart Association • *American Journal of Hypertension* • American Massage Therapy Association • American Society of Dermatologic Surgery • Ayurvedic Institute, Albuquerque • Toni Bark, MD • Bastyr University • Herbert Benson, MD • Richard Berger, MD • Diane Berson, MD • Bio-Electro-Magnetics Institute • Biofeedback Certification of America • Keith Block, MD • Richard Bloom, herbalist • Barbara Bobo, herbalist • Lori Bond, DAc • Roderick Borrie, PhD • *Bottom Line/Health* • *Bottom Line/Personal* • *Bottom Line/Tomorrow* • Boulder College of Massage Therapy, Boulder, CO • Boulder Valley Allergy Clinic • *British Journal of Plastic Surgery* • *British Medical Journal* • Andrea Candee,

herbalist, board member, Holistic Resource Network, Inc. • Deborah Carson, PharmD • Ronald Charles, MD • *Chest* • *Cleveland Clinic Journal of Medicine* • Barbara Close, herbalist • Comprehensive Tinnitus Clinic, Atlanta • Lisa Cosman, nutritionist • Randy Cummins, massage therapist • Mark Daniels, MD • Gary Danziger, R.P.T. • Marco de la Cruz, MD • *Dermatological Nursing* • Elliot Dick, PhD • John Douillard, DC • *Drugstore News* • Duke (University) Diet and Fitness Center • James A. Duke, PhD • Jocelyn Eberstein, MD • Douglas Finlayson, MD • Stephen Fortman, MD • Victor Frankel, MD, PhD • Alfred Franzlau, MD • Peter Gail, PhD • Steven Gawne, MD • Scott Gerson, MD • Tara Skye Goldin, ND • Tom Goode, ND • Joe Graedon and Theresa Graedon, PhD • Karen M. Grewen, PhD • Elson Haas, MD • Letha Hadady, DAc • Herb Research Foundation • David Hill, MD • Alan Hirsch, MD, Smell and Taste Treatment and Research Foundation, Chicago • Patrick Horay, DC • Bernard Hurley, PhD • International Breathwork Institute • *Journal of the American Medical Association* • *The Journal of Bone and Joint Surgery* • *Journal of Holistic Nursing* • *Journal of Neurology* • *Journal of Occupational and Environmental Health* • *Journal of Planning Literature,* The Ohio State University • Richard Kavner, OD • Raphael Kellman, MD • Doug Kennedy, DC • Nooshin Khoshkhesal-Darvash, ND • Douglas Labar, MD • *The Lancet* • Alfred Lane, MD • Neil Levin, nutritionist • Mania Levitan, MD • Erica MacDonald, physical therapist • Charles MacInerney, meditation teacher • Russ Mandor, DDS • Norman J. Marcus, MD • Brigitte Mars, herbalist • Alexander Mauskop, MD • *Mayo Clinic Health Letter* • Rob McCaleb, PhD • Gary Monheit, MD • Michael Murray, ND • Stephen Nagler, MD • Willibald Nagler, MD • National Athletic Trainers Association • National College of Naturopathy, Portland, OR • National Institutes of Health • National Jewish Medical and Research Center, Denver • National Sporting Goods Association • *Nature Medicine* • Marion Nestle, PhD • New York Botanical Garden • New York Hospital–Cornell Medical Center • *Penn State Sports Medicine Newsletter* • Glenn Pfeffer, MD • The Pilates Center, Boulder, CO • Richard Podell, MD • Robert Pritikin, Pritikin Longevity Center, Santa Monica, CA • James Quinn, MD • Nancy Rao, ND • William Regelson, MD • Richard Restak, MD • Kurt Reynolds, trainer • Rocky Mountain Center for Botanical Studies,

Boulder, CO • Katie Rodan, MD • The Rolf Institute, Boulder, CO • Jeanne Rose, herbalist, president, National Association for Holistic Aromatherapy • Jeanne Rose, herbalist • Zeda Rosenberg, ScD • Robert Rountree, MD • Debra Rouse, ND • Asim Dutta Roy, PhD • Peter Ryoy-Byrne, MD • Laura Sattler, aesthetician • Marilyn Saunders, DC • *Science* • Richard Shane, PhD • C. Norman Shealy, MD, PhD • Robert Sheeler, MD • Rosemary Shoong, bodyworker/energy healer • Sonoma Mission Inn and Spa • Jill Stansbury, ND • Debra St. Claire, herbalist • Philip Sutton, PhD • Donald Teig, OD • Brian Thompson, trichologist • Touch Research Institute • Varro Tyler, PhD • University of California at Los Angeles Medical Center • The Upledger Institute • Joseph Weber, MD • Kristine Whitmore, MD • Wilderness Medical Society • Reford Williams, MD • Elisabeth Williamson, yoga instructor • Sidney Winawer, MD • Elliot Wineburg, PhD • David Winston, herbalist • M. Michael Wolfe, MD • Bruce Yaffe, MD • Michael A. Young, PhD • and Gary Zammit, PhD.

CHAPTER 3: The Alan Guttmacher Institute • American Academy of Neurology • American Association for Nurse-Midwives • American College of Obstetricians and Gynecologists • American Society of Reproductive Medicine • Susan Barr, PhD • Bastyr University • Tamara Bavendam, MD • Lori Bond, DAc • *Bottom Line/Health* • Andrea Candee, herbalist, board member, Holistic Resource Network, Inc. • Barbara Close, herbalist • Tara Skye Goldin, ND • Letha Hadady, DAc • Harvard Women's Health Watch • Herb Research Foundation • Tori Hudson, ND• Vicki Hufnagel, MD • *Journal of Reproductive Medicine* • Susan Love, MD • Jan MacBarron, MD • Brigitte Mars, herbalist • Karen May, music therapist • *Medical Tribune* • National College of Naturopathy, Portland, OR • *The New England Journal of Medicine* • Nancy Rao, ND • Katie Rodan, MD • Jeanne Rose, herbalist • Rush-Presbyterian-St. Luke's Hospital, Chicago • Society of Behavioral Medicine • David Spiegel, MD • Jill Stansbury, ND • Beverly Whipple, PhD • and Hope Young, music therapist.

CHAPTER 4: American Urologic Association • Mitchell Benson, MD • James A. Duke, PhD • Ken Goldberg, MD • Harvard School of Public Health • Herb Research Foundation • Robert Ivker, MD • Johns Hopkins University School of Medicine • *Journal of Urology* • *The Lancet* • The Male Sexual Dysfunction Institute, Chicago • Man-to-Man prostate cancer support group, Denver • Brigitte Mars, herbalist • *Natural Health* • David Orentreich, MD • Michael Perelman, PhD • Robert Rountree, MD • Rush-Presbyterian-St. Luke's Hospital, Chicago • Sickle Cell Foundation of Georgia • The Sickle Cell Information Center • Patrick Walsh, MD • and John Whitesel, MD.

CHAPTER 5: Alliance of Genetic Support Groups • American Association for Medical Transcription • American Medical Consumers • American Medical Women's Association • American Preventive Medical Association • Fred D. Baldwin, PhD • Blue Cross Blue Shield of Colorado • *Bottom Line/Health* • Center for Patient Advocacy • Centers for Disease Control, Atlanta • CenterWatch • *Encyclopedia of Associations* • Group Health Insurance Association • Institute for Medical Quality (California; Ambulatory Care) • *Journal of the American Medical Association* • Medical Information Bureau • *Money* • National Committee for Quality Assurance • National Institutes of Health • National Library of Medicine • National Vaccine Information Center • *New Age Journal* • New Hope Communications • *SELF* • SOS International • Universal Travel Protection, Inc. • and The Wilderness Medical Society.

Index